Urban Poverty, Local Governance and Everyday Politics in Mumbai

This book explores the informal (political) patronage relations between the urban poor and service delivery organisations in Mumbai, India. It examines the conditions of people in the slums and traces the extent to which they are subject to social and political exclusion. Delving into the roles of the slum-based mediators and municipal councillors, it brings out the problems in the functioning of democracy at the ground level, as election candidates target vote banks with freebies and private-sector funding to manage their campaigns. Starting from social justice concerns, this book combines theory and insights from disciplines as diverse as political science, anthropology and policy studies. It provides a comprehensive, multi-level overview of the various actors within local municipal governance and democracy as also consequences for citizenship, urban poverty, gender relations, public services, and neoliberal politics.

Lucid and rich in ethnographic data, this book will be useful to scholars, researchers and students of social anthropology, urban studies, urban sociology, political science, public policy and governance, as well as practitioners and policymakers.

Joop de Wit is Senior Lecturer in Public Policy and Development Management, International Institute of Social Studies of Erasmus University (ISS), The Hague, The Netherlands. An anthropologist, his research interests are political science, governance, policy issues, urban poverty, and decentralisation. He has published the books *Poverty, Policy and Politics in Madras Slums: Dynamics of Survival, Gender and Leadership* (1996) and *New Forms of Urban Governance in India: Shifts, Models, Networks and Contestations* (co-edited with I.S.A. Baud, 2008) as well as numerous articles.

Cities and the Urban Imperative
Series Editor: Sujata Patel, Professor
Department of Sociology, University of Hyderabad

For a full list of titles in this series, please visit https://www.routledge.com/Cities-and-the-Urban-Imperative/book-series/CUI

This series introduces a holistic approach to studying cities, the urban experience and its imaginations. It assesses what is distinctive of the urban phenomenon in India, and also delineates the characteristic uniqueness of particular cities as they embrace change and create ways of experiencing modernities.

Taking an interdisciplinary route, the series evaluates the many facets of urbanisation and city formation and explores the challenges faced in relation to regional, national and global processes.

The books in this series present the changing trends in macro- and micro-urban processes; the nature of demographic patterns of migration and natural growth therein; spatial reorganisation and segregation in urban areas; uneven economic development of manufacturing and services in cities; unequal access to power in the context of formal citizenship; increasing everyday violence and declining organised protest; and breakdown of urban family life in juxtaposition with the reconstitution of community. They trace how new forms of socialities are replacing old forms of trust and solidarity and how these are being institutionalised in distinct and diverse ways within South Asia.

Also in this Series

Participolis
Consent and Contention in Neoliberal Urban Governance
Editors: Karen Coelho, Lalitha Kamath and M. Vijayabaskar

Dharavi
From Mega-Slum to Urban Paradigm
Marie-Caroline Saglio-Yatzimirsky

Beyond Kolkata
Rajarhat and the Dystopia of Urban Imagination
Ishita Dey, Ranabir Samaddar and Suhit K. Sen

Urban Poverty, Local Governance and Everyday Politics in Mumbai

Joop de Wit

Routledge
Taylor & Francis Group

LONDON AND NEW YORK

First published 2017 by Routledge

2 Park Square, Milton Park, Abingdon, Oxfordshire OX14 4RN
52 Vanderbilt Avenue, New York, NY 10017

*Routledge is an imprint of the Taylor & Francis Group,
an informa business*

First issued in paperback 2019

British Library Cataloguing in Publication Data
A catalogue record for this book is available from the British Library

Library of Congress Cataloging-in-Publication Data
A catalog record has been requested for this book

ISBN: 978-1-138-20749-3 (hbk)
ISBN: 978-0-367-17741-6 (pbk)

Typeset in Sabon
by Apex CoVantage, LLC

Contents

Preface

I carried out my first anthropological slum study in Madras in 1984 and kept engaged with urban poverty and governance in India ever since. A first step was my PhD research in the same city in the late 1980s. Rather than only targeting the urban poor, I now expanded my scope to include the interfaces between slum people and the local government in service delivery and policy making, noting the importance of informal patronage and political relations. Following my PhD I had a most instructive time in the 1990s in Bangalore as resident programme advisor of the Dutch-funded Bangalore urban poverty programme. From 2003 to 2006 I was part of a team leading an Indo-Dutch research project to investigate changing forms of urban governance in India, together with Isa Baud of Amsterdam University and Amitabh Kundu of the Jawaharlal Nehru University. The research cities were Delhi, Mumbai and Chennai (formerly Madras). The latter studied the evolution of public–private partnerships and new forms of urban finance. My focus was urban decentralisation where I gradually came to consider the local councillors as the key agents linking poor city people to organisations and institutions critical for them. In areas such as health, education, sanitation, and also police problems, councillors displayed a solid mediation and problem-solving capacity. But there was always a price, for instance bribes or the promise to vote for their parties.

Madras in the 1980s was still a relatively parochial place, where the local state for slum people was mostly the corporation and slum board, with little evidence of privately provided services. The private business sector was small, and there was no capitalism in its present dominant form; nobody talked much about middle classes. India then had a regime of protectionist and interventionist policies under 'Licence Raj' with low 'Hindu' rates of economic growth. All this changed with the opening up of India from 1991, the start of India's neoliberal trajectory. We saw this evolving in our research, with increased urban growth and indications that India's rich and poor were growing apart. Income polarisation increased; high-rise apartment towers and shopping malls emerged in cities alongside sprawling slums, which, however, did not seem to change much. India opened up to outside forces of globalisation, following global trends of deregulation and involving non-state actors – notably private-sector firms but also NGOs – to co-govern with the state. A general move occurred towards discourses and practices now labelled 'multi-stakeholder governance' with agreeable assumptions of pluralism and hopes for better, even 'good governance'. And where Mumbai goes, it did grow economically and capitalism struck roots, with lots more money going around. But 'bad governance' also increased, and the benefits of growth were not being shared equally across its classes.

So when faced with the choice to locate my follow-up studies in my 'home city' Chennai, in Delhi or in Mumbai, the latter city seemed to offer most. It was the most globalised Indian city where neoliberal policies, for example seen in public–private cooperation, took hold earlier than elsewhere. With half of its population living in slums, I knew I could study urban poverty in relation to basic services. Mumbai had a lively local democracy with 227 councillors elected to the council of the rich and powerful Mumbai City Corporation (BMC). But apart from this, I decided for the city as I like Mumbai and always much enjoy being there. One can sense it is a powerhouse where stakes are high, a place where people, rich and poor, are all on the move. Notwithstanding poor governance, the megacity remains an intense, vibrant and rich place of culture and street life. It has been labelled a rather tolerant 'city of dreams', attracting both the ultra-rich and dejected Bihari peasants. I kept visiting the city over the years and gradually collected a mass of primary and secondary data, which form the basis of this book. Increasingly I recognised the primacy of politics, which led me to probe local democracy dynamics with its culmination in fiercely fought ward-level elections.

I kept working with contacts and networks established during the Indo-Dutch research project, including local officials, councillors and slum contacts as well as academics and researchers. I worked with scholars of the Jawaharlal Nehru University and Mumbai University, in the latter notably with Abhay Pethe whose advice and Mumbai writings proved invaluable if only to confirm my initial assumptions. My interactions over the years with many staff of the Tata Institute of Social Sciences (TISS) were always useful, where I like to mention Amita Bidhe especially. I am indebted to the All India Institute of

Local Self-Government led by Sneha Palnitkar not only for lots of rich documentation but also for hospitality in my early research years. N. Sridaran of the Delhi School of Planning and Architecture was my window to Delhi and a rich source of urban knowledge. The Indo-Dutch research project coincided with an urban governance project of the Delhi-based Centre de Sciences Humaines, and many of the very rich research findings it yielded found their way into my book. Mutually beneficial and pleasant cooperation ensued with team members, one of whom the much missed late Jos Mooij of ISS, with warm relations enduring with Marie-Helene Zerah, Veronique Dupont and Loraine Kennedy. I kept benefiting from working with Isa Baud with whom I edited a book, while I cooperated closely with three of her PhD students working on Mumbai. Navtej Nainan wrote rich accounts on the local Mumbai state, the different faces of councillors and the far too close relations between powerful building firms and political parties. Padma Desai delved deeply into 'everyday' realities of Mumbai slum upgrading. Lots of details about ward office–level activities and the role of Mumbai's councillors there were uncovered by Tara van Dijk. One fine day I was lucky to meet Mr Deepak Dopat who leads a small but effective research organisation. Apart from many others who helped me gauge details and mechanisms at the slum and ward levels – notably slum-level NGO workers – he was most instrumental in my multi-year drive to put together the pieces of the puzzle making up everyday local governance and politics. Then, over the years I learnt a lot from the many friends I made in Chennai, Mumbai, Delhi, and Bangalore. I enjoyed their company at all sorts of occasions and got to know their views and concerns. These, as well as relevant illustrations and examples tabled by them, are perhaps not used but did feed into this work.

But all such great colleagues do not guarantee good research. One needs informants, and I was lucky to succeed in finding a large variety for this book, which moves from slum households to mediators on to Mumbai's many government institutions. I am very grateful first to the numerous councillors I met over the years. Little by little I came to understand how they work and what drives them. They would notice that the valuation of their performance in this book, based on strong evidence, is not quite favourable. Yet I like to note that an overall assessment is hard to make where they form a heterogeneous group of 227 actors, all working in their own way, in shades from white to black – just like the officials with whom they work closely. And I do acknowledge them as political survivors who come up and survive in rough, competitive and risky conditions. I met and learnt a lot from officials in many of Mumbai's governance agencies, especially those in the Mumbai Corporation (BMC) – the centre of municipal governance. I am grateful to them for sharing views and concerns and for enlightening me on both formal rules and practices, but also 'behind-the-facade' dynamics of informality. Last but not least I want to extent a word of thanks to Mumbai's slum people and neighbourhood social and party workers. I was with them in the huts, houses and streets of their slums in a city belt stretching from Borivali to Malad to Dharavi to Chembur. Always with a translator/assistant, I felt welcome there and at ease, talking individually or in tea shops/focus groups about slum life, slum politics and how men and women navigated complex slum conditions and associated opportunities and risks.

My book compiled all knowledge so collected into one comprehensive account, and I was unavoidably drawn to study what seemed a dominant system of 'informal governance', which figures large in this book. Things like corruption, nepotism and political patronage get plenty of attention where they occur in opaque networks of cooperating or colluding actors. Yet nowhere do I single out anyone as I target the overall system, the relations between actors, their agency and the interfaces between different 'life worlds'. My aim is to present one view as to how Mumbai seems to work and what are the operative mechanisms and trends. But since I often navigate relatively unknown and deep waters, this book is also a research agenda, noting many areas where more evidence is needed. Social justice concerns also form a motivation for my book, where I feel part of a growing group of academics and development practitioners observing alarming trends of globally deepening processes of social and political exclusion or even 'expulsions'. My book can be seen as a case study of exclusion mechanisms for one global city which are likely to operate elsewhere. Exclusion in Mumbai shows, for example, in that poor people are being squeezed between reduced public/social-sector services such as health and education and too costly private ones. While poor women and girls have always bore the brunt of urban poverty, such exclusionary trends affect them particularly severely. A final factor to mention is the agreement among most impartial Mumbai watchers that the metropolis could perform much better. It ranks poorly in a global city index, with governance seen as the key constraint. Not only poor people but all *Mumbaikars* would benefit from improved administration. But, in all this and in any plan for change or repair, it is vital to go beyond de-politicised discourses of governance and superficial accounts of democracy which only consider the 'formal'. To avoid the risk of wasting money or unwittingly being part of the problems, we need to start from actual, local, everyday realities and praxis and be clear as to how systems work and for whom.

I have been fortunate in working with talented academics who shaped my education and world views. Where the fields of slum studies and political anthropology go, I like to mention two. Jan van der Linden guided me into the fascinating world of the urban and slums. Before the concept of 'governance' even existed, he inspired me to use his 'Relations between Actors in Slum Upgrading' framework. My late neighbour Jeremy Boissevain's study 'Friends of Friends' and his work on patronage, political networks and the local mafia were another important inspiration. In this latter field I was lucky to find an active ally in Ward Berenschot with whom I share a strong interest in patronage and political clientelism and whose writings helped shape and sharpen this book. Thanks to Ward and also Abhay Pethe for providing valuable comments and advice on earlier texts of this book, helping to strengthen it. Sujata Patel, the editor of the Routledge Series in which this book appears, was a constant source of encouragement and gentle pressure while providing advice at critical junctions. She saw the potential of my book several years back and was patient enough to wait to see its final completion. Many thanks to Sujata and to Shoma Choudhury of Routledge for a very pleasant cooperation. Thanks too to Steve Graham and Chris Orton for allowing me to reproduce their Mumbai map.

One cannot write a book alone, and many people have directly or indirectly contributed with their interest, encouragement and suggestions. This is where I first like to acknowledge the importance of working in the International Institute of Social Studies (ISS), my academic home. I gained a lot from being part of its fertile ground for development-oriented knowledge, debate and global inputs on the part of my colleagues and our international students alike. ISS provided research support and made possible much of my fieldwork financially. One class I teach already many years is about the stuff of this book, entitled: 'People, Patronage and Politics'. We always have a great time in collecting examples from far too many countries where voters receive a remarkable range of 'freebies' as pre-election gifts and on the ways parties try to make voters keep their promise.

For many different reasons I want to finally mention special persons close to me as friends and neighbours and for steady interest and loyalty: Monique, Bas, Hans, Corrie, Susan and Ramesh, Ria and Charly, Simon, and Ester and Wim. My wife Els and daughter Marieke were always there while this book gradually took shape. My wife Els and daughter Marieke were always there while this book gradually took shape. I enjoyed their support in many practical ways, as well as their confidence and encouragement. They accommodated but also energized my rhythm of ISS teaching, trips abroad and intensive spells of book writing. All that, as they know, is deeply appreciated. I dedicate this book to them.

Amsterdam
29 February 2016

Abbreviations

AAP	Aam Aadmi Party, established in 2014, ruling Delhi since 2015
AC	assistant commissioner (or ward officer – WO)
ACB	Anti-Corruption Bureau
AE	assistant engineer (in ward office)
ALM	Advanced Locality Management – BMC policy with incentives to engage middle-class neighbourhood communities in neighbourhood management
AMC	additional municipal commissioners (four high IAS-level positions in BMC)
BEST	Bombay Electric Supply and Transport Agency
BJP	Bharatiya Janata Party
BMC	Brihanmumbai Municipal Corporation (also MCGM or Municipal Corporation of Greater Mumbai)
BPL	below poverty line (income-based indicator to define poverty)
BSP	Bahujan Samaj Party
BSUP	Basic Services for the Urban Poor programme under JNNURM
CAA	Constitutional Amendment Act (e.g. 74th CAA on urban decentralisation)
CAG	comptroller and auditor general of India
CBO	community-based organisation
CDP	city development plan (e.g. under JNNURM/BSUP)
CIDCO	City and Industrial Development Corporation of Maharashtra
CM	chief minister (of one Indian state)
CPI	Communist Party of India
CPM	Communist Party of India (Marxist)

CRZ	coastal regulation zone, where rules apply to protect vulnerable coastal stretches
CSO	civil society organisation (e.g. CBO, NGO, RWA)
DCR	Development Control Regulations for Greater Mumbai
DMC	deputy municipal commissioner (heads one of the seven administrative Mumbai zones)
DP	development plan for Mumbai (1991–2011, 2014–34)
EC	Election Commission
EVM	electronic voting machine
EWS	economically weaker section (as opposed to low-income groups and higher-income groups)
FHH	female-headed household
FIR	first information report (first step in police investigation)
FSI	floor-space-index: allowable building area per square feet of land
GoI	Government of India
GoM	Government of Maharashtra
IAS	Indian Administrative Service, transferable elite cadre career officials
ICDS	Integrated Child Development Scheme
IHSDP	Integrated Housing and Slum Development Programme
JE	junior engineer (in ward office)
JNNURM	Jawaharlal Nehru National Urban Renewal Mission
MBPT	Mumbai Port Trust
MC	municipal corporator
MCGM	Municipal Corporation of Greater Mumbai, now mostly named BMC
MHADA	Maharashtra Housing and Area Development Authority
MLA	member of the legislative assembly (state level)
MMR	(Greater) Mumbai Metropolitan Region
MMRDA	Mumbai Metropolitan Region Development Authority
MNS	Maharashtra Navnirman Sena (political party, offshoot of SS)
MP	member of parliament (Central Parliament in Delhi)
MPC	metropolitan planning committee (to be formed under the 74th CAA)
MSRDC	Maharashtra State Road Development Corporation
MUDP	Mumbai Urban Development Project
MUTP	Mumbai Urban Transport Project
NCP	Nationalist Congress Party
NDZ	no-development zone
NFC	National Finance Commission (on central–state relations)

NGO	non-governmental organisation
OBC	other backward caste, a group of relatively disadvantaged caste people, but of higher status than the scheduled castes (SCs)
OCG	organised crime group (mafia)
PAP	project-affected persons
PCP	public–community partnership
PDS	public distribution system of subsidised essential food stuffs
PIL	public interest litigation
PPP	public–private partnership
PWD	public works department
RAY	Rajiv Awas Yojana – slum development program
RCF	rail coach factory – Indian Railways
RPI	Republican Party of India
Rs	Indian rupees (one euro is Rs 75 and one dollar is Rs 67 in June 2016)
RTI	Right to Information Act
RWA	resident welfare association
SAP	slum adoption program of the BMC
SC	scheduled caste (former untouchables) or Dalits
SEC	State Election Commission
SFC	State Finance Commission
SHG	self-help groups
SJSRY	Swarna Jayanti Shaharu Rojgar Yojana – urban poverty alleviation scheme
SRA	slum rehabilitation authority
SRS	slum redevelopment scheme as implemented by SRA
SS	Shiv Sena, a political party
SSA	Sarva Shiksha Abhiyan, centrally funded education programme/scheme
SSP	slum sanitation project
ST	scheduled tribes
SWM	solid waste management
TDR	transferable development rights
ULB	urban local body
WB	World Bank
WCMs	wards committees
WO	ward officer, another name for assistant commissioner

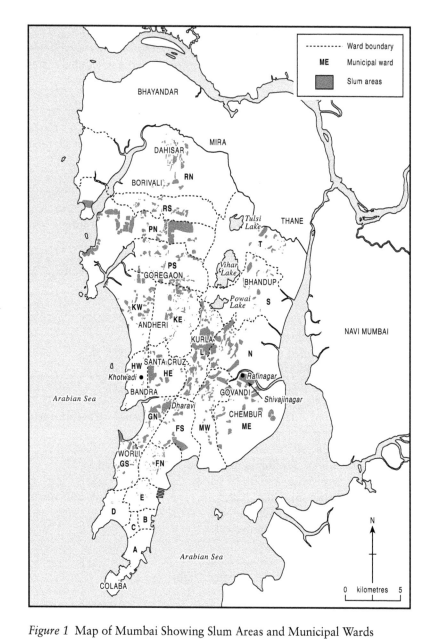

Figure 1 Map of Mumbai Showing Slum Areas and Municipal Wards

Source: This map was prepared by Chris Orton and is reproduced with permission of Steve Graham, Newcastle University, United Kingdom.

Introduction

In 1993, Mrs Amita from Bihar state bought a small plot of land in an emerging slum located in a marshy coastal area of North-West Mumbai. She paid Rs 10,000 to a Shiv Sena party worker, an agent linked to an influential party member. The land sale took place despite the fact that the area was, in fact, a no-development zone (NDZ) as a protected and vulnerable mangrove area. She agreed to pay Rs 80 monthly as rent or protection money. Amita was lucky when she was directed to another 'agent' who offered to informally get her a ration card for Rs 4,000. She now had access to cheaper foodstuffs in subsidised food shops, but more important it meant proof of being a Mumbai resident, which enabled her to obtain a voter identity card. After more people settled in, the water problem became urgent. At the behest of an opposition party agent, plumbers were paid to make an illegal connection to the water mains, which upset nearby middle-class colony people who worried about water quality. In 2003 the entire slum was demolished: 5,000 houses, 36 toilets, 2 temples, clinics and other amenities were turned to rubble by the Mumbai Corporation (BMC), but people returned. After the demolition, Amita found that the more powerful residents such as shopkeepers and cattle-shed owners captured larger pieces of land, moving away from the creek towards the drier, higher grounds and the main road. The poor were left with marshy plots and huts closer to the creek, making them more vulnerable to impacts of high tides – and to even more mosquitoes. Again, in 2004, 250 houses were demolished by the BMC, part of a massive citywide eviction drive that affected about 90,000 households. One thousand four hundred 'illegal' huts were demolished in 2013. But people – perhaps 40,000 – are still there today. Building firms are in touch with politicians in the hope that this formal no-development/NDZ area could become a possible future location for real estate development, through informal processes that had worked in other city areas.[1]

I begin this book on Mumbai's urban poor by introducing the main 'stakeholders' in the slums, municipal government and politics who will take the centre stage in its chapters. We see migrants trying to settle in a city; a slum evolves with its own internal divisions; politicians and party workers act as mediators to help provide services – ostensibly hoping for votes. Middle-class residents feel uneasy about the slum, and builders see prospects to make money out of real estate. The case raises many questions as to the reasons why politicians play such an active role and why this slum, on a clearly unsuitable and prohibited location, remains there for 20 odd years, even while it was demolished several times. How to explain the apparent coexistence of what looks like 'formal' rules such as no-development rules and 'informal' dynamics where illegal plots are sold and water mains are illegally tapped? This book hopes to answer such questions, by specifically examining the dynamics of politics and power, as well as governance changes resulting from recent national and global developments. The liberalisation of the Mumbai and Indian economy, a related exposure to the forces of globalisation and neoliberalism, and the increasing presence of vocal middle classes have strongly impacted Mumbai as a global city as well as its poor and slum people.

This is India changing with the good news of considerable economic growth over the past 20 years where its path of neoliberalism paid rich dividends. Unfortunately, the benefits of increased prosperity have not accrued, or 'trickled down', equally to all. One cannot escape to see processes of polarisation of incomes and assets between India's upper- and middle-income groups on the one hand and vast numbers of poor people on the other hand. In spite of the government rhetoric of 'inclusive governance', or 'housing for all by 2022', fears of processes of segregation are mounting. In Mumbai as in other cities, these can already be seen in the emergence of well-serviced 'gated cities'; large shopping malls; and fancy, glass-towered office blocks – which coexist with populous slum areas. Poor people here face the daily struggle to acquire wages and to live in substandard conditions and insecure housing and grossly inadequate basic services while relying on what many see as deteriorating public government schools and hospitals. This growing apart of poor and working classes from middle and upper classes is not limited to India or its cities; such trends are documented also in countries such as the United States, China and Kenya. It is only good that processes of income polarisation and exclusion currently get much attention (e.g. Oxfam 2015). One voice here is from Sassen (2014) who postulates that global money and investment flows lead to increasing 'expulsions of people', be it house evictions in Spain or the United States or people evicted after land grabs in Africa or Cambodia. Framing 'exclusion' as a form of discrimination, she feels that we see a movement towards deliberate expulsion ('foreclosure') of people, mostly as a result of the concentration of capital and power in companies which are supported by too helpful states. State elites and company elites often have the same interests. Politicians believe that growth is key, which can be achieved 'by merging more or less with the global business elite'. She expects a kind of global demarcation in areas where profits are made and, on the other hand, in neglected areas without prospects, which may disintegrate in processes of global marginalisation.[2]

It appears as if both dimensions of increasing inequality and expulsions can be witnessed in India, as well as a blurring of formerly more distinct roles, relations and identities of businesspeople and politicians. In the broadest sense, this book wants to assess the extent and nature of such processes for Mumbai as well as its determinants, by investigating the changing relations between the local state and its urban poor against the context of changes in India's political economy. Taking into account social, policy and political dimensions, this book hopes to contribute to a better understanding of such deeply worrying global trends by uncovering and illustrating the factors and mechanisms at work in the relatively limited arena of governance and political actors in one global megacity.

Engaging with urban poverty and governance in India

Ever since I engaged with the study of urban India from 1984 (de Wit 1985), I targeted the urban poor in the slums. My Chennai slum study 'Poverty, Policy and Politics in Madras Slums' traced the interfaces between two slums, city agencies and politicians in India's pre-liberalisation era (de Wit 1996). My work as project advisor of a Dutch-funded Bangalore Urban Poverty Alleviation programme (BUPP) taught me the hard way the obstacles of introducing modern, Western-originated buzzwords such as 'participation' and 'empowerment' in slums as complex human habitats (de Wit 2002). Over time I recognised more and more that the prospects for reducing urban poverty obviously start from the efforts, 'agency' and characteristics of the poor themselves but that the local state played a decisive role as to whether these efforts were enabled or rather undermined or even discouraged. Poverty is clearly much more bearable if provisions exist for support in areas such as health, education, water supply, and sanitation, certainly if these are uniformly available to all. But it was obvious that the Indian state was not providing such a uniform system or social safety net, even while a range of apparently well-drafted laws and policies – or 'schemes' – did exist. This puzzle of an apparently active state and policy machinery coexisting with persistent and dire poverty led me to move away from slum studies per se to instead target the nature and dynamics of the policy delivery system in relation to the urban poor. My focus shifted to state–society relations and the interfaces between cities and the poor, within a 'multi-stakeholder governance' framework to assess the dynamics and impacts of governance changes (Baud and de Wit 2008). I was particularly interested in the outcomes of the urban decentralisation policy under the 74th Constitutional Amendment, with its promise of improved governance in terms of proximity, local democracy and participation (de Wit *et al.* 2008). Whereas the 'governance' discourse proved helpful to identify the interests of and relations between weaker and stronger stakeholders, I realised its limitations as a de-politicised perspective underplaying two critical dimensions. One the one hand, it neglects power and power relations as reflected in, but not limited to, party politics and, on the other, the coexistence in most countries of formal and informal institutions and relations.

If governance targets stakeholders in their roles and capacities to 'co-govern' with the government, one would assume most attention for elected politicians, the key movers and agents of democracy. Elected to lead the government, they are expected to act as representatives on the needs and priorities of the voters, ideally all citizens. So while there are plenty studies on urban governance in India – especially its metropolises – surprisingly little seems to be known and published about the actual workings of urban democracy and the winners and losers of the evolving Indian democracy over time. After all, India is a 'new democracy'. The Western liberal democracy model has been transplanted there for only about 65 years. With a long tradition of caste-based hierarchies and historical patterns of inequality, it was never to be expected that Indian democracy would be very similar to that of Sweden, the United States or South Africa. One would expect some 'indigenisation' of the model, where Indian democracy can be considered as a 'variation of democracy' (Goankar 2007; Michelutti 2008; Paley 2002; Witsoe 2013: 4–5). Whereas there are many studies about the more procedural aspects of democracy such as election outcomes and where and why parties win or lose, few studies target the changing nature of urban politics, parties and politicians and increasing evidence of political corruption. One indication concerns 'vote-buying' practices, where voters receive pre-election inducements such as cash or other 'goodies' or 'freebies'. There is no doubt that such and other election strategies are very costly, but only very few studies probe the origin of the massive funds to support parties and candidates (Prabash 2010; Quraishi 2014). Urban democracy is affected by a shifting power balance with indications that Indian middle and upper classes are turning away from electoral politics and prefer to target local state officials directly or through their resident welfare associations. Their need for local government services is reduced through their increasing reliance on privately provided services such as private schools, hospitals, backup water supply, and electricity systems. In contrast, for poor people all over the world, the local state is very important as they typically rely or relied only or mostly on publicly provided state services.

Similar trends can be observed in Mumbai. More or less in concert with other state and parastatal agencies, it is the BMC that provides the services that are most important for poor people. In a way it is rather an old-fashioned corporation engaged with services such as water, transport, public schools, and hospitals. But it is no surprise that it cannot supply all services to all people. The city has grown very fast over the past 60 odd years from 3 to over 12 million inhabitants, accommodating many poor migrants. Both administrative and financial capacities have been and are under stress, and in a way it is remarkable that the city is as liveable as it is, considering the multi-faceted challenges it coped with over the years. After all, it is South Asia's most globalised city and a busy port and transport hub. Its economy grew by 4.6 per cent in 2013. Many companies have headquarters here, and it contributes significantly to India's tax incomes and growth. In a Global Cities Initiative report which compares Mumbai with other global cities, it is pictured as a 'city of dreams', and it is true that it attracts both the global high and mighty and dejected Bihari peasants. It represents a symbol of opportunity, modern life and vibrant culture. But Mumbai scores poorly on many indicators in the ranks of global cities and is seen to be both successful and underperforming, and at risk to compromise its long-term appeal (Clark and Moonen 2014). The latter source (Clark and Moonen 2014: 21) perceives its governance framework as the most fundamental obstacle, and my study intends to delve deeply into what constitutes Mumbai multi-agency governance and changes over time – with urban poverty outcomes as its benchmark but noting other areas where the city could do better.

One example is that BMC policy is changing too, where it embraces neoliberal reforms by giving ample opportunities to the private sector. Just like we see in other countries with a similar trajectory, it is the poor who are affected most here. Mumbai slum housing is now to be produced through public–private–community 'partnerships'; basic services come with user fees, and there is a mushrooming of private schools and clinics. At the same time indications are of a neglect or even closure of public schools, clinics and hospitals – making access to quality health and education even more problematic. This seems one reason that the urban poor are much more engaged with local democracy while voting more in elections. Access to local state institutions is sought by using mediators, who are most effective if linked to politics, notably local political leaders and municipal councillors, in Mumbai named 'corporators'. Electoral competition between parties in slums is considerable, with slums much more politicised than non-slum city areas. I argue that the propensity of poor and other people to use mediators to get access to the state is mirrored by a preference of state agents – officials and politicians – to allocate state benefits on a personal, case-by-case basis. Such dynamics are captured in the perspective of the 'mediated state' (Berenschot 2010). This perspective highlights supply-side problems for the state to cater to the needs of all, but also the power and dependency mechanisms where state agents position themselves as 'gatekeepers' to extract rents as bribes or votes. Rich people, poor people and businesspeople are all affected by the way Mumbai's local state works, but poor people have fewest options or alternatives. They depend on politically linked agents in their quest for public entitlements and state support and are the most active and committed voters locally. This raises the question as to whether the slum dwellers' political preferences and electoral support translate into policies or reforms addressing the structural determinants of their poverty. Or could it be that the poor are critical 'vote banks', helping elect politicians who turn their back on them as soon as elected, so condoning trends of socio-economic exclusion and spatial segregation?

Initial evidence is not encouraging. In an earlier study (de Wit and Berner 2009), I argued that, for many reasons, poor urban people generally fail to organise for sustained and effective collective action and that, in contrast, they 'position themselves for patronage', preferring to rely on vertical brokerage relations with local mediators. This, in turn, is accommodated but also sustained by politicians in what has been termed 'patronage democracies' (Chandra 2004, 2007). As elaborated in the next chapter, Chandra believes that politicians misuse their discretionary powers to allocate state benefits and opportunities to individuals, not in return for bribes but for votes with the image of 'elections as auctions'. The juxtaposition of formal democracy and democratic institutions such as the Election Commission, and such informal (dependency) mechanisms of (political) patronage therefore will be a key theme of this book, following perspectives stressing the critical role of institutions, for example as 'the rules of the game' in relation to governance and poverty (cf. Jones and Presler-Marshall 2012). The study of local democracy and local politics will naturally focus on the manifestation of power, which I assume to take place foremost through informal dynamics and 'everyday political practices'. Even though hard to study, I anticipated rewards in terms of depicting realities as experienced by all stakeholders and the 'behind the facade' mechanisms of formal electoral democracy, which may be more important than formal laws, rules and institutions.

I refer here to perspectives considering the formal state – represented by ministries, political parties, courts, the constitution, and municipal rules as facades behind or around which important informal institutions and dynamics operate. Examples are systems of corruption and nepotism, collusion between state officials and private firms, patronage relations, and incidences of vote buying and political corruption. The study of such informal dynamics has not been quite pronounced in India (a rare example is Harris-White 2003: 74, who studied the 'actually existing state' and who refers to the Indian state as a 'shadow state'). This is in some contrast to, for example, Africa where more research is done into what is called 'everyday governance' or 'everyday politics'. Looking beyond the formal state, the focus is on actual realities – formal, informal or hybrid forms – which determine 'who gets what, when, how', when it comes to access to services, housing, licences, pensions, and the like (e.g. Blundo 2006; Lund 2006 on 'twilight institutions'). Lindberg (2003) asks the question as to whether democratisation in Ghana contributes to the reproduction of neo-patrimonialism, rather than actually counteracting it. A study on South Africa, entitled 'Patronage Politics Divides Us', examines local politics by assessing dynamics of poverty, patronage and inequality (MISTRA 2014).

The study of urban India: too little attention for the poor, informality and politics

This book argues that informality is not a separate part or characteristic of the local state or its subjects but in fact an integral, if not dominant, trait of power-driven politics and governance. Far too little attention is devoted to such informal realities and mechanisms. It seems likely that the well-meant work of donor agencies and even NGOs is undermined by a stubborn reliance on the facades of formal institutions and processes, rather than on 'everyday realities'. This book wants to probe these by investigating what I believe are three understudied areas or 'black boxes' in the study of one Indian metropolis: the changing conditions and power position of the urban poor vis-à-vis other governance actors; the nature of local democracy by focusing on the roles of municipal councillors in relation to the urban poor; and the role of the private, corporate business sector as regards local politics and governance. On the one hand, this book wants to probe the 'everyday' micro-level political relations and governance mechanisms operating between poor urban households, slums as unique human habitats, and the municipality, in this case the powerful and rich Mumbai Municipal Corporation (BMC). But it also aims to examine the bigger picture, to take a broad helicopter view of city-level evolution starting from another apparent gap in the study of Indian urban governance, which is a lack of contextualisation. I try and bring together and interrelate diverse socio-cultural (caste, gender, identity) and socio-economic dimensions (poverty, informal-sector labour, land dynamics) with the aforementioned political mechanisms while tracing urban governance and policy outcomes.

Even while this book broadly considers urban politics and governance in relation to the urban poor, where the Mumbai municipal corporators (MCs) are considered key agents, the point of reference of this book is the city's urban poor and slum dwellers. Slums accommodate half of Mumbai's population, and I argue that both relatively well-established lower-income groups and poor people can be found there. But to a higher or lesser degree, all slum people face problems of shelter insecurity and inadequate services notably as regards water, toilets and health care. Among the far-from-homogenous slum people, divisions such as those of caste, religion, gender, income, and political affiliation may hinder organised claim-making action but also allow for internal exploitation inside slums where 'landlords' exploit tenants and local moneylenders disturb already-indebted households (Boo 2012; de Wit 1996). There is a need to establish who and where precisely are the urban poor of Mumbai, those of at the bottom of the city's vast pyramids of assets and resources. This book has a bias towards the position and critical role of women and girls as regards household management and overall livelihoods, making the case that urban poverty is most severe among women and girls, Dalits (the former untouchables) and minorities such as Muslims and recent migrants.

Yet this book is not a slum study, where its focus is on the interfaces of municipal governance in Mumbai by exploring the relations between the 227 elected MCs and the urban poor/the city slums. Following Gowda and Sridharan (2012: 235) and Weinstein (2014) in terming them 'political entrepreneurs', I ask the question as to whether MCs play a role in the inclusion of the poor in the social, economic and political fabric of the city. By impartially considering them as versatile and powerful 'spiders in citywide webs', I trace their political history over time – for example against the rise of the Shiv Sena political party, now dominating city politics. I picture them as political survivors, skilfully adjusting to changing times, and to changing stakeholders in governance and democracy, for example their strained relations with the upcoming middle classes and their associations. In contrast, it appears as if their relations with private-sector firms and the corporate sector are getting ever closer – to the extent that some see a blurring of positions where many Mumbai corporators receive election funding from private-sector firms, and many develop into prosperous businesspeople. It has been argued that the most powerful Mumbai governance stakeholders are not, in fact, its politicians, but rather the very powerful real estate and building business firms of Mumbai. Engaging in transactions in and on the scarce and hence extremely expensive city land, they construct middle- and upper-class housing and are actively involved in the lucrative business of 'slum redevelopment' (Nainan 2006, 2012). They are believed to be very close to the Mumbai political parties and politicians, which may take the form of deals between the party and a builder, who is 'enabled' or 'facilitated' by local politicians such as corporators. Indications are that builders and developers help finance the election campaigns of corporators and their parties in return for future secret deals and agreements. As noted, such funds may be used to provide inducements to voters in the context of India's dominant model of 'vote bank politics'. I argue that such practice is not new; I noted it in comparatively modest forms in my former Chennai research. Scott (1969) investigated the relations between politicians, the business sector and poor voters long back by applying the perspective of 'machine politics' to India. Yet it is puzzling that not more attention is given today to such dynamics, if only now that India's business sector has grown so powerful in a context of relatively unregulated governance, so much so that some are perceiving a trend of India moving towards a 'corporate state' (Ravindran 2013: 245) or having traits of 'crony capitalism'.[3] So whereas this book is partly a study of the policies and bureaucracy of the Mumbai City Corporation, I assert that the real action, the actual decision making and the articulation of interests and power, lays in politics and with politicians. The study of governance needs to be fully informed by its submission to politics, or, perhaps more accurately, politicians. Ultimately then, this is a study of local democratic practice in one Indian city, where it is assumed that things may be pretty similar in other Indian cities, but conceivably also in the cities of other developing countries. It is hoped that this study's methods and broad scope may inspire others to engage similarly with other megacities. I now present a brief overview of the state of current research on India's large cities and urban development to contextualise this book and to indicate where it wants to fill perceived gaps.

Urban poverty

It has been noted that there is something of an upsurge in the studies on the city in South Asia, with a range of books and articles targeting the Indian city, many of which seek to understand the economic, political and social life of cities mostly through the lens of neoliberalism and globalisation (e.g. Anjaria and McFarlane 2011: 5; Coelho *et al.* 2013; Desai and Sanyal 2012; Shatkin 2014). As mentioned, I perceive a neglect of three themes in the current studies: the everyday livelihoods of the urban poor; the omnipresence of 'informality', notably a neglect of corruption as an integral and essential part of India's urban governance; and, most striking, a neglect of politics and the critical role of politicians in urban governance, especially the working of vote bank politics where local democracy meets with service delivery dynamics for and livelihoods of poor people.

There is no doubt that India experiences far-reaching changes in terms of governance, with novel power configurations of stakeholders in the national and global private sector, in foreign direct investment, in public–private partnerships (PPPs), and in new ways of urban finance such as the massive Jawaharlal Nehru National Urban Renewal Mission (JNNURM) (Banerjee-Guha 2010; Baud and de Wit 2008; Sivaramakrishnan 2011). Shatkin and Vidyarthi (2014) perceive two emerging lines of inquiry, one of which targeting India's urban political economy in relation to spatial change. An example could be Roy's (2009a: 826) exploration of new geographies of theory as applied to South Asia. Here the concept of informality mostly figures in terms of the 'production of space', which produces an 'uneven geography of spatial value thereby facilitating the urban logic of creative destruction' (Roy 2009a: 826); Roy does not further elaborate or clarify this latter process. Another suggested theme concerns the contextual factors impacting the social and political dynamics of Indian cities. Many studies here are framed in post-colonial theory, focusing 'cultural resistance to externally imposed political and social projects' (Shatkin and Vidyarthi 2014: 3). Such inquiries may start from an interest in the 'subaltern', a complex term which may be taken to mean the poor and marginalised (e.g. 'the subalterns as the poor who devise strategies to contest the power of literate bureaucrats'; Gupta 2012: 37). The term may refer to the Indian population categorised as not belonging to the elites and to the conditions of the people outside the elite class, associated with a sense of subordination (Roy 2011a: 226). For all the frequent mentioning of the 'subaltern classes', and a concern that they are experiencing processes of exclusion, marginalisation or enduring structural violence (Gupta 2012), it seems striking that much of the recent writing on Indian cities neglects these groups not only in terms of their livelihoods but also as to how they perceive matters. One notes a preference to discuss urban developments in relatively broad terms, mostly in sweeping language of the 'neoliberal' globalisation or the 'post-colonial' globalisation (e.g. Roy 2011a).

This is in some contrast to a felt need to engage more with the study of urban poverty, where Coelho and Maringanti (2012: 40) argue that

> There is an urgent need for more careful and sensitive work, both empirical and theoretical, that explores urban poverty as shaped by struggles over resources and meanings and by city-specific political constellations defined by infrastructure projects, party and patronage networks and urban renewal processes.

Key themes mentioned include the changes in the dynamics and determinants of urban poverty, a need to count the poor and to locate them in spatial dynamics and attention for how the poor are governed. Nevertheless by and large one notes a lack of comprehensive studies providing solid evidence as to what happens to the urban subalterns, for example whether they do have or act on agency – despite enormous odds and oppressive structures. How, actually, do changes under the present neoliberal Indian regime impact the urban poor, for example in terms of ever more evidence of user fees and the privatisation of quality education and health care? What seems to be missing are in-depth, micro-level studies, first, of the subaltern urban poor as such, how they cope, how they adjust to governance and political changes. In my endeavour to triangulate my own Mumbai slum data and findings over 10 years of research with those of others, I was surprised to find only few recent slum or urban poverty studies (older monographs are Desai 1995; Lobo and Das 2001). Consistent probably with pressure on and time constraints of academics to publish articles rather than books, there are very useful recent but single-topic contributions, mostly and understandably focusing on one dimension such as water, slum relocation, gender and suicide, food security, and quite a few studies on the Dharavi slum. Very useful recent exceptions are the detailed ethnography of a Mumbai airport slum by Boo (2012) and a book with inside views from Dharavi (Campana

2013). It appears as if preoccupations with Indian city studies today largely miss grassroots/slum level and political realities, focusing more on issues of geography and 'space'. There are too few anthropological or ethnographic-type studies uncovering everyday struggles by the urban poor and the ways they perceive and practise politics. Many useful city studies lack a contextualisation as to how slum life links to politics, how elections link to builders and developers and how municipal governance is undermined by systemic corruption. A notable exception is the work by Berenschot (2010, 2011), whose excellent work on political fixers, the role of goondas and the 'mediated state' in Ahmadabad are an inspiration for this book, as elaborated later. Likewise, I benefited much from and built on the work of Khan (2005), Kumar and Landy (2009), Leftwich (2005), and Witsoe (2013). As a political anthropologist and long-term teacher on governance and public policy, I thought it might be good to apply something like a holistic perspective 'integrating the material with the nonmaterial or the pragmatic with the ideal' (Pardo and Prato 2012: 85). I saw the need for a text addressing issues of power, identity, gender, and inequality in relation to governance and democracy, linking and bridging several disciplines, notably anthropology, political science and policy studies.

Informality and corruption

Today, corruption is a dominant theme in India, if only as an election theme in the 2014 national elections framed as 'good governance', the recent Delhi election which brought to power the 'common man' AAP Party and the short-lived popularity of Anna Hazare's anti-corruption movement. It surprises to see little engagement with the theme in current urban studies. Even while admitting the existence of a sphere of informality (which contested concept is elaborated later), few studies target the omnipresence of informality such as the entrenched and systemic corruption, which has an enormous negative impact on the daily lives of the urban poor (e.g. hawkers, auto rickshaws, prostitutes). Beyond such 'petty corruption', there are far too many signs that public budgets are misused by politicians and officials, including entitlements for the poor (Debroy and Bhandari 2012). Gupta (2012: 78) disagrees with the distinction that Chatterjee (2004) makes between the state, civil society and political society; he argues that

> instead of taking the distinction between the state and civil society as a point of departure and then analytically mopping up the vast remainder with a third term (*political society*) I propose to employ

the discourse of corruption to argue that scholars need to reinterpret what they mean by terms like the state and civil society.

He believes that, in India, the discourse of corruption is a key arena through which the state, citizens and other organisations imagine the state; 'it is a mechanism through which the state itself is discursively constituted. Corruption is an essential lens for understanding the meaning of the state in the Indian context'. Following from this, I will assess this notion that corruption is not just an accidental and dysfunctional aspect of the state but in fact central to it against Mumbai realities. The distinction by Chatterjee (2004) between 'political' and 'civil' society is shown to be unhelpful and confusing, as realities are of major porosities in the roles and status of all city actors (Kumar and Landy 2009). Hence, I intend to go beyond less relevant discourses and fuzzy concepts such as 'imagined states', 'community participation' and empowerment to concretely ask the question what corruption means for Mumbai's urban poor and for all those, in fact, dependent on them: from local brokers and employers to corporators keen to be elected (this may be what Roy 2011a: 229 means by 'poverty capital'). Generally, studies of governance, democracy and urban development which neglect corruption, informality and illegality seem to be futile, and not only where India goes.

Local governance, local democracy and everyday politics

Neglected local governance

India is 'the world's largest democracy', so one would expect urban studies to at least take into account the role of politics and politicians in urban governance, but this is not always the case. This is a surprising lacuna if one considers the vibrancy of Indian democracy and the fact that politics is the bread and butter of Indians rich and poor, as one cannot escape notice in daily news coverage in newspapers and on TV. It also shows in a degree of neglect for politics in terms of assessing dimensions of power such as the basis of power in slums and of politicians, as well as forms of power use and abuse. Where the term 'urban' ultimately refers to a limited category of space such as 'the city', one explanation may be linked to the fact that 'local' governance and democracy studies are under-represented in India, as argued by Mooij and Lama-Rewal (2009: 93). They perceive a general lack of interest among political scientists interest in local-level politics in India, but it seems there is a more general lack of academic interest in the 'local'. This seems matched by little interest in urban local governance on the part of Indian policymakers and officials. If only for political and electoral (vote bank) reasons, Indian policies, welfare programmes and political activity have tended to favour rural populations more than those urban, where the majority of India's population (voters) lives. Rajivan (2013: 140) notes a fundamental disrespect and disregard for lower levels of government. Yet, interestingly, he is also open to the thesis that in fact 'we know the potential power of local leadership and figure that it is better to keep those guys under leash'. This needs to be kept in mind in assessing the powers of, as well as the constraints faced by, Mumbai's corporators. This surprising lack of interest in local governance and democracy among donors, national bureaucrats or academics appears to be a global fact, as argued by Boex (2010)[4] who states convincingly that 'all development is local'. It is critical to appreciate that all development efforts and the delivery of pro-poor services on which people rely on a day-to-day basis take place at the local level, at the level of 'street-level bureaucrats' (Lipsky 1980). Whatever national governments formulate as policy and priority and whatever budgets they earmark, it is only at the local level and through local governments that policy and budgets are translated (if not transformed or reduced beyond recognition) into concrete benefits for common people. If there is no inclusive development at the local level, there will be none. And whereas there are certainly solid local urban governance studies (e.g. Hust and Mann 2005; Ruet and Tawa Lama-Rewal 2009; Siddiqui and Bhowmik 2004 on Mumbai; Sivaramakrishnan 2000, 2006), there are fewer urban studies of local politics or local democracy. This seems to contrast with the notion of a 'considerable interest in recent years in the character and consequences of poor people's politics in India and throughout the global South' (Weinstein and Ren 2009: 407). Characterising such studies in terms of 'subaltern politics', 'deep democracy', 'political society', and the 'politics of inclusion', they argue that political theorists have examined how seemingly marginalised groups assert their centrality and make political claims on the state. In their view, two main sets of questions are being asked: those about the interests and organisational capacity of the urban poor and how political mobilisation is shaped by neoliberal globalisation, transnational activism and democratic decentralisation. A second set is about the state's responsiveness to these mobilisations. Ongoing urban transformations are seen to have created more inclusive spaces while forcing the state to engage more directly with the urban poor. However, just like was noted for slum livelihoods, attention to the nitty-gritty details of such 'transformations' and 'spaces' or of poor people's capacity to organise seems scarce (with some exceptions like Bhide 2006 and Harris 2005). What motivates the urban poor while voting in elections? Do they actually organise or mobilise under diverse and adverse conditions? Relations between the urban poor and local politicians, the role of mediators or political fixers in the everyday functioning of India's democracy and the precise nature and quality of local democracy as perceived and experienced by the urban poor also deserve much more scrutiny. But some recent studies do target the informal and often mutually beneficial relations between municipal councillors and the urban poor (Berenschot 2009, 2010, 2011), and this book is partly inspired by the perspectives presented here such as the mediated state and 'patronage democracy' (Chandra 2004, also Kumar and Landy 2009). Such authors target relations between state and society – or, rather, the blurring lines between both as well as the porosity of the assumedly separate boxes of 'executive, legislative and judiciary'. Yet, here too, the agency of the poor as voters and otherwise in what may appear to them as a remote shadow state with twilight institutions is not addressed sufficiently. Building on such work, I try to contribute to a better understanding of poor people's political behaviour and praxis, notably the role of identity, as well as of 'money' and 'muscle power' in elections. I want to go beyond shallow accounts as those by Krishna (2008: 10) on poor people and democracy, which ask the wrong questions, failing to address both the daily predicaments of the poor, the fundamental informal realities they live in, and how such an adverse context shapes their actions in what people tell them is democracy (cf. Witsoe 2013). While considering 'democracy shifts', the position and role of the Mumbai middle classes in elections and as regards councillors is examined. I contest the position that 'the middle class grows through promoting equality of opportunity, and having larger middle classes has shown to work positively for democracy' (Krishna and Booth 2008: 159). Against the background of these and other lacunae listed in the study of urban poverty, local urban governance and local/slum politics in India, I now turn to the objectives and set-up of this book. Key concepts and analytical perspectives used are further elaborated in Chapter 1.

Book objectives, research methods and book plan

Book objectives

The main concern of this book is to order and bring together a wealth of data, facts, trends, perspectives, and opinions on the poverty, politics and governance of Mumbai, as are available today.

I will note below that my fieldwork data and long-term urban engagement with India form the starting point and core basis of this book, but it could not have been written without the masses of information available from newspapers, journal articles, books, online publications, and so on. There are plenty of insightful, rich, thought-provoking articles and special books on diverse aspects of Mumbai, probably more than on any other Indian city. Academics, MA and PhD students, journalists and NGO workers have all written most usefully on slum policy, the realities of water supply, the evolution of the Mumbai mafia, practices of vote buying and BMC administration. Remarkably, and certainly conveniently, all of these are documented and in the public domain. Much of this is very useful. Yet, as indicated, there is a lack of comprehensive texts bringing together interrelated key factors and dynamics at different governance levels in their full complexity, while examining the interweaving and juxtaposition of formal and informal governance mechanisms. Early comprehensive studies provided a kind of baseline, which were gratefully used (Patel and Masselos 2003; Patel and Thorner 2003). I saw a need and an opportunity to examine these everyday dynamics of one Indian city in relation to its urban poor, which would help to see politics and governance for what they really are and bring about. To this end, first, I needed to combine perspectives and methods from several academic disciplines such as anthropology, policy studies and political science. Even while not quite innovative, there is an outline here of a method or approach which has the potential to yield much needed detailed knowledge on multiple aspects of poverty and the contextual determinants to alleviate it.

Related to this, and second, this book wants to provide an account, as impartial as possible, of governance realities of Mumbai as a kind of political anthropology case study. It offers one view as to how all the *Mumbaikars,* all stakeholders – rich and poor, common men or politician, together made and manage their city. The account seems critical, but it is evidence based where I have tried to stick close to how Mumbai people themselves see things and made sure to double-check facts where possible. I made ample use of their newspapers and journals, I watched their TV channels and over 10 years I talked to lots of people including poor slum widows to corporators to top BMC officials and Mumbai-based academics. Due to the complexity of its broad agenda, this book surely misses points, gets details wrong and may contain misunderstandings. I can only hope there is merit in my account, and I am fully open to discuss contested findings or conclusions. Even while its governance could and should improve much – most urgently and critically in caring for its poor people – Mumbai does work in its own way. In spite of its numerous constraints, corruptions and challenges, it remains a strong city. This is a city that works, a city that moves as all citizens seem to be on the move. To me it is a fascinating place which I found easy and pleasant to engage with. No one disappointed me in my quest for ever more details and deeper understanding of the city's mysteries and complexities.

This book casts a wide net and deliberately raises many issues, hoping to better understand the larger city context of poverty and local state dynamics and how such mechanisms link to and influence each other. Here and there I enter terrains explored less or address topics not studied much or only in isolation across the wide spectrum of poverty, local democracy and public administration themes. More evidence and in-depth research is needed on many topics, with the key ones noted in the conclusions. This book is therefore also a research agenda on the broad, multi-faceted agenda of India's uneven urban development. It charts understudied areas and notes topics lacking any or solid evidence. As noted, the everyday working of local, grass-roots-level democracy is an area needing much more attention, but also matters such as differences between poor men and women as patronage agents, or, in terms of informality, how and to what extent the lucrative 'transfer system' in the BMC affects its administrative machinery.

I believe that there is a lack of comprehensive city studies globally. It is likely that Mumbai realities have similarities with other large cities governed nominally as democratic cities, say Lagos, Mexico city or Manila. Probing and charting such cities through in-depth analysis of interrelated socio-economic and political traits and trends would yield critical knowledge to understand processes of inclusion and exclusion, no doubt, operating there too. This should help our understanding of poverty trends beyond poverty lines; the full and ugly impacts of corruption and help unmask many false or tenuous accounts as to the virtues and promises of local democracy globally. Democracy is here to stay, but if there are challenges or even defects, we need to see them for what they are. Only then will donor efforts for reform, or 'democratisation' and NGO efforts to organise or 'empower' people, be grounded in empirical, evidence-based realities as they should be. Since exclusion trends are global, we need solid micro- to macro- to global-level data to understand dynamics with a view to begin halting them. If only from a social justice point of view all efforts are needed here and this book hopes to inspire students and others to get engaged in this critical field.

Where India goes, the study area of urban poverty, urban development and urban politics seems less well established, certainly when compared to similar rural topics. Detailed studies of urban dynamics are too scarce, with a specially striking absence of solid monitoring and evaluation studies of big urban programmes such as SJSRY and JNNURM, and also the Mumbai Slum Redevelopment Scheme (SRS). Is anyone learning from past policy achievements and the more frequent policy failures? All this stands in marked contrast to projections that India's urbanisation rate may rise from the present 31 per cent (2011 Census) to as much as 60 per cent (adding 404 million people) by 2050. There is a clear and present need to invest more in studying urban issues, to learn from the problems and constraints in past and current policy and to develop forward-looking scenarios and associated future needs. This book also wants to argue the case for academics to engage with this huge and increasingly important – and fascinating – theme of urban development and politics.

Finally, at the highest level of abstraction, this book aims to contribute to academic and policy debates and discourses on governance, democracy and development. It is located in political science, cultural and political anthropology and policy studies. One theme addressed is the claim that democracy contributes to development (cf. Khan 2005; Leftwich 2005; Witsoe 2013). It illustrates the relationship between local democracy and poverty alleviation from a bottom-up perspective, where India is a rich test case as a functioning democracy in a country with massive numbers of poor people.

Research methods

This book is based on a combination of primary and secondary data. Even while a first study took place into the role and position of women municipal councillors in Mumbai in 2002 (de Wit and Holzner 2003), data collection for this book through interviews, surveys, slum-level group discussions and the like started in 2004 with a research project funded jointly by the Netherlands and India IDPAD[5] research programme. The project *New Forms of Governance in Indian Mega-cities: Decentralisation, Financial Management and Partnerships in Urban Environmental Services* explored governance shifts in Urban India (Baud and de Wit 2008; Kundu 2006). Concentrating on the background to and impacts of India's urban decentralisation, my focus was on the BMC administration, its local corporators, and the nature and performance of the newly established wards committees (WCMs) from 2000. Over three years many interviews were held with corporators, ward- and city-level officials, including top bureaucrats and junior engineers, while a questionnaire-based survey was held under corporators and ward officials with the support of M. Pinto. (Pinto and de Wit 2006). The research project also covered New Delhi, where changing arenas of urban governance were studied, (de Wit 2009a) and Chennai where the focus was mostly on local corporators but also on slum women self-help groups (de Wit 2009b; de Wit and Berner 2009). Apart from the one-time surveys, good relations were established with many corporators, in terms of visiting their offices and houses, witnessing the working of party offices such as the Shiv Sena *shakas* and joining meeting hours where corporators meet (poor) people of their constituency. Many such contacts have been nurtured and maintained up to the present day, representing a rich source of information on facts and trends. Following the end of the project follow up research was carried out over subsequent years in Mumbai for short periods with an initial focus on the slum adoption programme (SAP) under which, at least on paper, slum dwellers and their 'community organisations' were to be enabled and paid to keep their own slums clean (de Wit 2010a). Following Blundo (2006) I framed the programme as a grassroots-level example of 'the informal privatisation of slum services'. Follow-up visits were made to the major Mumbai relocation areas in later years. The evolution of a one SRS, initiated in 2007, was traced over time, starting with a baseline survey and tracing turbulent community dynamics resulting from the contested involvement of two building firms, each linking with one local slum leader/faction. These experiences and dynamics have fed into the present book, but the plans to add a chapter on these have been dropped for reasons of space (de Wit 2016 forthcoming). With a view to underpin the democratic and electoral dimensions of Mumbai's local governance, a study was made of the 2012 Mumbai municipal elections. Targeting one ward with many slums and working from there, we followed the campaigning of several candidate corporators, associating ourselves with some of them.

So while key methods to collect data over time have included participant observation, open ended as well as structured interviews and questionnaire surveys, these have mostly targeted politicians/corporators, officials and key informants such as academics, retired commissioners, private-sector entrepreneurs and contractors. It is one limitation of this book that it aims to start from the urban poor, but that it is not a slum study, in the sense of not being fully based on primary slum data. Always with an assistant, I spent lots of time in many slums in most parts of the city (in tea shops, near massive garbage dumps, at political meetings, in all types of dwellings), with plenty 'focus group discussions'. Yet I did not carry out my own slum surveys as I did for my 1996 Madras book. For that reason, Chapter 3 on the Mumbai slums is mostly based on secondary sources. I tried as best as possible to fill this gap by using secondary data from many other studies, just like how I filled gaps in hard to grapple topics related to informality and corruption. As indicated, only few in-depth Mumbai slum studies seem to exist, reason why I benefited much from the detailed slum study of everyday life and household struggles by Boo (2012). I made grateful use of the comprehensive 2009 Mumbai Development Report (MCGM 2009), and a range of articles targeting specific issues such as nutrition, domestic violence or slum sanitation, and articles, papers and reports from NGOs working in the slum (e.g. Campana 2013). Very useful too was Bjorkman's (2013) study of pre-election slum level money allocations. A second limitation of this book pertains to its endeavour to uncover as much as possible of the actual informal governance realities of 'rent seeking', brokerage and politicisation. Such dynamics and mechanisms have been brought out, but, as could be expected, it proved hard to get straight and frank answers from either politicians or bureaucrats on such sensitive matters. It was often only indirectly, in bits and pieces, during very informal meetings and over meals that clues, pointers and facts might be given: for example the nature and size of the expected cuts payable by a contractor to BMC officials; the amounts to be paid for a lucrative transfer; the way money is distributed to voters just before the elections. Such knowledge has continuously been validated/triangulated with other informants as well as newspapers, and the most likely outcomes are presented here. As indicated, I am open to correction and adjustment, and any errors are completely mine. Even if I caught some facts wrong, I hope at least to have uncovered the key operative forces and mechanisms.

Over all these years, support was provided by excellent research assistants and translators – who also collected data in periods between fieldwork. In addition I was in touch with NGO workers in several slums as another rich information source. I benefited much through working closely with the Tata Institute of Social Sciences and Mumbai University, the Jawaharlal Nehru University in New Delhi and the All India Institute of Local Self-Government (which published the Mumbai Human Development Report [MMCM 2009]). Grateful use was made of excellent data sources as represented in the work by PhD and MA scholars, especially Nainan (2006, 2012), but also Desai (2002) and van Dijk (2006, 2011a).

It is important to note that less attractive facts and trends as regards the BMC administration, cases of malfeasance or poor management, which are part of this book, are not new. These are and have been reported and documented by some of the earlier authors, and on an almost daily basis in the newspapers. If that is not convincing, this book's findings are corroborated by high-status official reports investigating BMC irregularities. There is, first of all, the damning report on the Thane Municipal Corporation (TMC; neighbouring the BMC and part of the Greater Mumbai area) drafted by the Nandlal Commission, which reported in detail on systemic corruption and systems of agreed cuts accruing to officers and corporators.[6] Another important negative landmark report was the committee investigating realities of Mumbai city planning led by retired Maharashtra chief secretary D'Souza in 1987. It scrutinised the Mumbai's development plan and 'is a scathing indictment of the Sena-ruled BMC. The Committee judged that builder's testimony has exerted undue influence in the drafting of the Development Plan' (Thakkar 2003: 261). The discussion in the BMC Council gave rise to ugly scenes and a virtual battle of words between ruling and opposition parties, but the report did nothing to improve matters: 'irregularities in matters of land continue . . . a prominent part is played by politicians in all these deals' (Thakkar 2003: 261). Another devastating report was published by a committee led by the former municipal commissioner S.S. Tinaikar, bringing out in detail the working of corruption in the BMC contracting and implementation of works with depressingly numerous cases of malfeasance and collusion of politicians–officials–contractors (Nainan 2012; Pinto and Pinto 2005: 513–14; Tinaikar 2003). The comprehensive, forthright book by Pinto and Pinto (2005) itself is an excellent source to understand the assumed but also real workings of the BMC. So it is not that this book should surprise BMC staff or observers. Generally, the majority of facts and trends in this book are in the public domain and accessible to all, where I took care to back up or triangulate my own findings and views with widely available secondary sources. My main job was to compile and then order this mass of data.

And, in addition, for all of India's challenges in governance and democracy, it is a liberal democracy in at least the sense of having unusually free and open media. TV stations, newspapers, online sites and journals openly and deeply report on and probe even the most sensitive and unholy corruption cases, scams and illicit deals and cases of 'the nexus' between powerful stakeholders. One may ask as to whether all this has actually helped reduce such negative, even disturbing, phenomena, but the media have greatly helped to inform this book with a

view to be alerted to, illustrate or underpin relevant incidents and critical processes. It will not be surprising to see plenty of references to the
Mumbai edition of the *Times of India,* but one will find references to
Indian Express, DNA, Hindustan Times, and *The Hindu,* apart from
quotes from journals such as *Frontline, Tehelka* and *India Today.* I
am aware of the risks involved: some papers are close to certain political parties and/or owned by self-interested private-sector firms; some
papers may not be expected to publish certain news,[7] so there might
be a bias in the articles used. To reduce risks here, I avoided clearly
biased reports, while cross-checking information with other media and
my own informants.

Plan of the book

Having set the agenda of this book, in Chapter 1 I briefly introduce the
key general and analytical perspectives needed for contextualising this
study and to ground it firmly in India's trends of urban poverty and
governance on the one hand, and in relevant current conceptual and
theoretical perspectives on the other. I depict urbanisation trends, the
size and nature of urban poverty and growing urban inequality. Shifts
in urban governance following India's wholehearted embracement of
a neoliberal regime are traced. The changing nature of Indian politics
is theorised next: the apparent emergence of a new type of 'political
entrepreneur' politician less bothered about the long-term welfare of
voters or constituencies, but self-interestedly focused on rent seeking
when in office, which may well explain the increase of dynastic politics. The chapter concludes by reviewing requisite concepts, theory and
perspectives which guide the presentation of the book and are verified
with its materials of the book. I compile a patronage-based analytical
frame, with related and partly overlapping perspectives of mediated
state and patronage democracy, with the concept of machine politics
to draw attention to the growing interest and role of businesspeople
in democracy.

Chapter 2 sets the context of Mumbai's municipal governance. It provides the facts about the population and conditions of housing and
services and goes on to describe the set-up and mandate of the BMC.
After depicting its several parts, committees and hierarchies, I assess the
outcomes of the efforts towards urban decentralisation: the formation of
16 WCMs sub-city Wards Committees, the changed relations between
corporators and ward-level officials and the disappointing impacts where
participation and accountability go. Other key Mumbai (and Maharashtra state-level) agencies such as the Mumbai Metropolitan Development

Authority (MMRDA) and the Slum Redevelopment Authority (SRA) and their often conflictual and tedious relations are also introduced here. Reflecting on what we may call the 'divided neoliberal city', I examine the growth and rising powers of the Mumbai middle classes and what this means for the half of the city population living in slums.

Conditions in these slums are explored in Chapter 3, including facts and data on land and housing, the nature and coverage of basic services such as water, electricity and woefully inadequate toilet conditions. Attention is given to changing patterns of school enrolment and health care provision away from the public (BMC) to the private sector, with serious implications for poor parents and patients. Of course not all six million slum people of Mumbai are poor – indeed, some say that many of them do quite well while not paying taxes. So I sketch internal slum divisions/hierarchies of income, assets, gender, and vulnerability and question the ability of the poor to organise for better services or even real change. Prospects here obviously start from power relations in each slum but cannot be seen as separate from the supra-slum-level context: whether or not people themselves contact agencies like the BMC; the role of brokers who can double as gatekeepers; and the nature and organisational basis of political parties and the police. It is already noted here that the most important slum relations in a ward somehow come together in the person of the corporator, notably from the ruling party – but even opposition-party corporators are shown to be as 'helpful' as they can. The chapter concludes with a review of past and current slum policies, which, apart from the controversial and non-performing SRS, are actually hard to identify and evaluate. Rather, there were and are many schemes which can be easily manipulated and misused in the context of a mediated state. What should be programmed entitlements by policy or law often become claims to fight for in return for lots of bureaucratic hassle, bribes or a need to express loyalty to a party.

Since I consider the corporators as the key agents, if not masters of Mumbai's local governance, the central and core Chapter 4 is fully devoted to their backgrounds, their ways of working, their activities, and the citywide formal and informal networks of which they are part. Assuming that ultimately Mumbai's political parties determine their entry into (and exit from) politics, I consider MCs' position in and duties towards parties and how relations are entertained with developers, builders and other private firms. The chapter deals with the locally considered very detrimental 'corporator–contractor–official nexus', while listing the average cuts or bribes circulating in such informal 'cabals'. Corruption is shown to be most likely in the land and housing sectors and in offices where people interact with the offices of the local state, but I point out that certainly not all BMC staff are engaged in malfeasance and that not all corporators are corrupt. And even corrupt corporators combine profitable money-making rackets with providing support to women suffering domestic violence or to facilitate access into schools, hospitals and jobs – be it mostly with a bias towards people loyal to them. As their actual democratic role is assumed to represent all (and not only the ruling party) voters, their concrete activities vis-à-vis the urban poor are assessed in some detail: are they agents of inclusion or exclusion?

The ways and means through which corporators are elected are the topic of Chapter 5, which investigates the 'everyday realities' of municipal elections. I describe the preparations and organisation of the local Mumbai elections in February 2012, where the massive formal machinery to engage nearly 10 million voters in citywide elections is contrasted with actual and largely informal practices of campaigning and voting. This is about illicit spending on allocating cash and other goodies to prospective voters, slum- and ward-level turf wars between candidates and their agents and the use of persuasion or what is called 'muscle power' or the 'fear factor'. As much as possible I trace the role of the private sector to support parties and candidates. Relations between them are shown to be entirely non-transparent, with too much evidence of shady reciprocal benefits around campaign financing. Once more it is shown that it is poor people who vote most, illustrating the awkward situation that they may help to power politicians who care less for them than for most other city groups.

The final conclusion wraps up the book by summarising its key arguments while answering questions raised in this introduction. These conclusions start by mapping changes in Mumbai's stakeholders in governance and politics, after which the conditions of poor slum women, men and children and their prospects are outlined. In terms of the agency of poor people, I suggest assumptions on differential patronage roles for men and women, which are proposed for further study. I then turn my attention to the relations between and conditions inside Mumbai's governance agencies, tracing patterns of formality and informality, and to the politics of service delivery through 'mediated local state agencies'. Final sections address the workings and impacts of local democracy and the changing nature of parties and politicians. I reflect on trends where politicians seem to move closer to businesspeople and firms – while politicians turn businessmen and businessmen politician. I suggest that poor slum people are by and large unaware of what 'democracy' could actually mean for them. They seem to pragmatically exploit those useful bits and pieces they encounter, including election goodies or making money by working for a candidate. In the context of the mediated state, most poor voters appear to go for the candidate with a reputation of being generally helpful and able to 'pull funds into our slum'.

Notes

1 The case of Ganpat Patil Nagar slum was studied during visits from 2004 onwards and through fieldwork by assistant N. Shewari. Recent events are documented in *Indian Express* (8 January 13) and *Times of India* (25 June 13). The controversial slum was again in the news when it was noted that it was marked in the draft 2014–34 Mumbai Development Plan as a residential zone – even while located in an NDZ Coastal Regulation Zone – 1. 'Who Is Accountable for Blunders in Draft DP 2034', *Times of India,* 22 April 2015.
2 Sassen Interview in NRC Handelsblad, 11 July 2014.
3 'Planet Plutocrat: Our Crony Capitalism Index. The Countries Where Politically Connected Businessmen Are Most Likely to Prosper', *The Economist,* 15 March 2014. Oxfam (2015: 10) discusses the capture of politics by the economic elite as a key factor to explain global inequality.
4 'The World We Want? Promoting the Notion That All Development Is Local', blog.metrotrends.org/author/jboex (accessed on 29 April 2013).
5 'Indo-Dutch Program for Alternative Development' (IDPAD). Our program was a joint effort by the JNU, Amsterdam University and ISS.
6 The Nandlal Committee Report, which had inquired into irregularities and corruption in the TMC from 1987 to 1996, named 54 corporators and 36 civic officials who had caused huge losses to the TMC. http://timesofindia. indiatimes.com/city/mumbai/PIL-planned-based-on-Nandlal-report/article-show/5035426.cms (accessed 25 August 2014).
7 Under the title 'Media Losing Credibility; Market Forces Coupled with Political Influence Totally Dominate the News Domain Today', Mr Srivastava argues that there is a need for a counter-media publication or TV news channel in a context where some media houses are part of large corporate and business houses, serving their interests above everything else (*The Sunday Indian,* 17 February 2012: 60). In the run up to 2014 national elections, Mr Kejriwal alleged that 'parties are paying the media' (*The Hindu,* 15 March 2014).

1 Locating Mumbai's poor in urban governance, politics and informality

Before concentrating in later chapters on this book's core matter of Mumbai's administration, conditions of its slum people and local politics, this chapter sets the broad overall context. First I discuss the overall Indian situation and trends of urban poverty and exclusion, along with national governance changes, all of which strongly impact the city. I survey current trends and complications in Indian democracy and elections. I then elaborate my analytical frame, which will help focus and guide this study. As noted already, it centres on the key relationship of patronage, which seemingly simple relation became the cornerstone of more ambitious perspectives. The mediated state concept highlights the central role of brokers in the individualised allocation of state benefits; patronage democracy adds politics by stressing that state benefits are also exchanged for votes. With a view to understand the increasing role of the private sector in politics and elections, I go way back to Scott (1969) who conceptualised the 'machine politics model'. A brief review of Indian democracy shifts closes the chapter, where I consider the growing political clout of the upcoming middle classes and the emergence of 'new politics', which seem mostly detrimental for poor people whose key asset is – or was – their vote.

1.1 Urban poverty, inequality and exclusion

It is for very good reasons that inequality currently enjoys a sudden spurt of attention globally, with evidence of a drifting apart of the rich and the poor in almost all countries. Piketty (2014) argues that when the rate of return on capital is greater than the rate of economic growth over the long term, this will result in the concentration of wealth and increased inequality, with social and economic instability as possible outcomes. Such trends are inherent to capitalism but were aggravated with global liberalisation. With low economic growth rates, wealth accumulates faster from capital than from labour, accumulating more among those already wealthy, so increasing inequality. Where labour is rewarded so low as in many developing countries, these effects will only be stronger. Sassen (2014: 76ff.) argues that global money and investment flows lead to increasing 'expulsions' of people, for example in house or slum evictions, following land grabs or as part of industrialisation projects. Recognising the value of the concept of exclusion as a form of discrimination, she feels that we see a movement towards deliberate expulsion (foreclosure) of people, mostly as a result of the concentration of capital and power with companies and sometimes states. State elites and company elites often have the same interest. Politicians are seen to think that growth is key and that it can best be achieved 'by merging more or less with the global business elite'.[1] Both dimensions of increasing inequality and expulsions can be witnessed in India and will be checked for their determinants and outcomes in Mumbai.

India can serve as an example where income and asset inequality has risen sharply in the recent years and where it is well documented that its poor people have not benefited like the rich from considerable economic growth in the past few years. Vakulabharanam and Motiram (2012: 47): 'The urban elite, constituting about 10–15% of the total population of the country, has monopolized almost the entire gains after the economic reforms.' For India as a whole they believe that the number of the 'poor and vulnerable' has actually gone up from 732 million in 1994 to 811 million in 2000 and to 836 million in 2005 – even while their proportion to the Indian population is decreasing. Vakulabharanam and Motiram feel that urban poverty is most widespread among casual labourers and the self-employed and, as is to be expected, in slums.[2] According to the 2011 Census, 377 million people live in Indian cities and towns (31 per cent of the population), representing a decadal growth of 32 per cent since 2001. Most sources estimate a fast urban growth in the near future, with the GOI/Planning Commission (2011: 2ff.) expecting the urban population to be about 590 million in 2030. This would imply a bit of a nightmare if present patterns of poverty, exclusion and ineffective urban governance were to persist.

In 2004–5, 81 million people of the then urban population of 309.5 million (or 26.8 per cent) had incomes below the poverty line (BPL; their monthly consumption was less than Rs 538). Over the past three decades (1973–2004), the number of urban poor in India rose by 34.4 per cent and the shares of the urban poor in the total number of urbanites rose from 18.7 per cent in 1973 to 26.8 per cent in 2004–5 (GOI/Planning Commission 2011: 2ff.). Haritas (2008: 462) mentions a national urban poverty average of 23 per cent.[3] While urban poverty appears to be increasing, rural poverty is decreasing. The Planning Commission (GOI/Planning Commission 2011: 4) indicates that the Gini coefficient – a measure of income inequality – is not only higher for cities and towns than the inequalities in the rural areas but it has risen continually since 1983. This confirms a general impression that urban inequality has increased, not least as a result of liberalisation reforms from around 1991. But not all poor urban people live in slums. The 2001 Census pegs the Indian slum population at approximately 42.6 million, forming 15 per cent of the country's total urban population and 23.1 per cent of the population of cities and towns reporting slums. Maharashtra state has the highest proportion of slum dwellers at 11.2 million, making up 26.3 per cent of the total Indian slum population (Bhatiya and Chatterjee 2010: 24).[4] Such slum settlements have a higher proportion (17.4 per cent) of scheduled castes (SCs) than non-slum settlements. Generally, poverty in India is highest among SCs and tribes, followed by Muslims. Forty-two per cent of SC people in urban areas live in poverty, as compared to 24 per cent for other categories, mostly other backward castes (OBCs) (Haritas 2008: 462). The segregation in Indian cities is confirmed by Vithayathil and Singh (2012) who note that historically disadvantaged castes disproportionally live in slums and that urban segregation is highest for both the highest- and lowest-status groups. One critical factor is whether people work in the 'unorganised sector' – with low and fluctuating incomes, high risks of exploitation and of personal safety such as violence or sexual harassment for women and girl domestic servants or building-sector workers with high risk of accidents. Another vulnerable group include the self-employed, even while one expects overlaps between people alternating between incidental informal-sector labour and running a road-side family shop, for example. Suryanarayana and Das (2014: 52) mention that, at the all-Indian level, relatively deprived social groups such as SCs and tribes have been left out of the growth process: 'Our findings . . . suggest that inclusiveness of the poorest in Indian mainstream growth process is still a forlorn hope.'

Despite several national and some state-level policies aimed at enhancing the position and well-being of women and girl children, India witnesses high rates of feminisation of poverty, seen to be related to an increasing exclusion of lower classes, lower castes and minorities. Women and children are mentioned to account for 73 per cent of those below the poverty line, while the ratio of women to men is 933:1,000 – getting worse in most Indian states (Haritas 2008). Haritas (2008: 463) indicates that poor urban women suffer dual exclusion: first as woman and next as being poor (and, in addition, possibly being a Dalit or Muslim). She mentions, inter alia, that 'poor women identify NGOs or political representatives to address issues of access to basic urban amenities, without considering their own political activity as a possible solution', which raises the question as to women's political agency, one of the issues addressed in this book. Such discouraging dry data and negative trends conceal the very problematic and precarious day-to-day conditions of poor urban people, linked to their exploitation on many counts. This has been noted, among others, by Bhowmik (2010: 194) who stresses the importance of the urban poor in contributing to the economy of cities, defending them against those who frequently accuse the poor and slum dwellers of draining city resources. He quotes from the India National Slum Policy:

> The poor represent an extremely important element of the urban labour force and contribute substantially to total productivity and labour market competiveness. It is vital that all Urban Local Bodies recognise the contribution of the urban poor in help- ing to build urban prosperity and make sufficient provision for them to have access to affordable land, house sites and services. The present planning and development framework is exclusive of slums and informal settlements. It views slums as 'problem areas' requiring corrective action. The legal framework with its origin in the pre-independence socio-economic contexts requires modifications and progressive change. There is a need for a greater commitment to institutional re-orientation by adopt- ing a more 'enabling approach' to the delivery of basic services accessible to the poor through the more effective mobilisation of community resources and skills to complement public resource allocations. Major areas of attention include: town planning, land management, poverty alleviation, basic service delivery and capacity building.

In a related and thoughtful article, Mr Revi[5] considers the present state of Indian cities, identifying the following constraints, which together actually appear as a full-blown crisis: a huge underinvestment in cities by both public and private organisations; low net rural–urban migra- tion rates, collapsing infrastructure and governance; terrible living and working conditions of the majority, especially the urban poor; and traffic congestion as well as a poor record of public safety and criminal justice. He argues that the main factor to explain why, despite this, a $1.2 trillion urban economy could be built in a few decades is the never-ending hard work of the urban poor, in a rare recognition of the critical role they play in cities:

> First, the immense hard work and productivity of the urban poor and informal workers, especially women. This is in spite of low levels of education and skills; very poor living and working conditions; insecurity of employment, housing and public services and no pretence of a social security net. Though the country's over 125 million informal sector urban workers produce nearly € 500 million worth of output, there are too few to speak to. Yet they produce almost as much as the organised industry and transnational firms. Unlike in new Brazil, few of India's urban poor have the real 'right to the city' that they have built and keep alive with their labour.

So there is a problem of growing urban poverty and a general increase in inequality in India at the same time that the economy has grown in an impressive way. However, there is obviously a risk in discussing or lumping together the problems of and prospects for millions of very poor, poor or upwardly mobile urban Indian households, and I start from the principled position that we need to move beyond binary theorisations of haves and have-nots. Even within oppressive structures, agency can be manifested; even the weakest of stakeholders may have a voice – or at least we need to check that. For example Anand (2011b: 543) argues that in both scholarly and popular literature, Mumbai has frequently been thought of (and measured) in binary terms – those who have more than they can ever need and others who have desperately little to live on. I agree that things are much more complex in reality when assessing the evolution or decline of a particular household or slum, and it is important to scan for ways in which people succeed in overcoming minor or major constraints. Yet for the urban poor as a class, conditions seem to have changed little if at all since a 2000 World Bank poverty survey, which highlighted relations of access between people and the local state. This survey of the poor in 47 countries revealed once more how ineffective the state is by documenting the experiences and perspectives of poor people. The latter do expect the government to provide infrastructure, health and education services, yet their lives remain unchanged:

Poor people report that their interactions with state representatives are marred by rudeness, humiliation, harassment, and stonewalling. Poor people also report vast experience with corruption as they attempt to seek health care, educate their children, claim social assistance or relief assistance, get paid, or receive protection from the police and justice from local authorities. In many places, poor people identify particular individuals within the state apparatus as good and certain programs as useful, but these individuals and programs are not enough to pull them out of poverty. The impact of a corrupt and brutalizing police force is particularly demoralizing for the poor, who already feel defenceless against the power of the state and the elite. There are gender differences in poor people's experience with state institutions reflecting societal norms of gender based power inequity. Women in many contexts report continued vulnerability to the threat of sexual assault.

(Narayan 2000: 8)

An echo of this for India was found in the editorial of a weekly,[6] referring to uncontrolled and unregulated market-led developments where cities are increasingly complex, mainly due to 'the dark lanes of underdevelopment that the path of reckless capitalism seems to produce'. Such market-led development leads to two failures: first, a majority of citizens are unable to live a decent life, while being confronted by a volcano of bad amenities and an unsympathetic bureaucracy. Second, capitalism has failed to correct regional imbalances, leading to pushing people from backward regions to the cities, such as Mumbai, which is seen as a mirage – but this can lead to polarising developments like anti-Bihari incidents instigated there by some political parties. So, in spite of plenty of rhetoric on 'inclusion' (e.g. the 11th Five-Year Plan 'Towards Faster and More Inclusive Growth'), processes of social, economic and political exclusion appear to continue, leading Coelho and Maringanti (2012: 41) to worry that this is all about a change from state-led to market-enabling modes of policy intervention. They believe that the language of inclusion, on the one hand, has the feel-good idea that all need to be included; on the other hand, 'true to its origin in the neoliberal paradigm', it implies a segregation in a two-tier system of services into those for full-cost-paying citizens and those for the poor. We need to assess to what extent such dynamics hold true for Mumbai's poor, what their prospects are in a fast-changing city and to what extent the local state enables processes of inclusion or instead sustains, or even deepens, exclusion.

1.2   Limitations of urban governance: the state, institutions and governance changes

Whereas the poor have their very own problems with and in the city, all Indian urbanites somehow face discomfort or constraints, ranging from road conditions and traffic queues, to air and noise pollution and a lack of open spaces and parks. Indeed, cities portray in sharp outline the dismal quality of administration, wholly inadequate levels of services and infrastructure and an almost complete lack of planning for the future – where the plans made are often not implemented (cf. Roy 2009b). A succinct assessment of India's urban crisis is given by Dhar Chakrabarti (2001: 263):

> Cities of India are facing the accumulation of past neglect when their affairs were not left to the citizens but to the extraneous forces of party politics and bureaucratic interference, when state control and the proliferation of parastatal agencies marginalised city governments, when cheap populist measures overshadowed sound financial considerations, when a kind of urban *laissez-faire* prevailed over discipline and control, when a culture of subsidy and concession was allowed to rule over cost effectiveness, when responsible and capable urban leadership was not allowed to develop, and when developing the capacity of urban managers was not a concern. . . . Unfortunately . . . city level democracy has not really been allowed to flourish. City governments were treated more as an appendage of provincial government than as governments in their own right.

Things do not appear to have changed for the better recently, despite, for example, massive investments under the urban investment programme JNNURM (Banerjee-Guha 2010; Sivaramakrishnan 2011), which came along with conditional policy relating to participatory modes of local governance, urban decentralisation and attention as well as funding for slums and the urban poor. A key factor in all this has been a multiplication of actors or stakeholders in urban governance, conceived as a new 'urban regime' by some (Nainan 2012). Other dimensions include the transformation in forms of city administration and governance, where Banerjee-Guha (2010: 208) perceives processes of undermining democratically elected bodies with an encroachment on constitutionally devolved areas of state government jurisdiction, under new arrangements which are often praised by India's business and industrial tycoons. I already mentioned that the organised urban middle class has become an important factor in governance, in addition to increasingly powerful actors relating to global capital, urban land and the building sector. Not only has the power balance in cities changed, but there are new configurations of actors where the state engages in public–private partnerships (PPPs) and in public–community partnerships (PCPs) and where it appears that there are marked changes in the way the urban poor and middle classes deal with the local state and local democracy (Baud and Nainan 2008; Berenschot 2010: 888).

This book links to urban governance discourses, building on earlier work (Baud and de Wit 2008) on urban governance shifts, while taking a political economy perspective on changing power configurations of multi-stakeholders. 'Governance' is defined (Hyden *et al.* 2004: 16) as

> the formation and stewardship of the formal and informal rules that regulate the public realm, the arena in which state as well as economic and societal actors interact to make decisions. It is a multi-stakeholder process with weaker and stronger actors who need to cooperate to solve collective (local) problems.

It may be noted that the fashionable 'governance' concept is pre-dated by political economy frameworks applied in city studies under the label of 'relations between actors in slum upgrading' (van der Linden 1983). A useful distinction is made between 'the rules of the game' or the 'institutional context' with its formal and, importantly, informal rules, on the one hand, and the more dynamic, political arena, where we can observe 'who gets what, when and how', on the other. Ample attention is given to the critical role of institutions, which includes an array of formal rules as laid down, for example in the Indian constitution, the municipal acts governing Mumbai and the development control regulations. I show and try to explain why many such formal rules are not or only partially observed, with a special focus on 'informal institutions': 'The socially shared rules, usually unwritten, that are created, communicated, and enforced outside of officially sanctioned channels' (Helmke and Levitsky 2004). Such institutions include norms and values underlying India's caste system and gender relations, but also 'institutionalised' informal rules governing systems of corruption and nepotism, for example the 'normal' or accepted rates to extort a bribe from a hawker or additional payments to obtain a licence or birth certificate. But institutions can also be specific organisations empowered to enforce formal or informal rules, for example central banks, courts, the caste leaders in a town, or a powerful mafia outfit. Relationships such as marriage and patronage have been institutionalised as important to regulating social relationships. One example bringing together dimensions of 'actors' and the force of changing 'values' is provided by Mooij and Lama-Rewal (2009: 83):

> given the elite nature of India's middle class . . . [this] can be understood as a process of social polarisation: the upper segments of the middle class became richer, indulge in more and more lavish consumption, and isolate themselves in gated communities, while the poor become poorer, perhaps not in absolute terms but certainly in relative terms . . . while . . . their worldview, aspirations and values are influential far beyond themselves.

In terms of new stakeholders or 'governance shifts', a distinction can be made between 'horizontal' shifts where the states engage non-state actors to support, co-produce or even take over the provision of services hitherto provided by the public sector such as PPPs and privatisation modalities. 'Vertical' governance shifts refer to changing relations between the state and supra-state, global actors and organisations (ranging from the IMF to WTO to regional bodies such as SAARC, global capital and transnational corporations), as well as to processes of decentralisation, where a national government transfers tasks, powers as well as funds to lower administrative levels (Baud and de Wit 2008: 6–20). There is a whole discourse to suggest that decentralisation – in its more ambitious form of devolution or democratic decentralisation – has the potential to enable more effective governance, in terms of service delivery, accountability, participation, and even pro-poor policy making. However, most studies on decentralisation conclude that it rarely fulfils these promises, and this applies especially to the espoused pro-poor consequences of complex decentralisation processes (Crook and Sverison 2003; Robinson 2007). The process of central authorities voluntarily giving up power to the benefit of local-level stakeholders and politicians is a political process much more than an organisational one, as it is fundamentally about power shifts across multiple levels – administrative, financial and legislative. As a result, initial enthusiasm about anticipated benefits has reduced considerably, with suggestions that they can even be harmful. For example, Hadiz (2004) criticises what he sees as de-politicised, neoinstitutional ideas and strategies that undermined Indonesia's decentralisation reforms. These are seen to have basically benefited regional elites and local mafia groups through opaque and informal power articulation processes. It raises the more general question as to whether administrative and social justice issues can be addressed by purely technical, organisational and fiscal solutions that neglect the use or abuse of power. Particularly, if we assume a zero-sum concept of power and if decentralisation were to empower the elites in the frequently found dynamics of 'elite capture', it would imply that the poor may not be benefiting but lose out. All this is relevant for the study of Mumbai's urban governance, as, from 2000, the city implemented urban decentralisation in the establishment of sub-city decentralised WCMs.

Governance is not only about inputs, outcomes and impacts, but values such as transparency, accountability and participation are important in themselves. This has given a separate and normative dimension to what is the neutral idea of multi-stakeholder governance and is captured in the 'good governance agenda'. Even while contested today, it highlights worthwhile donor ideals such as effective policy making, 'citizen's voice', human rights, and the need to combat corruption. I cannot go in more detail here and only note that concepts of governance and even more so good governance have lost much of their initial appeal, if only with its association with neoliberal reforms (Demmers *et al.* 2004). Many donors seem to have lost interest in promoting good governance, and the governance concept itself has become so fuzzy and multi-interpretable as to become almost meaningless. One concern is that the study and proper practice of public policy is neglected in the relabelling and prioritisation relating to public- and private-sector governance and its discourses (Frederickson 2005).[7] At the same time, working towards good governance remains imperative, if only as it is basically the poor who are and will be dependent on the state and hence stand to benefit most by enforced human rights, political accountability and reduced corruption.

But even if we only consider governance as an impartial, more technical process of multi-stakeholder interaction, there are inherent complications as documented well by Swyngedouw (2005). One concern is about democratic control and the risks of a democratic deficit: who controls the state now that so much has been privatised, contracted out or is being implemented through partnerships. The ultimate danger seen here is captured by the metaphor of the 'hollow state' (Nazar n.d.), which refers to the increasing use of third parties, both for-profit companies and nonprofit NGOs, to deliver social services, construct or maintain state infrastructure and generally act in the name of the state. It raises critical issues as to who is accountable for services delivered and whether the state retains legitimacy when it delegates so many tasks to other stakeholders. This, in addition to trends where states also surrender powers to multi-lateral agencies, international courts and under treaties such as WTO, undermining the 'voice' and means of accountability for state citizens. In terms of democracy, Swyngedouw (2005: 1999) worries that the democratic character of the political sphere is eroded by 'the encroaching imposition of market forces that set the rules of the game', in cases where coalitions of economic/social elites dominate. More powerful or well-connected groups and individuals may opt out of politics and directly target local governments for quality services. And while the concept of stakeholder is presumably inclusive and exhaustive, actual concrete forms of governance – for example those around a specific public service such as health care – are necessarily constrained and limited in terms of who can, or is allowed to, participate. I now reflect on such dimensions by tracing governance changes and associated impacts in India generally.

Governance changes and informality in India

In their study of poverty alleviation schemes in India, Véron *et al.* (2006: 1923) found that in many cases rent seeking has increased under economic liberalisation and had changed its character: corruption was now more likely to be initiated and controlled by actors in civil society, including businesspersons, than it was by state actors. Formal democratisation had created opportunities, incentives and pressures for elected politicians and officials 'to compensate for political uncertainty by building up a capital stake through corruption'. According to some, the evolving 'nexus' among Indian capitalists/businesspeople, politicians and government bureaucrats has led to the incidence of crony capitalism in India, as for example noted by *The Economist* (15 March 2014) and the *Frontline* magazine (21 March 2014, on the 'Reliance Factor', highlighting the unholy nexus between big business and political parties). *The Economist* states that India had a decade of epic corruption, ranking ninth on its 'global crony capitalism index', but managing to improve things: 'Recent graft scandals and a slowing economy have hurt many of its financially leveraged and politically connected businessmen' even while others have prospered. Crony capitalism is based on rent seeking and making money through political connections, with practices ranging from outright graft to poor regulation to the transfer of public assets to firms at bargain prices. Interestingly, the current Reserve Bank of India governor Mr Rajan took position against crony capitalism in the country, which he said creates oligarchies and slows down growth:

An important issue in the recent election was whether we had substituted the crony socialism of the past with crony capitalism, where the rich and the influential are alleged to have received land, natural resources and spectrum in return for payoffs to venal politicians. By killing transparency and competition, crony capitalism is harmful to free enterprise, opportunity, and economic growth. And by substituting special interests for the public interest, it is harmful to democratic expression.

His observations on India's democracy and politicians are also worth reproducing here. If there was some truth to such perceptions of crony capitalism, he said, a natural question arose as to why people tolerated it:

Why do they vote for the venal politician who perpetuates it? . . . One widely held hypothesis is that our country suffers from want of a 'few good men' in politics. This view is unfair to the many upstanding people in politics. But even assuming it is true, every so often we see the emergence of a group, usually upper middle class professionals, who want to clean up politics. But when these 'good' people stand for election, they tend to lose their deposits. Does the electorate really not want squeaky clean government? . . . Apart from the conceit that high morals lie only with the upper middle class, the error in this hypothesis may be in believing that problems stem from individual ethics rather than the system we have. In a speech I made before the Bombay Chamber of Commerce in 2008, *I argued that the tolerance for the venal politician is because he is the crutch that helps the poor and underprivileged navigate a system that gives them so little access. This may be why he survives.*

(italics added JdW)[8]

Corruption appears to be endemic in India, both in what can be termed 'grand corruption' and – obviously related – in 'petty corruption', which is a plethora of bribes payable for people seeking services or goods from the state (Das 2001; Debroy and Bhandari 2012; Nainan 2012). Gupta (2012: 78) considers corruption an essential lens for understanding the Indian state: 'Instead of treating corruption as a dysfunctional aspect of state organizations, I see it as a mechanism through which the state itself is discursively constituted.' Heston and Kumar (2008: 1257) refer to a Transparency International report on corruption. Fifty-seven per cent of respondents in India reported paying bribes for admission, extra pay for tutoring or donations to the school. Police corruption marked by political interference to subvert formal processes is high in India (53 per cent), whereas bribes paid for the first information report (FIR) and judiciary bribes paid to a court official were common. Doctors, hospital staff and nurses all took payments. Teachers, and, to a much smaller extent, management, were seen as the agents of corruption in education.

> Clearly the perception in these surveys is that the immediate service provider is the bribe taker in education, health, and police, while lower level employees tend to be the intermediary in the case of land administration, the judiciary and taxes.
>
> (Heston and Kumar 2008: 1257)

Kumar and Landy (2009: 116) believe there is a corruption-driven 'privatisation' of the state. Besides such petty corruption, which, for already poor people, is an unfair regressive tax, grand corruption, typically associated with rich, powerful and resourceful individuals, is feared to be considerable:

> The menace of corruption in the country is pegged at Rs 1,555 thousand crore (or USD 345 billion) in the last decade and majority of it has been laundered out of India using illicit gateways, a recent study has claimed. . . . Ascertaining the size of corruption in India with respect to money laundering, an individual spent over Rs 2,000 as a cost of corruption in 2009, which is 260 per cent higher than the amount borne by a citizen ten years back.

With a view to my later focus on the Mumbai corporators and their formal and informal activities and earnings, I finally refer here to the reputation of their councillor colleagues in another metropolis Chennai. Things were so bad there that Chief Minister Jayalalitha felt the need to publicly denounce the entrenched corruption practices of the Chennai corporation municipal councillors of her own AIADMK party, attacking them:

> for indulging in corrupt practices and exceeding all limits in committing irregularities. . . . [and] warned them that unless they mended their ways, she might be forced to dissolve the city Corporation Council. She gave them a dressing down at a closed-door meeting in the wake of complaints of corruption and illegal activities against city councillors, party sources said. . . . A section of

the media had carried reports that councillors were demanding money for works in their wards. . . . Underscoring that 'excesses' by DMK councillors during the previous regime played a major role in the DMK losing power, she said she had information that AIADMK councillors were collecting money from every possible source. 'When a multi-storeyed building is constructed, you go and collect commission. If a person stores sand or gravel in front of his house for construction purposes, you demand money from him,' she said.

(*The Hindu*, 19 June 2012)

1.3   Urban dependencies: the urban poor, patronage and access to the state

Patronage, brokerage and dependency

While the benchmark of this book is Mumbai's urban poor, and while I bring out the many challenges they face, the focus is not primarily on their severe constraints in terms of employment, basic services and housing. Rather, I want to know whether and how their constraints and struggles as regards services, survival and upward mobility are being supported by the state, that is public-sector city agencies (which some call 'public capital', as part of other livelihood capitals such as 'human' and 'social capital'). I frame this investigation in terms of 'access' to the state and in terms of the well-documented fact that the poor are limited in their ability to succeed in obtaining state services through formal channels or as a result of a routinely provided entitlement. This is partly a result of a severe mismatch between the 'supply' of services and the enormous 'demand' for services such as quality health care and housing, and we can hardly blame poor countries and municipalities in being unable to cater to the needs of all, certainly not in the fast-growing cities of the global South. In general, such a mismatch leads to people competing for relatively scarce services and, in turn, to waiting lists, people queuing and queue jumping – for example by offering bribes or applying influence through agents or fixers. What are in principle entitlements by policy or law may now become something like marketable services or goods with informal prices attached. Mechanisms may operate and become institutionalised where the price of a service increases with its value or degree of urgency, pricing out those with fewer resources. I later show that this can be one reason for the 'commodification' of many services. While the poor cannot well compete here, they have additional problems in their 'demand capacity' in what may be called 'social handicaps'. They are often illiterate or semi-illiterate (hence lacking relevant knowledge); poor (with fluctuating, informal-sector wages); of low caste, for example the Dalits who are over-represented in the slums; newcomers to the city (hence lacking useful contacts and networks); or members of a minority or women. I have argued elsewhere that, more broadly, many poor city people live in a largely 'informal world', where they are engaged in informal-sector work and live in informal, often unrecognised/illegal settlements, depending on informal and exploitative moneylenders (de Wit 2010b). More than others, they may first visit an informal doctor ('quack') in case of health problems, avoid the police in case of conflicts by approaching informal caste/community leaders or even organise protection through a local mafia group. Together, these facts lead to a fundamental vulnerability and severe exclusion risks, where people basically have to fend for themselves under conditions where nothing comes easy, where trust is in short supply and where the poor and less poor compete among themselves for scarce opportunities (well illustrated for a poor slum by Boo 2012). They operate in an environment characterised by unreliable institutions, negligent or even predatory government agents and multiple but volatile sources of household income – in Wood's (2003: 468) term, by 'destructive uncertainty'.

One might hope that the poor as a group or class – all facing very similar urgent challenges of city livelihoods – would unite and organise to claim both better services and deeper, structural improvements in their position. However, this seems to be rare, and even in those cases where NGOs support communities or community organisations, longer-term impacts have been less than impressive. Invariably all slums harbour heterogeneous populations. Divisions or even factions exist based on income, caste, religion, ethnicity and gender, while tenants have other interests than 'house or hut owners', and the coexistence of different political parties can become divisive before elections. As explained in more detail in de Wit and Berner (2009), I argue that relations between the poor and city agencies are marked by (and cannot escape) a pervasive patronage logic, which ultimately affects all efforts aimed at 'empowering' the poor or at engaging them in 'participation', be it by a foreign donor, a municipality or local NGO. Rather than being vehicles of empowerment and progressive change, slum CBOs and their leadership often block progress, controlling or capturing benefits aimed at the poor and misusing them for private (political) interests (e.g. de Wit 2010a on the misuse of funds to clean slums under the guise of CBO-based community organisation activity).

Instead of the poor organising and acting as a collective (which is more likely in case of a defensive reaction like resisting an eviction than of an offensive, 'claim-making' action), they seem to prefer to cultivate vertical contacts in the form of patrons or brokers who do have access to arenas of influence and power in a context where the formal state is remote. We may term them 'patron–client or patronage relations', when there is some stability over time between a poor person and another one with more resources and/or contacts, and where some degree of reciprocity and trust exists. So while such relations may offer some relief, they also help sustain poverty, for example when a patron is exploitative. This may present what Wood (2003: 468) has termed a 'Faustian bargain', a discounting of a possible better future in favour of survival in the present which contributes to chronic poverty: 'The dangers of not being a client, of not being protected, of losing "membership" of the local commander led community are immense. Better to be with the devil you know' (Wood 2003: 468). Yet it appears that such more stable patronage relations are less frequent in the monetised and anonymous context of large cities, where many poor households shift home quite frequently, for example as a result of gentrification. This is born out in my former Chennai research, where 'traditional' and respected leaders (de Wit 1996: 168–69) were shown to lose ground, and by Berenschot (2011: 393–94) who feels that the nature of political fixers is changing. Previously they were 'local notables' such as traditional upper-caste patrons, village strongmen and other 'big men'. It appears that 'traditional' mediators or agents – arguably marked more by authority, respect and non-political forms of prestige – have made way for 'new leaders' with a proven, much more instrumental capacity to get things done, but always at a price. Besides, increased inter-party competition has led to a proliferation of fixers linked to several parties, so that people can choose those most effective – and their parties.

Rather than stable patronage relations, the dominant form today seems to be the less durable 'brokerage' relation, where people seek out specialised agents who are reputed to be able to provide institutional linkages with key actors like BMC officials, the police and employers. Even so, given trust and a mutual interest, such relations may also become consolidated even if only for specific domains. Dependency of the poor on brokers is evident, especially in conditions of insecurity, need and crisis. The scope for patronage and brokerage is a function of a lack of resources or services; access problems to agencies and institutions; and finally a lack of enforced impersonal rules for the allocation of resources. Berenschot (2010: 890ff.) makes a somewhat arbitrary distinction between brokerage (needed to obtain or validate information/documents by the poor and facilitating the information flow between state institutions and citizens); patronage, which is the practice of exchanging access to state resources for political support; and particulatisation, referring to 'the practice of undermining the uniform application of laws and legislation to the advantage of private interests'. Such activities – especially the latter – form the basis for Berenschot's model of the mediated state to which I return later. In this book I use the concepts of 'patron' and 'broker' to distinguish the duration of a general relationship which need not be linked to politics and 'clientelism' or political patronage when such relations include the exchange of political support or benefits for votes. 'Clientelism – the individualised quid pro quo in which benefits are conditioned on political support – is characterized by the sustained relationships between brokers and the clients they organise' (Stokes *et al.* 2013: 92). The perception that the poor have little option but to use patrons or brokers is confirmed by Landy and Ruby (2005: 25), writing about Hyderabad, India:

> If one is poor and one is fortunate enough to know someone with power, there is no choice: for any public service, water supply or PDS (public distribution system) or whatever, this powerful one will be approached since he is the only one who can be used as a broker. The poor hardly visit the various specific line department offices, they go to meet the same broker each time.

Kumar and Landy (2009: 107–8) note that a broker can be both a 'gateopener' and a 'gatekeeper', and they coin the term 'vertical governance': the dominant vertical power relations of actors managing the city, all of them relating to patronage, brokerage and corruption (chains). It is seen as a function of a vertical segmentation of society, with porosities blurring the boundaries between the state and civil society and between state and market, which conforms Gupta's (1995) position. Evidence that brokers – as gatekeepers – actively discourage or block slum people in Delhi to contact government offices themselves is provided by Jha *et al.* (2005). Brokers and patrons are more effective if they are part of the political machinery. Indeed, a broker outside a party is probably highly ineffective as he (rarely she) will not have access to decision making – 'the people at the top' – regarding public services (housing, land, the police, etc.).[9] This brings in a political dimension to the informal relations of patronage or brokerage, referred to as electoral clientelism or political patronage. To conclude the construction of my analytical framework, I now direct my attention to the nature of local democracy, with its apotheosis in local, that is municipal elections.

1.4 'Vote for me and I get your work done'[10]: patronage democracy and the mediated state

This book is essentially about the nature of local democracy in India, assessing whether and to what extent it yields benefits for the urban poor. For good reasons, India is considered by many as the world's largest and most vibrant democracy, and this is confirmed by basics such as multiple parties at both national and state levels, with new parties being formed (and others fading) and multi-party elections supervised by a well-respected Election Commission, while media are quite open and critical (Quraishi 2014: 1ff.). Most of all, sitting politicians can be and are defeated in elections,[11] being replaced without any delay or doubt by a new set. This is not the case in many new democracies, certainly not in what are seen as 'illiberal democracies'. Seen this way, India could almost be seen as another 'liberal democracy',[12] but if one looks closer, not all is well. Serious questions need be asked about the nature of representation, the degree of inter-election activities and the quality and accountability of politicians in prioritising citizens' needs and designing suitable policy. Where elections go, many accounts of Indian elections focus on the hustle and bustle, the planning and scheming of parties and politicians, voting patterns and changes and the impacts of election outcomes. But most are superficial and touch neither actual grassroots dynamics nor widely reported informal practices of electoral manipulation and political corruption.

> The explanatory power of formal democratic institutions for democratic process features is more limited than many had hoped . . . institutional arguments have little to say about substantive alignments that rally citizens around rival contenders or the strategic appeals made by leading politician's in each camp.
>
> (Kitscheld and Wilkinson 2007: 1)

Taking account of more informal dimensions yields other, perhaps more truthful, perspectives, for example this assessment by Varshney (2011):[13]

> However, for all its achievements, India's democracy has considerable flaws. If electoral competitiveness were the only yardstick to judge a democracy, India today would qualify as a great success.

Over the past two decades, the incumbents have repeatedly lost elections. Since incumbents can control the state machinery that conducts elections, it is clear that elections are genuinely competitive, and that popular will, barring individual exceptions, is clearly expressed. What happens between two elections, however, is very different. India's democracy has become Janus-faced. Political power is used at the time of elections to please citizens. During the years between the elections, it is often used to accumulate wealth, treat citizens in an unfeeling manner, and humiliate adversaries crudely. Following their bosses, the permanent bureaucrats – administrators and policemen – act as accomplices in this project. Empowered at the time of elections, the citizen often feels powerless until the next elections arrive. Entry into schools and treatment in hospitals often depends on whether a politician or bureaucrat can call on your behalf, or whether you have a bribe to pay. Corruption also marks the issuance of driving licenses, property registration, enrolment in the employment guarantee scheme and payment of wages. The list can go on.

Others worry about what they see as the deteriorating quality of politicians and political parties (Banerjee 2012: 46):

Indian politician's behaviour and public standing have seen a long steady decline compared to the cohort of educated, idealistic and conscientious politicians who brokered national independence and authored the constitution. Political parties are increasingly dominated by kin and nepotistic networks and have blocked the rise of new talent, and in too many cases the sins of greed and avarice appear to have displaced any desire to serve the public good.

Chandra (2004: 1) is quite gloomy when she refers to a 'malign' democracy in India, which 'has malfunctioned in a serious way for India's most vulnerable citizens' (Chandra 2004: 4–5). This, however, is about the 'form' of India's democracy, more accurately its 'outcome/impact', and not the 'nature' of India's democracy, where it actually works quite well in the formal organisation of elections, voting, counting, and delivering a verdict which is respected by all parties. Chandra characterises India as a 'patronage democracy' and, as is discussed below, its elections as 'auctions':

India's is a 'patronage-democracy' in which elections have become auctions for the sale of government services. The most minimal goods that a government should provide – security of life and property, access to education, provision of public health facilities, a minimum standard of living – have become, for large numbers of people, market goods rather than entitlements. This is a violation of modern norms of governance. Worse, this violation affects citizens unequally. And worst of all, this violation has become routinized in everyday imagination, so that it is now no longer perceived as illegitimate. Just as democracy in India has become business as usual, so has the politics of patronage.

Former chief election commissioner Quraishi (2014: 398) agrees by arguing that India has 'Good Elections, Flawed Democracy': 'Political Parties, originally based on ideology and social movements, steadily started losing their moorings as their focus shifted to capturing the government at any cost without delivering governance. Consequently, public trust in them began to decline' (Quraishi 2014: 395, where he mentions that, of all public institutions, trust in political parties is lowest at 46 per cent). 'We have a sad scenario of poor voters and rich candidates, some of whom do not even find it necessary to submit their income tax returns' (Quraishi 2014: 273). Chhokar (2015)[14] makes a useful distinction between 'procedural' democracy (adult franchise, elections, secret ballot) and 'substantive' democracy, which refers to 'the internal democratic functioning of the parties, which purportedly represent the people'.[15] Prabash (2010: 88) brings in another dimension of the role of money-in-elections but confirms the 'market for votes' idea. He feels that the electoral process is being de-politicised, so that ideology, policy preferences and public opinion hardly matter, while 'with the help of money, elections are turned into a great spectacle and the electoral arena converted into a big market space where money mediates between the candidates and the electorate'.

Following a long-time neglect of informal political dynamics including political patronage and political corruption, the excellent work by Kitscheld and Wilkinson (2007) was important in once more focusing attention on what they perceive as the fundamentally informal dynamics of politics in many developing countries. In one chapter of their book, Chandra (2007: 85–86) elaborates a model of politics which she calls a 'patronage democracy', a system in which the political leadership is chosen through competitive elections, and where the state has a relative monopoly on jobs and services. Elected politicians then enjoy significant discretion in allocating jobs and services at the disposal of the state – on an '*individualised*' basis (italics in original). Chandra considers this as a form of rent seeking and corruption where the returns to politicians for supporting individuals take the form of votes rather than bribes. Just like Berenschot (2010), she sees the Indian state as still quite powerful and important. I may note at this point that the Indian economy was liberalised to some extent from the early1990s but that the state retained important powers. Vital administrative fields are still regulated by both central and state governments, for example sensitive sectors such as real estate and land acquisition (Gowda and Sridharan 2012: 233), and I may add regulating, licensing as well as planning and budgeting for development. From the perspective of the poor, the local state still offers, in principle, a variety of public services such as health, education, mother and child care, and 'ration/fair price shops', while specifying rules as to who is eligible to live in a slum legally and what documents are needed to be eligible. Both Chandra and Berenschot then postulate a key role for elected politicians in the allocation of resources and services, who use their discretionary powers to channel public benefits to selected persons or groups (which could be vote banks). What should be regular entitlements for people – leading from many laws and policies and schemes often starting with ample funding for the poor – have, in their view, now become currency in the relations between people and brokers/politicians – the latter benefiting in terms of not only money but, importantly, also votes. A candidate translates whatever party leaders say on general policy matters into a personalised, particularistic message: 'Vote for me and I will get your work done' (Chandra 2004: 3). A process of 'marketisation of basic services' has taken place: voters believe they can count on state services only when the politicians they have paid with their votes are in power, and not otherwise. Most affected are the poorest and most vulnerable groups who neither have a 'voice' (by way of consultation or participation) nor can 'exit', as middle classes and elites can do. The latter seek resort to private-sector services (water, education, health, security) or use their non-political contacts and leverage, for example simply calling an official directly in case of need.

In such views, Indian democracy is marked by an uneasy but strong interdependence of democracy and informal patronage ties. A politician has a stake in democracy as the way to build up personal, individual power by addressing voters or 'clients' individually. An indicator of a lack of efforts in India to reduce such processes includes the continued existence – in spite of ample evidence of gross misuse – of 'discretionary' funds for all levels of politicians, such as the Area Development Funds of Mumbai corporators, which amounts tend to increase time and again (e.g. Kumar and Landy 2009: 120ff.). These are funds politicians (MPs, MLAs, MCs) receive each year, to be spent under specified guidelines in the politician's constituency, but without much control as to how they are spent (with evidence of large-scale misuse) and who uses the created facilities. Kumar and Landy (2009: 120ff.) argue that such discretionary power undermines institutional and democratic decision making (in the municipal council, legislature or parliament), while strengthening a personalised competition for power as well as perpetuating patron–client relationships. The key operational term here is 'individual discretion'. There is a parallel here with the work of Berenschot (2009: 124), who refers in this respect to 'the mediated nature of the state':

> As the expanding state institutions lacked the resources and information to make services easily available to all, poorer residents in particular came to rely on political actors to facilitate their interaction with the state.

For aspiring politicians to win elections, they need to efficiently and instrumentally have some control over state operations as part of what Berenschot (2009: 124) calls the 'particularisation of the state to target specific beneficiaries'. But where he appears to suggest that state institutions faced a 'supply-side problem', one may note that such institutions were weak from the start, as a result of the origin of the Indian state in a colonial state with 'very low infrastructural power' and relying already on an army of regional and local power holders and brokers. I agree with Chandra (2007) then that pre-existing, colonial and informal discretionary channels persisted and further expanded after independence, adding more and more levels and relations into webs and pyramids.[16] Such informal systems persist as a result of incentives affecting politicians. These evolved to become the most effective way to build up power and status for individual/aspiring politicians, who can subsequently use this to advance their status and careers in the party and government (Chandra 2004). One could argue that the sudden imposition or transplantation of the Westminster-type democracy to India has yielded, over time, a variation of democracy, as suggested by Witsoe (2013: 4–6). Witsoe considers India's democracy against India's state formation, and I endorse his vision 'of the myriads of struggles over dominance and subordination that accompany everyday political practice' (Witsoe 2013: 17). Relevant too here is the work of Grindle (2012) who traces variegated and not always sustainable paths of states to overcome the dominance of almost universal historical patronage systems, and India is a case which has not succeeded. In India, an indigenised model of democratic politics evolved and was firmly consolidated. It works, but there is a need to assess as to how inclusive and representative it is and how it is evolving presently to adjust to India's neoliberal trajectory.

1.5   The private sector and democracy: the political machine perspective

I need to elaborate one more dimension of India's democracy and elections here, which is the origin and role of the massive amounts of money to finance India's elections at all levels. It is part of another line of inquiry to assess the value and implications of 'the political machine' or 'machine politics' perspective. This classic concept was already applied by Scott (1969), and it has always surprised me that it is not given more prominence in political science writings today, with the ever-increasing role and powers of the private-sector and 'business elites'[17] and the close ties between politicians and business, for example in the United States where the notion originates. Stokes (2005) revived a discussion on clientelist parties, which she equates with political machines, where she builds on the classic Scott model. Scott (1969: 1155) suggested that machine politicians promote the interests of wealthy elites in return for financial assistance:

> the machine politician could be viewed as a broker who, in return for financial assistance from wealthy elites, promoted their policy interests while in office, while passing on a portion of the gain to a particularistic electorate from whom he 'rented' his authority.

Scott too considers patronage as crucial for machine politics in terms of 'self-interest as political cement: the patronage' (Scott 1969: 1151). He refers to India in 1964 where politicians 'made use of the available patronage (not to mention licences, contracts, franchises) to maintain their electoral strength' and to other countries where parties have become a gigantic patronage organisation. In this perspective, the electorate is seen to have little sense of community interests and has a preference for immediate, personal inducements. On the other hand, that brokers develop reciprocal obligations to the private sector and wealthy elites 'has made the pursuit of longer-run development objectives more difficult'; it may lead to fiscal deficits and a trend that business seeks favoured or monopolistic positions – free from competition (Scott 1969: 1155). This position tallies well with Berenschot's (2010) view that India's local politicians are far more interested in dealing pragmatically and quickly with ongoing requests and crisis, more like 'street-level politicians'[18] than with designing, implementing and monitoring development policy. The machine politics perspective emphasises a lack of ideology, an exclusion of class politics, the primacy of pragmatism and opportunism, and a capacity to target heterogeneous populations, where the poor are many and the middle classes are few (Scott 1969: 1149ff.). As a result, it is not surprising that politicians prefer investing in easily accessible and dependent poor people with many urgent needs. The operation of such political machines and machine politicians meets with the very pragmatic praxis and often miserable conditions of the poor living in largely informal conditions, in heterogeneous settlements where survival and self-development are core (Gupte 2012: 208; Stokes *et al.* 2013: 161).

One dimension of machine politics is the targeted allocation of material incentives in return for votes, either in targeted policy benefits or in outright vote buying (Berenschot 2009; Hicken 2011; Nichter 2008; Schaffer 2007). It is readily agreed that this is bad, for example as it distorts who is elected in the first place (Geddis 2008: 142), while it affects the basic incentives for those who are elected and the institutions that are supposed to regulate such incentives. But in India not everybody agrees as was shown by a union minister who was accused of 'allegedly inducing voters to take bribes' as he had encouraged voters during a speech to accept the liquor, sarees, shirts, and Rs 5,000 in return for votes. He said: 'This is the time when illegally earned money can go to the poor.'[19] The context was the Bihar state elections where a party leader framed his anticipated victory as a 'victory of principles over moneybags'.[20] In a depressing chapter 'Money Power in Politics', Quraishi (2014: 259ff.) lists 40 'illegal expenses during election', ranging from providing cash to voters to paying rival candidates not to campaign (seriously). Stokes (in Geddis 2008: 143) adds that it insults the autonomy of the poor and that it may make them vote in ways counter to their long-term interests – 'if they sell their vote to their richer compatriots'. But the matter is more complex, in that some see the money or other goodies or freebies offered for votes as some kind of buy-off on the part of politicians for governance failures (Debroy and Bhandari 2012: 16), while others emphasise the more symbolic nature of the 'gift' in terms of trust, future bonds and expected reciprocity (Breeding 2011: 73). Bjorkman (2013: 35–36) believes that 'the expectation for reciprocation upon receiving a (vote bank) benefit is just as symbolic as the gesture of the vote bank benefit itself'. Material inducements or cash for votes are often not given one to one to voters, but rather to what is called 'vote banks', which can be defined as:

> A loyal bloc of voters from a single community, who consistently back a certain candidate or political formation in democratic elections.

Such behaviour is often the result of an expectation of real or imagined benefits from the political formations, often at the cost of other communities. Vote bank politics is the practice of creating and maintaining vote banks through divisive policies. As this brand of politics encourages voters to vote on the basis of narrow communal considerations, often against their better judgment, it is considered inimical to democracy. The term was coined in India, where the practice of vote bank politics is rampant.[21]

I return to some such perspectives that relate to micro- (election booths) and individual-level election issues by way of introducing Chapter 5 on Mumbai's 2012 local elections. There I will discuss what is called 'perverse accountability', when voters can be punished for voting – mostly against the expectations and calculations of the winner – for a candidate who lost the elections (Stokes 2005). Stokes (2005: 317ff.) makes another important point on the way machine parties are normally organised, which, too, can be checked with Mumbai grassroots realities. The typical political machine in her view is bottom-heavy, decentralised while relying on an army of grassroots militants. Parties are expected to be effective to the extent that they insert themselves in local social networks, marked by a tentacle-like organisational structure. This is in line with Khan (2005: 719) who notes that pyramidal patron–client networks are likely to emerge as the most rational form of political organisation. Such views tally well with the aforementioned mediated state perspective, which overlaps with that of the patronage democracy, in that (chains of) brokers are a lifeline for anyone seeking a state service or benefit, where political mediation is part of the state's 'everyday operation' (Berenschot 2009: 113ff.). Networks of politicians, brokers, agents, and local party offices are used to transfer the election promises, policy benefits but especially material inducements to the earmarked, prospective voters. Finally, a machine party and politician losing the elections – and hence its powerful position to command and allocate state resources – normally survives if only by maintaining ties with its voters, even if its politicians/mediators can offer much less. Stokes (2005: 319) suggests:

it does not end if the machine can carry over public funds from the party's time in power or if it can make use of resources donated by private actors who expect policy concessions from the machine when it is back in power.

1.6 Elections and election funding: black money, builders and the transfer industry

Surprisingly, while many authors and Indian academics do refer to large expenses made in providing pre-election material inducements, the question is rarely asked where the money comes from.[22] This, while there are and have been plenty indications as to close links between the state and its officials and politicians on the one hand, and private sector actors, elites or 'powerful interests' on the other. This is confirmed by Harris-White (2003: 96).

> As the state becomes weaker, so elements in it attempt to buy off powerful challenges from the informal economy by selling rights to the State's political transactions. Politicians have long realised this and have inserted themselves as brokers, paid by powerful interests to *prevent* regulation and taxation, and paid by officials to influence their transfers and promotions. These payments are returns to investments in the electoral process, and they also reinforce a politician's capacity to see off challenges.

So who are the powerful or business interests and how and why are they so interested in politicians and elections? One incontestable source would be the well-respected Election Commission, whose commissioner (CEC) is quoted in a newspaper in the context of a consultation on political party funding.

> CEC Mr. Brahma said, in view of the high cost of election campaigning in terms of media advertisements and public rallies, that the use of 'big money' in politics is a major concern today. 'If wealthy individuals and the corporates pay to the political party or the candidate in order to make him listen to them, this undermines the core principles of democracy and transfers the economic inequality to political inequality'[23]. . . . Following the consultation, the CEC gave a statement 'that the use of black money during elections had to be checked as it created imbalance in a democratic system'. . . . 'Black money impinges democracy. Black money and muscle power disturb level playing field. Though money cannot guarantee votes, the one who can spend more has an upper hand'.[24]

So something is obviously wrong, as confirmed by Quraishi (2014: xiii): 'Vast sums get flung into an election both within and *outside* the Companies Act. This is where black money mingles with the white, making the whole thing as grey as smog.' He frames the key question: 'Once elected with the help of another's money – be it an individual or a company's – can the victorious candidate look the donor in the eye and say "No" when that donor asks for an inappropriate concession?.' In this view, the 'power of wealth' becomes a 'tyranny' for both the losing and winning sides. I refer to Prabash (2010) as one of the scarce sources directly referring to the link between business groups and politicians as in corporate contributions to politicians and parties, and who asks 'the million dollar question . . . . where these galactic sums come from'. He argues that they find their origin in corporate contributions and corruption (Prabash 2010: 91), relating it to the influence of money power in Indian elections and a growing pressure of business interests in Parliament and State legislatures. Arguing that a new breed of politicians in the form of 'political entrepreneurs' has emerged,[25] he suggests that there are processes of de-politicisation, 'an ethnicisation as well as fragmentation of the party system', and that economic liberalisation has contributed to the manipulation of the electoral arena by vested interests. This confirms the Chandra (2004) thesis of elections as 'auctions', but Prabash calls it 'a big market place'. Massive amounts of money are being spent on central and state elections; in a 2009 survey, one-fifth of voters stated that candidates or party workers offered money to vote in the past decade.[26] A survey by Bihar's chief electoral officer revealed 'that almost 80% of people feel that taking money or gifts to vote for someone is not wrong'.[27]

The most obvious source of such largesse is black money: an Indian general election is 'one of the most expensive shows on earth . . . and the fuel powering this frenetic activity is almost all black money', says Guha Ray (2009: 1), who feels black money has an overwhelming presence in the political arteries of the Indian economy. Funds to invest in elections may come directly from parties' reserves and business circles; it may also be transferred before the elections from abroad or dis-invested in assets where money was parked temporarily. More than 60 per cent of corporate funding to all political parties is provided as black money: 'Top Mumbai-based companies are now funding elections in states where they have big business interests' (Guha Ray 2009: 4). Says one NGO working on democratic reforms: 'Politics is actually a big game of money. Those spending heavily are doing so only as an investment and expect a ten-fold return on their money' (Guha Ray 2009: 7). It is, however, not only the business class itself volunteering to invest in the support of political parties or candidates; politicians are also demanding such contributions, which again frustrates another part of the business class. They worry whom to support: 'Election results are of vital importance to contractors: if they bet on the wrong party, they stand little chance of securing lucrative government contracts afterwards' (Berenschot 2010: 900). Contractors need to be close to politicians; they may have to pay around 10 per cent of a contract obtained through a politician. These dynamics are confirmed by Gowda and Sridharan (2012: 226), who assess Indian legislation to deal with election campaign expenses since 1951. In their view 'these laws may have perverse impacts on the electoral system: they tend to drive campaign expenditure underground and foster a reliance on unaccounted funds or "black money" '. It fundamentally distorts democratic principles: 'This tends to lead to an adverse selection system, in which those willing and able to work with black money dominate politics.' Since 1975 India is seen to have witnessed 'electoral arms races' where parties tried to outspend each other with all sort of inducements such as free liquor during campaigns (Gowda and Sridharan 2012: 232). The business sector had no incentive to change things, if only as companies liked the secrecy to pay any candidate without upsetting rival ones. Besides, there is a critical issue here in terms of the discretionary powers of politicians – which was noted to increase the incidence of informal dependency relations for poor people. But, however well funded they are, private-sector firms also have to queue up to obtain licences, contracts, concessions, and the like (Gowda and Sridharan 2012: 237). In reaction, they have a general ongoing interest to keep different competing political parties and their politicians in a generous mood by paying sums to many of them (which may be followed by more specific machine politics deals/contributions later). So, in terms of how it all started, it is not that the business sector can be seen as the (only) cause of 'machine' payments: politicians expect these in return for their 'efforts'. By now it appears to have grown into a system with its own informal institutions, incentives and sanctions, perhaps even business cycles.

There are, however, other and time-tested ways for politicians to make money – as noted way back by Wade (1982), but few follow-up studies seem to have been done – which is by managing the transfer of bureaucrats. It is the politicians of India who decide on the transfers of officials, with basically three options. Ideally the transfer follows bureaucratic rules and is merit-based and money plays no role. But what may happen is that politicians receive a bribe from an official who is keen to move to a better-paying position (i.e. where illegal earnings are more) or that an official gets a 'punishment transfer', for example when his or her performance is not to the liking of a politician or a group of other officials. Das (2001: 130) mentions that the process of transfers is so lucrative that it is called 'the transfer industry' (cf. Kishwar 2005: 130):

> It is true that many times the transfers are made on caste lines and in most cases for monetary considerations. Elected representatives develop some kind of a contract, fixing the amount to be paid for the officer to remain in a post for a particular period.

Berenschot (2010: 898ff.) believes that politicians benefit in two ways from their powers over transfers. It helps them manipulate or enforce obedience and loyalty from officials, which is also a way to make sure policy benefits can be channelled without disturbance to the specific voters they have in mind. Besides, it yields handsome sums to be invested in elections and campaigning – and accumulating in (family) wealth and power.

I need to finally consider – and eventually check with evidence – another critical by-product of the dominance of machine politics and the workings of a patronage democracy. This is its unavoidable focus on the short term (the five-year politicians' horizon), and its focus on policy 'implementation' (how already budgeted funds and policy plans are used) rather than the equally important policy stages of 'formulation' or policy design (whether, for example, policies are formulated with a vision and feasible strategy about the roots of poverty) and policy monitoring and evaluation. This follows from Scott's (1969: 1155) classic formulation: 'The machine became specialised in organising and allocating influence at the *enforcement* stage' – and implicitly not formulation stage – while it 'has made the pursuit of longer-run development objectives more difficult.' Hence, the focus on votes, and the terms of agreement between business and politicians becomes an end in itself, dangerously undermining the representative dimension of liberal democracy where the needs and priorities of voters come first. In line with this observation, it appears as if today, as part of India's urban governance, two factors work against the adoption of public policies relevant for development, in terms of enhanced welfare for all – and especially the urban poor. One is what Prabash (2010: 88) calls the 'de-politicisation' of politics. Politicians are either themselves de-politicised, or they have become instruments in the hands of others, notably the business sectors 'which attach high value to direct representation in Parliament in the era of economic liberalisation'. Here, he notes an increasing presence of business representatives especially in the lower house of parliament (Prabash 2010: 92).[28]

He identifies a risk that policies – and I may add city planning and budget allocations – are determined more by the influence and power of big business than as a result of a political process where people/the electorate elect representatives/policymakers/legislators on the basis of their needs and priorities. In his view, elections are no longer a contest of ideas and public policies as money has replaced the former role of ideas and policy alternatives. Where such money dynamics and vote buying systems are dominant, they cut back the core democratic connection between voting and alternative policy or development paths: 'Under vote buying, public policy will tilt away from the interest of the class of vote sellers; their votes do not communicate policy preferences prospectively, nor do they communicate judgements of policy or performance retrospectively' (Stokes *et al.* 2013: 248). All this tallies with the trappings of the Berenschot (2010) 'mediated state model' of local politics, where, as already mentioned, local politicians are no longer policymakers, but have evolved into street-level politicians. Starting from budgets and opportunities available – and forever trying to maximise them as in their discretionary funds, their business is basically the particularistic allocation of state benefits (at some price).

The emergence in India of the 'political entrepreneur' and trends where politicians turn into businessmen and businessmen into politicians undermines Scott's simple three actor political machine model. Today, business people may try and stand for elections for MLA and MP positions, whereas many MLAs and MPs have (developed) extensive business interests – and it is not that this trend is unique to India (e.g. Kenya or the United States). It leads to a dangerous blurring of positions and more scope for undue influence mongering and misuse, and to 'revolving doors' between public and private domains. This risk is noted by Oxfam (2015: 10) in a chapter on 'The Capture of Politics by the Economic Elite' including 'the revolving doors between business and politics'.

1.7 Democracy shifts: the Indian middle class and the urban poor

Any societal change will see winners and losers. In India it has, by and large, been the land- and capital-owning elites and the (salaried) middle classes to benefit most by India's high rates of growth – that is in the relatively limited number of fast-growth sectors. An interest has ensued in the role of the Indian middle class in urban governance and democracy (Anjaria 2009; Baud and de Wit 2008; Chakravarthi 2007; de Wit 2009a, 2009b; Kundu 2009; Srivastava 2009).

If only as the concept of 'middle class' is notoriously hard to define, there is a lack of uniform data on its size, but as noted, it may have grown from 162 million to about 254 million people in 2005 (19.3 per cent), of whom 210 million would have been middle-class people and 44 million high-income people.[29] A crucial question is as to whether enriched and 'empowered' middle-class people would be interested and if so capable of enforcing better governance and a better democracy. A classic view of democratisation propounded by Barrington Moore (1966) is that it is the bourgeoisie which is the key agent of democratisation. One might wonder therefore whether growing middle classes in countries such as China, Indonesia and Nigeria could help deepen democracy or demand a more 'liberal democracy', with free and fair elections, the rule of law and generally a governance context of accountability and reduced corruption. Initial indications in terms of democracy here are not encouraging. For India, it was noted already that Indian elites and middle classes vote much less in the Indian elections than lower-income groups, or altogether turn away from what they may perceive as suspect, corrupted or even criminal politicians. According to Heuze (2011: 70) the Mumbai 'petty bourgeoisie' still voted in large numbers in the 1960s and 1970s; he notes since then a growing alienation of the so-called middle classes from the field of parliamentary democracy. D. Kundu (2009: 283) mentions 'strong evidence showing that while middle-class people in India have withdrawn increasingly from electoral politics, poorer people are remarkably active participants'. *Asia Times* reports on voter turnout patterns:[30]

> India's rich and middle class urban voters have failed to show up in large numbers to exercise their franchise in the country's general election. . . . Urban middle class voters have indicated that they are laggards in comparison to the rural or urban poor. . . . And what makes this rise in voter turnout significant is that it is spurred by the rise in participation in elections by the poor, women, lower castes and *Dalits* and tribals. The most vulnerable sections of Indian society are increasingly enthusiastic about voting. The newspaper stresses that it is not religion but class that forms the dividing line, with the rich and middle classes lacking the faith the poor have in elections, and that urban apathy has grown. Importantly it says: 'for all their whining about the quality of politicians (like the fielding of criminal and corrupt candidates) . . . India's educated and more privileged sections don't do anything about it on polling day: they simply stay away.'

A similar view is held by Gupta (2012: 293): 'Democracy has created a situation where electoral funding is mostly from capitalists . . . but the popular vote comes mainly from poor rural and urban voters.' Things appear to be similar at the local level and in municipal elections and politics, as noted by John (2007: 3993) who refers to what is called 'social municipalism': 'initiatives by middle class residents, especially women and retired people, to improve their neighbourhoods in the face of "the failures of local governance"; initiatives that seek to bypass or supplant both the electoral process and popular local politics.' Well-to-do citizens tend to bypass local politicians for whom they have little respect and whom they distrust and try to contact municipal officials directly either personally or in organised forms such as resident welfare associations (RWAs), which have multiplied in Indian cities.[31] In cities like Delhi (*bhagidari*) and Mumbai (Advanced Local Management groups – ALM), such groups are actively supported by the state (Baud and Nainan 2008: 13; de Wit 2009a). Indications are that they are less open minded and less focused on working towards enhancing overall city welfare, and less pro-poor than one might have hoped.

More broadly, significant local governance shifts are noted by Harris *et al.* (2004) who refer to 'new politics', which entail a growing role for 'civil society' and their organisations (like RWAs) instead of for traditional political parties and labour organisations. Such novel ways of organising are seen by some to have more potential for genuine participation than the representative electoral democracy of 'old politics', which in many countries are seen to have become corrupted, failing to solve the urgent social problems. However, such trends can be assumed to work out negatively for the urban and rural poor, who have problems organising and who are squarely in traditional politics where politicians have vested interests to keep them. Just now that the poor are establishing themselves in local and even state politics, with Dalit parties, powerful political leaders from the OBCs, and evidence that the poor continue to support and act in local politics and elections, a political segregation can be discerned between the poor and higher-income groups – along with increasing inter-group income inequality. Harris (2007: 2722) confirms that middle-class people withdraw from electoral politics and that poorer people are remarkably active participants: 'Representative democracy has empowered some historically subordinated groups at least.' But that does not make him optimistic: 'The new politics of empowerment – the mode of governmentality of the post liberalisation state of India – does not incorporate the urban poor, nor articulates their political practice' (Harris 2007: 2723).

So the poor (have little choice to) remain most active politically – if only to obtain benefits in India's patronage democracy. The middle classes and the rich seem to largely opt out of voting and rather organise on their own while joining/supporting anti-corruption movements and parties which, from their perspective, can be well understood. But there is also another perspective where Kumar (2009: 127) perceives the anti-Bihari and more general anti-migrant sentiments among middle classes as a broader assertion of cultural superiority of the urban upper and middle castes and classes who are marked by a 'gated-community consciousness', which is suspicious, if not afraid of the dangerous and dirty 'other'. Such a sentiment is assessed also by Mander,[32] who ponders the capacity of India's middle class to look away when confronted with enormous injustice and suffering and Indian society's cultural comfort with inequality. He feels that large sections of the elite and middle classes are prejudiced against people of 'lower' castes, urban slums and working-class migrants from poor states. He notes a 'strange new social common sense' where it is the rich and privileged in new India who 'are being led to feel oppressed and short-changed by the poor, rather than the other way around'. There is a dominant discourse along lines like: 'We work hard and earn an honest living and then we are taxed to supply freebies to the undeserving poor.' This view holds that the poor should work hard and pull themselves up through their own efforts. Mander agrees that existing inequities and injustice do indeed reflect a failure of the state and its laws, policies and institutions, but that these are due to the 'social' sanction given by the influential middle and upper classes.

> It means that it is not enough to fight for stronger laws to end corruption, without recognising and resisting ways in which the middle and upper classes are not just victims of corruption, but also participants in and beneficiaries of it.

Whatever the merit of this view, if we compare the poor and middle classes, facts are that the former are typically bribe-payers, whereas there is more chance that a middle-class income earner is a bribe-taker: at least he or she has more choices.

This chapter, on the one hand, sketched the overall Indian context of poverty, governance and democracy against which I now introduce Mumbai realities in the next chapter. Besides, I outlined my analytical framework of concepts and perspectives covering the broad agenda of this book. It is designed to help target key issues and trends as seen important by academics, practitioners and journalists, as well as to assess the value of diverse viewpoints and positions. We move from the general to the more specific and, in the next chapter, zoom into megacity Mumbai, mapping municipal governance and its recent changes.

Notes

1 Sassen Interview in NRC Handelsblad, 11 July 2014.
2 'Against the Grain'. 2007, *The Hindu*, 21 August. Arjun Sengupta, Chairman of a NCUES Commission, mentions that the number of Indians in the marginal group consuming less than Rs 15 per day increased from 186 million in 1994 to 207 million in 2005; the vulnerable group consuming less than Rs 20/day increased from 290 million to 392 million. He confirms the total number of 836 million poor people and estimates the middle class to have grown from 162 million to about 254 million people in 2005 (19.3 per cent). Of these he counts 210 million middle-class people and 44 million high-income people, assumedly 'the elite' (cf. NCEUS/Sengupta 2007).
3 A more meaningful and comprehensive way to measure poverty is 'the empowerment line' framed by McKinsey Global Institute (MGI; *The Hindu*, 20 February 2014), which estimates the economic cost per capita to meet a minimum requirement of consumption of eight basic services – food, health care, education, sanitation, water, housing, fuel, social security, and 'others' including clothing and entertainment. This, for India, results in a higher actual incidence of urban poverty at 44 per cent, contrasting with the Planning Commission estimate at 25.7 per cent.
4 K. C. Sivaramakrishnan, 'No One Owns the City', *Indian Express*, 14 May 2014:

> in the last 10 years India's urban population has grown from 266 to 377 million. The slum population has also increased. Counting the slum population is like shooting the rapids on the Ganga: you can go up to a high of 93 million or a low of 68. Urban and slum growth has occurred across the country.

5 'Winners and why they made it'. 2013. *India Today*, March, p. 38. Mr Revi is director of the Indian Institute for Human Settlements, Bangalore.
6 *Economic and Political Weekly*, 16 February 2008: 5.
7 His text is entitled: 'Whatever Happened to Public Administration? Governance, Governance Everywhere.'
8 'Crony Capitalism a Big Threat to Countries Like India, RBI Chief Raghuram Rajan Says'. 2014. *Times of India*, 12 August.
9 'Congress Faces an Existential Dilemma: What Is the Point of a Party of Patronage When Not in Power?' *The Economist*, 21 June 2014, reflects on the fate of the Congress Party after its battering in India's 2014 general elections.
10 Gratefully quoted from Chandra (2004: 3).
11 The fact that India has the 'constituency' or 'first past the pole' election system may explain to some extent that major political shifts seem to take place when a sitting government is defeated. However, if one calculates

vote strength as in actual percentages of votes, shifts are often not that sizable, as shown in Chapter 5.

12 Freedom House website, https://freedomhouse.org/report/freedom-world-2012/methodology#.VY5crUavZYU (accessed on 12 September 2014).

13 'India's Battle for Democracy Has Just Begun; The Urban Middle Class Is Now the Base of the Anti-Corruption Movement and Has the Resources to Last, Writes Ashutosh Varshney.' 2011. *Financial Times.* 29 August. http://www.ft.com/cms/s/0/7158efa8-cf41–11e0-b6d4–00144feabdc0. html#ixzz2fhrqDXEZ (accessed on 18 February 2014).

14 J.S. Chhokar, 'For a Thriving Democracy', in *Governance Now*, 1–15 April 2015.

15 Ibid.

16 Boo (2012: 20) adds an interesting perspective on what she sees as an increased need for mediators:

> But in the twenty-first century, fewer people joined up to take their disputes to the streets. As group identities based on caste, ethnicity, and religion gradually attenuated, anger and hope were being privatized, like so much else in Mumbai. This development increased the demand for canny mediators – human shock absorbers for the colliding, narrowly constructed interests of one of the world's largest cities.

17 See Bjorkman (2013: 14) for an assessment and Stokes *et al.* (2013: 175ff.).

18 Lipsky (1980) argued for the central policy role of street-level bureaucrats. The policy process ultimately depends on street-level bureaucrats (municipal, district officials, policemen) whose daily practices operationalise policy guidelines and dictates into the concrete material processes/benefits people experience. These bureaucrats influence how policies are implemented and how rules are enforced with what results by transforming general policies into concrete decisions. But this final step in the policy process allows for opportunities for individual professional gain and rent seeking, which depends on the precise level of discretion, complicity of superiors and subordinates and the degree and mode of accountability. In contrast, local politicians are expected to be engaged in prioritizing citizen needs, designing or adjusting policy in a general way, aiming at the welfare of whole constituencies, while leaving implementation to street-level bureaucrats. Berenschot sees a blurring/changing of roles here.

19 'EC Notice to Gadkari for "Inducing Voters to Take Bribe" ', *Times of India,* 6 October 2014.

20 'Victory of Principles over Moneybags: Sharad Yadav', *Times of India,* 8 November 2015.

21 http://en.wikipedia.org/wiki/Votebank (accessed on 23 September 2013, providing an adequate definition).

22 Roniger (2004) addresses the role of the market economy, but fails to address this matter.

23 'No State Poll Funding Sans Radical Reforms', *Indian Express,* 24 March 2015.

24 'Poll Panel for Stringent Law to Deal with Political Funding', *Indian Express,* 31 March 2015.

25 Gowda and Sridaran (2012: 235) mention that the preference of political parties for wealthy candidates can give rise to a new breed of 'political entrepreneurs' who 'are ready to invest in running for office in the hope of controlling the levers of government to further enhance their personal wealth'.

26 Guha Ray (2009) states that the 2014 general Indian elections were the most expensive ever and, globally, ranked second after the 2012 USA elections. 'Informed sources told *Tehelka* that an estimated Rs 10,000–15,000 crores (US 2–3 billion) has been earmarked by political parties for "unofficial" purchases of individual votes' (p. 3). 'Estimated per candidate expenditure is Rs 3–15 crores; the price of a vote is now Rs 2,000–5,000 per voter (on average); candidates openly distribute money in the garb of personal functions.' 'Conglomerates like the Birlas and Tatas have separate electoral trusts, through which they donate money to political parties' (p. 6). '60% of companies are financing political parties with black money' (p. 3).

27 '80% of People in Bihar Feel Taking Money for Vote Is Not Wrong: Survey', *Times of India*, 7 October 2015.

28 There are indications that more and more business people themselves try and stand for elections for MLA and MP positions, whereas many MLAs and MPs have developed extensive business interests (Interview with Mr Sarkar, 18 September 2013). This makes the trapping of the relatively simple three-actor machine politics model more complex as business elites may double as business people and politicians at the same time. This risk is noted by Oxfam (2015:10) as 'the revolving doors between business and politics'.

29 Arjun Sengupta, 'Against the Grain', *The Hindu*, 21 August 2007.

30 www.atimes.com, 25 April 2009 (accessed on 7 April 2010).

31 Cf. Berenschot (2010: 888), who mentions that richer citizens have the means to deal with (or circumvent) the state without political intervention as they have more influential contacts and monetary resources.

32 H. Mander, 'Forgotten Brethren: In the Middle Class Expectations of 21st Century India, People on the Socio-Economic Margins Should Stay There, Because That Is Their Lot', *Outlook*, 20 April 2015.

2 Mumbai megacity
City, people and governance changes

Mumbai is home to 12 million people, around 20 million if the people of the entire massive metropolis 'Greater Mumbai' are included. It is an amalgam of people from all Indian states, religions, identities, and income levels, with pavement dwellers living close to sleek modern towers housing millionaires, all crammed together onto a relatively small area. No surprise that it has been called a 'maximum city' (Metha 2004) and a city of extremes, and any government would be hard put to govern such a complex, extremely heterogeneous and potentially divided population and area. The city faces severe mismatches between the supply and demand of essential services and overall infrastructure. Land is so expensive that it has become the key city arena of both contestation and profit making, spurring dynamics of informality and rent seeking by powerful city groups. This chapter provides the socio-economic and governance context needed to understand the juxtaposition of poverty, politics and governance in the metropolis. Facts and trends as regards demography, employment and incomes are presented first, followed by a review of city administration, dominated by the Mumbai Corporation of Greater Mumbai (MCGM), better known by its former name BMC or Brihanmumbai Municipal Corporation. Its main players such as the municipal commissioner, the powerful standing committee and the BMC council are introduced. Urban decentralisation legislation was implemented from 2000, and I will describe the twisty road towards the formation of the main institutions and actors and assess their overall performance. But the BMC is by no means the only organisation governing the city; powerful state- and central-level agencies and parastatals are assumed to co-govern, with an increasingly large role for the private sector. I will show that, unfortunately, this is a city with too many bosses and too little coordination and efficiency, where agencies are politicised and often self-interestedly compete for funds and opportunities.

2.1 City, people and planning

With divergent estimates between 12 and 14 million people within the municipal boundaries – and about 20 million in the larger Greater Mumbai Metropolitan Region (MMR) – the city is a pressure cooker of people, houses/slums and cars. It is a maximum city indeed jammed into a limited area of 438 sq. km and an overall population density of 27,800 (MCGM 2009),[1] and an estimated 30,900 as per the 2011 Census. Fifty-four per cent of the population lives in slums. The Mumbai region – including several municipal corporations – grew by 30 per cent between 1991 and 2001,[2] but the growth slowed down to 12 per cent in 2001–11. Mumbai is the capital of Maharashtra state and dominates this state in many respects, certainly in terms of GNP, trade, tax basis, and the number of cars. The city occupies a dominant place in India's economy and finance where its share in all India's foreign trade is 40 per cent; 33 per cent of all taxes are collected here (MCGM 2009: 41). It is the commercial, industrial and cosmopolitan centre of India, with the largest film and TV industry of India known as Bollywood. It is the most cosmopolitan Indian city; boasting lots of festivals and foreign links to the worlds of arts, music and design. This is where the global elite easily mixes with the Indian elite in posh five-star hotels or even more luxury private apartments. Mumbai is a good example of a global city (Clark and Moonen 2014; Sivaramakrishnan 2011:53), which figures in a Knight Frank Wealth Report. It ranks Mumbai in 2012 as the 16th most expensive city in the world in terms of owning prime residential property with a price tag of about Rs 57,000 ($905) per square feet.[3] In terms of the super-rich, Mumbai ranks seventh, with a total of 2,700 millionaires, expected to increase to 5,000 or a 137 per cent increase. In the same city, approximately six million people live in slums; two to three million are extremely poor.

One reason for such expensive real estate is a substantial mismatch between supply and demand, which in turn has everything to do with extremely high land prices – which are partly caused by the peculiar geography of the city, but hugely exacerbated by the lack of socially oriented land, housing, planning and management practices. The city centre land mass is surrounded by seas, limiting its expansion except towards the north. While Delhi and Chennai have expanded outwards relatively easily, the key urban area of Mumbai remains 'the island city' or, simply, 'the city'. This is the city built around the original seven islands of Mumbai, starting with Colaba in the south, with as northern boundary the neighbourhoods of Mahim and Sion. To the north of this are the 'suburbs', which can be divided again into western (such as Borivalli) and eastern (such as Thane) suburbs. It is in the city where most government buildings are located: the Maharashtra state government departments and the *Mantralaya* meeting hall for the members of the state legislative assembly (MLAs) as well as the BMC headquarters with the meeting hall for the city's 227 MCs. There has been city expansion just north of the city, both in terms of office space (e.g. the Bandra-Kurla complex, cf. Banerjee-Guha 2010: 214ff.) and in upmarket housing, but this has been accessible only to the very rich. Most people looking for reasonable (but still expensive) property do so in the northern or eastern suburbs. Those working in the city travel south each day by either the incredibly busy suburban trains or buses, which together ferry nearly 10 million persons across the city daily (MCGM 2009: 158). Others may opt for using their cars, at risk of losing much time in massive traffic queues at peak hours with staggering pollution from thousands of fuel-inefficient vehicles. A key reason for Mumbai's specific mix of urban challenges is weak governance, which allows for very poor – if not a fundamental absence of – long-term urban planning:

> The unchecked growth of build-up areas in Mumbai that defy most planning, zoning and environmental regulations is one of the major causes of the structural vulnerability of Greater Mumbai. Added to this are weak and vitiated planning practices. . . . The central tenets of long range planning have been systematically violated in Mumbai. This has choked off natural areas that provide its core ecological services: water, food, clean air, waste absorption, and protection against the tide and weather, in favour of more profit for its developers and realtors and greater rents for its regulators and property owners.
>
> (Revi 2005: 3913–14)

A newspaper reported that only 5–7 per cent of the plans included in the 1991 BMC development plan (DP) were implemented in the city's 24 wards in over 20 years.[4] As I elaborate later, the prospects for the DP 2014–34, which was developed in early 2015, do not look too good either. An initial plan was presented by the BMC on 16 February 2015. Among several issues, critics targeted a few of relevance to this book, first the fact that, amazingly, the BMC had decided not to map the city slums as part of the 'existing land-use exercise'. Yet, as Bhide (2011) argues, this is nothing new.[5] So while the 1,000-page DP has 336 maps, there are no maps of the city areas where half of the city population is living, which appears like an exercise in 'exclusionary planning'. This, even while it is understood that it is complex to map and plan for city slums, some of which on BMC lands, others on the land of other agencies or in private hands.[6] Another major criticism is captured in an article 'BMC to Open FSI Floodgates despite Infra Woes', referring to the fact that by expanding the floor-space-index (FSI) in a range of city areas, the incidence of vertical building and high-rise towers (from 70 now to 120 metres/40 stories) will increase much.[7]

According to Das (2003: 220), land in Mumbai has been systematically captured by private builders who even manipulate land records and land-use plans and is developed for commercial projects and housing high-income groups. He argues that slum lands are seen by the authorities as the most convenient source of land for public works and new commercial development 'under a policy of privatisation of all development', which benefits giant companies and big investors. Patronage relations are seen to play a role (Das 2003:221):

> With the price of urban land sky-rocketing, there is a scramble to acquire pieces of it. New packages of urban land are continually created by the various urban development authorities, with the land being made available not only below the value commensurate with state inputs to development, but even below the prevalent market prices. This creates a scramble for such land and an opportunity for politicians and bureaucrats to extend patronage while making a killing.
>
> (Das 2003:224)

Such new land is released into the market in a strategic way, so as to benefit most from prevailing land scarcity, and some such land is acquired or reclaimed illegally such as Mumbai's nominally protected mangrove swamps and coastal regulation zone (CRZ), in processes as outlined at the start of this book. There was some hope that the city as a whole – including vast numbers of urban poor – might benefit from the availability of the large unused land tracts that were part of the former textile mill factories. To the disappointment of many, it appears as if big capital and large investors managed to lay claim to most of these lands. Maneckersha (2011: 29) refers to a growing clout of realty barons who appear to be engaged in the development of ever more new townships with flashy fully serviced apartment towers or in constructing amazingly expensive apartments in the island city. Yet she reports that, by 2010, there are reportedly nearly 32,000 unsold flats and that housing activists maintain 'that smaller and more affordable flats are simply not being built'. There may be some continuity here, as noted by Narayanan (2003: 203–4), that, in those days, only over 6 per cent of the MMR households could afford 'formal housing' and that there were also far more housing units than there are buyers, as people simply could not buy these. 'When one says that the private sector meets up to 90 per cent of Mumbai's housing needs today, one is taking into account a substantial number of "informal housing units", including slums and pavement dwellings' (Narayanan 2003: 203–4). Such slums and makeshift pockets of huts all over the city are the result of encroachments organised or allowed not by migrants or other low-income people themselves but by local slum leaders and slum lords, mostly with the knowledge or blessing of a corporator. Then Chief Minister Deshmuck met a group of MLAs where he instructed the Mumbai commissioner and police commissioner to take strict action against their staff who abet the proliferation of slums:[8]

> The delegation (of Congress MLAs) also demanded action against slum lords who have made crores of Rupees over the years by selling public land to unsuspected slum dwellers. If the authorities want, they can easily get the names of the slum lords from the shanti dwellers. Slum lords are the people who, in collusion with corrupt staff in the BMC, collector's offices and the police department, are exploiting poor slum dwellers.

But poor households or migrants are by no means the only ones engaging in 'illegally' occupying city lands; this also applies to middle-class households and the rich. For example, the High Court addressed a public interest litigation which claimed that there were 3,000 unauthorised structures, including bungalows, along a Malad road and that the BMC had neither identified these structures nor taken action. The court ruled that a lack of personnel cannot be a reason not to deal with complaints of unauthorised construction.[9] As a result of these hyper-intensive, largely informal land dynamics beyond any development (DP) or other plan, combined with an elite domination of real estate, housing is very costly and a major concern for all Mumbai citizens. A final constraining factor affecting the entire Mumbai building sector is the extremely complex and cumbersome process to obtain building permits and commencement certificates. It takes 27 steps and 162 days to obtain a construction permit in Greater Mumbai, making up 46.05 per cent of construction costs. Developers indicate that it is not only that they have to pay money under the table – to the BMC building department, which is widely perceived to be its most corrupt (Pinto and Pinto 2005: 188, 194) but also the 'interminable wait' and the number of counters to visit, which is 'throttling the industry'.[10] For all these reasons the limited supply of formal housing mostly benefits the rich, that is the upper middle classes, Indian elite business groups, politicians, and multi-national companies, while the urban poor have been crowded out of formal housing according to Pethe *et al.* (2014: 120). Yet they argue that the urban poor have successfully engaged with the state through political negotiations, vote bank politics or what Benjamin (2008) calls 'occupancy urbanism'. Such factors help explain how it can be that as many as six to seven million people live in the numerous slums and these are not only the poor. Many households that qualify as middle class in terms of incomes and assets have little option but to live in slum or chawl-like conditions (there were 700,000 applicants for 3,500 relatively cheap state-built apartments; MCGM 2009: 38).

> The country's financial capital and also the richest city, Mumbai, has a humongous 14.5 lakh families living in slums, said Chief Minister Prithviraj Chavan in the Legislative Council on Wednesday. Assuming five persons per family, the total slum population stands at a whopping 72.5 lakh. These slum dwellers account for 58 per cent of the total population of 1.24 crore, but are squeezed in a meagre 37 sq. km or 6.13 per cent[11] of the total city area.[12]

This pressure on the scarce land has led also to a lack of public space in the form of parks and open spaces and to severe constraints to plan and construct urgently needed new roads, bus and metro lines. All this is happening, but mostly at a very low pace and with large cost overruns, for example, on the elevated metro lines now under construction.[13] A recent Jones Lang Lasalle Report reveals a severe mismatch between investments in real estate – which are very high – and far too low investments in basic civic projects.[14] Unsurprisingly, most *Mumbaikars* have plenty of complaints about the BMC services: 'Mumbai isn't happy' is the title of a report based on a survey by the NGO PRAJA. Twenty-eight thousand inhabitants gave all 14 BMC-provided civic services a below-average rating, with issues such as cleanliness and sanitation; poor-quality hospitals, schools, and colleges; water supply; traffic jams and public transport; pollution; waterlogging; power supply; and public gardens.[15] This is despite the fact that there *are* plans as well as concrete projects aimed to improve things. As explained in the course of this book, projects are implemented slowly and poorly 'owing to the lack of political and bureaucratic will, absence of focused and organised policies, vested political and corporate interests and differences within the ruling parties'.[16]

2.2   Rich and poor in Mumbai's economy

The Mumbai population is a mix of various groups, of whom 43.7 per cent were categorised as migrants in the 2001 Census, as not having been born in Mumbai – but 37 per cent of these migrants came from Maharashtra state (63 per cent from other states). The next largest group of migrants hails from Uttar Pradesh at 24 per cent, followed by Bihar and Karnataka (GOI 2013: A-42). Most migrants have a rural origin (MCGM 2009: 19). The idea that the original Marathi population declined at the expense of newcomers was being put to political use by some 'sons of the soil' political parties such as Shiv Sena and the MNS. Yet the recent population changes did affect the position and ideology of such parties, which now – pragmatically – also scout for the votes of non-original *Mumbaikars*. The large majority of BMC city area people are Hindus (67.4 per cent), next Muslims (18.6 per cent), Buddhists (5.2 per cent), Jains (4 per cent), and Christians (3.7 per cent) (GOI 2013: A-25). The percentage of SCs in Mumbai is 5.5 (GOI 2013: A-27). However, two-thirds of them live in the many city slums (Mahadevia 2013).

The Mumbai Human Development Report (MCGM 2009: 40) observes: 'Mumbai's economy can be the envy of several States and Cities.' The per-capita net income was Rs 65,361 at current prices in 2006–7, which is one and a half times Maharashtra's per-capita net income of Rs 41,331 and twice the country's average per-capita income of Rs 29,382. Pethe (2010: 7) argues that the economic growth of Mumbai has been remarkable, which led to reduction in poverty. He notes, however, that this growth came with a clear increase of inequality and increasing real estate prices: 94–95 per cent of Mumbai households cannot afford a formal-sector house.

Following general trends, Mumbai witnessed a decline of employment in the primary sector (agriculture and related) and secondary sector (manufacture and construction) – now at 25 per cent (see Banerjee-Guha 2010: 209ff.). The tertiary sector of services grew fast (now 74 per cent), including transport, restaurants, communication, banking, and tourism, so that Mumbai's economic growth over the past few decades took place alongside de-industrialisation (Vakulabharanam and Motiram 2012: 48). Partly as a result of globalisation and neoliberal reforms, there appears to have been a polarisation in the labour market too. On the one hand, Mumbai has attracted high-end sophisticated industries and organisations linked to the global economy with very well-paid formal jobs in the ITC sector, tourism, finance, and car-related work (MCGM 2009: 51). Employment also grew in the informal sector – where most poor people and migrants work – but it is marked by irregular and unpredictable work, long working hours, unsafe conditions (e.g. in the construction industry and for female domestic servants), and often downright exploitation in terms of payments. Boo (2012: 20) puts it like this: 'Wealthy citizens accused the slum dwellers of making the city filthy and unlivable, even as an oversupply of human capital kept the wages of their maids and chauffeurs low.'

As an overall indication for India as a whole, Vakulabharanam and Motiram (2012: 4) indicate that unorganised workers comprised 92 per cent of the total workforce;[17] another source indicates that the informal sector accounts for 68 per cent of the total employment in Mumbai.[18] Workers engaged in this urban informal sector form the bulk of the urban poor. But I need to stress that the 'informal sector' is far from a homogenous category. Extremely diversified, it covers a range of jobs – some at rock-bottom wages, others in fact with a good days' income – for example for people with good skills as plumbers or carpenters or in a strategically located food stall. Rejecting a dualistic framework, Vakulabharanam and Motiram (2012: 4) argue that the informal and formal sectors are linked up in many, often less well-understood ways. They highlight the fundamentally flawed position of the state, which on the one hand may try to regulate street vending while also considering it as a source of revenue, 'while on the ground, it is predatory and rent seeking (extracting bribes)' (Vakulabharanam and Motiram 2012: 48; cf. Bhowmik 2010). The unorganised or informal sector should not be perceived like one static reservoir, which can simply absorb present workers and incoming migrants. Rather, conditions are rough, driven by subsistence needs where some workers are ready to work for even lower wages than others; there is also plenty of underemployment and unemployment. It may be one of the perhaps understandable grudges of established people in Mumbai to see their own work taken over by desperate newcomer migrants, ready to take work at lower rates just to survive. A report on the impacts of globalisation on Mumbai indicates that 'this process has been accompanied by increase in casualization, contract labour, subcontracting and lengthening of working hours' (MCGM 2009: 51). Self-employment has also increased in the past decades – jobs such as hawkers, waste pickers, small shopkeepers, and beggars. Too many children are working for wages in spite of legislation preventing this, for example many girls employed as domestic servants and many boys making long hours as captives in sweat shops. Indications are of a feminisation of labour as seen in the increased number of women as main workers (working more than 183 days a year, MCGM 2009: 48). The combined efforts of all these informal-sector workers can be seen as an enormous subsidy to the more formal sectors of the Mumbai economy and to its well-off citizens who can avail of many critical services at very low cost. A case in point concerns Mumbai's solid waste collection, where rag pickers and waste pickers handle more than one-third of the city's waste (Manecksha 2011: 28). Such employment patterns translate into a growing apart of city incomes, which confirms all-India trends.

An indication of Mumbai income groups is given in de Souza (2011: 7), who makes an interesting distinction in what are often simply termed 'middle classes'. Of the total Mumbai city population of 14 million, 7 million are classified as slum population (which actually includes well-off people too; cf. Gupte 2012: 193); 3.5 million are counted as 'lower-middle classes', and 3 million as higher-middle classes; 500,000 people are counted as 'ultra-rich'. Patel (2015: 63) mentions that Mumbai does not have an expenditure profile across all households, let alone an income profile. Yet the article has a table on income groups, which brings out the following five classes. People with a monthly household income of Rs 2,500 to 5,000 make up 38.8 per cent of Mumbai's population, 25.7 per cent have incomes from Rs 17,500 to 30,000; 14.4 per cent of inhabitants earn from Rs 32,500 to 67,500. Incomes from Rs 70,000 to 97,500 are earned by 9.6 per cent of Mumbaikars, with 7.2 per cent earning between Rs 100,000 to 120,000 (ibid.: 63). The (earlier) survey in Baker *et al.* (2005: 8–9) finds 27 per cent of Mumbai households with household incomes below Rs 5.000, with an average of four household members. At that time such income was above the Maharashtra urban poverty line at Rs 594. One important finding is that 8.8 per cent of such households were headed by women, whereas it is 4.5 per cent on the average for all Mumbai households, and only 1.3 per cent for incomes higher than Rs 20.000. But we need to keep in mind that incomes are only one indication of poverty or wealth – it leaves out assets/capital, free or guaranteed access to public services and the possibility of having black money, which is more likely for the rich. As noted by the Mumbai Human Development Report (MCGM 2009), it is not quite easy to determine the degree of (extreme) poverty. Forty per cent of the slum population – 6.5 million people – is reported to have per-capita incomes below the poverty line (BPL), amounting to about 2.5 million people. At least 1.2 million of them have (had) per-capita incomes as low as Rs 592.00 per month (in 2006) (Mahadevia 2013: 13; MCGM 2009: 44, 57).[19] And this does not count non-slum poor, who live on the streets or in undocumented slums. As we will see in the next chapter on Mumbai's urban poor, other indicators of poverty beyond controversial poverty lines are also negative, for example that malnutrition among children below five years living in Mumbai slums in Mumbai is considerable and that 27 per cent of girls were underweight (MCGM 2009: 119). Besides, with a remote and indifferent state which does not much enable or facilitate livelihoods, the poor have to basically fend for themselves in terms of many critical services. All in all, an estimated three million women, children and men in Mumbai are very poor – already and if only in terms of incomes – or having low-nutrition food and/or go hungry. That makes a massive number of people for one of the richest Indian cities and an appropriate focus of this book.

I now have a closer look at the main municipal Mumbai body – BMC, the oldest Indian corporation. Compared to the Delhi and Chennai municipalities, it is an 'old-fashioned' multi-tasked agency responsible for a wide range of services. It is the key institution for the poor, both in terms of many basic public services that it provides and also politically as the home of the city's 227 local corporators or *Nagar Sevaks* (city servants) elected to represent the rich and poor in Mumbai's wards and neighbourhoods.

2.3   City governance: the Mumbai Corporation (BMC)

In terms of formal organisations and files that are moving, municipal administration in India at face value seems well organised. Yet in reality it is beset with a multitude of fundamental problems seriously undermining its effectiveness, efficiency and transparency. This is true for smaller municipalities of India, many of which are more or less bankrupt and where corruption is rife, but no less for India's globalised mega-cities. In fact, there is a long history of writings reflecting on India's 'urban crisis' (e.g. Dhar Chakrabarti 2001). It is good to note and reassuring that by and large cities have been growing and developing in the face of huge challenges of population growth, land shortages and limited budgets without an acute crisis or apocalypse. But this should not detract us from noting the gradual, insidious accumulation *and* increase of severe urban problems, such as urban poverty, infrastructure, climate change and floods, pollution, and waste management. Financial constraints are common to all Indian cities, but possibly less so for Mumbai, seen generally as a relatively resourceful place. But the city's position as India's financial capital, with tremendous pressures on basic services, land and housing, leads to high economic and financial stakes for all 'governance stakeholders' in its governance and politics. These stakeholders include formal and informal groups, such as a criminal underworld with *dadas,* slumlords, informal contractors, shady land speculators, and the 'mafia' (Weinstein 2008) – believed to have links to parties and corporators, not least those of the Shiv Sena (Hansen 2001: 98, 225). I now examine the evolution of the BMC and subsequently dwell on other agencies with relevance to the urban poor such as the MMRDA, MHADA and the SRA. While describing the BMC in terms of its formal structures and mandates, we need to keep in mind that behind this formal facade all is not well – where informality could well be the dominant governance domain as elaborated particularly in Chapter 4. In a comment on the BMC elections, *The Economist*[20] states: 'The BMC, which supposedly runs the city, although there is scant evidence of that, has an annual budget of $4 billion and is a byword for graft.' Corruption will be shown to be pervasive in many departments, offices and official transactions in an informal, shadow market economy of governance. With a massive annual budget (larger than that of several Indian states), and without debts, BMC is an attractive place to govern. This fact was emphasised in media reports relating to the 2012 local elections, with a discourse picturing Mumbai as a very important prize to win, implying great riches for victorious politicians.

The Brihanmumbai Municipal Corporation

By the standards of other large Indian cities, the Mumbai Corporation is both powerful and rich – it is India's richest civic body, 'virtually a State within a State' (Pinto 2008: 7) employing 140,630 persons (Shetye 2006: 219). It is directly in charge of almost all municipal services such as water supply, roads and public transport through its BEST (Bombay Electricity Supply and Transport) department. It manages public schools, hospitals, solid waste management (SWM) and drainage systems, public parks, and the cleaning and maintenance of all such public facilities and assets (Shetye 2006: 215). Importantly, BMC is in charge of the regulation of construction (licences, encroachments, illegal structures), providing licences for shops and establishments and for revising and implementing the city's DP. This should help reserving space for public amenities and open spaces as well as guiding vertical growth – even while it is the Maharashtra state government which ultimately decides on land and planning matters. The

BMC annual budget is larger than the budget of some Indian states at about Rs 33,000 crore or Rs 330 billion.[21] PWC (2012: 26) indicates that, of the total budget, 3 per cent is spent on slum improvement; 42 per cent on public works (drainage, roads, traffic, and bridges); 16 per cent on civic services; 2 per cent on primary education, 4 per cent on health, and 3 per cent on SWM.[22] It is important to already mention that many budgeted expenditure items are relatively fixed and cannot easily be changed, for example salaries, recurring operational administrative expenses, building maintenance, or transport costs. Perhaps 'only' Rs 70 billion would be available for 'development works', which might become the target of corrupt practices in some BMC departments as depicted later.[23]

The commissioner

The BMC is marked by a power-sharing model, described as 'commissioner type' (Pinto 2008), which is heavily in favour of the commissioner, the standing committee coming second and then only the 227 councillors who are called MCs. A mayor is elected for one year by the MCs and essentially plays a titular and ceremonial role. Another important BMC functionary is the municipal secretary who resorts under the standing committee (Shetye 2006: 221).

The BMC is an old-fashioned hierarchy, which is still governed under the guidelines and rules adopted by the British, specifically the Municipal Corporation Act of 1888. At the time a choice was made to vest most powers in one powerful commissioner and to create a deliberative body in the municipal council, which, however, is less powerful than the commissioner.[24] Seen this way, the BMC model is not quite democratic, as it is the executive who takes most initiatives (Pinto and Pinto 2005: 9) and with commissioner powers superseding those of MCs. Yet the latter do have the right to suggest proposals to the commissioner and to sanction his proposals (Nainan 2012: 73). He (there was never a woman commissioner) controls much of the BMC organisation, assisted by four additional municipal commissioners, each in charge of specific domains (MCGM 2009: 9–10). In consultation with BMC heads of departments, ward officers (WOs), chief engineers, and chief accountants, the commissioner drafts the annual budget. This is then discussed, negotiated and approved by the standing committee, next by the full council. Hence, the BMC has a powerful executive wing with a large machinery of departments and officials, as well as a less powerful, rather more controlling, deliberative wing. The commissioner is appointed by the state government for a term of three years, which can be extended for three more years. Since the state government appoints this powerful official and his co-governing additional municipal commissioners, who are all IAS officials, it may be clear that the state has overriding powers in BMC. Added to this is the fact that the loyalty of most IAS officials tends to be towards the executive wing of the government, which also applies to the top BMC leaders 'who feel less responsible to municipal councillors' (Nainan 2012: 78). Detailed formal guidelines govern the (limits on) financial powers of the commissioner and all other functionaries and BMC committees. The BMC area has been divided into seven administrative zones, each headed by a deputy municipal commissioner (DMC), and into 24 wards, which, since 2000, are administrated by 16 wards offices, headed by the WO or assistant commissioner (AC).

The BMC standing committees and other committees

As per the municipal act, the BMC council has a number of obligatory committees, but it can also create others. The former set includes the standing committee, the improvement committee and the BEST committee, as well as less prominent committees such the education and tree committees.

The standing committee is the most powerful committee. Its key mandate is financial, and it meets weekly to deal with all the financial matters of the civic body, including the clearance of the BMC budget. All proposals with budgets over Rs 1 million need clearance here in consultations between the council and the commissioner. The standing committee exercises executive, supervisory, financial, and personnel powers; it sanctions contracts, invests funds and scrutinises estimates of income and expenditure prepared by the commissioner (Pinto and Pinto 2005: 24–25). For all practical purposes, it is in charge of the day-to-day management of civic affairs, by exercising executive, supervisory, financial, and personnel powers, and its decisions are generally accepted by the commissioner. But informal processes of negotiation and adjustment are at play, and standing committee proceedings are very politicised where the dominant parties have little qualms using their powers, as discussed later. A case in point is the allocation of the so-called area development funds, which are the personal discretionary MC funds that can be spent, by and large, as per their liking. Already in 2008 conflicts arose here, when dominant parties allocated more money to themselves.[25] Things got worse in 2015 in a controversial ruling where collected corporators agreed to a large expansion of their discretionary corporator funds, with the chairman benefiting most.[26] Pinto's remarks (2008: 46) are relevant here when she notes:

> committees are known to extend their boundaries at the expense of the Corporation, become powerful centres of decision-making and develop strong linkages with the administration. In fact, what the Corporation cannot do as a deliberative body and the Commissioner cannot do as the Chief Executive Officer in matters of policy-making can be done by the committees.

The improvements committee is powerful too as it deals with property and the acquisition of land required for public purposes; the education committee is in charge of primary education and has powers to appoint officials in the BMC education department and levy education cess (Shetye 2006: 220). Over time, the council has established additional committees such as the public health committee, the women and child welfare committee and the works committee (Kennedy *et al.* 2009: 175–76; MCGM 2009: 8). The committees have representatives in ratio to their strength in the council.

In a study on the nature and role of Mumbai's women corporators (de Wit and Holzner 2003), we already established a pattern that in the powerful, well-budgeted BEST committee, women counted for only 18 per cent of members in 2001. In contrast, the education committee had a 50 per cent women membership; the public health committee 47 per cent; the education committee 65 per cent; and the women and child welfare committee 100 per cent (cf. Hajare 2002: 13–18). The present standing committee has 36 members since 2012, only 6 (16 per cent) of whom are women. It is anybody's guess whether they were elected on their own merit and act as more 'autonomous' political agents or rather are 'proxies' or 'puppets' managed by male kin. Hajare (2002: 13–18) comments that 'positions of financial importance are in the hands of men'.

The municipal council

The BMC municipal area is divided into 227 constituencies or wards, of which a corporator is elected for a five-year term. There is then one corporator for 54,970 people in Mumbai in 2011. The corporation's elected members lay down policy frameworks, frame bylaws, sanction the budget, oversee the administration and are members of the aforementioned council committees. Since the 1992 urban decentralisation reforms under the 74th Constitutional Amendment were adopted for Mumbai in 2000; one-third of the MCs are women. Just before the 2012 elections, this reservation was increased up to 50 per cent, so that today there are 113 women corporators.[27] The reforms provided for the formation of 16 WCMs, so that since 2000, MCs have a dual role to discuss on general matters of policy, personnel and finance at the level of the plenary BMC council, and to monitor and discuss civic matters at the level of the WCMs (de Wit *et al.* 2008). But they also have to consider their own working conditions and emoluments, with indications that expectations are increasing, including a higher honorarium, laptops and air-conditioned cars.[28] The council naturally played an important role as regards Mumbai's decentralisation reforms. These will be examined now, descending from the central government, to Indian states, on to city-level governance and its by-now well-institutionalised WCMs.

2.4   Urban 'decentralisation': Mumbai's wards committees

It all starts with the adoption of the 74th Constitutional Amendment Act (CAA) by MPs in Delhi in 1992, an act providing a broad framework for urban decentralisation and for strengthening India's urban local bodies (ULBs), which were perceived – as mentioned in the act – to be very weak (cf. Sivaramakrishnan 2000). Given India's federal set-up, after its central acceptance, all states had to enact conformity legislation to adjust the act to state conditions. Already at this stage, many states watered down the ambitions and potentials of the act (3iNetwork 2006: 52), so that many states established only very weak and powerless institutions, implementing provisions grudgingly, minimally or not at all (Sivaramakrishnan 2011: 141ff. for an overview).

Assessing the 74th CAA is complicated where the act itself does not explicitly specify its objectives, but its preamble does refer to devolution (the most ambitious decentralisation form, also labelled democratic or political decentralisation) and to a more vibrant democracy, which is linked to 'self-government'.[29] Hence, time-tested indicators of devolution can be applied (de Wit *et al.* 2008: 68ff.; GOI/Government of India 1992) in terms of 'bringing governance closer to the people' or increased 'proximity', the actual transfer of power and funds, an increased mandate and role of elected representatives, and increased democratic accountability. The act did specify the contours of a new and stronger institutional framework for local self-governance, with six key provisions for the states to implement (de Wit *et al.* 2008:

67ff.): create ULBs where none existed yet and decentralise tasks to these bodies from a state list of tasks; establish WCMs at neighbourhood level in 300,000 plus cities; establish a state finance commission (SFC) to regulate the revenues (taxes, budgets) and expenditures as regards ULBs; establish a State Election Commission charged to organising and monitoring regular ULB elections; establish a metropolitan planning committee (MPC) as a broad, democratic forum for planning metropolitan areas; and regulate that at least one-third of ULB council seats are reserved for women and, in ratio to their population strength, for scheduled tribes and castes.

The state of Maharashtra established a State Election Commission in 1994 to oversee municipal elections. An SFC was also formed in 1994, but Pinto (2008) feels that it was not taken quite seriously initially and that it might generally be less relevant for Mumbai with its own relatively stable incomes mostly from octroi[30] and taxes.[31] The establishment of a MPC was delayed for many years, where the state government apparently found it unnecessary to create yet another body in addition to the existing, quite powerful Mumbai Metropolitan Regional Development Agency (MMRDA) (Pinto 2008: 51–52). Mostly as a result of pressure in the form of conditions to obtain JNNURM funding, an MPC was recently established in Mumbai, but according to Sivaramakrishnan (2011: 54) it is 'remarkable for its significant disconnect with the MMRDA which carries on its own exercise on the future of the Mumbai region'.[32] Where the position of BMC as an ULB is concerned, the state government entrusted it only with very limited tasks under the so-called 12th Schedule (Sivaramakrishnan 2011: 213). The BMC remains in charge of services of roads, water, health, and education but has only partial say over critical concerns as urban planning/town planning, planning for economic and social development and the regulation of land use and building construction. These tasks remain mostly with the state government (where the chief minister [CM] always manages the urban development department) and the special (non-democratic) parastatal agencies such as MMRDA, MHADA and SRA. However, the BMC does draft a DP as already noted, which includes area planning and the nature of FSI use, and it grants building licences. With a view to the poverty and slum focus of this book, it is important to emphasise here that urban poverty alleviation, slum improvement and upgrading and the safeguarding of the interests of the weaker sections of society fall outside the mandate of the BMC as an ULB – and hence beyond the powers of Mumbai's local corporators (de Wit *et al.* 2008; van Dijk 2006).

Wards committees

It took eight years for the Maharashtra government to establish WCMs as stipulated by law, apparently with considerable reluctance. The matter was quite politicised, and its impacts were carefully considered along political party lines. Until 1999 the Shiv Sena party was in power in the state and the dominant party in the BMC, and it seems to have been un-interested to take action. In fact, it was the then opposition parties supporting decentralisation (see Nainan and Baud 2008: 135). I have found no reports that MCs from any party were actively pushing for WCMs – even while they would be most affected. It was after the NCP–Congress party coalition came to power in 1999 that WCMs were formed in 2000 (see Nainan and Baud 2008: 126; Shetye 2006: 222, 250). However, it was done in a politically motivated way, keeping in mind the short-term impacts of power on ruling and opposition parties in each of the 16 committees to be established. Politicians went so far as to organise things in such a way that very few WCMs would have chairpersons belonging to opposition parties (only four), while a majority of 12 WCM chairpersons were with the ruling party (Shetye 2006: 251).[33] And while there were already 24 administrative ward offices by then, it was decided to establish only 16 WCMs. So if the WCMs are to be seen as adding a democratic component to local administration, in a way there was a form of centralisation, grouping together various wards.[34] Even this limited degree of 'urban decentralisation' met with resistance from the state government, and was partly the result of civic action, deliberation, lobbying, and litigation (Shetye 2006: 223; van Dijk 2006: 40).

In the ultimate state government policy document, Mumbai WCMs are designed to include as members all corporators elected from the wards that make up each WCM area. They meet monthly once under a chairperson elected from their midst for one year. Their mandate is laid down in a list of tasks and duties (PRAJA 2012: 11).

Concretely, WCMs are to (1) dispose expeditiously of matters relating to water supply, drainage, cleanliness, and storm water drains and other basic amenities and local civic amenities, as well as the renaming of roads; (2) consider proposals of expenditure on different heads of budget provisions relating to the wards, recommend the same and forward them to the municipal corporation; and (3) give administrative approval to the plans and estimates up to Rs 500,000 for civic works in the area of the WCMs for which budget provisions are sanctioned by the corporation (see MCGM 2009: 9). All this indicates that we cannot really speak of 'devolution' where powers, tasks and related funds are delegated to newly formed elected bodies. I argue instead that WCMs became relatively powerless but also harmless talk shops to discuss a limited number of local-level issues and expenses. We would define the half-way house Mumbai modality as 'deconcentration plus' (see de Wit *et al.* 2008; Siddiqui and Bhowmik 2004: 145).[35]

Ward office and wards committee

So what do things look like following these modest administrative reforms? Until 2000, Mumbai was administratively divided into several zones and 24 administrative wards, in a hierarchical system which can be seen as a form of pure 'deconcentration'. The 24 WOs (or ACs) were the heads of the ward administration, but directly ('upwardly') accountable to the BMC, implementing policies and projects as formulated by the higher levels of BMC decision makers (Pinto and Pinto 2005). Apart from the new political context, the position of the AC has not changed in itself. He or she is in charge of the delivery of various civic services provided by his office, to address any civic matter in his or her ward, while overseeing the tendering of civic works and the selection of contractors. Within the BMC hierarchy he or she is accountable to the DMC, the head of one of the seven BMC zones. Each ward office has a unit of every major BMC line department (e.g. health, education, slums, water works, licensing, building and factories, environment/SWM, in total 17 ward units/sections (Pinto and Pinto 2005: 225ff.). The AC coordinates these functional departments of the WO through a secretariat, administering the office through the finance/accounts department and the complaints office. However, consistent with the aforementioned limited mandate of the wards office, the planning and construction of major roads and bridges, capital works of all engineering departments and tax matters remain the responsibility of the BMC head office, often working independently of the ward administration. As an example, a WO (AC) of the M-ward reported with regret that he was initially neither adequately informed nor prepared for the influx of project-affected people into his ward (field notes, 23 January 2005). Nothing much has changed financially either. In contrast to the large mandate and budgets of the BMC, the administrative and financial powers of the WCMs are quite limited indeed, if only as the size of 'decentralised' funds is very small. An analysis of the budget of one ward revealed that the WCM controlled only 6 per cent of the total budget of the ward (van Dijk 2006). There is no separate budget for the ward office. The overall BMC budget has different budget lines, and it is under these budget lines that provisions are made for the ward office areas. It is here that the wards office is expected to submit proposals for the overall BMC budget. It ideally prioritises works to be carried out in their constituencies and requests the WO administrators to make a financial estimate, which is then sent to the BMC – which, together with the standing committee, may or may not include it in the overall city budget (Nainan 2001: 75). Once a sanction is given, 'the budget allocated to that Ward can be spent on the works by the WCM only if the work is below Rs. 500.000' (Shetye 2006: 249). Higher-cost projects need to be approved by the zonal office/DMC or, if still larger, by the standing committee.[36] It is important to note that this spending limit is much lower than the discretionary funds (corporator's fund) available for each MC until recently at the value of Rs 6 million annually. This was raised to as much as Rs 10 million,[37] already a sign that more value is attached to individually managed discretionary funds than the general BMC funds whose outlays are up for discussion (PRAJA 2012: 55). While proposals for these corporator's funds are also discussed in WCM meetings, there seems to be a consensus that few questions are asked, with corporators keen to avoid interference in their respective ways of doing things (Van Dijk 2011a: 40).

So nothing much changed in terms of additional tasks, duties or funds at the level of the city wards. The most important change was actually more political and in terms of local MC presence. Corporators – as individuals but also as a group in the WCM – claimed and obtained increased powers over the executive officials at the ward level. Before, such ward office officials were upwardly accountable to the DMC (in one city zone) and BMC headquarters, less so to the council. Now ward-level officials have new – or at any rate more visible and active – masters in the wards committees' chairpersons and corporators. Let us now dwell on the performance of these new 'institutions of self-governance', but first contextualise Mumbai's accomplishments against the wider all-India picture.

Assessing Mumbai's urban decentralisation

If the 74th CAA wanted to bring governance closer to the people, for Mumbai this did not work out much. Since Mumbai had a municipal population of about 13 million people by 2012 and 227 electoral wards in the city, each of the 16 WCMs has 14 corporators on the average, and each WCM hence has to represent or cater to the needs of about 875,000 people. Already in terms of numbers, this is a daunting, if not impossible, task where a corporator represents 61,000 persons on average (Van Dijk 2011: 51). It may be already one reason that WCMs have not really taken off. Indeed many *Mumbaikars* are unaware of these new institutions, and Pinto (2008: 556–59) has a good point in stressing that they have *not* developed into a 'bee hive' of local neighbourhood governance. Phatak and Patel (2005: 3903–4) note already in the early years that 'their functions are not yet discernible'. Continuity from colonial times is maintained: councillors were allowed in the municipality, to give them a voice, 'while ensuring that real power remained firmly in the hands of a Government appointed officer'. Another reason for a lack of people's interest in WCMs is arguably that, surprisingly, its proceedings are secret. Public is not allowed to participate in WCM meetings so I also missed the chance to observe their working and what follows is evidence obtained otherwise.

WCM meetings are chaired by a chairperson, elected for one year from among all WCM members – normally from the majority party. The chairperson is in charge of organising meetings, preparing agendas and linking with higher levels of the city administration (and of his or her political party). The chairperson receives the same salary (Rs 4,000/month) as other MCs. Pinto (2008: 58) indicates that the WCM chairman can be quite powerful, despite the lack of executive, financial and emergency powers (field notes with Pinto, 16 December 2004). Administrative officers and, when needed, engineers attend WCM meetings on request so as to inform MCs on technical feasibility of MC proposals (Shetye 2006: 239). As noted, Van Dijk (2011a: 40) mentions that in theory, the WCM should prioritise the most needed facilities in all WCM wards, which would lead to a match between what is needed and what can be financed in the neighbourhood as a whole. In reality all proposals mooted by any MC seem to be accepted and supported: 'MCs stay out of each other's business because if they want to get work through the Committee it is best to approve other's works.' However, there are indications that politics come in the way, where in some WCMs' opposition party MCs are not allocated funds for the work they would like to propose. Van Dijk (2006: 77) refers to MCs of opposition parties, indicating that the projects they propose were assigned a lower priority. Yet another report refers to efforts to explicitly organise a fair distribution of funds, to avoid conflicts with the opposition (Shetye 2006: 236).

There is mixed evidence as to the degree to which and where the corporators are seen to have been empowered through the formation of the WCMs. One obvious factor is that WCMs never had a real chance leading from its very limited powers; another that they function on party lines or, perhaps more important, that WCM members promote a personal agenda. Besides, within the clear and well-institutionalised BMC hierarchy, these new, powerless bodies were perceived with a bit of disdain. In our survey of Mumbai corporators, there was a general satisfaction with the establishment of WCMs, but at the same time most of them felt their powers were still very limited both in terms of delegated funds and in powers to manage local affairs with more autonomy. Kennedy *et al.* (2009: 179) report: 'For now the evidence does not support the argument that decentralisation has led to the empowerment of councillors' (see van Dijk 2006: 88). But it is important not to generalise, and evidence is not sufficient to make final statements. Zerah (2006: 13) shows that all MCs in her survey agree that their allotted funds are insufficient, but they do agree that the 74th CAA has given them more power. Remarkably, however, and consistent with my own field notes and reports, she feels that 'few of them discuss the process of decentralisation in terms of their own ability to direct budgets and to decide on large policy decisions'. This confirms my findings that MCs contesting the very systems and structures or powers of WCMs or making this an issue in WCMs or in the plenary BMC council seem to be rare. Zerah's paper (2006: 14) is a good source to appreciate variations here in her assessment of the performance of three wards offices. Critical factors determining the quality of administration include the effectiveness of coordination, the nature of the leadership exercised by the WO (AC), the voice of citizen groups, and the socio-economic composition of the ward population. Besides, an increase of MC powers does not actually need to be positive, as noted by a WO (field notes, 17 December 2003):

> The Ward Officer/AC was mostly positive about the impacts of the 74th CAA: there was more discussion on ward level priorities and there were lesser delays. He was however worried about 'more political pressure' which made local planning problematic: 'each MC now wants to implement things in his/her ward, and this may lead to scattered, fragmented activities in the larger WCM area, so that e.g. some urgently needed roads are not constructed. Before the WCM, our BMC engineers and officials would simply plan and implement as per local needs' – as if the local and *general* prioritisation and meeting of needs was more effective before WCMs were formed.

One returning issue in our surveys of MCs and ward officials alike concerned the overall capacity to get work done. One AC informed us that things had become more complex following WCM formation (field notes, 15 September 2005): 'Things did improve following the 74th CAA, but it is far from perfect and more administrative reforms are needed. There are too many levels and layers and administration now just takes too long.' Another AC complained that he was severely short of staff but that there was a BMC freeze to employ people and his people had to cope as best as they could. Capacity is a complex matter, ideally encompassing an alignment of human resources and the organisation of the WO, with the broader BMC and public-sector context (Grindle and Hilderbrand 1995). Reality is a far cry from this, which led Pinto and Pinto (2005: 508) to be rather pessimistic about municipal wards management:

> The reason why Municipal Wards perform so poorly is because the persons who run them, and those at the higher level who supervise them are either of poor calibre or are too lethargic to operate as more than slaves of their In-trays. As ACs (heads of Wards Offices) are now highly paid and enjoy perks like a large residential flat, chauffeur driven car, residential phone, cell phone, etc. It is best that some MBAs with 5 years' experience in executive positions be selected for these posts.

Changed corporator and official roles at the ward office level

In a democratic type of local governance, key players are local politicians and officials, but these have markedly different ways of working, different attitudes while reacting differently to incentives. Officials can be expected to start from 'what is possible', given the budgets, the rules and the need for 'due process'. In our surveys and interviews over time, ward officials often told us that they would prefer to work on the basis of their own inspections and what they hear from other officials and from citizen complaints through the ward office complaints officer. In contrast, many corporators are seen to start from 'this needs to be done', then setting about by hook or crook to organise this or that footpath or nullah (open drain) wall repairs. They are driven more by the – often more personal – questions and issues they pick up on the rounds of their wards, from the people who come to their personal offices or party *shakas,* or issues conveyed through their local agents and party workers/*karyakartas.* As can be expected, their perspective is political and not devoid of opportunism as elaborated in Chapter 4. They are biased towards their own networks, political supporters and party members and specific areas such as election booth pockets where they may invest in view of past voting patterns – and with a view to the next elections. From his or her perspective, success for a corporator means being more effective than others, like one MC boasting to be able to draw large funds to his or her ward (Pinto and Pinto 2005: 13; Zerah 2006).

Nainan and Baud (2008: 131) suggest that officials feel that MCs lack the proper education to take good decisions, but I would argue that education is only one factor here. The corporator's personality seems more critical here, and how he or she is embedded in the local context. Some are able to 'manage' officials well; others harbour a deep sense of frustration and irritation with officials. Indeed, following the WCM establishments, many observers initially noted serious adjustment issues, for the officials to get used to pushy and demanding corporators, for the latter to get used to procedures and due process. A collective fear appears to have existed in that each group would be missing out on previously institutionalised corruption patterns (see Pinto and de Wit 2006). Nainan and Baud (2008: 131) refer to tense MC–official relations, with elements of jealousy and officials weary to obey orders or even provide information to MCs.[38] I have the impression that a gradual process of adjustment has occurred over time between the MCs and officials and that cooperation is more likely today. Dynamics of water supply in Mumbai slums as recorded by Anand (2011b: 552) provide some proof here. He believes that MCs, ward officials and engineers deeply understand their mutual dependence: the former mediate the demands of slum dwellers and in fact do important screening and appraisal work for busy water department engineers. Corporators exert pressure on the latter to provide water to slums, even where it is not in fact permitted by the rules. But the key common interest that binds them together are the dynamics of illegal money making in different types of corruption rackets, within a parallel payments system of 'cuts', to be discussed in Chapter 4. Hence, the engineers and officials also depend on corporators for things *they* need sanctioned such as requests, applications and not least a range of tenders for projects of roads, pathways and sewage lines with more or less substantial contracts and related informal earnings. It is not entirely clear as to whether this gradual process of MCs and ward officials adjusting is good news. One well-informed informant (field notes, 31 January 2005) said: 'This whole decentralisation thing has no benefits for the citizens; before it was mostly local officials demanding money and now also the corporators are much more demanding, while they are also jealously watching each other.' Today, by and large routines seem to have been evolved where MCs and officials interact pragmatically on a regular basis – especially during weekly inspection rounds of the wards. We still got reports that MCs can be pushy and impulsive in the way they work while neglecting proper procedures – which applies more to newcomers. But there are recent indications of more serious corporator–official conflicts and not just about sharing informal spoils. One example is the protest of the municipal engineers' union against attacks against its fraternity.[39] It started with an alleged assault by an MNS corporator in Dadar on a civic engineer, who was then hospitalised. The engineer had been slow to respond to an 'emergency call' to demolish a temporary shed that was 'blocking' a part of the corporator's shop front in Dadar. The engineer's union president said, 'In the last one year, there have been 12–13 incidents of politicians assaulting engineers,' including a corporator holding an engineer hostage in his office. The *Frontline* journal[40] refers to the 'dubious relations' between politicians and officers of the administration and perceives growing intolerance among elected representatives towards decisions taken by officers.

But politicians are quite versatile, and a corporator has a powerful weapon to use against ward officials in the form of the threat of or actual transfer away from his or her present position by way of a punishment. Corporators may alert their higher-party friends that such official is making a problem and that he or she is no longer needed. One official said:

> If we try to work in a just and fair way for the common interest of our area, we may incur the displeasure of an MC who has his vote bank in mind. . . out of fear of reprisals or a transfer, we may give in.
>
> (field notes, 16 December 2004)[41]

A WO who had been in his post for 14 years said that he was not being allowed a transfer and denied promotion because 'I have angered too many MCs who in return are demanding exorbitant amounts of money' (Van Dijk 2011a: 35). It seems best then to characterise corporator–official relations in terms of subtly shifting balances of power, as well illustrated by Zerah (2006: 13): 'Just to rule is not power. If a councillor is raising his point and the officer does it, this is also power. Officers will act upon that and powers are there.'

2.5   Mumbai's multi-agency governance and its pitfalls

At the time of the municipal elections in 2012, there was much discussion on the actual roles of BMC and other Mumbai agencies as to the importance of the BMC as regards Mumbai governance:

> As the Shiv-Sena-BJP alliance readies to return to power in the BMC, the question many experts are asking is whether its corporators will have any real role in the city's planning and development. The civic body, they say, is being slowly stripped of powers while the idea of local self-governance and decentralisation gains currency elsewhere. . . . Experts point out that the real power today flows not through BMC committees, but from the corridors of *Mantralaya* and the offices of MMRDA and MSRDC.[42]

The Vote Mumbai Campaign website[43] puts it like this:

> The elected Corporation has only deliberative powers for policy making but no say in execution or planning. In this our elected representatives are powerless and have to go to the lowest rung BMC executive with joined hands to get any work done. Multiple parallel agencies like PWD, MSRDC, MMRDA, MHADA etc. truncate the work of the Commissioner and BMC. They are directly controlled by the state and are not answerable to the citizens of Mumbai. Also central agencies such as MBPT & Railways, AAI, Defence, who occupy a large chunk of land, are not accountable to the BMC (for municipal governance/services).

These, as well as earlier remarks on the limited mandate of the BMC as an ULB and the WCMs as regards neighbourhood management, point to the need to briefly provide the features of other key public-sector agencies governing the metropolis (for an overview, see Pinto 2008: 53). The focus will be on their possible roles as regards the urban poor, the city slums and urban poverty alleviation efforts.

Multiple agencies governing Mumbai

The Indian constitution holds that the domains of land and housing, urban development and provision of civic infrastructure come within the mandate of state governments who are legally empowered to formulate and execute related policies (Risbud 2003: 4). Hence, the state government has a solid grip over Mumbai governance through its various departments (state-level ministries). The key department is no doubt the urban development department, which is traditionally managed by the state CM. It is in charge of town planning and urban development and urban water supply and sewerage – even while in Mumbai, the latter is managed by the BMC. Its mandate also includes housing policy, land ceilings, rent control, slum upgrading, and supervision of foreign-aid projects (Risbud 2003: 4). So capital-intensive and potentially profitable key concerns of land and housing are managed by the state and its legislators/MLAs (many of whom live in Mumbai but have their constituencies all over Maharashtra) housed in the *Mantralaya*. In core urban planning and management decisions on mega projects, the nature and use of transferable development rights (TDRs) and FSI, the Mumbai DP, and development control rules (DCRs), they have a large say. It was MLAs who raise the MC women quota to 50 per cent. And, as noted, the state government has firm powers over the BMC, if only as it appoints the BMC commissioner, deciding on the appointment and transfers of top-level IAS BMC officials.

And even while state government dominates urban development policy, the 'central government' plays (used to play) a significant role through the devolution of resources to state governments within the framework of National Five-Year Plans.[44] Besides, the centre implements several centrally funded urban poverty programmes, such as SJSRY, Rajiv Awas Yojana (RAY) and ICDS (more details in Chapter 3). The centre is also a large landowner in Mumbai, including lots of railways land. It owns and manages Mumbai's transport lifeline, the Mumbai suburban train system and the Mumbai airport. The MMRDA is in charge of regional planning, coordinating and supervising development efforts in the MRR. The region includes, apart from the BMC municipality, 7 municipal corporations, 13 municipal councils, parts of Raigad and Thane districts, and over 900 villages (Pinto 2008: 51). It has 9 MPs, 54 MLAs and approximately 1,200 corporators from the numerous local bodies (Sivaramakrishnan 2011: 54). The MMRDA is in charge of ambitious (donor-funded) projects such as the Mumbai Urban Development Project (MUDP) and Mumbai Urban Transport Project (MUTP), both World Bank funded. The parastatal agency is completely controlled and managed by the state government through an appointed metropolitan commissioner and lacks direct democratic representation or accountability. Not all is well with its activities, for example recent reports that Mumbai's recently opened monorail link between Chembur and Jacob Circle is not safe in terms of its construction and prone to earthquake risks; it suffered enormous and partly unexplainable cost overruns, while its operations and maintenance costs are far more than the Delhi metro train.[45] MMRDA is a smaller agency than the BMC. The former had a 2009 budget of Rs 66 billion; BMC's budget then was Rs 168 billion (Pethe *et al.* 2011: 191). MMRDA has to cooperate closely with agencies such as the BMC and the Mumbai Housing and Area Development Agency (MHADA) and the collector on issues of landownership. MHADA is the main agency supplying public housing and is led by officials fully nominated by the state government. It was established in 1977 by merging the former Maharashtra Housing Board, the Bombay Building Repairs and Reconstruction Board and the former Maharashtra Slum Improvement Board. The 'Office of the Collector of Mumbai' is the revenue authority of Mumbai and has jurisdiction over the titles and deeds relating to landownership, while managing open spaces/vacant government land.[46] It is also responsible for issuing identity cards to slum dwellers, the collection of service charges from them, the granting of entitlements to government lands and removal of unauthorised structures from public land/authorising demolitions (Pinto 2008: 52; Risbud 2003; van Dijk 2006: 55). Mumbai's water supply and sewerage systems are managed by the 'Maharashtra Water Supply and Sewerage Board', another parastatal agency reporting to the state government urban development department. Pinto (2008: 51) notes:

> All is not well with the functioning of the Board. For instance, schemes take years to operationalise and loans fixed for one local body get diverted to meet the needs of another. The State Government has now permitted local bodies to undertake work through the Board or private sector agencies in a desperate bid to improve the Board's performance.

This is one example where a malfunctioning agency is the reason for seeking refuge with the private sector, which would explain the popularity of the public–partnership approach, notwithstanding all their opacities and hard-to-gauge complications (Romero 2015). A case in point is the 'slum rehabilitation authority' (SRA), established in 1995 by the Maharashtra government under the Maharashtra Slum Areas Act 1971. It has endeavoured to redevelop slums under a public–private–community partnership (SRS) model with mixed and certainly meagre results, as shown later. It obtained the status of planning authority for redevelopment schemes and is responsible for reviewing the state slum situation, undertaking slum surveys and formulating and implementing schemes for the redevelopment of slum areas. Here it obviously needs to cooperate much with the

BMC and MHADA. Again, this potentially critical agency for Mumbai's slum dwellers is a parastatal, directly controlled by the state government, with the CM as the chairperson and led by an IAS rank chief officer. According to Pinto (2008: 51) the SRA enjoys a privileged position and constitutes a very powerful body headed by the CM. SRA policies and (meagre) outcomes are discussed later when dealing with slum policies.

Relations between agencies: many independent kingdoms

One of the most distressing problems of Mumbai's governance is the degree of non-cooperation between the multiple agencies in charge of various governance domains. Much of this originates not, in the first place, with the administrators of these agencies, but with Mumbai's assertive politicians. Besides – and ironically – problems are compounded by 'an overbearing interference by the State Government of Maharashtra via the parastatals established by it under different departments' (Pethe *et al.* 2011: 190). A useful introduction was found in a newspaper[47] reporting on the reasons for the normally massive delays in implementing large-scale and urgent infrastructure projects in Mumbai – for example a water transport link between Mumbai's northern and south-western suburbs, several highways and a new airport:

> 'Those projects could have completely overhauled the commute system but owing to the lack of political and bureaucratic will, absence of focused and organized policies, vested political and corporate interests, and differences within the ruling parties (the state is governed by a Congress-NCP coalition) work on them has not gone far beyond the drawing board'. One reason for the delay in a waterway project is a conflict between the MSRDC Agency which is controlled by the NCP; but it is the Congress controlled Urban Development Ministry which has to approve the plans. In the case of the proposed new airport in Navi Mumbai an empowered group of ministers is sitting on a tender document: 'the reason was that that the central authorities ruled by the Congress wanted a higher stake in the development, but the NCP-ruled CIDCO, the executing agency, had already claimed the major share'. Similarly, as regards another sea link project that was revived in 2004, there are complications between the NCP ruled MSRDC, and the MMRDA which is controlled by the Congress.

Hence, a fundamental factor underlying a harmful lack of inter-agency cooperation and coordination is political, that is the relatively narrow interests of Mumbai's politicians. The key contestation is between the two most powerful agencies, the BMC and the MMRDA – both of which, inter alia, are governed through a state government–appointed commissioner. Yet contestations are political and linked to which political party 'owns' an agency. It may be assumed that such owner-ship entails an expectation that money can be made informally if and when contracts are signed and payments are made.[48] As the earlier case illustrates, even within the then state government ruling coalition, coalition parties Congress and NCP, differed openly on how projects are implemented and who gets what share – often therewith blocking or delaying urgent decision making.

> Shiv Sena corporators 'resent any positive publicity that the MMRDA – which is under the state government with the rival Congress-NCP parties – receives for its work in the MMR. . . claiming that the latter is trying to undermine BMC by taking over the development of the city and its suburbs'. Various BMC special committees with Shiv Sena members 'often threaten to withdraw cooperation that MMRDA requires in order to successfully imple-ment its projects if their demands are not met'.
>
> (Pethe *et al.* 2011: 192)

Another example is where the BMC council city improvements com-mittee threatened to refuse to agree that the MMRDA would be using the space around the upcoming metro rail for commercial purposes if it was not given 50 per cent of the profits made by such enterprises (Pethe *et al.* 2011: 192). In another case, the BMC standing committee demanded a share in profits made by the MMRDA on its land deals. All these contestations occurred in a context where the BMC 'is ruled by Shiv-Sena/BJP and the State by Congress/NCP, and that such con-flicts were absent when Shiv Sena was in power in both in the period 1995–99, which was marked by great cooperation between BMC and MMRDA' (Pethe *et al.* 2011: 192). It is, however, not only the BMC or its corporators which may be the cause of conflicts and boycotts. It is believed that the MMRDA could certainly be more helpful or tactful. Projects it has (more or less) completed may be suddenly 'handed over' to the BMC for maintenance in the full knowledge that it cannot be democratically punished for such action as it is not an elected body where citizens might take offence (Pethe *et al.* 2011: 192). Sivaramakrishnan (2011: 54) also seems to feel the MMRDA is bullying the BMC: 'In Mumbai, despite opposition from BMC, the MMRDA took on project responsibilities and acquired considerable financial clout from money spinning projects like Bandra-Kurla complex.' Sadly, today 'interactions between BMC and MMRDA are riddled with conflicts that fester due to the absence of arrangements for conflict resolution'. Interference by the CM appears to be limited to talking to the two top men he himself appointed as commissioners, 'which may be futile since it is the elected councillors in BMC rather than the bureaucrats who are not forthcoming in cooperating with MMRDA' (Pethe *et al.* 2011: 192–93). Desai (2002: 106) adds to this the element of centralised mindsets: 'As new authorities continued to be created, their initiatives are being throttled by crucial decision making powers that remained centralised at higher levels.' But problems are not only political. The parastatal agencies are truly kingdoms onto themselves, with accountability neither to in-house elected representatives nor to MLAs or MCs, but instead to the state government. Pinto (2008: 53) believes that they often lack transparency in their functioning and are 'ridden with corruption', highly bureaucratised while lacking knowledge of and experience with grass-roots problems. She feels the parastatals weaken the BMC as a multi-functional ULB. Their inter-agency problems seem to be a result of contested and overlapping civic and urban functions, with field officers showing very little interest in coordinating activities with others at the local level.

As already noted, in a belated response Mumbai did recently (and opportunistically) establish a metropolitan and planning committee (MPC) under the 74th CAA, which is supposed to precisely coordinate multi-agency and multi-area governance under democratic guidance. An MPC is to develop a draft metropolitan DP for all municipalities and panchayats in a metropolis, including physical planning, sharing of water and other resources, integrated infrastructure development, and environmental conservation (Phatak and Patel 2005: 3903). Such an MPC has elected representatives from all local bodies in the area as members, which, in Mumbai, would include corporators. Plans for a Mumbai MPC never took off, until, following public interest legislation, an MPC was established, but Sivaramakrishnan (2011: 54), as noted, feels that the MPC is disconnected from the MMRDA, which carried on with its activities in the MMR. Pethe *et al.* (2011: 190) believe that 'the State Government has been reluctant that the MPC becomes completely operational as it would dilute its control over the Mumbai Metro Region'. A key constraint then seems to be 'political will'.

2.6   Changing governance arenas: the ascendancy of the private sector, middle classes and global elites

This book is about the governance of Mumbai and the nature and implications of a specific juxtaposition of multiple actors in the city's governance arena: 'Governance refers to the formation and steward-ship of the formal and informal rules that regulate the public realm, *the arena in which state as well as economic and societal actors interact to make decisions*' (Hyden *et al.* 2004: 16). A distinction is made here between the 'institutional context' with its formal and, importantly, informal rules, and the more dynamic arena in which we can observe 'who gets what, when and how' in the politics of multi-stakeholder processes where actors act upon their interests and power (Baud and de Wit 2008: 6). As I argued elsewhere for New Delhi (de Wit 2009a), we can speak of 'Changing Arenas for Defining Mumbai' as well. The already very weak political power basis of the urban poor is being undermined by the organised political efforts of Mumbai's middle classes and elites, as well as by a new regime and associated ideology. Like other Indian mega-cities, in a short time Mumbai became a global city, intensely intertwined with global capital and influenced by the values and aspirations of globally oriented or global citizens. Mumbai's global integration came along with neoliberalism and a market-based ideology, part of the global hegemony of neoliberal thinking and associated practice favouring a lean public sector, while enabling the private sector to partake in public service delivery (Banerjee-Guha 2009). Nainan (2012: 186–87) argues that a new regime of market-based governance, or a 'new urban development regime', emerged in Mumbai's governance. She locates its beginning in the leadership of the former chief minister Sharad Pawar around 1989. He had a good rapport with all Mumbai stakeholder groups – including the private sector and CSO groups – which, together, took the shape of a 'liberal land coalition'. He was instrumental in framing the new DP of Mumbai with new discourses and policy instruments such as the applica-tion of the TDR and the FSI indicators and de-reserving large tracts of Mumbai land. Subsequently, large landowners and new building firms and companies engaged ever more with the state in setting goals and priorities for urban development, looking for financially attractive interventions and projects for private investment. The model of PPPs (including the private sector and CSO groups) gradually grew into a dominant development model, extending beyond land management onto power, roads, harbours, airports, and telecommunications (Pinto

2008: 59–60). Two processes can be seen: governance shifts towards 'multi-stakeholder' governance including important roles and growing powers for the private sector and some, but not all, NGOs.

From this time we can observe gradually rising incomes of mostly middle-income households who capitalised on increasing prices/value of the assets they had (housing, land, savings) and were able to earn good incomes in existing/expanding and new industries (e.g. ITC) and the growing service sector. The latter trend has been called 'middle-classisation':

> Given the elite nature of India's middle class . . . [this] can be understood as a process of social polarisation: the upper segments of the middle class became richer, indulge in more and more lavish consumption, and isolate themselves in gated communities, while the poor become poorer, perhaps not in absolute terms but certainly in relative terms. . . while . . . their worldview, aspirations and values are influential far beyond themselves
> (Mooij and Lama-Rewal 2009: 83)

Even while nobody will deny that Mumbai's rich and poor are growing apart, few sources quantify this, leading to considerable confusion as the precise nature and size of the 'middle class'. One source (fieldnotes 20-10-2011) estimated Mumbai to have 3.5 million people as 'lower-middle classes' and 3 million as 'higher-middle classes', with 500,000 'ultra-rich'.[49] It appears that Banerjee-Guha (2009: 106) refers to this class:

> Urban elites, composed of assorted groups hailing from diverse entities like business, industry, media, or films, are increasingly and vociferously making their presence felt in the discourse on 'urban' and getting integrated into the neoliberal planning manipulations. They have links and engagements beyond the city and make their presence felt by 'colonising space' in the peri-urban areas like farmhouses, luxurious entertainment complexes, and wealthy gated communities.[50]

However we define the 'middle class', there is no doubt that their prominence has led to lots of changes in India – in the media, culture, lifestyles, and even obesity patterns – but I need to consider the political dimensions of their newly gained powers – articulated mostly – but certainly not only – in local organisations or RWAs. RWAs of diverse sizes and shapes have been formed in most Indian cities, normally representing the interests of their members as regards day-to-day problems faced by the residents of a neighbourhood, apartment block or compound such as a 'gated community'. One type of RWA typical for Mumbai is the advanced locality management (ALM) model, of which there were 648 members according to Zerah, of which about 150 were active (2009b: 248; see Pinto 2008: 60), which are street- or building-level associations registered with the BMC. The ALM model found its origin when the BMC got interested to involve communities in keeping local areas clean by segregating waste at source and organise its collection and composting. Such efforts were complemented by the wards office (the sister 'participatory' slum SWM programme was the ill-fated SAP, see de Wit 2010a). By now the ALM model has evolved, and active ALMs may play an active role in the supervision, management or even control of their areas in a wider sense, and such RWAs have become an accepted new stakeholder group in city governance. Opinions vary as to whether they have replaced the state in city governance or whether they are a more innocent type of BMC-supported local action committees. The starkest statement on the nature and powers of RWAs is by Anjaria (2009: 391) referring to citizen groups and residential associations in Mumbai: 'It is these civil society organisations, not the state . . . who are the agents of increased control over populations and of the rationalisation of urban space.' Civil activists use the rhetoric of citizen participation but undermine the 'radically heterogeneous forms of democratic political participation the city offers'. While the former statement seems too strong to be proven valid, the latter statement finds support, for example, from Harris *et al.* (2004) who, as I noted in Chapter 1, refer to 'new politics'. They perceive risks in an emphasis on the potentially exclusionary character of a governance regime based on 'civil society' and social movements, at the expense of the traditional 'old politics' of political parties and trade unions.[51] Tawa Lama-Rewal (2007: 59) argues that 'these associations, promoting the political participation of the "middle classes", end up empowering the already powerful'. She feels, first, that they are seen as un-democratic (Tawa Lawa-Rewal 2007: 55) as they operate as self-styled elite clubs formed by self-selection and co-optation, often excluding tenants, while they are representative neither of their areas nor of the city as a whole. They are also not democratic as they tend to by-pass elected representatives such as MLAs, and especially the municipal councillors, whom they distrust and look down upon. Additional proof for this is the fact that the Indian urban middle classes and elites hardly vote in municipal elections (de Wit 2009a; Mooij and Rewal 2009: 93; Tawa Lama-Rewal 2007: 53–55), while avoiding municipal councillors and preferring to contact municipal officials either directly personally (or rather by phone) or in organised forms such as RWAs. Indeed, according to Zerah (2009a) relations between the Mumbai ALM units and elected corporators are marked by mutual disdain, the latter seen as corrupt and lacking vision as they are uneducated. Still there is communication as RWAs realise that they exert considerable influence locally.

More important for this book is that RWAs are seen to play an exclusionary role, especially in relation to the urban poor and the slum dwellers. In Delhi RWAs may link up with the police to agree that lists are made of persons who would be allowed to enter the locality (Srivastava 2009: 343ff.), including authorised maid servants, hawkers and plumbers. Slum needs and priorities may get sidelined because RWAs have good political connections and/or class affinity with ministers, so that the latter's problems get prioritised. Zerah (2009a: 867) found that ALMs are not quite inclusive. Their opposition to an urban project takes the shape of a NIMBY (not in my backyard) type of protest, whereas they are all in support for larger urban restructuring to make Mumbai more a city like Shanghai (see Weinstein and Ren 2009). Most of the court interventions sought by ALMs had two major objectives: the enforcement of no-hawking zones and the displacement of slums that were held responsible for the major 2005 Mumbai floods.

But for all the drawbacks and negative pointers of RWAs vis-à-vis the city slums, it is not as if they have taken over the 'rationalisation of urban space' from the state, as Anjaria (2009) argues. First, there is a sense that RWAs, by and large, have a utilitarian approach, focusing on immediate urban service issues, not addressing larger policy issues, reason that Tawa Lama-Rewal (2007: 59) refers to the 'parochial' nature of the RWA concerns. 'As soon as the problem is resolved, they often stop their activities' (Smitha 2010: 77). Second, city authorities and politicians do not seem keen to allow even more power to accrue to citizen groups and RWAs. That, finally, the middle classes exert agency to add their voice to city governance seems legitimate, if only as they see around them that other stakeholders such as politicians, officials, real estate developers, and contractors are exerting and quite successfully enhancing their powers, in relations frequently referred to in the English language newspaper as a 'corrupt nexus'. It is not so surprising that they are suspicious, if not actually enraged by the performance of politicians at all levels, including the 'dirty politics of MCs' (John 2007); the dismal nature of the Mumbai administration; and the corruption cases and scams that dominate the headlines a bit too often. That they vote less in elections can also be explained by the fact that, once in the polling booth, they find no credible or clean candidate of their liking, if only as the main candidates are from well-established party machines. Understandably, they may hope for new, fresh parties or leaders. Following the victory of the Aam Aadmi Party in February 2015 Delhi state elections, there was talk of the party expanding more into Mumbai, which might potentially shake up things if only to broaden political choices. Today this seems less likely. The Mumbai middle classes – whether or not organised in an RWA – have to necessarily cohabit with six million or so slum dwellers, and here too we may need to recognise that legitimate concerns and frustrations exist. It is not that it may be nice to live next to a new slum that emerged next door, while suspecting an MC is behind it. But as to be expected with such complex phenomena and processes, things are ambiguous as noted before when critical questions were raised about the apparent middle-class capacity to look away from enormous injustice and suffering, a prejudice against lower-class people and what it means that one could hypothesize that they are more likely to be bribe-takers than givers.[52] A concrete example of such complexities is a dispute about taxes, as reported in an article 'Why Are Slums Spared by Property Tax?'.[53] It is about a meeting of middle-class activists and residents in the relatively affluent Vile Parle neighbourhood.

> Dissatisfaction was expressed that slums illegally encroaching on public land are not included in the BMC's new property tax bracket. This, while the State Government rules that 85% of all properties have to pay tax, which is confirm JNNURM guidelines. One activist asked: 'why are 60% of slums exempted from the current property tax structure? Is vote banks politics responsible?'. Another speaker referred to the fact that slum dwellers who are rehabilitated in SRA buildings, return to their slums, sometimes illegally selling their flats already within 10 years, and wondered why such people have tax concessions for 20 years: 'Is it the motto of the state government and BMC that property stealers should be rewarded and honest tax payers be punished?'

As a sign that the middle classes can and do act politically on their concerns, some RWAs have become active in local elections, as reported by Zerah (2009a: 866) for Mumbai ALM groups. During the 2007 municipal elections, ALMs were actively involved at the city level in a 'Vote Mumbai Campaign' to motivate middle-class residents to vote. They organised meetings in electoral wards with residents and candidates to compel the candidates to voice their priorities and make commitments on residents' demands. In one ward, an ALM fielded its own candidate. I will come back to the role of RWAs and ALMs and what are called 'citizen candidates' in the 2012 municipal elections in Chapter 5. But that middle-class pushed candidates are named 'citizen candidates' already raises the question as to whether the remaining majority are lesser, non-citizen candidates.

To conclude this chapter and to illustrate just how fundamental the shifts of stakeholders, ideology and powers were, I look back at landmark events in 2004–5, when a group of business actors, state politicians, officials, and middle-class groups/civil society groups rallied around a new vision for Mumbai in a movement entitled 'Bombay First'. It commissioned the McKinsey firm to draft a comprehensive analysis of the city as well as a plan for the future, which was entitled 'Vision Mumbai; Transforming Mumbai into a World Class City'.[54] The report provided a comprehensive and holistic approach to Mumbai's development agenda, including suggestions on governance, infrastructure and the economy (Pinto 2008: 61).[55] One of the aspirations was to bring down the number of people living in the slums from the current 50–60 per cent to 10–20 per cent, to increase housing affordability, and to dramatically increase low-income housing availability (1.1 million low-income houses), while upgrading housing stock. The report was received with mixed reactions where enthusiastic 'liberals' opposed low-income and slum organisations activists, who labelled the report a 'builders' plan'.[56] The state government embraced the report nevertheless, and implementation started by demolishing slums:[57]

> The ambitious 'Shanghaisation' of Mumbai is finally under way. Chief Minister Vilasrao Deshmukh kicked off the project, which was initiated by the previous Democratic Front government, by announcing a Rs.31,000-crore package in early December 2004 and subsequently launching a massive clean-up drive of the metropolis. While the end result could benefit all its citizens, the initial impact is bound to be the hardest on the city's poor and voiceless. So far more than 45,000 shanties have been demolished, displacing nearly two lakh people, but freeing up to 300 acres (120 hectares) of land. Activists, social workers and urban planners question the government's callousness in evicting people who were a precious vote bank until recently. Does the solution to Mumbai's problems lie in clearing the urban poor and building projects to be used by less than 40 per cent of the population – they ask. Or, is this is just a ploy to free precious real estate?

Yet for all the energy of stakeholders to push or oppose the plans, the money paid to consultants and the misery brought about as a result of massive slum evictions (more details follow in the next chapter), it appears that the whole plan has avaporated. There was little, if any, follow-up to the report: nothing much has changed. It is believed that, as so often, many slum households returned to their original slums. In the next chapter I have a close look at the Mumbai slums as divided heterogeneous communities to see where and who the poor are and how people sustain livelihoods in taxing habitats with inadequate services.

Notes

1 http://www.census2011.co.in/census/city/365-mumbai.html, accessed 14 May 2013.
2 'For Migrants in Mumbai, Voting Is a Luxury', *Times of India,* 15 March 2014, mentions that 1.57 million migrants from outside Maharashtra came to Mumbai in the period 1991 to 2001, which amounts to nearly 15.7 per cent of the total population.
3 'By 2024, Number of Billionaires in India Expected to Swell to 3371', *Deccan Herald,* 10 March 2013.
4 Dilnaz Boga, 'Urban Poor Ghettoised: NGO', *DNA,* 18 December 2012.
5 'What Does the BMC Have in Store for Your Future?', *Hindustan Times,* 16 February 2015.
6 Bhide (2011: 79): 'The experience of the development plan in Mumbai in particular and the country in general has been one that has been characterized by non-implementation.'. . . 'The development plan "virtually" denies the existence of a slum. Slums are totally invisible under the brush strokes of the yellow, green and blue of the development plan.' As a consequence, 'the plan acts as a ground for denying basic services to the slum' (Bhide 2011: 81).
7 'BMC to Open FSI Floodgates Despite Infra Woes', *Economic Times,* 17 February 2015.
8 'Vilasrao Gets Tough with Slum-Abeting Staff', *Times of India,* 12 December 2004.
9 'BMC Cannot Cite Shortage of Staff for Inaction against Illegal Buildings: HC', *Times of India,* 18 April 2015.
10 'BMC to Cut Permissions Needed for Building Projects by 50%', *Times of India,* 30 April 2014, quoting a 2014 World Bank Report, which ranks India at number 184 out of 189 countries in terms of doing business easily.
11 This percentage of 6.13 per cent has been circulating for a long time; some BMC officials indicated during interviews that it is probably higher, at perhaps 10 per cent or even 12 per cent, if all unauthorized low-cost constructions are added.
12 *Financial Express,* 26 July 2012.
13 *Hindustan Times,* 13 February 2013.
14 'Mumbai Splurges on Land, Ignores Infrastructure Needs', *Times of India,* 3 April 2012. Real estate investments amount to Rs 27,000 crore, mostly

in big-ticket land deals, and not including SRA and other redevelopment projects; and investments in basic civic projects counting Rs 15,000 crore since 2005. The Lasalle Report states, 'While land in Mumbai is a gold mine, funding of infrastructure is in the pits'.

15 http://www.mid-day.com/news/2012/jan/150112-Mumbai-isnt-happy.htm (accessed on 8 March 2012); see also 'City Bears Brunt of BMC's Poor Performance', *Times of India*, 4 January 2012.

16 *Times of India*, 16 February 2012.

17 Quoted from a report on India's vast unorganised sector which applies this definition: 'Those working in unorganized enterprises or households, excluding regular workers with social security benefits, and the workers in the formal sector without any employment/social security benefits provided by the employers' (NCEUS/Sengupta 2007: 3).

18 http://infochangeindia.org/urban-india/backgrounder/the-informal-sector-and-urban-poverty.html (accessed on 5 March 12).

19 The survey in Baker *et al.* (2005: 8–9) finds 27 per cent of Mumbai households with household incomes below Rs 5,000, with an average of four household members. At that time such income was above the Maharashtra urban poverty line at Rs 594. One important finding is that 8.8 per cent of such households are headed by women, whereas it is 4.5 per cent on the average for all Mumbai households and only 1.3 per cent for incomes higher than Rs 20,000.

20 *The Economist*, 25 February 12.

21 For an assessment of the 2011–12 BMC budget, see 'City Bears Brunt of BMC's Poor Performance', *Times of India*, 4 January 2012. 'BMCs Big Budget Focuses on Small Wins', *Hindustan Times* reported on 5 February 2015 while discussing the 2015–16 budget. The budget outlay is Rs 33,514.15 crore. Important for this book is to note the decrease in the budget for education (from Rs 2,660.44 to Rs 2,501.35 crore). There is a new initiative to 'empower the girl child' under a new campaign; 'however, there are no details on how the civic body plans to execute the project'.

22 The BMC budget is very hard to understand, as it is divided into several hard-to-understand sub-budgets, as if 'there is a deliberate effort to create confusion' (field notes IDPAD seminar, 29 November 2003). Sources indicate that many MCs do not at all understand the budget (field notes ward office interviews, 18 December 2004); the official indicated that this may be one reason that MCs are more interested to engage in mundane matters such as changing street names.

23 *Times of India*, 11 February 2012: Mr Vinod Tawde mentions that the BMC has a budget of almost Rs 22,000 crore, of which almost 65 per cent is spent on salaries and maintenance of administration duties; the remaining Rs 7,000 crore remained for development work.

24 Pinto and Pinto (2005: 12ff.) refer to the commission that ultimately designed the 1888 act. One member 'feared that vesting executive authority in a municipal council would be a retrogressive step, plunging the municipality into a gulf of mismanagement, inefficiency and jobbery such as the wildest rumours have not dreamt of'. In this he was supported by a justice who stated, 'My Beau Ideal includes a strong Executive responsible to the Corporation and an enlightened Corporation watchful over its Executive.'

25 This is elaborated in Chapter 4, Section 4.5. In 2008, the Shiv Sena Standing Committee chairman succeeded to 'garner funds of Rs 8 crore for his

Ward as other corporators get only Rs 30 lakh' (*Mumbai Mirror*, 13 March 2008). He obtained the maximum share of funds of 8 crores out of the estimated Rs 325 crore available for the discretionary 'Area Development Corporators' Funds'.

26 This was when the plenary MC council demanded an increase in their discretionary councillors' funds before passing the budget, which led to budget cuts in the other sectors. *Hindustan Times* (9 April 2015) in an article 'BMC May Not Be Able to Buy Reserved Plots, as Corporators Get Funds' reports:

> The Civic Standing Committee has diverted more than Rs 200 crore for corporators to take up local ward work. In fact, Standing Committee Chairman and K-West Corporator Yahodhar Phanse has given himself a large chunk of Rs. 17 crore. . . . The Standing Committee has now allotted Rs 1 crore each to all the 227 corporators.

The MC Opposition leader said: 'The ruling party (SS) in the Standing Committee is misusing its powers. The distribution of funds to corporators was not done properly, and taking a huge amount of money from one department is not fair.'

27 There are also quota systems for SC/ST people, which I will not further discuss. The rationale and arrangements for women and such SC/ST quota systems are contested under indications of misuse, for example the submission of bogus caste certificates, and the perception that many women MCs are 'proxies' or 'puppets' for men, as will be discussed in the elections chapter (Chapter 5) (cf. Ghosh and Tawa Lama-Rewal 2005).

28 'Now, Corporators Demand Free Medical Treatment for Them', *DNA*, 23 December 2015.

29 The CAA states:

> In many States local bodies have become weak and ineffective on account of a variety of reasons, including the failure to hold regular elections, prolonged supersessions and inadequate devolution of powers and functions. As a result, Urban Local Bodies are not able to perform effectively as vibrant democratic units of self-government.

The Constitution (Seventy-Fourth Amendment) Act 1992, http://indiacode. nic.in/coiweb/amend/amend74.htm (accessed on 7 August 2014).

30 'Octroi' is like a municipal customs fee, a tax raised from any goods imported into Mumbai. With the planned introduction of an all-India general sales tax, it seems unavoidable that Octroi will disappear and that the city has to identify new taxes/income sources, which is not going to be easy.

31 I will return to the SEC in Chapter 5 and not further discuss the SFC, which relates to all state ULBs, and where Mumbai occupies a special place in view of its large own incomes as in octroi and taxes (Pinto and Pinto 2005: xxv; for recent details see PWC 2012).

32 K. C. Sivaramakrishnan, 'The Devolution Deficit: Why We Need to Revisit the 74th Amendment', *Indian Express,* 1 May 2013, who argues that the intent of the amendment was to institutionalize democratic decentralisation

but that this has failed for many reasons, such as its very design, and also states considering it as an incursion on their powers. He notes that municipal planning committees have been established only in Kolkata and Mumbai, but 'even in these areas, they are practically non-functional'.

33 It is quite telling that an important governance reform is implemented in such a way that the immediate political power balance is not disturbed, whereas, of course, the WCMs were to be 'institutionalised' to emerge as local institutions of general administration. It confirms a more commonly observed short-term time horizon for politicians, at the expense of implementing solid, issue-based, long-term workable reforms, with a clear objective and plan.

34 Praja suggests that one first thing to do in terms of democratic decentralisation is to create 24 WCMs, with a view to increase people's voice (www.praja.org: 2, accessed on 12 May 2013). Shetye (2006: 218) mentions that Mumbai is entitled under the act to set up 25 WCMs.

35 For reasons of space I will not deal with the provision that WCMs can co-opt NGO/CSO representatives as non-voting members (for this see Shetye 2006: 241ff.; Nainan and Baud 2008: 138).

36 Many feel that this spending limit is far too low: for that reason WCM corporators may break up larger proposals/projects into smaller bits and get these approved – but this is only possible when all/most MCs and the various parties can agree (field notes CBO member interview, 29 November 2003). One example was a community hall costing Rs 1.6 million; it was split up into four parts and so approved by one WCM.

37 'Now, Corporators Demand Free Medical Treatment for Them'.

38 Other factors are at work here, and practices differ from case to person to person. One factor is that parties dominating a WCM may differ from the BMC-level majority party – for example a WCM dominated by Congress-NCP and the BMC council by Shiv Sena (Shetye 2006: 247).

39 'Wants MNS Councilor Disqualified', *Times of India*, 3 August 2013. In a comment, the newspaper views the attack as a pointer to the depth in which our parties, politicians and politics have sunk: 'The line between goons and politicians is blurring.' It shows Mumbai turning into a zone of total lawlessness.

40 'Civil Service Woes', *Frontline*, 17 April 2015: 115.

41 Pinto and Pinto (2005: 505): 'Transfer is a weapon that politicians often use to control good officers and to penalize those who do not toe the line.'

42 *Times of India*, 20 February 2012.

43 www.votemumbai.org/wardcommi.asp (accessed on 11 February 2007).

44 The central government under Prime Minister Modi abolished the National Planning Commission and the practice of developing Five-Year Plans in 2014.

45 'Despite Spending Rs. 3,000 crore, Monorail Not Safe, Says CAG', *Times of India*, 11 April 2015.

46 'Playground vs Parking Space Debate Heats Up,' *Hindustan Times*, 2 February 2015. The article reveals that Mumbai had 2.318 hectares of open space out of a total space of 43.771 hectares, amounting to 1,86 sq.mt. for each citizen. The same newspaper reported on 5 February: 'Left with just 300 acres, collector fights to retain land in the suburbs', that hundreds of acres of collector's land have allegedly been taken over either by slums or by unscrupulous builders. The collector – the biggest landlord in the

Mumbai suburbs – has decided to build reinforced concrete walls to keep encroachers out.

47 *Times of India,* 16 February 2013.
48 This is not to deny that there can be issues between MHADA and BMC also, for example that MHADA constructs housing in a low-lying area, which is prone to water logging. It is the BMC which is then in charge of cleaning and maintaining the area; it will complain to MHADA but often in vain (field notes, 2 February 2005).
49 '30 of India's 68 Billionaires Call Mumbai Their Home', *Times of India,* 11 March 2015. As per the 2015 Knight Frank Wealth Report, India has 68 billionaires, number 7 on a ranking of 97 countries. Mumbai's billionaire population will grow 110 per cent by 2024. Fifty per cent of the investments of India's ultra-rich are in real estate.
50 Whitehead and More (2007: 2431) state: 'Private land is highly concentrated, which has its roots in the colonial period. Parsi merchants and philanthropists acquired a lot of land. Today, about nine developers and trusts control all available private land in Mumbai island.'
51 In an interview with *The Hindu* (15 August 2007), Harris says that 'Ironically, . . . [middle class values] came to resemble those reflected in the self-seeking actions of the politicians they so despised'. He refers to an inverse relation between socio-economic status and electoral participation.
52 H. Mander, 'Forgotten Brethren: In the Middle Class Expectations of 21st century India, People on the Socio-Economic Margins Should Stay There, because That Is Their Lot', *Outlook,* 20 April.
53 *Times of India,* 11 February 2013.
54 See http/www.bombayfirst.org/LCKinseyReport.pdf (accessed on 20 April 2004), which portrays a vision of Mumbai to be like Shanghai. Various city development plans of other cities in the Mumbai region included goals of becoming world-class, slum-free cities. For Mumbai also see Vreeswijk 2006: 32ff and 238–39).
55 I may recall that these Mumbai developments coincided with the efforts of the then BJP union government to project India's potential and favourable prospects under the label 'India Shining'.
56 A series of seminars followed the report's presentation, one of which at TISS. One seminar contribution was by me (de Wit 2004) that the need of the hour was no grandiose plans, but the incremental – serious and as clean as possible – implementation of the various policy schemes and plans already underway or budgeted, and the proper enforcement of extant legislation and rules.
57 Reported by 'For a New Mumbai, at Great Cost', *Frontline,* 17 January 2005.

3 Included and excluded
Mumbai's poor and slum dynamics

Having provided the larger context of Mumbai's governance, political economy and changing power configurations especially of and for its wealthy 'citizens', we need to map the realities of that other half of the population: the poor and poorest people in the slums. I will list the key areas of concern for poor women, men and children in terms of secure housing and access to things like water, health and education facilities. Slum conditions are pictured as some kind of 'informal world'. In the absence of reliable, let alone uniform state support, slum people make do with informal solutions such as for shelter, toilets and loans. They navigate a risky and, for many, adverse slum and city context of a remote BMC ward office and an unfriendly police. The scope and also the many constraints to organise for collective action are considered, as well as how these are affected by everyday local politics. Specific attention will be given to the patterns of inclusion and exclusion inside slums and beyond and to how power is played out locally.

3.1 Poor slums and established slum colonies: an overview

Even while the use of the word 'slum' is contested,[1] for the purposes of this book I follow the long-term Indian practice and use the word 'slum'. I apply the government of Maharashtra definition, which is helpful to the extent that it agrees that slums are unsuitable for human habitation. As noted by Weinstein and Ren (2009: 423), it highlights physical conditions of a housing area (and not often more pressing legal or service-oriented dimensions). The Slum Areas (Improvement, Clearance and Redevelopment) Act 1971 refers to a slum when:

> The buildings in any area, used or intended to be used for human habitation are in any respect unfit for human habitation, or by reasons

of dilapidation, overcrowding, faulty arrangement of streets, lack of ventilation, light or sanitation facilities or any combination of these factors, detrimental to the health, safety or convenience of the public of that area.

But the word 'slum' is also unhelpful as it tends to ignore the large differences between Mumbai slums, as well as whether people subjectively feel they live in a slum. In reality, many Mumbai slums have existed for decades and probably a majority of slum dwellings are more or less quite liveable, with established (even if problematic) services. They have been homes to one or more generations. Many such people do not consider themselves 'slum dwellers', which may be reflected in the names they themselves use, such as *wadi*, colony, *koliwada,* or *goathan*. This is not at all to deny the existence of many down and out poor and under-serviced slums or slum pockets (*zopad patti*), which are associated more with (more recent) 'encroachment'. Such areas are scattered all over the city; others are informal 'substandard' extensions of an existing slum. Way back in Madras (de Wit 1985), such slums were called 'raw slums'.

Weinstein (2013: 295–97) notes that the number of Bombay people in the slums grew from very few in the early 1950s to about 500,000 in 1961, rising to two million in 1971, reaching already about six million by 2001. In the mid-1950s, a slum clearance project was implemented (arbitrarily labelled an early proof of slum eviction by Weinstein 2013: 296). As per the earlier slum definition, approximately one out of each two persons living in Mumbai lives in the slums. They are close to 54 per cent of the housing stock (MCGM 2009: 55; Vakulabharanam and Motiram 2012 mention 56.9 per cent). But nobody seems to know exactly how many people live in the vast variety of makeshift huts, incrementally growing *kacha* structures or poorer *pucca*[2] houses and I can only present rough estimates here. Anand (2011b) mentions that approximately 55 per cent of Mumbai residents presently live in slums and another 25 per cent in low-quality, dilapidated housing including chawls. According to Nijman (2008: 76) by 2003, an estimated one million people lived in the aforementioned *zopad pattis* or are completely homeless. Fifty-five per cent live in more permanent slums; 82 per cent of the population live in one-room dwellings and over 80 per cent of the city's people live in 'overall substandard housing'. However, all these numerous huts, shacks and chawls are believed to occupy only 6 to 10 per cent of all Mumbai land, pointing to extremely high levels of population density (Zerah 2009a: 854). Contrasting the trend to use static slum definitions, Gupte (2012: 195–97) usefully underlines the dynamic nature of slums and their people. Slums are never static: they emerge, grow and develop (even into two- or three-storied small buildings with little iron staircases, e.g. in Dharavi); people come and go – but they can always be demolished – witness the Ganpat Patil slum case at the start of this book. Slums face a 'lack of basic state service provision combined with unhealthy living conditions and hazardous locations; the households dispose of very low living space per person, while they are socially excluded from citywide services and networks' (Gupte 2012: 195–97).

But it is important to note that I do not think all Mumbai slum people would feel socially excluded. Plenty of people with reasonable, even stable incomes and assets – TVs, motor bikes, individual bathroom in some *pucca* structure – simply got stuck in a slum dwelling due to the lack of any affordable alternative.[3] As explained earlier, most slums have a mixed population, ranging from well-off to poor people, one reason that it is so hard to develop uniform policy (e.g. the case of slum taxes). Some observers see four broad slum categories, starting from the date of establishment and corresponding and evolving 'cut-off dates'. Many people in slums that came up around 1976, 1985 and 1995 are doing relatively well, as they managed to consolidate their positions while enjoying protection (even while surely poorer or financially struggling households must have left such slums in gentrification processes). Problems are more for post-1995 and certainly for more recent slums – and individual households. In fact, as land is so very expensive, many slum households especially in 'the city' sit 'on gold', as the plots where they live can be very expensive. For example, I heard that the price of a Bandra slum plot was Rs 12 million and that some slum properties are sold for as much as Rs 960,000 to 1.5 million.[4] Such wide diversity is obviously hard to manage and gives rise to all sorts of unexpected dynamics.

The precise number of slums in Mumbai is not clear; one report mentions 1,959 slums, another 2,245 slum pockets as per the MCGM (2009: 58–59) report.[5] Almost half of the slums are on land owned by various government agencies (BMC 16 per cent, state government 22 per cent, 10 per cent mixed public), while private landowners own the other half, or about 47 per cent (MCGM 2009: 59). Das (2003: 210) specifies that 2,500 slum settlements cover only 6 per cent of the city's total land area and are located on private land (50 per cent), state government land (25 per cent) and municipal corporation land (25 per cent). The remaining slums are located on various central government and state housing board lands.[6] Two more distinct habitat types also accommodate the urban poor: the chawls and the Mumbai streets.

Even while neither is normally grouped under the slum label, conditions here may look pretty similar. MCGM (2009: 61) reports that '52 per cent of Mumbai households with incomes less than Rs. 5,000 live in slums, and 38 per cent in *chawls*'. These are single or multi-storied single-room tenements mostly in the southern parts of the city built for the workers in the textile mills and other factories at the time when Mumbai was an important industrial centre. They have, by and large, been neglected ever since, partly as a result of very low rents that were rarely raised. Chawls are marked by grossly inadequate conditions of leaking, crumbling walls, stagnating pools, and very insanitary conditions. On the positive side, these units are strategically located in the central parts of Mumbai, and the original owners have 'virtual ownership' at a very low cost (MCGM 2009: 58; see Joseph 2011: 6ff.). The most miserable of poor city households would be pavement dwellers and the homeless: the former simply erected temporary huts on any of the cities' roads; the latter sleep under bridges or station platforms – including street children. However, one must assume they also want to be upwardly mobile and hopefully end up eventually in a regular slum given incrementally growing incomes and/or useful contacts. Recent migrants will be over-represented among them, hoping to be absorbed by the city sooner or later. It is reported that the number of homeless households is decreasing, from 60,000 in 1971 to 24,000 today (MCGM 2009: 63), which seems too low a number. My 2003 field notes indicate that at that time the SPARC NGO was said to work already with 22,000 pavement dwellers with a view to their relocation. Pinto (2008: 42) mentions that approximately 1.5 million live on the pavements, which again seems on the high side. The Mumbai Human Development (HD) report (MCGM 2009: 16) mentions another non-slum but vulnerable group of urban poor: mostly men as recent or circular migrants, who come to the city to work, send their earnings back to their families, and who may return themselves after saving enough. They may live together in cheap lodges, or just rent a bed for certain hours boarding houses or hostels. Their numbers are not known as they are not normally registered.

The city's slums are located throughout the metropolis. Only one ward out of 24 city wards in the southern island city has no slums (MCGM 2009: 68ff.). Most slums extend in a north–south belt in the western suburbs, and next – and counting – in number come the eastern suburbs. But over the past decade we see a gradual shifting to and concentration of slum/urban poverty areas in a few suburbs, notably the eastern suburb wards of M-east (Chembur) and the north-western P-ward (north) (Manecksha 2011: 26).[7] On the one hand, slum households may be relocated as project-affected persons or PAPs when the land of the slum is needed for unavoidable projects such as the World Bank–funded Mumbai Urban Transport project (MUTP), or other construction projects including metro lines, bridges or (often underused) overhead sky walks. Another number of slum households were relocated after their slum was affected by SRS under the SRA agency. Some of such households (probably a minority) were accommodated through a land-sharing modality 'in situ' on their slum land itself, but many more were shifted to a more remote location, for example under the innovative but controversial TDR model of urban housing since 1991. The good news is that such households, if they can prove to be eligible (proof to have been in the city before a certain 'cut-off date', see later), obtain alternative accommodation in the form of a 225 sq. ft. housing unit (increased to 269 sq. ft. in 2008). The bad news is that the vast majority of such units are located in far-away and already impoverished areas, with grave risks of creating ghettos of the poor. Op top of this, the process of allocation is riddled with corruption where slum households, officials, politicians, and even the urban rich benefit from such far too few and small housing units (more details on SRA are provided in Section 3.7).

Rumours circulate in the Annawadi slum studied by Boo that it will be redeveloped under the SRS scheme. Eligible households who could prove that they lived in their huts since 1995 or 2000 would obtain a tiny apartment, but with running water, which made them a valuable asset: 'Hence overcity people (in contrast to the *undercity* slum people,) had been buying up shacks in the slums and concocting legal papers to show that *they* were long time Annawadi residents'. Most such speculators were to use them for rental or investment purposes, expecting to earn ten times the investment price. A small time politician bought a block of huts on behalf of a major developer, 'hiring thugs on commission to persuade the occupants to sell'.

(italics added Boo 2012: 225)

An estimated 60,000 people were relocated over the past decade, and as per one survey, one-third of them to locations more than 15–20 km away from their original slum (26 per cent of those inhabitants now spent more time commuting). Such processes of relocation and redevelopment are by no means over as noted in MCGM (2009: 70). Approximately 50,000 households will be affected due to road and railway transport projects; 60,000 to 80,000 households may need to be relocated as a result of the airport expansion programme. SRA statistics indicate that 150,000 'units have obtained approval for rehabilitation'. If and when finally a redevelopment plan for the large Dharavi slum area might be approved and then actually implemented, this will affect another 57,000 households. (Manecksha 2011: 26) refers to the process of Mumbai's slum people's relocation as indicative of the city's growing exclusionary character. She mentions a slight dip in the slum population of wealthy south Mumbai, while in M-east (Chembur, Mankhurd) the slum population grew by 48 per cent and that today 85 per cent of the population there are slum dwellers. Similarly, the slum population of the P-north ward grew by 39 per cent, with slum people now making up 75 per cent of the population. Relocated people are facing many hardships in their new locations, in terms of employment, access to water, water in toilets, and increased illness. A solid and detailed study by Ayyar (2013) highlights the problems women face in one such location, the ill-famous Lallubhai compound in the M-ward, with 72 massive multi-storied buildings crammed together in a very small area. We visited the site several times and carried out spot-check interviews and focus group discussions there (field notes, 15 February 2012 and 23 February 2014). A mix of diverse population groups live there after their shifting from slums, chawls and pavements in different areas of Mumbai. Large groups of Dalits, OBCs and Muslims now live there, having migrated from regions of Maharashtra, Tamil Nadu, Karnataka, and Uttar Pradesh. A newspaper reports on the inspection of one such five-story block for PAPs, describing it as a vertical slum, lacking adequate spacing, water, elevators, and toilets.[8]

Slums then come in all sorts of shapes and sizes, ranging from recently occupied and slowly growing pockets with the most 'downtrodden' to well-established slums and large low-income 'colonies' where lower-income groups reside with facilities such as toilet blocks and piped water. A survey of the literature brings out the determinants of their nature, liveability and prospects. Factors are as to whether or not the slum people in majority can prove to have lived there before the most recent 'cut-off date', which stands at 2000 presently – and whether, therefore, the slum has been provided any facilities (toilet block, water supply, electricity, mother–child care centre); whether the slum is located in an otherwise well-off area with employment possibilities for men and women; and whether it is prone to flooding during the monsoon months and accessible with cheap local transport. Another factor is whether a slum is of a mixed caste/income composition or whether the lowest castes (Dalits), Muslims and the poor dominate. A final factor is the absence or presence of local brokers/political agents active in the slum who link it to supra-level slum opportunities: in other words, whether a corporator or active social worker can help pull down funds to that particular slum (see Risbud 2003: 9; van Dijk 2011a: 38). All reports agree on an important role of local and state politicians in allowing people to settle on land and to offer them some security. Pending a later discussion on this when considering the role of corporators as regards the urban poor, one view – which is certainly as to how the middle classes look at this – is presented here:[9]

> A politician's hunger for votes is almost always the reason behind a new slum coming up. This is abetted by a section of corrupt officials, who look away from the problem till a settlement grows too huge that it cannot be demolished.

The Mumbai Human Development Report (MCGM 2009: 59) puts it this way:

> The present cut-off date for notification of slums is 1995. The issue is simple: people have colonised lands with impunity or with local political and administrative connivance. The city government is unable to deal with the problem of slums, given the constraints of funds and political patronage that enables new slums to emerge.

3.2   Who and where are the urban poor?

Not all people living in slums are poor, and not all poor people live in the slums. And as this book starts from conditions of and prospects for the poor, I now venture – handicapped by limited and fragmented data – to uncover urban poverty facts and trends. MCGM (2009: 44) agrees that the precise extent of poverty remains to be determined and that existing data are confusing. A 1998 survey pegged Mumbai poverty at only 8.5 per cent, another at 10 per cent for the Mumbai population as a whole (say 1.2 million poor). A baseline study by MMRDA in the Mumbai slums concluded that 40 per cent of households had incomes below the poverty line (with about six million people in the slums, this would make 2.4 million).[10] A slum survey by Bhatiya and Chatterjee (2010: 24) found that 27 per cent had monthly 'household' incomes up to Rs 2,500; 52 per cent up to Rs 5,000; 11 per cent up to Rs 10,000, while 9 per cent reported incomes over Rs 10,000/month. They frankly admit that actual incomes might have been higher, as it was observed during data collection that many households had TVs and refrigerators, while 28 per cent possessed a mobile telephone.[11] Their survey brought out that 99 per cent of respondents possessed a valid proof of identity: 56 per cent had both a voter's card (which today is the key item) and a permanent ration card (which is no longer given so much importance as legal proof). Chatterjee *et al.* (2012) carried out a cross-sectional, interviewer-administered survey of adult female respondents from 283 households in slums across three Mumbai municipal wards. Food insecurity, as measured by the Household Food Insecurity Access Scale, was established in more than half of households: 59.7 per cent (n = 169) households were categorised as severely food insecure, 16.6 per cent (n = 47) as mildly to moderately food insecure and 23.7 per cent (n = 67) as food secure. Households where a woman was the primary income earner were more likely to experience severe food insecurity. Household incomes are a notoriously poor indicator of general household welfare where women and girls are normally poorer than men and boys, but disaggregated intra-household data are lacking. A key question here is whether earning men and sons make all their earnings available or spent a considerable part on personal consumption, as seems likely from available evidence (as elaborated later, spending on alcohol by slum men is said to be high – Kapadia 1996: 1436 and Bisiaux 2013: 58, while Boo 2012: 157 implies it is common in the Annawadi slum she studied).

So what is the profile of a poor Mumbai household? Perhaps the major poverty problems and challenges are faced, as just noted, by households where women are alone or with a poorly earning or alcohol-using husband, besides widows, deserted wives and divorcees. This would be consistent with the findings of my earlier slum studies in Chennai (de Wit 1996). A next category might be the Dalits (former untouchables) who may not number so many in Mumbai,[12] but most of them do live in slums or on pavements, and they are believed to be least able to achieve upward mobility. Ayyar and Khandare (n.d.: 20): 'The caste hierarchies play a dominant role in strengthening and realizing the chances of upward mobility. Dalits being the lowest in socio-economically status remain deprived among the slum dweller population.' One key factor that sets them apart already materially is that, unlike most other caste groups, they rarely owned or even could own property – like land or an owned house, let alone some sort of enterprise. One could argue that they share this crucial handicap with the women of India who, by and large, don't have much property as land or house on their name – even while current formal legislation regulates equal daughter–son inheritance. Empowerment will not be quite easy without economically useful assets.

For centuries Dalit men and women were simply labourers doing all sorts of hard, tedious and dirty work at very poor wages, neither allowed nor able to save much or to achieve a higher more respected status. They were subject to harsh regimes, regulated by strict and often nasty sanctions. As argued earlier for the Chennai slum Dalits (de Wit 1996), like all castes they developed their own mindsets, culture and praxis, where one could argue that in their case these are often defensive and much less offensive in terms of claiming rights (as SCs) persistently.[13] Finally, it appears that they find it hard to mobilise and organise, where observers feel they also suffer and suffered from poor (political) leadership as illustrated later by their voting in the 2012 Mumbai municipal elections. This seems in contrast to another relatively poor and vulnerable community of poor Muslims (labelled a 'minority'). Based on interviews and observations I tend to believe that they manage better to unite against what they may see as a threat or to capitalise pragmatically on opportunities. This could be to vote (also as a group) for a well-connected corporator, even if he or she is from Shiv Sena or BJP, known for an anti-minority attitude. But not all Muslims living in the slums are that poor; many have their small-scale enterprises there with all workers and facilities at hand.

Another very important – yet hard to observe – factor is whether a household has contacts and assets in 'their native place'. To the extent that many Mumbai people – rich and poor – are migrants, their background critically determines how easy they can enter, merge and come up. For example, in a poor Malad slum with a majority Tamil population, we found that many households kept close contacts with far-away Tamil Nadu families, for example that a wife delivered her first child there as is customary. Children were sent there for study and earnings, and agricultural goods were brought back. Generally, what may look like a poor household does not have to be one, with people always emphasising that things may not be what they look like – you can't see poverty from the outside or by talking to a poor person. Other factors explaining poverty entail, first and foremost, the degree to which the state/BMC supports households in terms of free, subsidised health and education services. For individuals and household literacy is key, if only to be aware of opportunities and the wider city context. Poverty is more likely when a household is a tenant, rather than 'owning' a hut/house;[14] when members are casual daily labourers in the informal sector; when it is hard to obtain cheap credit in the absence of a collateral; or when one is handicapped or lacking social support in terms of social capital or organisation membership. Most slum households have debts and reserve monthly money to pay the interest and if possible repay the loan. A sudden 'stress event' can catapult an average household into misery and debt, such as an accident or slum fire.[15] To conclude, I quote from a report on our multi-year fieldwork on an SRS in Malad (de Wit 2016) where we drafted a list of the slum households most vulnerable to suffer from or be adversely affected by the project (Desai and de Wit 2007: 14):

> Although the SRS policy does not differentiate between owners and tenants, in reality, the tenant households, lacking any legal status, had no claim to a formal tenement in the new scheme. They would be evicted from their hutments once the scheme commenced. They had neither representation in the CBOs nor support from the leaders, the builder or Ward Office. This group, the most vulnerable, was invisible in the scheme. The second most adversely affected category were older residents without valid official proof of their residency. Despite residing in the slum before 1995, they neither possessed any valid documents nor did they have the financial stability to acquire the same via fraudulent means. This group typically consisted of the poorest of the poor – single women, households with very old members, those with a woman main earning member and alcoholic husbands, daily wage earners or those having intermittent, unsteady work. The latter group also did not have a close connection with the slum leadership and therefore no clout for negotiating their status in the scheme. These households were not eligible in either of the lists drawn by the two competing builders.

3.3   Security of tenure and the market in residence proofs

Under Maharashtra law, slums as a whole can be 'declared', registered or 'notified', granting the slum a degree of security by law. Today, 93 per cent of all slums are notified which allows the Mumbai authorities – mostly the BMC – to provide basic services to these slums, such as street water taps and internal roads. Households here then have to pay Rs 20–22 as 'nominal charges' (MCGM 2009: 59), which is an indication that slum people do pay fees – as some kind of tax. The people living in non-notified slums are vulnerable to eviction – without relocation – and the BMC does not normally provide them with basic services. Yet exceptions are always possible given that there is protection, that is a powerful patron, who, for whatever reason, is sympathetic to the slum dwellers, and current legislation recognises the right of any person to water supply. But such an overall slum right does not one-to-one translate in household slum rights; this right is related to so-called cut-off dates. Individual households settling in a slum after that date have no formal legal right to the land, slum services or relocation. The practice divides households into those who can prove they lived in their slum before that date from those who cannot. The distinction may not mean much for the day-to-day realities of most households, but can suddenly assume importance, for example when a slum is taken up for redevelopment or relocation. The very first cut-off date was set in 1976, in a time when there was a shift from seeing slums as a problem (leading to slum clearance boards and policies; see de Wit 1996: slums as a solution). Photo passes were issued to those eligible, and in notified slums the inhabitants were 'in principle' eligible to municipal services: electricity, water and garbage collection, but also the right to relocation after demolition. On the one hand, it was a positive step towards shelter security, but on the other a distinction was made for the first time between eligible and ineligible slum households – those with and without housing rights. This remains controversial to date (Anand and Rademacher 2011: 1758). Importantly, slum notification and the establishment of cut-off dates is ultimately a political process, where politicians have an important stake. Corporators and their parties may advocate extending the cut-off date for electoral vote bank reasons to charm slum people, so that the practice of cut-off dates – seemingly unpredictable and arbitrary – illustrate the relations and negotiations between slum dwellers and politicians.[16] Cut-off dates were extended in 1980, to 1985, to 1990, to January 1995, and presently up to 2000. It appears as if today the importance of the cut-off date has shifted from the level of entire notified slums to the level of individual slum households, each having to prove it actually lived in a slum before the cut-off date to be eligible for relocation. One activist is quoted in a newspaper:[17]

> Extending the cut-off date is just an appeasement solution. It hampers effective implementation of slum redevelopment schemes. . . . Most slum colonies have a mix of eligible and ineligible residents. The ineligible ones often oppose redevelopment plans of the other group. Even before a developer emerges on the scene, an internal conflict has already arisen.

The nature of proof has changed over time. Initially the SRA authorities accepted various documents such as the identity card/photo pass, voter's identification, ration card and electricity bills. But in 2007 the Election Commission removed the ration card from the list of proofs to enable people to vote – probably in the knowledge that such cards can be made and bought illegally. However, a newspaper reported that 'after protests from political parties, it was re-introduced'.[18] Nainan (2006: 3) reports that illegal ration cards can be obtained through informal networks at Rs 2,000 to Rs 5,000 per family. A few years later Kumar and Landy pegged the amount at almost Rs 8,000 (2009: 116). The money was distributed as follows: Rs 500 goes to the typist, Rs 2,000 to the agent, Rs 4,000 to the rationing officer, Rs 1,000 to the assistant rationing officer, and Rs 1,000 to the inspector. The Maharashtra state government had weeded out 2.9 million bogus ration cards[19] in the state, with the highest number of 650,000 in Mumbai.[20] Ironically, the majority or 2.2 million fake cards were from households with above-poverty-line incomes. These are not exactly people in need of a card for food or to prove a hold in the city – well-off Indians have the luxury to settle anywhere. A newspaper reported that 6,000 blank ration cards had been released by the *Tehsildar* in rural Maharashtra a few months before the assembly elections in October 2014:

> He did the illegal act under a heavyweight politician of the then ruling party, the Congress, Phundkar (a BJP Legislator) told Express. According to him, the blank ration cards were distributed among people from the BPL to lure them to vote for Congress.[21]

3.4   The informal slum world, slum hierarchies and gender relations

Having provided the basic data as to how many slums may be there and what poverty patterns prevail I will now reflect on the nature of slum life. How do different caste and ethnic groups live together in congested and ill-serviced areas, and how do men and women together manage households under often adverse conditions? Social networks will be shown to be both inclusive and exclusive, which is related to issues of formal but more importantly informal or factual power. I trace the role of mediators and assess the scope for the poor to organise and make a fist to claim their rights. Four notions guide the text, first:

> What characterizes the social life of the urban dispossessed is not simply anomie, alienation and a 'culture of poverty', nor a particular penchant for embracing (extremist/violent) politics, but primarily the practice of 'informal life' – a social existence

characterised by autonomy, flexibility, and pragmatism, where survival and self-development occupy a central place.

(in Gupte 2012: 208)

A second related notion is the realisation that poor people operate in an environment characterised by unreliable institutions, negligent or even predatory government agents and multiple but volatile sources of household income – in terms of Wood (2003), by 'destructive uncertainty'. As they have to cope not just with short-term shocks but also unpredictable future hazards, avoiding unnecessary risks is absolutely imperative, which may lead to a strategy of 'staying secure, staying poor' (see Gill 2007). This book pictures the many debilitating constraints and challenges faced by the very poor, as if they were simply and only victims of massive, unchangeable structures – of exploitation, domination and patriarchy. That this is wrong is my third anchor point. Even the poorest woman has agency and will keep looking for and act on opportunities for herself and her household, the Dalit labourer sees scope to improve his position through a better employer and cases in this book portray women taking on corrupt officials or aspiring to become a corporator. Poor people are invariably survivors, or, to use that fashionable concept, they are 'resilient' – even if they have little choice. We must not forget that slums are not new – the first Tamil slum school in Dharavi was established in 1924; the first Maharashtra Slum Act dates from 1971. People have been flocking to the city in the prospect of work, incomes and a better life. Many migrants joined relatives already there, knowing what to expect. Others may have simply left their towns or villages being pushed away by droughts, land grabbing for dams or would-be industrial zones, or to escape caste atrocities committed by those more powerful (for a good overview of such push-and-pull factors, see Ayyar and Khandare n.d.: 17). As indicated, most still entertain relations with or go for voting in their native places. In all, we are talking about people cleverly investing their meagre capacities the best way they can: checking alternatives and cultivating both extended family relations and critical outside (political) contacts carefully. Finally, they are an integral part of Mumbai, and whatever exclusions poor people experience, economically they are implicitly welcome and factually included: the city would not survive without their votes and hard work. Imagine all labour gone into any of the city's shining glass towers or the efforts to clean and cook in all those apartments. Hence I agree with Anand (2011b: 543) that we need to move beyond binary theorisations of haves and have-nots. We need to avoid a Mumbai image marked only "by the extremes of those having more than they can ever need and others who have desperately little to live on".

Inclusion, exclusion and internal slum exploitation

I have argued elsewhere that the urban poor of India largely live in what I call an informal world – and in what could appear like an urban jungle (Boo 2012; de Wit 2010b). A vast majority work in the informal or unorganised sector, which is unregulated by definition; many live in informal settlements where eviction is a threat; they rely on moneylenders, informal shop credit and local saving schemes for finance; quite a few children are in informal schools like madrasas or small slum schools, while some people with health problems first contact a local healer or quack. Formality seems rare: that one man with a permanent BMC job and that one household which did obtain a legal SRS unit as per formal rules. Knowledge, literacy and aware-ness are major issues – reason that I consider proper education the one fast track to 'empowerment'. Many slum people are not aware (and not informed) of formal opportunities, such that slum women may not even be aware of an *anganwadi* in their own slum (see Heston and Kumar 2008: 1248). Generally one can argue that the most poor are most 'socially handicapped' – as in being of low caste, illiterate, a woman, or a member of a minority – which makes them dependent on others, which could (need not always) lead to them being an easy prey for predatory officials, policemen and politicians. So they look for protection and support and may succeed in linking with an employer, mediator and political agent in what may start as an incidental media-tion, but which can develop into a more permanent (or patronage) relation, based on perceived trust and reliability.[22] The lower one's status (money, caste, covered by protection) and the lesser (power-related) contacts the more risk to suffer impunity from stronger folks and having to pay bribes. The poor are almost only bribe-payers; they are no longer poor once they become bribe-taker. It is likely that the poor pay more in terms of bribes and petty corruption relative to their incomes than the middle classes. Heston and Kumar (2008: 1248) correctly argue:

> Even though the sums involved are often trivial, the indirect effects of petty corruption are much more insidious than usually por-trayed. When authorities extort payments from hawkers, small shopkeepers, squatters, their source of power stems from lack of

accountability and a great deal of discretion, especially when dealing with poorer segments of society.

Yet, for all these issues and daily hassles, slums or chawls as areas of informality are not traps or dead-end streets for most; they offer chances, security, networks, and survival opportunities as mentioned by Manecksha (2011: 27). Households are not static and can be upwardly mobile. Boo (2012: 62) mentions what is seen as three ways out of poverty:

> As every slum dweller knew, there were three main ways out of poverty: finding an entrepreneurial niche as the Hussains had found in garbage; politics and corruption, in which Asha (*already a slum boss, aspiring to become a SS corporator*[italics added]) placed her hopes; and education. Several dozen parents in the slum were getting by on roti and salt in order to pay private school tuition.[23]

But slums can also turn into something like an unpleasant, even nasty prison, where hostile landlords are claiming high rents, where mafia-like *goons* threaten people or criminals take the law in their own hands, with the police only watching or actively engaged. Social networks may support people but can also be exclusionary for reasons of gender, caste, ethnicity, or political affiliation. It all depends on where you are in the slum hierarchy, where incomes and assets may be less important than power and relations – even while these may obviously coincide. Generalisations are risky, especially as Mumbai slums may be counted as some of the most heterogeneous slums globally, harbouring an astonishing diversity of people from wide-ranging backgrounds and characteristics. Dimensions or potential divisions include ethnicity/language, caste, religion, gender, income/employment, political affiliation, owner/tenant – and of course not everybody gets along with everybody anyway. Unfortunately, very little is known as to how the six odd million slum people live and survive and how they themselves experience slum life and social relations. Divisions listed may not mean much in daily life, but can suddenly assume significance: tenants and owners in opposition after an SRS scheme is announced; citywide agitations targeting religious groups as happened in the past; Dalit or Muslim youth being targeted for little, if any, reason during a police raid. There is the important ethnic factor, which, along with religion, has been misused especially by the Shiv Sena party to 'divide and rule' (Gupte 2012: 206–7). The latter has a quote that ethnicity is 'the most potent energizer, embodying and radiating religious, linguistic, territorial and class and caste identities and interests . . . as an umbrella under which personal, familial, commercial and other local scores are settled'. In my view, this, unhelpfully, almost equates 'ethnicity' with 'identity', but I endorse the importance of both, as will be seen, for example, in municipal election voting. Very little is known about the caste composition in the slums, which obviously differs from slum to slum. Ayyar and Khandare (n.d.) list the castes present in their four research slums, noting that 'most of the slum dwellers belong to the lower socioeconomic strata of Indian society. Dalits, the ex-untouchables form the major chunk of slum population in Mumbai as they belong to the lowest social and economic hierarchy' (Ayyar and Khandare n.d.: 3). I gratefully quote from their insightful text on local social networks (Ayyar and Khandare n.d.: 28–29):

> Thus, slums might have heterogeneous populations but they live in homogenous clusters belonging to the neighbourhood dominated by caste and kinship ties. With a passage of time, the densification of neighbourhoods is webbed and fortified in the form of social networks. These networks are primarily kinship and neighbour-hood networks. They are helpful in numerous ways in negotiating with the civic authorities or accessing information on availability of jobs in the market and so on. Indeed these networks are not only support systems of the urban poor. Through these networks the urban poor can survive in a hostile city life. But these networks are essentially limited as they are based on common factors such as caste, religion, language. There is an apparent exclusion in this inclusive based social mechanism in slums.

It is therefore important to note that inclusion (solidarity, sharing and exchange) and exclusion (kept out of meetings, saving groups, useful contacts or information) and internal exploitation (moneylenders or saving groups charging high interests to poorer households) all occur in any-one slum. There is the case where a slum-street community looked after an old woman when she was hit by a bike, including a hospital watch, and keeping pressure on an opportunistic, devious police (field notes, 12 March 2013). Sudhakar (2012: 3) confirms solidarity and support:

> When a (slum) resident is admitted to hospital or is ill, he/she is supported (financially and by visiting) by almost every family residing in the area, confirming the unity of people in the area. Lot of sharing takes place in the neighbourhood. Taking cold water bottles from the refrigerator, wearing a neighbour's saree, taking chairs from someone's house, etc. are common here. Some of the

slum dwellers had well placed relatives residing in the flats or in their native place. One of the young women said: 'my brother is an officer in the government, my parents have a large piece of land and they support us whenever we need money.'

Yet, it would be too much to expect that the juxtaposition of so many people with different backgrounds and loyalties in tiny cramped areas would not lead to internal conflicts or to the exploitation of the poor by the rich – as happens elsewhere. Desai (2002: 119–20) mentions that slums can be marked by groupism, hostility and deep schisms – which may be articulated and deepened for selfish reasons by local slum leaders and powerful outsiders. Friction may arise out of internal differences of income or ownership status. Daily squabbles and fights take place over access to or use of scarce or overused services, notably water and toilet use. Moneylenders operate in all slums, well aware of the financial position of each (often already more or less-indebted) household and fine-tuning their demands and interest rates per case. Van Dijk (2011b: 111) refers to slums as stratified spaces where 'a better off and better connected strata are able to capture most of the benefits', which brings in notions of 'gatekeeping' where information and opportunities are not shared but captured, as in 'elite capture'. Boo's (2012: 237) assessment:

> Instead of uniting, poor people competed ferociously with one another for gains as slender as they were provisional. And this under-city strife created only the faintest ripple in the fabric of the society at large. The gates of the rich, intermittently rattled, remained un-breached.

Caste is one critical variable to understand local slum divisions and slum hierarchies: 'Caste-based social networks significantly operate to exclude and segregate others that are not part of their caste. Access to resources is routed through caste-social networks' (Ayyar and Khandare n.d.: 22) so that those lowest in the caste hierarchy and already vulnerable by birth are excluded, limiting their access to important resources or 'life chances'.

The position and problems of women and girls

Where relevant I have already mentioned or hypothesised that poverty and slum life are most problematic for women and girls, be it in terms of toilets, access to schools or health care – with specific issues of reproductive health, sexuality, pregnancy, and motherhood. These itself already imply degrees of vulnerability different from those for men and boys. It is beyond the scope of this book to go deep into gender discourses, and I only refer to a useful basic classic distinction between 'practical versus strategic gender needs' (Moser 1995). The first 'practical needs' category comprises needs normally, but wrongly, attributed to women resulting from current divisions of labour in households – what is needed for cooking, child care, cleaning, washing, and looking after the sick and elderly – but which are, in reality, simply household needs. All members benefit if they are met; both men and women could do the work. We may find that women in the slums face the full double problem: neither are men much engaged in household chores at all, nor do women have good facilities to help them in a lot of tough, tedious, repetitive but unescapable duties. The value of all this is neither recognised nor rewarded. A second more fundamental category comprises 'strategic gender needs', which start from the subordination of women to men and associated structural and socio-economic patterns of women discrimination/exclusion, endorsed in dominant male-oriented patriarchal norms and values. Examples include that daughters inherit much less than sons; that property and loans are registered on the man's name; that women suffer from unequal power relations resulting in domestic violence, and that, in terms of 'voice', women are grossly under-represented in politics and governance. An additional notion is 'the triple role of women' (Moser 1995), which assumes that women are, by and large, mostly responsible for 'reproductive work'. This concerns conceiving, delivering and raising children, plus all household work such as cooking, washing and catching water from the tap or tanker. This, in many cases until such time that a daughter can start supporting – so that she too gets socialised (sometimes kept from school) into homework. In addition, poor women often have 'productive tasks' as many poor women work for wages, mostly in the informal sector (V. Patel n.d.: 15 mentions 92 per cent): domestic servants,[24] hawkers and small food shop owners, producing simple products like handicraft. Third, more than men, women are often charged with or take on 'community management work', where it is often the latter to keep an eye on all slum kids and interfere when needed, who clean the water tap area or gutters or engage with officials when they have business in a slum. It appears that mostly women are engaged in micro-credit or joint saving schemes and groups (or 'bishis') – and rarely men.

It is critical not to start from the notion that households are basically stable, harmonious and united units or that they are all the same. Rather, households are little arenas (power ranges from flexible to zero sum) by themselves with men, women, children, and often elderly people together shaping how things are done. One cannot generalise: one sees harmonious households with lots of sharing between men and women; there are more and more female-headed households where a husband has died (sometimes too early, e.g. due to alcoholism) or has eloped; some men spend all earnings on their families – others don't; most elderly live with children, but increasing numbers of old men and women are on their own and very poor. Against this backdrop, I now present what I found by way of evidence to understand the position of women and girls in the Mumbai slums and how men and women appear to relate to each other. Women already have a lot of work to keep their dwellings and adjacent areas in some order (MCGM 2009: 138).

In terms of health, MCGM (2009: 138) goes on to mention the bad news of an increase in the maternal mortality of women, which increased between 1995 and 2005 – but combined with the good news of a decline in the infant mortality rate. Sixty per cent of Mumbai women are anaemic (MCGM 2009:139). The key reason for maternal mortality is seen to be deterioration in nutrition standards, which in turn may be linked to the non-functional public distribution system (PDS). In addition, all over India, women and girls who cook such amazing food get to eat last with more chances to eat less. A programme that could and should be most useful for mothers and children is the National Integrated Child Development Scheme (ICDS) under which there are pre-school nurseries – 'anganwadis' – with the provision of food, managed by paid women. However, yet again, both at the national level and at the slum level things are not at all in a good shape. MCGM (2009: 142) mentions that coverage at the ICDS centres is poor and that not all centres that are sanctioned are functional. As additional evidence is scanty, I refer to an old source (Udupi *et al.* 2000: 25) to bring out the mechanisms:

ICDS is available in the slum, but awareness of it is low, 34 per cent of the children are covered under the scheme, but at the same time and in spite of the presence of a state scheme and staff, 49 per cent of the slum children are malnourished. There are 32 anganwadis, but overall 'parents are quite unhappy with the existing anganwadi's'. So they may send their children to a private nursery school, despite a higher financial burden, 'because they believe that the children will at least learn something'.

(Udupi *et al.* 2000: 24)

Even in this most critical and vulnerable area of mother and child welfare, where pregnant women are in need of all support, corrupt practices appear to exist as noted, in general, in the following quote. I have no specific evidence on Mumbai.

> Debroy and Bhandari (2012: 53–54) mention that 'in a typical *Anganwadi* centre, Rs. 1.200 to Rs. 1.500 is collected every month as a bribe'. It is paid by the centre leader to female observers, the Child Development Project Officer, then district social welfare office and officers in districts and divisions: 'this is a standardized and fixed bribe amount. In case a complaint is lodged, visits are made to the *Anganwadi* centre and the bribe amount increases'.

For very good reasons there is increasing recognition of the 'problems of the girl child', that very vulnerable category of girls to young women facing too many daily challenges and worries in households and cramped slums. Their personal ambitions may clash with household or community norms; they are socialised to get married, to be moved one day to an unknown husband and his household all alone. I refer to a case study (the Vacha study) mentioned in V. Patel (n.d.) as to the situation of a sample of girls attending municipal schools (i.e. they would be more likely poor or lower class):

> Vacha interviewed 2.600 girls in 33 BMC schools from 11 wards. . . . Among total number of girls, 13 per cent lived in Female Headed households, i.e. in those homes main economic burden of families was shouldered by widows, divorced, deserted and unmarried women. In many of these households, sons were in private schools & daughters in BMC schools. All girls interviewed helped in housework in terms of cooking, cleaning and caring, fetching water and getting ration from PDS. In the sample, 60 per cent of girls dropped out after class VII as they could not cope up with Mathematics, Science and English. Inadequate food intake, low Body Mass Index, proneness to accidents & illnesses, eye & dental problems were marked features of their lives. Whenever they fell ill, they were mostly given home remedies, not medical attention from qualified doctor. Vacha study also highlighted the absence of child resource centre in all wards of Greater Mumbai.

Patel (n.d.: 23) calls attention for the fact that women, more than men, bear the major brunt of the dislocation and relocation projects in Mumbai as a result of road and flyover construction, slum demolitions and abolition of informal-sector markets in the past decade. All in all, women and girls in the very heterogeneous Mumbai slums are quite vulnerable indeed and a small misfortune or misstep (as perceived by others) can have grave consequences. MCGM (2009: 250) and Patel (n.d.: 24) mention that the variety and intensity of crimes against girls and women in Mumbai have generally increased in a relative sense (rape of minors, outraging modesty, dowry-related mental and physical harassment, or suicides and rape) – indicating that the police data are likely to contain just the tip of the iceberg. One factor to explain the unbalanced Mumbai male–female sex ratio could be India-wide practices of female feticide. Khan (2013) confirms the rise in crimes and violence against women, referring to the class-biased publicity that different cases get.[25] Other crimes mentioned include child sexual abuse, abduction of adolescent girls for forced motherhood, begging, petty crimes, pornography, labour concentration camps, trafficking of girls and women for prostitution, bonded labour, and organ trade. Whereas state support for women is already extremely limited and misused on top of that, there are indications that the women's agenda and efforts to address gender inequality get a very low priority both in state and in the Indian union budgets. An article on 'A Budget for Women'[26] shows that union budget allocations for women- and children-focused programmes have been more or less stable over the past years (not growing), but 'schemes focussed exclusively on women either received reduced allocations, or were not implemented'. The allocation for ICDS is to be reduced from Rs 166 billion to Rs 86 billion.[27] Expenses on public health – which is more a concern for women than men – are budgeted to fall from Rs 220 billion to Rs 180 billion as compared to 2014.[28]

It is not surprising then that stress and the prevalence of common mental disorders are reported to be high among Mumbai's poor and low-income population, particularly women, however strong and 'resilient' they are projected to be (see Parkar *et al.* 2008). Factors to be mentioned here include multi-tasking; commuting in the over-crowded buses and trains; the triple burden of wage work; house work and child care and nurturance; conflicts in communities over water, electricity and toilets; and the possibility of ongoing sectarian violence on caste, ethnicity and communal lines within communities. But problems are not the same for all women; much depends on the specific place of the woman and the household in the socio-economic hierarchy of the slum community. Issues for a local leader's wife or the wife of a husband with a fixed job are very different, indeed, for those of a Dalit woman whose husband is a daily construction worker or hawker on an intermittent basis. But what about the men who have been in the background so far? Ultimately and however much agency we would like to attribute to women, men (fathers, husbands, sons) appear to be the key agents for women's welfare as things stand today.

Gender relations

Available scanty evidence from the Mumbai slums appears to indicate that gender relations there are similar to what I found in my Madras (Chennai) slum studies in the 1980s (de Wit 1985, 1996). Men and women jointly manage their households as best as they can, and with a bit of luck they are not faced with 'stress events' such as accidents and deaths – which would force them into the hands of brokers and unscrupulous moneylenders. Around this assumed idea or norm, there are all the myriad of variations. Many of them are problematic or negative, as well illustrated by the households in Boo's 2012 slum study, with all their ups and downs. People may react more to street-, community- and city-level events, opportunities or threats than being in control and able to 'exert agency' and make a plan to come up. Little is known about intra-household dynamics in the slums, but there is a sense that women are dominating the management of households – consistent with their assumed more 'private' roles, where men are active in the 'public domain'. Women tasks are many and often stretch from early morning until evening. There is no doubt that women form the backbone of households and sub/street-level communities, yet this is not recognised generally or articulated by themselves – even while women may be well capable to 'manage their husbands through what is called "pillow power" ' (field notes, 1 February 2005). Besides, 'women play a significant role in creating main and surplus income through their own networks. Women also have capabilities to manage inadequate income, create surplus income through saving groups and so on.' (Ayyar and Khandare n.d.: 21, 28). Consistent with an assumed division between 'public' and 'private or community' roles, the tasks of men seem generally less multifaceted and mostly 'productive' and 'public': earning incomes and safeguarding the upkeep and preferably the upward mobility of the household. It may be argued that this role expectation is a rather challenging one for poor slum men working in the informal sector, facing daily constraints to find work and adequate incomes. At the same time, men may be less prepared to face such hardships; boys seem more sheltered from hard work and sacrifice than girls. The latter's choices are limited, and they learn the hard way what it means to ultimately be a second-class citizen or household member. In my Chennai slum studies (de Wit 1996), I hypothesised that the incidence of alcoholism among slum men might be a function of the frustrations of some slum men to conform to the male ideal or role model of an effective father, protecting and uplifting his household.[29] I also recognised a link between slum status, where alcoholism seemed to be a bigger issue in more recently established, 'raw' slums without facilities and security, but there is no evidence to assess such detailed facts for Mumbai. The degree and impacts of alcoholism are not quite clear, but it is certain that alcoholism affects gender relations and the roles of men as per an old source:

> It emerged that most of the women in the street worked as domestic servants. But the men often contributed nothing even if they worked because they spent their money on drink – 'they drink alcohol!' (*'darupeetay hai!'*). Thus primary responsibility for supporting the household fell on women in the majority of households . . . a statement . . . repeated by women in both the other streets we visited. The men drink and spend most of their earnings on drink. . . . In probably 60 per cent of the households women are the main earners.
>
> (Kapadia 1996: 1436, 1440)

That alcoholism is a Mumbai slum issue was illustrated on 20 June 2015 when approximately 102 slum men died after consuming illicit alcohol. In the study by Shrivastava and Shrivastava (2013) involving a sample of 274 married Mumbai slum women, 35.4 per cent of the women reported that their husband was an alcoholic (67 per cent of these experienced domestic violence) and 64.5 per cent did not. Of the 97 alcoholic men, 63 per cent engaged in domestic violence and 37 per cent did not, according to the authors, showing a high causal relationship. All this is inter alia by no means to deny that alcoholism occurs or that there are problem drinkers among the more wealthy Mumbai classes. Overall the authors report a proportion of 36.9 per cent of domestic violence in the slums. The most common form of violence was verbal in 87 cases (86.1 per cent), followed by physical in 64 (63.4 per cent). MCGM (2009: 76) finds that alcohol use is higher at 36 per cent in slums than in non-slum areas at 29 per cent. Twenty-three per cent of women in slums have ever experienced spousal violence, which is higher than in non-slum areas at 15 per cent (MCGM 2009: 77). The main reason for women not to report the domestic violence was noted to be 'maintaining the integrity of the family', which relates to the patriarchal norms and values governing Indian family life. In their study of gender and suicide in a Mumbai general hospital, Parkar *et al.* (2008: 500) mention that 'alcohol and drug problems in the community are greater than the rates of alcohol and substance abuse suggest'. There are marked differences in the reasons that bring men and women to consider ending their lives:

> 'Men typically explained Deliberate Self Harm with reference to work problems, financial problems and problem drinking. Women typically discussed domestic problems, in-law relations and victimisation'. Problem drinking affected women living with men who drank. The authors argue that social and situational factors appear to play a relatively larger role than psychiatric illness in self-harm and suicide in Mumbai, as compared to other countries. The most important reasons for women's mental problems include problems with in-laws after marriage (21 per cent) and with their spouse (18 per cent).
>
> (Parkar *et al.* 2008: 504)

There is little, if any, research on the ways and means of men in Mumbai slums; they figure more in the background and come to life only as political agents, brokers, party cadre, and corporators as depicted later. There is a lack of detailed micro-level household studies to bring out the roles of slum men in decision making and in sharing child caring and education tasks which render the risks for unfounded generalisations on the domestic roles and attitudes of men considerable. Yet I like to explore one domain relevant to my preoccupation with the concept of and practices around patronage. There is reason to assume that it is a key task for men to carefully – and perhaps secretively – nurture essential vertical relationships with useful other men, brokers, agents, and politicians. Such relations are the best way to cheap credit, an informal deal or windfall or access to a hospital. They can also be maintained as some kind of insurance, say some sort of Plan B, not for normal days, but in case of a household crisis or accident or more broadly to have 'safeguards' in a sometimes menacing or hostile slum setting when features of crime, caste or religion may suddenly become an issue. This assumption is supported by Ayyar and Khandare (n.d.: 27):

> There are powerful social networks and weak social networks. Certain social networks (bridging) mainly those of men's networks access resources that are shared by the powerful in the network. Often the poor and the most vulnerable like single mothers, physically handicapped members, women, widows, divorcee women are excluded from processes, leading to increased vulnerabilities of the most vulnerable.

I will argue next that the horizontal option to engage in collective action hardly figures for slum men – in contrast to some NGOs and many academics who assume that community participation strategies can significantly contribute to wider poverty reduction (de Wit and Berner 2009). But there are indications that this differs for women (de Wit and Berner 2009: 941). Women are assumed not to engage in such vertical ties – even while there are examples of women corporators, local leaders, brokers, and moneylenders, but these seem rare (yet in the slum studied by Boo 2012 two ambitious local women leaders appear, so we need much more research on such patterns). Rather, women are perceived to be more able to form and sustain horizontal or group relationships, as has been documented in many examples of saving and credit and self-help groups and by Ayyar and Khandare (n.d.).[30] More support here is provided by Roy (2004: 165), who argues that 'masculinist patronage' forms the social basis of informality in Kolkata slums (see also Haritas 2008). Roy generally believes patronage is a key feature of slum life and politics, with a 'constant recharging of patronage', where before each major election, the colonies are treated to infrastructural improvements (Roy 2008: 149). Quoting from a revealing discussion between a wife and her husband:

> While he insisted on having garnered great political concessions from powerful men, his wife quietly complained about the back breaking work generated by the absolute lack of everything in the settlement: lack of water, lack of toilets, lack of livelihood. In Calcutta squatter settlements, masculinist patronage seals the deal. . . . Squatter men participate in club politics, transforming their once subordinate role as landless peasants into the possibilities of being an urban voter. . . . They participate in patronage politics as men, as patriarchal heads of households. . . . This participation in patronage allows for the simultaneous stabilization of regime and family, sealing the dependence of squatters on fickle minded political parties.
>
> (Roy 2008: 162–63)

But the slum women are not convinced about the efficacy of their husbands:

> We work all day and they stay at home. They have become just like the *babus* we work for. We are simultaneously men and women, earning for the household like a man and taking care of the house like a woman.

Of course I am not suggesting that slum men are always and everywhere actively searching for useful contacts, but it is more their domain and maybe more like making and maintaining useful friends – who in turn are 'friends of friends' and potential entries into useful coalitions (as pictured in the classic political anthropology study by Boissevain 1974).

3.5 Power in the slums and the scope for people's organisation

Slum powers

One might hypothesise that over the past decades a change has taken place in Mumbai slums from a situation where more traditional forms of 'authority' – as in a commonly accepted trust in and respect for local leaders and politicians – have been replaced by more hard and rough forms of 'power', and that the image of the local leader and politician has changed likewise. In relation to this, Hansen (in Gupte 2012: 200) framed the concept of 'infra-power', based on his work on Mumbai. It is defined as 'power from below', achieved through individual and/ or social agencies outside the state agencies, but it is much more than that. He argues that, apart from spatial dimensions, 'it is the non-obvious, non-formal, and often ephemeral forms of organisation, knowledge, connections, solidarity and mythology that organize and weave together urban localities, if not entire cities'. The concept is applied by Gupte (2012: 200) to explain why slum people may not contact formal state agencies or the police to solve urgent problems, such as threats, extortion or tenancy problems. For example, formal tenancy contracts with registration numbers and stamps and all are said by a lawyer to be worth nothing much: 'It is the verbal contracts with the local goonda which actually count' (Gupte 2012: 201). Such conditions apply, for example, to many chawls, in some of which no household has a formal contract and where their only contract is a verbal one with the local goonda. Local people know well who has power (Gupte 2012: 202); they recognise 'the power to get things done – an ability to bend or break the rules (laws) as one sees fit'. Such power has a basis on things such as proven toughness or performance, and as an example Gupte mentions a 'handyman' who says, or anyway is reputed, to have murdered seven persons. Such a power definition neatly fits the expected powers of MCs: 'Corporators with the highest status are those who provide the most for their core constituents and who are able to bend or break the most rules' (van Dijk 2011a: 38). Relevant here is a quote by Boo (2012: 28):

> In the West, and among some of the Indian elite, this word, *corruption* had purely negative connotations; it was seen as blocking India's modern, global ambitions. But for the poor of a country where corruption thieved a great deal of opportunity, corruption was one of the genuine opportunities that remained.

Yet such power is invisible and can be held and exercised incidentally or over a longer time; 'it specifies an agency outside of the formal channels, sovereignty beyond the state, know-how of the city not only to get things done, but importantly also to provide security in times of need.' Infra-power can translate in the 'good things of life' for the already powerful (money, bars, girls). For the poor access and linking to such power can mean protection from violence, a secure place to live and access to employment. Importantly, non-state infra-power is seen to be held by formal state agencies and actors such as policemen, labour union leaders and politicians too – including corporators (Boo 2012: 203).

The logic of difficult collective slum organisation

A final question to address here is whether the urban poor are organising in any effective way to solve their myriad of problems – some individual, some collective – can they join forces to command power if only in numbers? I have discussed such prospects for mobilisation and participation elsewhere (de Wit and Berner 2009), arguing that it is easier, more rational and hence more effective for poor people to individually contact intermediaries than to engage in collective action. This is for all the known reasons of a lack of time and information; free rider issues; divided communities (listed before), and lacking a common, uniform platform or ideology. But the most important factor seems a lack of un-selfish, committed and reliable local leaders, who sincerely want to represent and support their followers. Local, street and neighbourhood leaders, party workers, and social workers in my view all operate through a 'vertical Patronage logic'. They convey requests, information and informal/illegal payments and earnings up and down between slum people, party bosses and corporators. Opportunities to engage in collective action are again smaller for the

poor(est) and those of lowest caste, leading first from their more limited numbers and reputation as 'minority', while being hampered by
lower aspirational mindsets and social handicaps listed in Chapter 1.
The number of successful and sustained community-based actions and
groups seems very limited, as confirmed by Das (2003: 226, 229). He
feels that slum dweller organisations have failed to develop and sustain
committed leadership to take on the 'short-term opportunism of vested
interests'. Factors listed include the heterogeneity of the Mumbai slum
population, levels of aspirations and the location of a slum. And while
it may be easier to discuss concrete issues of toilets, water and land
rights with people and perhaps mobilise them, this is much more difficult and rare for actually more important structural issues as health
policy, communalism, inflation, or informal-sector wages regulation.
Das (2003) argues that ultimately the basis of slum organisations is a
focus on material gains, which weakens them and their struggles while
making them 'vulnerable to donations and largesse in various forms'. I
understand this to include patronage-based, top-down/vertically provided benefits, for example prior to elections. These again undermine
any horizontal local mobilisation of the poor around concrete grievances and the deeper determinants of their poverty and lack of welfare:

> The relationships between organizations and slum dwellers are
> often weak and short lived. . . . These severe restrictions to con-
> tinuing political work allow opportunists and self-styled leaders to
> gain ground and continue with their petty machinations, contrary
> to the larger interests of the struggle. . . . Das provides the example
> of the Slum Rehabilitation Scheme as an example of a project that
> brings about an arena which divides communities, and which pro-
> duces self-styled leaders who claim to represent slum communities
> and who associate with various agents, developers and builders,
> inducing corruption.
>
> (Das 2003: 228; see Desai and de Wit 2007)[31]

It appears as if the good organisational work carried out by NGOs
such as SPARC and YUVA in the past is no longer so prominent or
effective. It is beyond the scope of this book to deal with this, other
than to say that the work of NGOs, however useful, cannot be a sub-
stitute for state action. Desai (2002: 127) is not quite appreciative of
the NGOs working with the Mumbai slum residents. NGOs are seen
as unable to build strong networks or share experiences and ideas; they
have a limited reach with reports on 'distant rivalry and competition
amongst them'. On the whole, 'the overall impact of NGO activities

has been, more or less minimal'. A larger, more complex issue here is noted by Kumar and Landy (2009: 128) in that the concept of 'civil society' is hard to apply when a state and state–society relations are very 'porous'. This makes the distinction between the state (retired officials may start NGOs), politicians (who may start their own 'CBOs' with slum-level political allies or cronies – as illustrated by de Wit 2010a[32]) and the amorphous category of 'civil society' very complex. Most collective action by the urban poor appears to be defensive in nature, for example large protests against the Mumbai mass slum evictions of 2005, both at the level of brave people facing the police and bulldozers and massive rallies to accuse and protest against the state. In contrast, 'offensive', or claim-making action seems rare, just like the willingness to organise in the context of a slum programme. There is an interesting case in Anand and Rademacher (2011: 1756) reflecting on the efforts of Mumbai civil society organisations and their frustrations to work with the urban poor. It confirms the complex challenges to work with poor slum people as I experienced myself while working in Bangalore in a Dutch-funded project aimed to establish partnerships between city agencies, slum NGOs and newly created slum CBOs (de Wit 2002). What started as an ambitious initiative to 'enhance the claim making powers of slum people' through 'empowerment and participation' gradually came to be seen and used by slum people and their local leaders as a vehicle for picking selected benefits and an access channels to city agencies. It made us wonder whether there is such a thing as 'progressive patronage' (de Wit and Berner 2009):

> For activists who have a history of sympathizing and working with settlers, contemporary settler [*slum dweller, jdw*] politics and strategies are often deeply troubling. Many settlers, motivated by the promise of financial gain, no longer align themselves with the long-term goals for which activists have long fought on their behalf. Pratibha Tai is one of the many housing activists disillusioned with the current state of housing politics in the city. She is seeking other channels of legitimacy these days, as she explained in a 2007 interview: 'Our NGO does not work directly in *bastis* [slums] anymore,' she said, 'after working for so many years organizing people, *morchas* [protest marches], getting them ration cards, starting groups, our work got appropriated by political parties . . . They [settlers] were smarter than us. They took our help for ration cards, got papers and now tell us it's ok – that we are not needed – they will handle their matters on their own.' "Pratibha conveyed an acute sense of betrayal and disappointment that

after spending years helping organize the residents of Sitawadi, they seemed to have abandoned her NGO for political parties. Yet embedded in her narrative of a weakened housing rights movement was also some evidence of its own compromised success'.

(Anand and Rademacher 2011: 1756)

Obviously, this is just one voice and can only be seen as anecdotal evidence. None of this is to deny that today many NGOs work in Mumbai slums, but it seems as if they keep a lower profile while engaging in basic but critical work. Distinctions between NGO workers and 'social workers' who can be active at election time (Chapter 5) may not always be so clear. Over time I noted activities such as supporting the proper implementation of available schemes, supporting people as regards the judiciary or high court and filing public interest litigation cases. Starting from local needs, they may be both engaged in service delivery and advocacy issues such as education, health, and women rights. I see an important function as 'watchdog' too – an outsider engaging with the slum, hopefully noting and acting on cases of individual or community anxiety or suffering. All in all, we may safely assume that the urban poor are pragmatic people – investing their time and attention in the most promising options, sometimes an NGO or CBO, sometimes joining a 'morcha' or simply contacting the Shiv Sena *shakha* and seek support there. Most social and political mobilisation presently occurs through parties (most effectively by the Shiv Sena and MNS with their decentralised, grassroots presence as elaborated in Chapter 5). This goes to show that party appeal and the deep-felt appreciation and adoration for charismatic, if not populist, party leaders like the Shiv Sena Thackeray family, is a consistent component of mobilizing (poor, heterogeneous) people as voters, which is in turn consistent of the 'machine politics perspective'.[33] And people can be mobilised and get genuinely enthusiastic when they see and feel that a candidate is actually with and for them. This happened in 2014 to slum activist Medha Patkar who was an MP election candidate for the Aam Aadmi Party in North Mumbai. The case goes to show that people are quite willing to organise and invest once they recognise a candidate they like and trust (Punwani 2014: 13): 'She never asked us for money'; 'we feel we have a stake in her campaign'; 'it is our loss if we don't elect her.' This points to the extremely important role of proper leadership for achieving poverty-reducing impacts, but such leadership is only too rare and seems to be throttled and bended to adjust to a dominant politicised and vertical patronage

logic. The calibre of many candidates in elections is low or even suspect, which obviously hinders mobilisation and true representation.

So I can agree that Indian cities are 'fast emerging as critical zones of
contestation', with a miniscule but exceedingly powerful global society and a huge majority of marginalised and dispossessed as seen by
Banerjee-Guha (2009: 106). But I am not convinced that we witness
'claims by the dispossessed, struggling for entitlement and alternatives'
as a response to an aggressive, neoliberal discourse and praxis by the
corporate sector and the rich, in what she calls 'repressive and revan-
chist urbanism'. These claims seem rather invisible. Similarly I have
my doubts regarding Weinstein and Ren's assessment (2009: 426) that,
even in an electoral democracy, the struggles around the right to the
city are only partially grounded in electoral politics. In my view, the
more frequent instances 'direct agitations, public protests, and legal
petitions', they see as the way in which political presence is asserted in
the context of urban renewal are only too rare where the urban poor
are concerned. I would argue that there is not much significant and
successful action beyond or unconnected to electoral party politics, by
and large the only game in town.

3.6   Basic services for the urban poor and the role of the police

By way of initial introduction, I quote from a survey among Mumbai's
urban poor (Karn *et al.* 2003: 3585), which paints a rather grim picture of slum conditions some time ago, but I am afraid not much has
changed for the better.

> In this respect, living environment of urban poor could be basi-
> cally characterised by nearly 70 per cent households living in
> flimsy shacks and temporary dwellings, 2 sq. meter housing space
> per person, 28 LPCD water consumption, 1.5 per cent households
> having access to sewer and only half of the people having access
> to toilets. Similarly, health status were shown as nearly 11 per
> cent people sick at any point of time; and TB and asthma patients
> numbering as many as 18 and 11 per thousand population respec-
> tively. The annual cases of water-related disease such as diarrhoea,
> typhoid and malaria is estimated as 61.468; 126 cases per thou-
> sand of population respectively.

Such statements conceal large differences between a variety of
slum types as noted, and more details are provided in this section

to confirm the overall scenario. But all slums are affected by the weather, and I may first note the importance of weather and location. Any slum may not look so bad or inhospitable on a sunny day in October. But go to that area after a few weeks of heavy monsoon rains, and the picture flips into a dismal one of leaking roofs, toilets now completely overflowing, slipping your way through small slum lanes, pools everywhere. Now one understands why some slums or slum pockets always looked poorer and less developed: these are low-lying areas or areas prone to annual flooding. This is where more desperate (recent/migrant) households decided to set up shelter, with all associated daily headaches and bouts of misery. In contrast, the sweltering hot Indian summers and occasional heat waves are a major concern for slum people who often lack fans and where refrigerators and air conditioners are rare and limited to richer households. With women and girls slum homemakers, such outside conditions impact them most. And, in terms of labour, slum men who probably work outside a lot are much more affected by the weather than middle-class men.

Against this background a review of services is presented here which may or may not be provided by various agencies – but foremost the BMC – to the Mumbai slums. Housing and slum (improvement) policies over time are examined at the end of this chapter. I may repeat once more that poverty is not just a lack of incomes/assets but that the level and quality of basic services critically impact the degree and misery of poverty. If any state provides good, cheap/free services, many people would not be that poor and would have some safety-net feeling as if they could never fall too deep into misery or destitution – but India does not provide such a security or some 'bottom floor' at all. One can fall quite deep indeed; one is utterly helpless if devoid of money or contacts. This aspect is addressed by Manecksha (2011: 27) mentioning that 62 per cent of the children in an eastern suburb of Mumbai are malnourished. She notes the irony that slum people spend a large proportion of their earnings on basic services 'which the BMC can legally provide at regular rates'. For the all-India level these dynamics are recognised by the GOI/Planning Commission (2011: 14), which notes that out-of-pocket expenditure for health pushes individuals further into poverty. Data from the 61st Round NSS survey show an increase in urban poverty by as much as 2.9 per cent if out-of-pocket health expenditure is accounted for. Maharashtra is mentioned as one of the states showing high out-of-pocket health expenditure as a cause for significant increases in urban poverty.

Water

Just like in housing, also where basic services and infrastructure are concerned there is a marked difference between formal and mostly adequate supply to more well-off people and the more informal and inadequate supply to the masses of people in Mumbai's slums. While Mumbai must be complimented for having an excellent water supply system, only 18 per cent of urban poor households have access to piped water at home – as against 92 per cent for non-slum households (MCGM 2009: 71). The municipality does provide water to notified slums, but mostly through shared community taps – and sometimes by contracting water tankers to bring water, after which residents (women) line up and obtain vessels against a small payment. Boo (2012: 53) mentions that in the slum she studied, the BMC supplied limited amounts of water through the slum faucets for 90 minutes in the morning and 90 at night, with people lining up for a long time. 'Local Shiv Sena party men had appropriated the taps, charging user fees to their neighbours' – yet another example of the informal privatisation of a public service. Where BMC water supply is insufficient or not available, slum households resort to private water suppliers. All in all water expenditures for slum households are higher than for better-off households 'because of indigenous arrangements made by users, paying exorbitant prices to private suppliers' (MCGM 2009: 71). But realities are more complex than this, and micro-level evidence shows that individuals or groups of slum households may succeed in organising a satisfactory and relatively reliable supply of water. Arrangements here are informal and critically rely on the support of the local corporator, who, as in the supply of other basic services, has the power to influence and align all stakeholders involved: the plumber making an illegal connection, relevant BMC officials and local slum leaders (Anand 2011a, 2011b; Bjorkman 2013).

Toilets, sanitation and solid waste management

It is already a bit of misfortune to live in a crowded area, in small houses with flimsy walls in which all household activities – from children learning to cooking to sleeping and sex – have to take place. It is yet another felt disgrace – especially in India with pronounced notions of status-linked purity – to have to line up each morning with a bit of water to visit one of the few slum toilets, which, again, is more problematic for women than men. It has been documented that there should be 125,055 'seats', but there are only about half of that (a deficit of 64,157 slum-level toilet seats (MCGM 2009: 74). Slum dwellers face a massive problem as regards toilets, be they poor or not too poor. As per the MCGM (2009: 72), 82 per cent of non-slum households have access to toilets; this is only the case for 47 per cent of Mumbai's urban poor. Census data indicate that 75 per cent of non-slum households have a toilet in their homes; this is only 32 per cent for slum households.[34] It is no surprise then that 79 per cent of slum households share a toilet, and a YUVA survey showed that 73 per cent depend on 'public toilets', where, on average, 81 persons make use of each seat (the range is from 58 to 273 persons/seat: MCGM: 72). McFarlane (2008: 94) mentions that six million people live in Mumbai's informal settlements, crammed into 1,959 slums and occupying 8 per cent of the land, and that 63 per cent of the city population or 3.9 million people exclusively depend on public toilets. That is already bad enough, but sadly, most of such public toilet blocks (or 'public convenience units') are in poor to very poor condition. Indeed, the city is littered with underused, unused, broken, or dysfunctional units, where universal key problems are non/insufficient water, non-cleaning and non-maintenance. Only 14 per cent of all public toilets do have adequate water; elsewhere people bring their own water. So they are overused, unhygienic and (should be) in fact unusable. People may be forced to defecate in the open, which is quite normal for children, embarrassing for men and very difficult, even risky for women and girls, if only as men may be watching them (see for an overview of actual realities Tiwari 2015).

Health

In view of the multiple risks and deprivations they face, one would hope for targeted health interventions for the urban poor and then especially for women and girls. Compared to men, they are the main agents of health care in households and arguably more vulnerable to diseases due to lesser food intake, their vulnerable reproductive system and specific delivery and maternal needs. But slum conditions are a health concern for men and women alike:[35]

> Information on maternal and child health indicators among slum-dwellers shows that their health conditions are 2 to 3 times worse than the average health levels in other urban areas in the state of Maharashtra. . . . According to estimates, health agencies are only reaching roughly 30 per cent of the urban poor – that too in comparatively less poor slums. For example, a study conducted

by Nair Hospital in an urban slum located in E Ward (Byculla) found that 44 per cent of new born babies had low birth weight compared to 21 per cent, [which is] the state average for the rest of urban Maharashtra. In another slum called Cheeta Camp in M-East ward (Chembur), three quarters of the women in the reproductive age group were anaemic, compared to the state average of 49 per cent in Maharashtra. The report notes that the actual situation in slum pockets is not clear. Unplanned deliveries, delays in reaching health facilities and deliveries by untrained personnel all contribute to injuries and loss of life during birth. These problems persist despite the concentration and proximity of public and private health facilities.

Other disturbing facts revealing a grossly inadequate health care system for the poor – in current 'Millennium or Sustainable Development Goal' times – are that only 62 per cent of mothers in slums receive post-natal care within two days of the last birth compared to 77 per cent in non-slum Areas. Slum children are slightly less likely to have been fully immunised than non-slum children. Due to nutritional deficiencies, children are 14 per cent more likely to be stunted in slums than in the non-slum areas and about 40 per cent are more likely to be underweight (MCGM 2009: 76). Public hospitals and nursing homes are stretched to their limits, leading to all staff being overworked, stressed and almost unavoidably less friendly (MCGM 2009: 112).

> Raja was one of the few slum dwellers in the slum studied by Boo with a permanent job as a public toilet cleaner, until he collapsed one day. 'His heart was bad. The sanitation department laid him off, saying that if he got a new heart valve and a doctor's clearance, he could return. Mumbai's public hospitals were supposed to do such operations for next to nothing, but the hospital surgeons wanted under-the table money. Sixty thousand rupees said the surgeon at Sion Hospital. The doctor at Cooper Hospital wanted more.'
>
> (Boo 2012: 24; for an account of the appalling conditions inside Cooper hospital: 99–100)

Kennedy *et al.* (2009: 174) refer to a recent study indicating that public services remain inadequate for the poor in Mumbai. Nearly one-third of reported ailments remained untreated; high levels of malnutrition persist among children and women in the reproductive age; inconvenient locations of health post hinder their accessibility. They (Kennedy *et al.* 2009: 174) refer to a long tradition where hospitals were managed by non-profit charitable trusts. From the 1970s these have been 'corporatised', which coincided with a massive expansion of private hospitals. The MCGM report (2009: 111) confirms this, adding that presently the business houses are actively exploring health care as a profit industry. More generally India witnesses processes of commercialisation of health care, where it has become a commodity and less of a public good: 'Medical care is turned into an "industry" whose primary purpose is to make the highest levels of profit . . . doctors are becoming less of professionals and more of businessmen.'[36] Over the past decades, the growth of the public hospital sector in Mumbai declined in proportion to population growth. Kennedy *et al.* (2009: 174) give the impression that this is linked to a decrease in the level of curative care: 'By the 1990s, curative care was being neglected in Mumbai, most notably by underfinancing such care in public hospitals' and as a result of the introduction of enhanced user fees. They note that 'the BMC clearly favours privatisation' (Kennedy *et al.* 2009: 174) as caused by both supply and demand factors. Policymakers and government officials are seen to have a mindset oriented to a belief that the private sector has a large role to play in health care, while paucity of state budgets results in pressure to reduce state health care inputs. Today, patients often have to pay for their own medicines and diagnostic tests in public health care and user charges are being paid. It may already be noted here that it is common for the poor to contact corporators to intercede in their favour to obtain access to BMC hospitals (Kennedy *et al.* 2009: 175). According to the PRAJA 2014a Health White Paper, less than 25 per cent of Mumbai's people use government dispensaries and hospitals; a majority uses private facilities.[37] As a result, we see a very clear and major shift from a traditional public health care system towards a dominant private health care system.[38] But while private hospitals and nursing homes far outnumber public health services, they too do not succeed to deliver sufficient quality health care in terms of patients and locations, with a clear divide in that facilities are available more in rich city wards. Ward D (a rich, island city ward) with a population of 388,000 people has 85 private nursing homes and 7 hospitals; ward H/East with 694,000 people and 75 per cent slum dwellers only has 35 nursing homes (MCGM 2009: 121). The report notes that these private facilities are often far too expensive for the poor households, 'who nevertheless resort to them as the public facilities are inadequate', representing a cruel choice for poor people faced with health problems. But the report also notes that the poor may compromise: 'For the lowest income group, accessibility and affordability is a more important a consideration than quality' (MCGM 2009: 123).

Education

Just like with health, also in education a clear pattern can be discerned of an increasing proliferation of more expensive and often better-quality private education institutions. One sees a gradual decline in quality and numbers of currently less popular and less well-reputed public or municipal schools. In spite of massive and growing numbers of urban poor and migrant children, such nominally free schools are hardly growing. The BMC has the mandate to cater to the education needs of all its citizens, but from the perspective of the poor it is failing them miserably. This, in spite of the Right of Children to Free and Compulsory Education Bill 2008 and the 86th Amendment of the Constitution of India in 2002, where universal primary education was included in the ambit of Fundamental Rights under Chapter III of the Constitution.[39]

As per the 2001 Census, literacy rates in Mumbai were 82 per cent for men and 72 per cent for women. Overall literacy rate for Greater Mumbai was 77 per cent in 2001 (Patel n.d.: 7). The highest female literacy of 80 per cent was found in C-ward (a rich ward in island city), and the lowest female literacy of 58.4 per cent was found in M-east ward – the ward with most slums and the highest number of relocated households. The BMC runs 1,188 schools, which enrol over 600,000 students, half of whom are girls. But all is not well with education for the urban poor. In their study into financial inclusion in four Mumbai slums, Bhatiya and Chatterjee (2010: 24) find that 49 per cent of the respondents had not received any education. Twenty per cent had studied up to class 5; 25 per cent from classes 6 to 10 and only 6 per cent had managed to study in class 11 and above. In contrast, MCGM (2009: 94) mentions that the number of out-of-school children in Mumbai is very small, only about 5–6 per cent. It points to large variations, where in areas without schools – mostly again in the M-ward – 35 per cent of children are out of school. Municipal schools face severe constraints, due to very limited budgets or budgets not spent well. There is a lack of play grounds, classrooms can be extremely crowded amid reports that teachers may not always show up (in India generally this is the case on any given day for 25 per cent of primary school teachers as mentioned by Patibandla 2013: 59).[40]

Many schools work in two shifts, where a classroom is used twice a day. Boo (2012: 63) notes:

> Nearly 60 percent of the state's government school teachers hadn't finished college, and many of the permanent teachers had paid large under-the-table sums to school officials to secure their positions. The Corporator was among the politicians who preferred to capitalize on these abysmal schools instead of reforming them. Among the business interests he tended on the site was a government-aided private school.

For a fascinating case study of the problems faced by an NGO running an informal school in a community of mostly Muslim Biharis in East Mumbai see Saigal 2008). She nicely brings out community dynamics and mind-sets, as well as the socio-cultural and identity dilemma's faced by the women teacher.

The public distribution system

In principle, the poor – but also non-poor – who have a ration card are eligible to purchase basic foodstuffs such as rice, wheat, oil, and kerosene from PDS 'ration shops', which, in theory, would be a great support for poor households. Unfortunately, most reports on the PDS system are negative, with Kumar and Landy (2009) arguing that the PDS is not so public: 'Not everybody has access to it, and there is an informal "privatisation" of the system through stealthy appropriation of resources . . . in favour of shopkeepers, traders, corrupt officials and politicians' (Kumar and Landy 2009: 110). It is hard to obtain a card through formal, official channels (in one Mumbai slum one-third of inhabitants had no card; in another slum only 1 per cent had a card). They stress – as I did before – that a ration card is an important identity proof, a tool of survival for those living in illegal slums and especially important for Muslims as it 'proves their Indian nationality' (Kumar and Landy 2009: 110). In Mumbai, cards can be obtained by paying Rs 5,000–8,000[41] or more depending on the degree of forging to be done. Kumar and Landy present a fascinating study of the real working of the PDS system in terms of a 'corruption chain', with known and clear ways to allocate the bribes (Kumar and Landy 2009: 116) and shrewd people investing to be part of the lucrative system. Once in, they necessarily have to collect bribes to repay their investments and gain a profit in the bargain. An earlier slum-level micro-study by Udupi *et al.* (2000: 22) confirms severe PDS problems. For 93,000 people, there were 12 outlets, but common problems included irregular supply of essentials, poor-quality food stuffs, malpractice by shopowners, lack of storage space, un-cooperative users, and violence and intimidatory tactics. It seems fair to conclude that a system meant for BPL people hardly reaches them, that apparently many benefits and monies disappear in the wrong hands and that money-minded stakeholders such as corporators who have no formal role in PDS are anyway benefiting by partly controlling it (Kumar and Landy 2009: 113–14). As one example of 'how the poor are being robbed in the name of welfare and graft', Debroy and Bhandari (2012: 51) explain that an incentive towards leakage is built into the PDS system, as it is too easy and too attractive *not* to sell the subsidised food stuffs in the open market, which immediately yields good money. And here too, it is impossible to obtain a licence for a PDS price shop without political contacts.

Justice, security and the police

In her classic text, Wratten (1995: 24, see also Narayan 2000) addresses the general problem of poor urban people's vulnerability arising from the non-intervention of the state and police. She argues that the urban poor will have more contact with state agents and the police than their rural counterparts and that the former experience the state in negative ways. This can be both an elusive and oppressive bureaucracy, which attempts to regulate the urban poor's activities without understanding their needs. The state can also appear as corrupt or venal policemen, demanding money in order to turn a blind eye to illicit income-generating activities such as brewing or prostitution – rather than as servants of the public. These remarks tally well with what is known of urban poor–police relations and interactions in Mumbai and, unfortunately also more generally, of India's justice or security systems. According to D. Kapur[42] in a general Indian assessment:

> 'For most citizens, laws are invisible; their encounter with the justice system is foremost with the police, a venal and demoralised arm of the state, equally reviled and derided until it is most needed'. He goes on to say that if there is one principle that unites 'the principals of the police and politicians of all hues and stripes, it is that a competent, autonomous police force is a threat to their common interest'.

A very serious ambivalence surrounds the Mumbai system of law and order for poor people. Manecksha (2011: 27) captures this by referring to the implementation of SRS programmes, where, she feels, thousands of slum people are being evicted but not rehabilitated. People are forced to start from scratch often in 'fresh slum colonies' without the necessary documents. It is pointed out that they 'are forced to take recourse to government officials and the police, when it is this very section that is denying them justice'. While one would hope the police to defend the weak against the strong and powerful, precisely the opposite seems to be the case in a rather cruel, unfair irony. The Maharashtra police do not exactly have a good reputation, which was confirmed, for example, in Anti-Corruption Bureau (ACB) figures.[43] The police is mentioned as the most corrupt government department for 10 years, with examples mentioned such as the practices of 'encounter killings' and policemen 'forcing small-time businessmen to cough up money from ATMs'. According to the National Crime Records Bureau, 1,418 ('reported') custodial deaths took place in India between 1999 and 2013, with around 23 per cent of these (or 333) from Maharashtra. For most of the past 15 years the state topped custodial death charts. What is worse – but confirming my impression that the chance to have some sort of justice decreases along with one's social status – the people dying in custody almost certainly after horrendous torture are almost invariably poor minority persons, notably Dalits and Muslims. An article[44] referred to the query of the Mumbai High Court as to why the victims of custodial deaths in Maharashtra are only from minorities:

> Observing that custodial deaths are occurring routinely, the High Court added, 'It seems to be happening only against certain persons from the minority community'. A division bench of Justices V M Kanade and P D Kode made the remark after they informed advocate Yug Chaudhry of their decision to appoint him as amicus curiae (friend of the court) in a case where a 23-year-old resident of Nalasopara (East) mysteriously died in Thane Central Jail. Chaudhry answered: 'I have done my research and it shows that the cases are mostly of Muslims and Dalits'. The court questioned why such deaths are happening in Maharashtra. Referring to the case at hand, it said, 'It is not reported as a custodial death but as a natural death'. The number of such cases is unknown, the court noted.

Mumbai reported 40 cases of custodial deaths in 2011 alone. Shockingly, 'among these, 32 of these accused had not been remanded in police custody by a court, pointing to alleged illegal detention by cops'.

One such case was a 35-year-old man, allegedly tortured to death at the Dharavi police station on 2 December 2012. A lawyer is quoted to say that the conviction rate for policemen in such cases was almost zero, 'fuelling a blatant violation of human rights by the police'.[45] While it is certainly helpful that a court worries about this, judges are no policymakers (where it has been noted, for India, that it is not rare that courts instead of ministries or states – ultimately – decide on policy matters). So poor people have all reasons to stay away from the police and to avoid at all cost to end up in a police cell. They would be utterly and hopelessly at the mercy of tough, insensitive, indifferent officers who may join to 'interrogate' a 'suspect' of whom they know very well, or made sure, that he or she has no connections of importance to worry about. This explains why family members of a 'suspect' will rush to the police station to affect the release, but they will not normally be entertained: 'Who are you? We don't know you.'[46] Almost always someone 'in the know' has to be brought, which could start by contacting the ward corporator, or through him a local leader/social worker. The police may demand upward of Rs 5,000 for releasing the suspect; the mediator takes up from Rs 1,000 (personal communication, NGO worker 24 February 2012).

So while a lot of harm is being done to poor people in police stations, it is not that the Mumbai police make the streets safer for poor people. I already mentioned cases where a policeman raped a middle-class college girl and another law-keeping officer raping a teenage rag-picker six months later.[47] More broadly it appears as if the police have a stake in condoning illegal activity, as this is precisely when people are most insecure and vulnerable and bribes can best be demanded.[48] Hansen (2001: 151) argues that:

> postings at certain stations can be strenuous, full of hard work and danger, but also a source of considerable rewards and bribes from the brisk flesh trade and drug economy in parts of central Mumbai. . . . The police departments depend vitally, therefore, on their networks of neighbourhood informants, networks that are created and maintained through an on-going flow of *hafta* (literally means 'weekly', as slang for local bribes) and other economic transactions.

An illegal bar with bar girls may happily be open all the time, paying a weekly or monthly *hafta* to the police. The police may even sometimes stage a raid, but it is all stage managed for the benefit of the public (and media), showing the police being active (field notes Malad,

15 June 2006). For the poor who are engaged in hawking or who have road-side stalls, the police are mostly seen as money makers.[49] Well-entrenched 'everyday corruption' systems exist in deals and negotiations between illegal hawkers, municipal workers and the police, where hawkers pay *hafta* as a set fee or a portion of merchandise to conduct business and survive. This affects a lot of poor people where it is estimated that 2 per cent of Mumbai's people are engaged in street vending, while an estimated Rs 4 billion is collected from them by municipal and police officials (Ayyar 2013: 52). Policemen may start to like one's restaurant and come over frequently to eat free of charge. They got the power; they won't go away: refusing is risky. Boo's (2012) slum study provides fascinating micro-level observations as to how the police act in a case of suspected murder, how they look for witness statements that suit them and how miserable conditions are in a court and city jail. She (Boo 2012: 107) quotes Abdul as thinking 'the Indian criminal justice system was a market like garbage, Abdul now understood. Innocence and guilt could be bought and sold like a kilo of polyurethane bags'. One observer makes a comparison between the formal police as a formal government institution and the obviously informal area-based local slum lords as part of the mafia. He raises the uncomfortable question as to whether the mafia could be more reliable than the police:

> Like governments, the mafia too collects protection money. But, unlike bad governments, it is honour-bound to protect those from whom it has taken the money. As a result, when a girl is under threat of molestation in a slum, her father would prefer to go to the local slumlord and request him to protect his daughter, than approach the police station. The mafia earns this respect because it actually protects its constituency – using both legal and extra-legal methods. Not surprisingly, when this slumlord stands for elections, his constituency will vote for him, irrespective of how many police cases the state may have filed against him. For the slum-dwellers, he is the protector, not the police, not even the government. But, sadly, if the slumlord does get elected, there will soon be a new contender for 'slumlord-ship' in the same constituency. Obviously, the contender will have to demonstrate that he can be trusted much more than the government, which now has the former slumlord as one of its representatives. If the 'good' old slumlord who got elected also gets tarnished by the smear of bad governance, shouldn't it be time for us to sit back and ask: why does a 'good' slumlord become ineffective and tainted once he

becomes part of the government? Is there something in the government that allows people to become protectors while they are not in government, but get transformed into oppressors when they become part of the government?[50]

3.7 Slum and low-income housing policies

As an interim conclusion, it can be noted from the earlier discussion that social and welfare slum policies in Mumbai leave a lot to be desired. Sadly, rather than supporting poor people, they become benefits to struggle and pay for, contributing to exclusion (e.g. where the police seems to target already vulnerable minorities more) instead of than inclusion. Whereas policy or provisions exist on paper and in budgets, they reach the poor only in limited, distorted ways, after cuts and bribes have been deducted and often only after mediation. To complete this chapter, I will consider the slum and low-income housing policies of Mumbai over time, in order to understand as to whether the local state has looked after the poor in terms of shelter and habitat more broadly.

Early years

All large Indian cities faced fast growth following independence, and the years 1950–70 saw a massive increase in the number of slums and slum dwellers. Initially slum people were considered illegal squatters, and demolitions and evictions were the norm. The general response was to 'clear' the slums (de Wit 1985, 1996: 53ff.). Over time a gradual (World Bank–supported) policy shift took place towards slum improvement and arrangements to recognise/register/legalise slums from the early 1970s into the 1980s. The adoption of the Maharashtra Slum Areas (Improvement, Clearance and Redevelopment) Act 1971 is one example here (Desai 2002: 102; the government not as a provider but facilitator). A Slum Improvement Department was established in the BMC, and basic amenities were provided in slums. Slum dwellers were given photo passes, evidence for some form of recognition. The first ever 1976 slum survey reported 1,671 slums with 2.8 million slum dwellers (Desai 2002: 114). But the Slum Upgrading Programme resulting from the policy change was no success. Against its plans to cover 100,000 households, only 22,000 households benefited (Desai 2002: 193). One reason may have been the way the Urban Land Ceiling Act was implemented in Mumbai – and which, according to Narayanan (2003), benefited the large landowners, the big builders and developers and industry as well as politicians and officials.[51] She mentions that government-constructed housing declined from 4,000 to 1,500 units a year between 1970 and the late 1980s. The shortfall was met by the private sector, whose share in housing increased from 50 to 90 per cent, much of it obviously informal slum housing. Anand and Rademacher (2011: 1769) note that MHADA constructed only 4,000 flats a year in Mumbai since its inception in 1977, with the number decreasing in the last two decades (see Desai 2002: 94 for an overview of all housing provided). And while state agencies acquired only very little land for public housing, large land areas were quietly purchased by large building firms. These had prior knowledge that such land – which was frozen under the NDZ status of 'no development' in the city's DP – would be de-reserved sometime in the future: 'We have our own 'links' inside the GoM' (Desai 2002: 91). The then small landowners sold cheaply as there would be no development and large profits were made following the de-reservation, which made possible large private housing schemes (Desai 2002: 88; Nainan 2012 on de-reservation policy). In 1988–91 the powerful Chief Minister Sharad Pawar ruled the state with the then undivided Congress party, which, according to Nainain (2012) marked the beginning of a neoliberal regime.[52] His government introduced legislation and policies allowing for a larger role for private landowners in slum redevelopment (Nainain 2012: 240), while actively de-reserving land which now opened up for private investment (Nainan 2012: 87): 'Such sweeping changes were supported by private sector landowners and developers.' Two new policy instruments entered the discourse and praxis of urban development and housing policy at this time. The concept of FSI was coined, indicating the allowed size (number of floors and surface) of a building in proportion to plot size, adjustable to the nature of a locality (one might want to allow higher buildings in the city centre).[53] The other instrument was TDR, an instrument to value land at a specific location for use elsewhere. If such land is used for another purpose, that value can be exchanged through certificates at another location.[54] An example is compensation given to private landowners whose properties are reserved by the BMC for public amenities like parks and playgrounds. The owner receives equivalent construction rights, which can be used anywhere north of the plot he or she surrendered. Both instruments are very much in the picture today, indications of a 'change of regime' as argued by Nainan (2012), especially in that the doors were opened for substantial – and ever-growing – private-sector engagement with government agencies.

The slum redevelopment scheme

During the election campaign before the 1995 MLA elections, Shiv Sena Supremo Balsaheb Thackeray announced that, if voted to power, his party would 'provide a free and formal house to every eligible slum dweller of the city of Mumbai' (Desai 2002: 239). This obviously drew considerable attention as at that time six million people would be affected. Shiv Sena and the BJP party won the elections (many believe the 'free housing' slogan was critical) and formed a coalition at the state level. True to its word, the new government started to implement the policy and a special authority was established in 1995: the SRA. At the same time, the BMC Slum Improvement Department was disbanded (Pinto and Pinto 2005: 406).[55] Conceived as a powerful agency, the SRA was located at a high level in the Urban Development Department (headed by the CM). It was entrusted the tasks to acquire land – both from public and private organisations; coordinate between agencies; sanction redevelopment projects; build temporary transit tenements; and monitor and evaluate implementation of what are called SRSs. Basically and interestingly, it starts from a tripartite relation between a slum 'community', a private-sector builder/developer and the SRA – by any means a complex, multi-actor 'community–public–private partnership'. After a slum is selected, one or more architects draft a plan for one or more builders, which is put to the community. Political parties are known to help provide access to such a slum through local patronage relations and the corporator who mediates in the process. In one slum redevelopment case two parties competed for the project: 'Each political party supports its own builder, as a result the residents are divided between a Congress promoted builder and the one supported by Shiv Sena' (Nainan 2012: 159ff.).[56] The proposal obtaining the consent of 70 per cent of the slum people is adopted. Two models are possible: slum dwellers are relocated in situ in a form of land sharing. In such cases the original slum land is divided into a separate closed area with small towers of 225-sq. ft. apartments (now raised to 296 sq. ft) for eligible slum households and a larger fancy area with expensive apartment blocks. Alternatively, for slum redevelopment projects for high-density slums and for PAP housing, the TDR instrument was further liberalised to allow transfer of land rights. Certificates could now be offered for the surrender of lands as well as for construction, where the landowner was compensated with TDR certificates equal to the area surrendered or constructed (MCGM 2009: 70; Nainan 2012: 135). Relocation almost invariably means that affected and eligible slum households are re-housed temporarily in so called transition camps – either on the initial slum land that was cleared or in a more remote relocation area. These are makeshift housing blocks of temporary materials of four to eight stories, accommodating many households in small rooms with shared facilities. It is not rare for households to stay here for many years, as many, if not most, redevelopment and relocation projects are plagued by serious controversies and delays. Yet, against the grandiose perspective of a city free of slums, the outcomes of SRS in terms of low-income housing have been dismal. All agree that it has been a boon for the private sector and, in combination and through informal opaque links, for politicians and officials. Pinto and Pinto put it this way (2005: 409):

> Builders have only taken up slums that are located in prime areas that fetch them astronomical huge sums of money. In one project in Andheri (West), slum dwellers who approached a builder in 1997 are still languishing in transit camps. In the meantime, the builder has used a portion of their land to set up a sprawling commercial centre including a bowling alley. In short, the SRA has not much to its credit. Barely 27,000 slum families, constituting less than 2 per cent of the 1,200,000 families eligible for rehabilitation in the city, have been shown as rehoused by private developers under the governments faltering slum policy over the last decade.

Different numbers are mentioned as to the housing units created. One report[57] notes that

> In the 15 years that the SRA has been at work in Mumbai. . . the agency has built less than 170.000 homes. That's a far cry from not only the city's slum population of 8.6 million people, but also the original target of 50.000 homes in five years.

Anand and Rademacher (2011: 1753) mention that approximately 50,000 in situ and 80,000 ex situ tenements were completed under the SRA by February 2008. MCGM (2009: 70) estimates that 155,000 units have obtained approval for rehabilitation. The SRA website does not provide numbers. Not all is well then with the SRS policy. Many planned SRA projects are not completed as a result of very complex webs and incompatibilities of stakeholder interests and relations in such public–private–community partnerships. Hence, projected units may never be built or completed and many slum households stay in transit camps for long periods, which can be traumatic (see Doshi 2012: 95, for 'the politics of patience'). The far too few 225-sq. ft. slum units actually constructed are obviously in very high demand, and many are already informally sold as soon as a scheme is underway, once 'owner-ship' lists are final after lots of wheeling and dealing. Many sources suggest that the scheme was biased towards the builders and not slum people, including Doshi (2012: 85) noting that benefits to develop-ers far outpaced the benefits to other parties. Pinto and Pinto (2005: 409) opine that the TDR mechanism was ill designed and that clever operators managed to misuse the arrangement, mentioning an accusa-tion that SRA had illegally released excess TDR worth more than Rs 250 crores to a few builders. Trading in TDR certificates in their view emerged as a lucrative market for some well-connected builders and traders (for more details, see Nainan 2008, 2012).

In conclusion, facts are that, first, over the past 18 odd years, very little housing was developed for Mumbai's slum or low-income popu-lation, while it is an open question as to how many slum households actually live in units developed under SRA units today – and how many ended up in the wrong hands as tradeable 'market' commodities. Second, such units have been developed at huge cost – first of all finan-cially. If one would calculate and add all amounts earned by builders and landowners – who are seen as the main beneficiaries – under the TDR and FSI rules, one would get an obscenely high cost per unit. One might assume that, if the state itself had started to map and use its own public (BMC, MMRDA etc.) land and applied a simple land-sharing formula, engaging contractors to build slum units and selling the remainder on the market, lots more units could have been created – in locations all over the city and for the common good. And the state would have made handsome profits. Even while this would require much more careful and detailed investigation, which is beyond this book's scope, observers worry that the state has, by and large, trans-ferred its own public land at throw-away prices to the building indus-try, land which can be used only once. A third point is about long-term social and economic costs of TDR and FSI policy on city planning, densification and geographical inequalities. Indications are that SRA policy and instruments contributed to a spatial segregation between rich and poor people. As a PPP, the SRA policy is biased towards the private sector: 'The market decides where TDR is used and where PAPs are resettled' (Nainan 2012: 152). If I may recall that in 2004–5 more than 90,000 slum dwellings were demolished and their inhabitants evicted, as the manifestation of yet another, more rough city gover-nance regime, one may have to conclude that slum people haven't really benefited much at all from formal habitat policy, even while it was framed and implemented in their name.

National poverty and other programmes in Mumbai

Apart from locally designed and implemented slum policy, there are national central government programmes, notably the SJSRY urban poverty alleviation programme. It had all the modern elements of empowerment, self-employment and community participation in self-help groups (SHGs) aimed at saving and obtaining credit/bank loans. The SHGs were to delegate a representative into 'community development societies' at the ward level to enhance accountability and feedback loops. The centre financed 75 per cent and the states 25 per cent of costs. But serious implementation problems are reported, as listed among others in the GoI/Planning Commission (2011: 18–21; see Van Dijk 2011b: 111, for a comprehensive account how the programme failed in its lofty objectives). Apart from 'supply-side' implementation problems, serious 'demand-side' access problems existed to be even eligible for SJSRY, which also apply to other poverty alleviation programmes. I quote Shah (n.d.: 4–5) on access problems by the urban poor to join such schemes:[58]

> None of these schemes benefit the really poor, who continue to slip out of the safety net for a variety of reasons. 1. The paper work required to make an application is so enormous & expensive that it is virtually impossible for a poor illiterate woman to put her application together. 2. Most applications are rejected on technical grounds of some paper or other not attached. The applicant is not even informed of the reasons for the rejection of her application & there is no provision for appeal or clarifications. 3. An ordinary application under one of the above mentioned schemes requires the following documents: Certified copies of the Ration Card, House tax receipt, Proof of Residence, Birth Certificate, Death Certificate of the husband in the case of widows, Certificate of the BPL Number, Income Certificate from the *Tehsildar*, Statement & *Panchnama* by the *Tehsildar* and Statement & *Panchnama* by the BDO. Collecting these papers costs the women anywhere between Rs. 500 to Rs. 1000 which immediately excludes the poorest, as it includes filing an Affidavit on Rs. 20 stamp paper, which then has to be notarised. Now, that filling of an application under the relevant schemes is privatised, a sum of Rs. 40/- is to be paid for obtaining *vastavya chadhakla* i.e. proof of residence and income certificate in the case of Mumbai. Further, the hidden cost that the aggrieved woman has to bear is as follows: 4. Trip to the Collector

to obtain the application & Rs.10/- to the writer to fill the form. 5. May or may not have to pay the officers for their certificates but it will definitely mean more than one trip to the Collector's office. 6. Trips to collector's office, to obtain the forms for the income certificate, payment to the writer, filling the forms, 2nd trip to collector's office to swear the affidavit, for procuring his signature for the income certificate, 3rd trip to *tehsildar* office to submit the forms & finally multiple trips to collect the certificate. Obtaining an income certificate costs anywhere between Rs.50/- & Rs.150/-. The family benefit scheme automatically disqualifies a woman with more than 2 children. Often the greater the number of minor children the greater is the destitution, yet the woman is punished, although she has little control over the number of children she bears.

So even while the SJSRY programme has been in existence since 1997 and was revamped in 2009, there are grave doubts as to its impacts and achievements. It is likely that similar constraints characterise other centrally funded schemes, such as the SSA education programme – if only for the poor to get access, which may now be increasingly complex if only due to smaller central budgets.[59] All such bureaucratic conditions make the poor (especially very poor, illiterate people) more dependent on those who can 'help' them get access. As shown in the next chapter, corporators welcome such proposals for support – to obtain a certificate, a recommendation to be admitted – either for a small fee or in exchange for promises in terms of party and/or election loyalty.

It was in 2005 that the then central government recognised the need to – finally and more seriously – engage with the urban sector, by launching the massive JNNURM, with a budget of Rs 1,000 billion[60] (Sivaramakrishnan 2011: 15). Mumbai benefited more than many other cities at the tune of Rs 1,800 crores. It has four distinct components, two of which relate to slums and the urban poor: the BSUP (Basic Services for the Urban Poor) programme and the Integrated Housing and Slum Development Programme (IHSDP).[61] I cannot go into much detail here, and I refer only to few initial indications of achievements and constraints. According to GoI/Planning Commission (2011) the programme gets mixed reviews. While it renewed focus on the urban sector throughout the country, it helped bring about an enabling context for urgent reforms in many states and cities. Under the BSUP programme, investment was targeted towards the provision of basic services to the urban poor in 64 cities, including Mumbai. However, 'critiques of JNNURM focus on the lack of community participation, capacity building and lukewarm implementation of reforms' (2011: 21). Some key bottlenecks recognised include the overall capacity of the centre, state and cities to implement the ambitious programme:

> One issue highlighted across all evaluations of JNNURM was the lack of capacity at all levels of government and the lack of capacity and engagement with city-level stakeholders such as households, communities, NGOs and the private sector.[62]

I will limit myself here to quoting from a comprehensive UN-Women (2012: 12) report, which highlights gender issues in JNNURM's implementation and the failure to enhance democracy:

> JNNURM pays specific attention to the participatory dimension of local democracy, yet its contribution in the matter has not been conclusive so far. For instance, one of the conditions for cities to be eligible was the elaboration of the City Development Plans (CDPs). CDPs were supposed to reflect the priorities of all stakeholders, which implied extensive consultation with city dwellers. JNNURM also makes it mandatory for eligible cities to implement a Community Participation Law (CPL), meant to achieve what wards committees could not, namely institutionalize a local participatory space, the area *sabha* (area assembly) where the local corporator and municipal officials would interact on a regular basis with representatives of the local residents. However, independent reviews show that the consultation process proved to be extremely flawed in most cases: consultation meetings were organised in such a way that they made the participation of the poor, or the uneducated, very difficult; when they did take place, many of their conclusions were not incorporated in the final CDPs. Furthermore, the current JNNURM guidelines do not make any conscious effort to ensure that groups representing women's needs and rights are included as stakeholders (whether they speak for rich, middle income or poor women). It was therefore difficult in the CDP /Detailed Project Report (DPR) process to appreciate why and where women should be involved.

In summary, the potentially very important and well-funded BSUP programme under JNNURM is shown, once more not to stand up to expectations. Shortcomings noted for a long time under the SJSRY programme are re-appearing here as if no lessons are being learnt.

Particularly striking is a deplorable and hard-to-understand absence of monitoring and evaluating as to what money was spent on what, who benefited and whether impacts were in line with programme objectives. For example, I could not find data on new housing created specifically under the BSUP programme in Mumbai. The ministry website mentions that 52,494 dwelling units were completed under BSUP as per March 2012 in the state of Maharashtra,[63] but other details are lacking.[64]

A new central urban programme RAY was initiated by 2012, taking into account some of the problems faced under JNNURM. The initial design was quite ambitious in terms of asking the states to legislate slum household mortgageable property rights (for which a model law was drafted), in situ slum redevelopment or upgrading, creating land banks, and low-income loan schemes, all this with community consultations and approvals (Chamaraj 2015: 35–37 also for more details on proposed adjustments). However, states were not forthcoming to cooperate, for example, claiming a lack of land, with Mumbai unwilling to change its practice of cut-off dates, so that general eligibility was not possible. It appears as if RAY has made only very little headway and that mostly initial pilot projects have been and are being implemented by states.

At the time of writing, the urban development intentions and plans of the Modi union government are slowly emerging. JNNURM will be closed, as well as RAY. Two new major initiatives are expected: the development of 'Smart Cities', with 'projects of wider impact based on area development'. Besides, a new Urban Development Mission for 500 cities under which basic urban services and amenities are provided is foreseen.[65] This has left the states in some uncertainty as they are still implementing BSUP and RAY.[66] We will have to wait and see what is in store for India's urban poor and slums in the near future where the union government is concerned. But whatever innovative or potentially effective programme or law it adopts, it is the states that implement and ultimately municipal corporations which are closest to the people. Not only politics but also governance is ultimately local, especially for the poor.

As regards another focus of this book on decentralisation, the union government has taken over the advice of the 14th National Finance Commission to devolve more funds to the Indian states, according to a new allocation framework. This important reform is expected to have large impacts on both India as a federation and its constituent states. On the one hand, it can be seen as deepening devolution by 'empowering state governments' financially and also politically in more freedom in spending central funds. Yet, as a common issue in decentralisation literature, there are doubts as to whether the new powers and funds will be put to good use. Two Indian experts perceive risks:[67]

> Professor Mahendra Dev says that resources to states have risen due to the devolution, but is not sure these will be used for social development. 'Earlier, utilisation of central scheme funds came with some directions and the states had to contribute 25 per cent of the funds but now they may want to spend that on something else. If they spend the resources on populist measures the resources will go to waste. That risk remains'. Development expert Saxena agrees: 'Unless centrally sponsored schemes are wound up, state fiscal freedom is a mirage . . . who knows the rogue states may use those funds for more airports in ministers' constituencies, or to send MLAs to Switzerland, or appoint a large number of Class IV staff on patronage basis.'

Some are worried that the union government is weakening India following this ambitious decentralisation reform, while India needs a strong state. Coupled with a very strong voice of the private sector in the corridors of power and in financing elections, one might argue that India is at risk of becoming a 'hollow state', where state power is undermined, while other stakeholders and administrative levels are empowered. And at the same time there are indications that decentralisation beyond the Indian states towards their local governments – that is to further strengthen panchayats and ULBs – is not part of the agenda. Referring to the 14th FCC recommendations, M. A. Oommen[68] says: 'The recommendations relating to Panchayati Raj institutions and urban local governments. . . . appear to be retrograde'. He mentions that the union budget 2015–16 will cut allocations to the Panchayati Raj ministry.

Now that I have provided the basic facts, overall picture and trends where Mumbai's slums and poor people are concerned, I will now return to Mumbai BMC, where an earlier effort at urban decentralisation under the 74th Constitutional Amendment led to the formation of WCMs and a relative strengthening of the position and powers of its 227 corporators. The next chapter explores how these corporators use their powers today and whether improved wards-level governance with benefits for the urban poor has been one of the impacts.

Notes

1 Gupte (2012: 192) agrees that the concept of 'slum' has negative connotations, as in associations with 'deprived' and 'dirt, criminality, pilferage' and that those living there are 'squatters and encroachers' whose rights

are tainted by illegality and ineligibility. Anand (2011b) chooses to use the relatively non-descript concept of 'settler'.

2 *Pucca* refers to things constructed from durable materials, that is stone or concrete rather than from materials such as thatch, plastic and carton wood, as seen in pavement dwellers' huts.

3 Anand (2011b: 544): 'After 3 decades of settlement, life is less precarious than it was previously for many living in Mumbai's older settlements. Many residents no longer identify themselves as poor.'

4 Interview of BMC official, 16 April 2015.

5 In a later footnote I mention that 'the 2000 (slum) survey data with the collector's office was lost in the Mumbai floods of 2005'. A slum sanitation survey was carried out much earlier by Montgomery Watson. As indicated, slums were not mapped for the 2014–34 DP.

6 Mr Prabhu, former MHADA chairman, mentions that in 2004 more than 5,000 illegal shanties came up on government land; in 2003 it was approximately 60,000–70,000. He argues that officials had always been aware of this occupation and even made money from it – he asked: how did they permit this in the first place? (in relation to the sudden incidence of 2004–5 Mumbai slum demolitions, cf. 'For a New Mumbai, at Great Cost', *Frontline*, 28 January 2005, p. 48).

7 One factor is the TDR mechanism. For example, relocating a slum area in South Mumbai yields a right to develop housing in another city area (multiplied by a factor), and today there is a clear pattern that high-end housing comes up in the southern and western areas and slum housing in a few unpopular and poor areas, such as M(E) and P(N) wards (cf. Nainan 2012).

8 'Mankhurd PAP Building a Vertical Slum', *DNA*, 9 June 2011. The buildings house about 9,300 residential tenements. 'These buildings are designed to make the poor even poorer,' said Malape.

> There is poor natural lighting and air circulation. The condition of sanitation is also terrible. A stench of excreta hangs in the air. The residents suffer from emotional distress and chronic sicknesses. The closeness between buildings not only leaves no space for fire engines but in fact facilitates the spread of fire and smoke. Passages between adjacent buildings are just 3 meters wide. The most striking violation is that 39 buildings that are ground-plus-five structures and have 5,914 residential tenements have no lifts. The few lifts that are there do not work. The colony gets water for just 15 minutes daily.

9 *Times of India*, 8 January 2013.

10 The Planning Commission defined the poor as those who live on Rs 28 per day in urban areas and Rs 22 in rural areas.

> This laid bare the intentions of the Govt. These were not poverty line figures, but destitution level benchmarks: unless you dropped dead, for the Government of India, you did not qualify for aid as a poor person. Can we agree in this country on a floor of human dignity below which we will not allow any human being to fall?

A. Raman, 'A Vernier Scale for Hunger; An Unfinished Log of Efforts by Governments Not Entirely Determined to Wage the Prolonged Battle That Must Be Waged to End Hunger', *Outlook*, 11 March 2013. (A daily per-capita income of Rs 28 makes Rs 4,200 per month for a five-member household).

11 We checked with a slum social worker the average household expenditure profile for his slum: rent 1,200; water and electricity 800; food 5,000; medicine 200; clothing 400; interest and loan repayment 1,200. This one anecdotal example seems to indicate that households today need at least about Rs 9,000 per month to manage (field notes, 17 April 2015).

12 Vithayathil and Singh (2012: 65) estimate the percentage of Dalits in Mumbai at a low 4.88 per cent. Nainan notes (2012: 148) that the largest concentration of Dalits in Mumbai is to be found in the M-ward in the east of the city. This started with the in-migration of Dalits following a drought in 1972, and the influx of low-caste people continues with the ongoing large slum relocations.

13 Even while it may be agreed that the overall position of Dalits/SCs has improved since India gained independence, there is no time for complacency as many of them today face horrendous problems and everyday constraints and humiliation: 'India's National Crime Records Bureau says that a crime is committed against a Dalit by a non-Dalit every 16 minutes. It says every day upper-caste men rape more than four Dalit women; every week, 13 Dalits are murdered and six Dalits are kidnapped. In 2012 alone, the year of the Delhi gang-rape and murder, 1,574 Dalit women were raped.' 'Of Udwin, Mehta and Attenborough', *Deccan Chronicle*, 11 March 2015.

14 Rents depend on hut/house type. Cheaper units in poorer slums in the suburbs which are dirty, face acute water shortages and poor access may go for Rs 900/month. Rents go up when more facilities are available and in slums towards the city: from Rs 2,000 and upward from Rs 3,000 for better units in better slums, for example in South Mumbai. In more established colonies *pacca* units may go for Rs 5,000. In all cases an initial deposit has to be paid, ranging from Rs 20,000 to 100,000 (field notes, 3 March 2013).

15 It appears that interest rates amount to about 10 per cent monthly without any collateral; it may be 2–4 per cent in case of a pawn. Most slums have thriving jeweller shops, which double as money lenders. One Mrs Sonavane from Dharavi pawned her home for Rs 10,000 to a money lender 20 years ago when her husband died in an accident. Thirteen years later she repaid the loan and re-claimed her house, after having paid Rs 60,000 to the 'micro-lender', which amounts to an interest rate of almost 100 per cent (Campana 2013: 95).

16 However, not all parties are in favour of easy extension such as SS and MNS, which may worry that extension gives housing rights to new coming – hence non-Marathi – migrants to Mumbai, which is not what these parties want.

17 'Cut-Off Politics Has Hampered Slum Rehab; In 18 Yrs, SRA Has Rehabilitated Less Than 4% of Slum Dwellers', *Indian Express*, 28 February 2014.

18 '29 Lakh Fake Ration Cards Seized Last Year', *Times of India*, 8 February 2010. It notes that there are yellow ration cards for below-poverty people and orange cards for above-poverty-line households.

19 Ibid.
20 *Indian Express* (9 March 2004) reports that BMC Mayor Deole ordered a probe into allegations that around 2,500 bogus photo passes were issued by civic officials in the K-west ward office.
21 'BPL Ration Cards in Modi's, Sonia's Names,' *Indian Express,* 9 April 2015.
22 Landy and Ruby (2005: 2) argue that poor people use the same broker in Hyderabad to get access to the PDS shops and other important institutions. I take this as an indication that ultimately trust and reliability are key (cf. Wood 2003).
23 Cf. Krishna and Bajpai (2015: 75) who argue that English competence is a must for upward mobility.
24 'In 2000, the estimated number of Mumbai domestic workers was about 600,000 out of whom 80,000 are full-time workers. About 40 per cent of the domestic helps were girls under 15 years of age. Many of them are female heads of their respective household. Abuse, generally verbal, and to an extent physical, sexual exploitation, and the absence of occupational health and safety standards are marked features of their labour processes and labour relations' (MCGM 2009: 146).
25 'Recall that a similar sort of outrage was expressed when a middle-class college girl was raped by a policeman on Marine Drive in April 2005, but that it was missing when a teenage rag-picker was raped, also by a policeman, near the airport only six months later' (Khan 2013: 12).
26 *The Hindu,* 25 February 2015 on the 2015–16 Central Government Budget.
27 'Public Funds to Push Neo-Liberal Agenda', *Frontline,* 3 April 2015: 43.
28 'Whose Bharat Is This?' *Outlook,* 16 March 2015: 33.
29 This assumption is confirmed in Parkar *et al.* (2013: 499): 'For men, the frustration of unfulfilled responsibilities typically arose from unemployment and the inability to provide for his family and himself. Such men felt that they had become an unacceptable burden on their family.'
30 This, however, does not stop one of the two women slum leaders in Boo's slum study (2012: 28) to cheat and exploit poorer slum women. She had formed a self-help group with mostly better-off women, and the money pooled was lent at high interest rates to poorer women whom they had excluded from their collective. Women solidarity cannot be assumed.
31 In our study of a Malad SRS, we documented similar dynamics of two secretive local leaders each conniving with a different builder, not so much to get a good deal for the wider slum, but to take care of his family members and local allies and to position for benefits such as more tokens exchangeable for SRS units (de Wit 2016).
32 Zerah (2006: 14): 'Many municipal employees highlighted the vested interests generated by the Slum Adoption Program and the role that political patronage plays in the selection of the CBOs. *However, others consider that 'politicians are also cooperating to make NGOs'* (italics added).
33 My Chennai slum study (de Wit 1996) unavoidably dealt with the hugely popular and charismatic ex-film star MGR of the AIADMK party, now led by the charismatic leader Jayalalitha, an example of a powerful woman politician, towering over party leaders and ministers alike.
34 '17% of Urban India Lives in Slums: Census', *Times of India,* 22 March 2013.

158 *Mumbai's poor and slum dynamics*

35 http://armman.org/mumbai (accessed on 4 March 2013).
36 Interview with Dr Gadre and Dr Shukla (who wrote a book *Voices of Conscience from the Medical Profession*) in 'Falling Medical Standards', *Tehelka*, 14 March 2015: 52–54.
37 See also http://www.slideshare.net/milindmhaske/health-white-paper-2012–14500442 (accessed on 16 March 2015).
38 This is the case both for Mumbai and for India generally:

> Estimates based on studies show that India's expenditure in the private health sector is as much as 4 per cent to 6 per cent of the GDP, in sharp contrast to less than one percent of the GDP which the governments spend. Only 17 per cent of all health-care expenditure in India is borne by the government, making it one of the most privatised healthcare systems in the world. (MCGM 2009: 109)

39 Two relevant clauses: Article 21A: Right to Education: 'The state shall provide free and compulsory education to all children of the age group of six to fourteen years in such a manner as the State may determine.' And Article 45: 'Provision of Early Childhood Care and Education to the Children below the Age of Six Years': 'The State shall endeavor to provide early childcare and education for all the children until they complete the age of six years' (MCGM 2009: 79–82).
40 From Boo (2012: 13)

> Zehrunissa expected Mirchi to pass ninth standard at the third rate Urdu-language private school for which they paid three hundred rupees a year. They'd had to pay since spreading educational opportunity was not among the governments strong suits. The free municipal school near the airport stopped at eight standard, and its teachers often didn't show up.

41 I already mentioned that Nainan (2006: 3) pegged the price of an illegal ration card at Rs 2,000 to Rs 5,000 per family and that Kumar and Landy found the amount was Rs 8,000 a few years later (2009: 116).
42 'The Law Laid Down; India Has Law But Little Order, Laws But Limited Justice. Where Did It Go Wrong?', *Outlook/New York Times*, 7 January 2013.
43 Mateen Hafeez, 'Police Has Been Most Corrupt Government Department for 10 Years: ACB', *Times of India*, 30 January 2010.
44 'Why Victims of Custodial Deaths in Maharashtra only from Minorities, Bombay HC Asks', *Times of India*, 1 August 2014.
45 Shibu Thomas, 'State Records Most Custodial Deaths in 10 Years', *Times of India*, 15 February 2013.
46 For a sad example of the case of a poor, not-connected chawl man who dies in a police cell, see Joseph (2011).
47 'Recall that a similar sort of outrage was expressed when a middle-class college girl was raped by a policeman on Marine Drive in April 2005, but that it was missing when a teenage rag-picker was raped, also by a policeman, near the airport only six months later' (Khan 2013: 12).
48 'Sunil often eavesdropped on Kalu's conversation after dark and in this way learned that policemen sometimes advised the road boys about nearby

warehouses and construction sites where they might steal building materials. The cops then took a share of the proceeds' (Boo 2012: 45).

49 One of the more ambitious slum women in Boo's study with a small business meets a male sub-inspector of police at the police station. He regularly demanded bribes from the family, since – as per 'formal' rules – people squatting on airport land were not allowed to run a business. 'You owe me for so many months,' he said when he saw her. 'Have you been hiding from me? Now that you are here we can settle your account' (Boo 2012: 92).

50 R. N. Bhaskar, 'Policy Watch: The Language of Money', *DNA*, 28 September 2014.

51 However, in that same period, the state was in a position to acquire large tracts of land in Navi Mumbai: 'This proves that should the government choose to do so, it can easily acquire land for development' (Boo 2012: 201).

52 Recalling the role played by Sharad Pawar, Mr S. S. Tinaikar, former BMC commissioner, called him 'the biggest collector', referring to the contributions that chief ministers of every state are required to provide to the party bosses (Nainan 2006: 102; cf. Tinaikar 2003).

53 This is proposed in the recent Mumbai Development Plan, where more FSI is allowed in urban nodes around metro stations and the like.

54 For details see Nainan (2012: 132–35). She notes (Nainan 2012: 231):

> In TDR, the financing required for the public amenity is raised by the government's issuing of TDR certificates, which are then sold on the open market. These TDRs are bought by plot owners who would like to increase the built-up areas on their plots.

55 While introducing SRS and establishing the SRA agency, all previous policies and agencies were disbanded or closed. Hansen (2001: 209) regrets this where all other more low profile, less-expensive and also more feasible programs to upgrade the slums were terminated in the flurry of publicity surrounding this new project.

56 I may already note that such dynamics underline rather very close builder–party relations. I will return to this in the next two chapters when discussing corruption and election funding.

57 'SRA Issues Showcause to 300 Builders; The SRA Has Identified Over 400 Such Projects', *Indian Express*, 7 September. To pull up builders whose projects have been pending for years, the Slum Rehabilitation Authority (SRA) has sent showcause notices to over 300 builders who have failed to begin housing projects for the past five years. The SRA has identified over 400 such projects. 'We are in the process of identifying and sending notices to builders whose schemes are stuck for various reasons. While builders whose schemes are delayed due to bureaucratic hurdles will be allowed to continue with the scheme, others will be barred from taking up such SRA projects,' said SRA chief executive officer Nirmalkumar Deshmukh. As per SRA data, only 197 of the 1,524 schemes allotted have been completed since 1996 when the authority was set up.

58 She refers to the Indira Gandhi Niradhar Yojna, Sanjay Gandhi Niradhar Yojna, Shravan Bal Yojna, and the Family Benefit Scheme and the Suvarna Jayanti Shehri Rozgar Yojna (SJSRY) program (Shah n.d.: 4). I have not been able to confirm the facts mentioned, but if only half of these apply to separate schemes, access is virtually blocked.

59 'Whose Bharat Is It?', *Outlook,* 16 March 2015: 33, consider the 'unprecedented cuts in social spending' in the 2015–16 union budget and notes that 'the biggest cut, in percentage terms, has been in education: for primary education (Sarva Shiksha Abhiyan) a budget of Rs 22,000 crore implies a reduction of 22 per cent'.

60 Representing an investment of Rs. 100,000 crores covering 65 cities. Compare Haritas (2008: 467) on Area Sabas.

61 Banerjee-Guha (2010: 208) assesses the program's guidelines and notes segregation in the massive JNNURM program, which has one ample-funded component of infrastructure provision with private-sector participation and another smaller one – and led by another ministry – which includes Basic Services to the Urban Poor (BSUP) programme.

62 If taken as a separate statement on urban governance and its changes following neoliberal reforms, this reflects ominously on what we now call 'multi-stakeholder governance'.

63 Besides Greater Mumbai, also Pune, Nashik and Nagpur are project cities.

64 http://pib.nic.in/newsite/erelease.aspx?relid=81775 (accessed on 9 September 2013).

65 'Smart Cities Project by Next Month: Venkaiah', *The Hindu,* 17 March 2015.

66 'Poor Verdict as Deadline Expires: 8 Years on, Slum Free City a Decade Away', *Times of India,* 11 March 2015.

67 A. Desai, 'Banking on Tall Promises; Low Deficit Ratio, High Growth, More Tax Revenue Could Just Be a Dream', *Outlook,* 16 March 2015: 32.

68 M. A. Oomen, 'Fiscal Omen of Local Democracy', *Indian Express,* 23 March 2015.

4 Political entrepreneurs

The Mumbai corporators in their political and financial context

After having introduced the formal institutional governance context of the BMC and related agencies in which the 227 Mumbai corporators operate in Chapter 2, I will now look in detail at their actual functioning and performance. What kind of people are they, what are they assumed to do and what do they actually do – both in a formal sense and, apparently more critically, in a variety of informal if not illegal activities? How does all this relate to the wishes and needs of their various political parties and other local governance actors and to the private sector which may finance some of their election campaigns? Last but not least, how do they deal with the wishes and needs of the many urban poor, both the people most in need but also the most enthusiastic voters?

Formally of course, and in terms of 'liberal democracy', the corporator as a *nagar sevak* (city servant) is elected to serve the wider interest of (all) voters/citizens in their constituencies: he or she is, or should be, a representative,[1] a policymaker, decision maker, communicator, facilitator, negotiator, power broker, and leader. He or she has to deal with local, constituency level grievances; actively participate in ward-level and BMC council meetings; and participate in special council committees dealing with things such as finance, public works or education. In earlier chapters I already explained that the Mumbai MCs are not all that active in several such committees, with exceptions such as the powerful standing committee. Their participation in the key institution of neighbourhood governance in the form of WCMs was shown to be lacklustre, or let us say that there is no evidence they aspire(d) to make this recent democratic forum successful or thriving. Rather, and unfortunately, we will have to recognise that the Mumbai corporators do not generally have a uniformly positive image or reputation. They are seen to be corrupt, illiterate and self-interested (John 2007; Nainan 2006; Pinto 2000).[2] As indicated, it appears that Indian urban middle classes are losing interest to vote in municipal elections while avoiding and looking down on corporators. They mostly contact municipal officials directly or through RWAs (Baud and Nainan 2008: 13). At the same time, most sources refer to MCs as remaining critical to the urban poor, which is linked to the aforementioned general failure of the poor to organising themselves into effective, broad-based organisations, which could counter the powers of middle-class organisation (Bhide 2006; de Wit and Berner 2009; Harris 2005). With evidence that rich and poor are drifting apart spatially, in terms of services and of representation in democracy, the question arises as to how MCs react to such developments, notably where poor people are concerned. After all they constitute their main vote bank. In this respect Nainan and Baud (2008: 126) note 'it would be factually correct to say that by and large the slum dwellers' votes are responsible for electing political representatives at the city level'. I will show that corporators have adjusted skilfully to city governance changes over time, fitting remarkably well in present-day conditions of dominant informality, which I will unravel in its related corruption and collusion practices. But while the overwhelming evidence points to an overall negative MC image, I will try here to present a balanced picture, starting from the reality that they come in different shades from being committed and helpful to very crooked. All combine constructive, supportive activities to sustain their political careers with more or less important profitable 'side' businesses. At the same time, they are subject to the changing dynamics and compulsions arising from the wider Mumbai institutional, financial and socio-political context where money and power are key drivers.

4.1   A profile of Mumbai corporators

Background and profile of MCs

Based on my own and other surveys carried out on the Mumbai MCs, I present some (by no means exhaustive) details by way of illustration of who they are. A combined survey (N = 32, 17 men and 15 women) of MCs in several Mumbai wards by de Wit (2010a), de Wit and van Dijk (2010) and Van Dijk (2006) brings out following patterns of age, profession and education of the Mumbai MCs by 2005–6. These corporators may not be there today after the 2007 and 2012 local elections, so this is more like a snapshot by way of illustration. As for work, eight male MCs reported as profession 'construction', 'developer' or 'property business, cement businesses', with almost half of them engaged in real estate. Other professions include 'repair shop', 'landlord/farmer' and 'owner of shops and a ration shop'. Only two MCs were full-time politicians. As for the (15) women MCs, the main profession was social worker ($N = 3$) – one woman had her own business and others were housewives, saleswomen and one medical doctor. All women studied up to 10th standard and beyond (including five BAs and two MAs); education levels for men were markedly lower with only three MCs with BA-level education. The average age of women MC in our survey was 43; for men it was 47 years. This seems to confirm Haritas's findings (2008: 460) that many women MCs in Mumbai are relatively well educated and well-off, having comfortable socio-economic status.

A survey by Ghosh *et al.* (2005: 75ff.) brings out that, at that time, most (53 per cent) Mumbai MCs come in the 41–50 years age bracket, followed by 30 per cent in the 31–40 age bracket. A majority of 38 per cent studied up to class 12, followed by 24 per cent who studied up to class 10. In terms of employment, the dominant profession was 'self-employment' (28 per cent, and a high 61 per cent for male MCs), followed by social work (30 per cent for women, no men here). Another survey ($N = 13$, 8 men and 5 women) of MCs in one Mumbai WCM shows an average age of 45 (van Dijk 2006: 62). Education levels ranged from a low class 7; seven MCs with class 12; and as many as five MCs with a BA, MA or MBA. Most common castes were represented, with two Muslims in this WCM. From the eight male MCs, two were in the construction business, four had a shop or a business, one was a landlord, and one was a medical doctor. Women jobs ranged from librarian to social worker (one) to clerks/administrative support staff. In a survey among MCs in Delhi and Bangalore, John (2007: 3988) found that the most common occupation among male MCs – including the husbands of women councillors – in both cities was contractors, developers and factory owners. It may come as a surprise that so many male MCs in Indian cities are engaged in building or developer activities (and if not themselves, it is often a brother or son who conveniently has a building company). We will see later that there is no co-incidence here where the work of an MC is very closely tied to the construction budgets and other earning opportunities at the level of the wards office. Some even argue that one key motivation to enter politics is the wide scope to earn incomes as argued by Pinto (2000) that councillors are quite corrupt, 'as many of them got into the Corporation with the expressed intention of making quick money'. Siddiqui and Bhowmik (2004: 141) confirm that their socio-economic background shows that they are in business rather than education-based occupations (Siddiqui and Bhowmik 2004: 187).

This is not to deny that there is some need for MCs to earn incomes as the sitting allowance they receive from the BMC is relatively limited at Rs 10,000 per month. This contrasts with present-day accepted norms and practice that MCs maintain an elaborate office – which underlines his or her status as separate from the common man. This would normally include a main office at home, a small ward-level consulting office to receive and contact citizens with complaints and requests, one or more (certain type) cars, and a wardrobe with suitable garments. In addition, MCs have a staff of advisors, both fixed and temporary ones, for example at election times. Depending on status and way of working, one or more bodyguards may be employed – which, together with cars and a nice house, double as popular status symbols. These double as attributes and signals of power, which are part of an – often carefully managed – public image repertoire which includes adjusting body language to different occasions and to persons of diverse status. The working context of Mumbai city brings along plenty complications in terms of time and expenses (heavy traffic, incredibly crowded trains and taxi or auto fares add-up). More strategic expenditures are for presents and contributions to weddings, funerals and inaugurations and cash to support clients and supporters in case of emergency. Such expenses are listed by Nainan (2006: 13) as 'political costs', referring to investments so as to remain attractive to voters after winning elections. Less tangible 'good will' brokerage activities and referrals to local leaders/party workers, officials or the police are part of this, but also the concrete costs of supporting school admissions or getting a job for a slum boy. But, as detailed later, probably the major chunk of MC earnings goes as contributions to his or her political party, which has helped the MC into his or her position and expects something in return. Money is flowing; money needs to be made. As we will see, having a business, or being 'self-employed', is very well compatible with a political career: MCs can delegate the work to others; they have earnings as MCs and get back to business in case they lose elections (see Ghosh and Tawa Lama-Rewal 2005: 77).

How to become a corporator

One may assume that a combination of low remuneration, large stakes in costly land and housing plans and deals and a general centralised culture of opacity and secrecy contribute to what is seen as systemic corruption in Mumbai's city governance. This chapter assumes that this applies equally to the role and performance of the city's corporators. I picture them as shrewd operators, as spiders in citywide webs and as 'political entrepreneurs' in adjusting to shifting power configurations. What do we know of MCs before recent neoliberal reforms took hold? Some say that the incidence of corruption has increased with the coming to power of the Shiv Sena with its relatively less experienced and populist type of politicians (Desai 2002; Nainan 2001: 44). Siddiqui and Bhowmik (2004: 175) trace what they call 'the deterioration of BMC councillors' over time.

> The real deterioration in the level of municipal politics began simultaneously with an influx of migrants to the city, and the consequent proliferation of slums, which became the vote bank for political parties. This was further exacerbated by the fact that educated intelligent citizens did not participate in civic affairs, and did not even bother to vote. They therefore left it to the slum dwellers and less discriminating voters to elects councillors. Naturally, the quality of councillors began to deteriorate. . . . The deterioration in quality of councillors was gradual, and till the end of the 1970ies there were at least 30–40 per cent of them who were responsible, respectable and dedicated politicians genuinely wanting to serve the community. After the 1985 elections, when the Shiv Sena gained absolute control over the Corporation, the number of such councillors could be counted on one's fingers.

They go on (Siddiqui and Bhowmik 2004: 175) to describe how MCs at the time were perceived and indicate that they were valued more by the poor than the Mumbai middle classes. By 2000, MCs are shown to be relatively well connected in neighbourhoods, certainly more than MLAs or MPs. About 60 per cent of the poor 'know about their existence', and of these, 38 per cent assessed their efforts to support the poor as good to very good; 34 per cent rated them as average and 23 per cent rated them as bad to very bad. In contrast, 62 per cent of the Mumbai intelligentsia rated the MCs as bad to very bad; 22 per cent as being of average quality and only 14 per cent believed they were good to very good. The reasons that MCs rate poorly sound familiar: they are busy with party politics and pursue their self-interest, neglecting their corporator work; they lack sincerity, honesty and accountability; they are not aware of their responsibilities; they are immoral, some of them directly or indirectly involved in crime; they are not concerned with the plight of the poor; and they lack training on leadership and city management (Siddiqui and Bhowmik 2004: 176).

All efforts to start a MC career start with the family, more so for women than for men as they need to either combine domestic chores with politics or organise support otherwise. Besides, women (wives, daughters) may be drawn into politics at the behest of their father or husband who sooner or later finds that his constituency (where he may have been elected many times) is declared for women candidates only. This fact alone – the loud and clear unwillingness of many sitting male MCs to step back and let others be democratically elected – already speaks for the democratic attitude of some MCs. It is one indication that there is more to the job than representing people and solving local issues. Some (not all) MCs may consider their constituency their personal fiefdom for five years, earning good incomes, building up solid networks of useful and rewarding contacts, and enjoying high and respected status; they do not want to lose all that. And in a context of (very) limited trust and intense political competition the family is considered the ultimate safe heaven. So (temporarily) passing on accumulated political capital to wives, sons and daughters can be seen as an increasing trend of 'hereditary politics' or 'dynastic politics' in India. It affects political families at all levels – MC, MLA and MP (e.g. in the Shiv Sena Thackeray family and the Pawar family for the NCP). But MCs may also want to keep political (and accumulated financial) capital in the family with a longer-term ambition for higher careers, as it appears that many MCs seem to aspire to become MLA or MP (Pinto and de Wit 2006 where M. Pinto calls them 'birds of passage').

The next most important network is obviously the political party as the source of all opportunities – getting a ticket, support to winning elections, information in joint meetings with party members at ward and BMC level and chances for a career. The party is probably more important for the corporator position than those of MLA or MP as it is the entry level into politics (van Dijk 2006: 65). MCs are normally party members for many years before qualifying as MC candidate and need to build up credit within the party to make a chance – as competition is fierce. In general, they have to balance the demands of the party with maintaining good relations with grassroots-level actors in their constituency where they depend on votes. Exemplary rapport with higher-party echelons is even more critical for MCs seeking a higher political career. The party demands are many and unavoidable. Important here are tying the party line, voting along with the party on important issues and getting close to and praising the leadership (which, in India, may sometimes be quite extreme in terms of sycophancy). There is a financial side too where MCs contribute money to the party – for example channelling part of the kickbacks or cuts that the MC receives upward into the party hierarchy. Nainan (2006: 5) mentions that all political parties require their elected members to generate fixed amounts to be handed to the party weekly or monthly, which at times may generate stress. It appears then that most MCs do need good and reliable incomes, which, as we will see, can be from ward-level contracts, shopkeepers or hawkers. According to Nainan (2006: 5) corporators and MLAs receive a fixed amount of the costs of all public projects undertaken in their constituency area. Further evidence was a respondent in a ward office (R/N; 6 April 2005) mentioning a corporator there paying Rs 100,000 monthly to the state party leader.

The decisive step to become an MC is to obtain a ticket to stand for the municipal elections. As indicated in more detail in Chapter 6, there is no uniform way to obtain a party ticket, but it seems certain that a candidate has to be very familiar with the party and, preferably, with the constituency from where he or she wishes to stand. Yet, in the context of a very personalised, particularistic and trust-reliant political context, most aspirants have a long-term prior association with another political leader or 'godfather' (see John 2007: 3988), and the party approves each candidate. Van Dijk (2006: 65) confirms that 'all the MCs had been party members for years prior to being fielded for office and all but one were approached and encouraged by their party to run, rather than them approaching the party first' (see Ghosh and Tawa Lama-Rewal 2005: 83). Starting from such minimum qualifications, efforts can be undertaken to obtain a ticket. Arrangements range from auctions where a ticket is awarded to the highest bidder to arrangements where tickets are allocated in a top-down fashion by the party leadership (where financial considerations may or not play a role), to a model where trusted party workers are rewarded with a ticket as a result of great dedication and popularity within a particular neighbourhood. Nainan (2006: 5) indicates for Mumbai that 'the rupee price of successful politics is indeed very high as each candidate first pays his political party for the ticket – this means payment to senior leaders'. For the municipal elections in Delhi, Ghosh and Tawa Lama-Rewal (2005: 91) write that 'even when you don't have to buy your ticket from the party, there are large campaigning costs to be financed by the candidate'. In those cases where tickets were up for sale: 'Wild figures circulated about the price at which some tickets were being sold by political parties for the 2002 Delhi municipal polls from Rs 100,000 to Rs 10 million' (Ghosh and Tawa Lama-Rewal 2005: 91). To quote Nainan (2001: 77):

> Entry into the formal political arena even at the local level through election is expensive; payments have to be made at every stage, to get a party ticket and to fight for the elections. All these expen-

ditures are seen as investments towards reaping these back once local elections are won. The political arena is known for its patron-client relationships and payments and cuts for everything.

Obviously, if people are ready to make such large investments to be an elected political representative there must be more than a craving need to serve voters only. Intense competition surrounds the struggle for tickets as a way to great riches and possibly higher political career. One indication of this is the manipulation of caste certificates. Apart from women reserved constituencies, others are reserved for SC and ST candidates and it happens that higher caste candidates forge a caste certificate to be able to still stand from there (see Pinto and Pinto 2005: 20 for bogus caste certificates).[3] A newspaper reports:[4] 'Disqualified corporators ignore notices sent by civic body for funds allotted to them and the city's taxpayers have to foot this bill.' The story is that there are many corporators who submit fake certificates and get elected from reserved categories. If they get caught and are disqualified they have to refund all benefits received from the BMC such as allowances, BEST bus pass and identity cards: 'Seventeen elected ex-corporators who were disqualified after election, have not refunded their allowances. *DNA* has a copy of the notices sent by the BMC to 17 such corporators asking for refund.'

Women corporators

Things are different for women candidates: they can try and obtain a ticket as mentioned, but by far the best way to a ticket is to stand in a women MC-reserved seat, combined to being the wife or daughter or sister of the MC who represented the constituency before. The state of Maharashtra, of which Mumbai is the capital, introduced a 33 per cent reservation of MC seats along with the 74th CAA in 2000 but has gone one step further and raised this to 50 per cent in 2012. Its precise rationale remains unclear. In my discussions on this I heard some say that this shows the emancipatory nature of the Maharashtra state while some said it is a ploy by state MLAs to make life difficult for the local MCs in the context of intra-party competition. Even more cynical voices hold that male MCs are OK with the rule as it may allow them to work behind the scenes on their various profitable money making endeavours while their 'proxy' women are nominally playing the corporator role. This latter hypothesis assumes that male MCs are quite confident that elections in their constituency can be won whether he himself or a woman family member stands. This assumption – perhaps inconceivable for what looks like a local democracy with competitive elections – appears to hold true by and large. It could be an indication of the extent to which elections are 'managed', through informal dynamics of personalistic ties, power and money. But the situation may be more mundane where there are reasons to believe that voters generally know that it makes no difference at all whether they vote for the wife (or other woman family member) or the former MC incumbent. Says one informant: 'Male corporators are the boss; they have the power, the inside knowledge and know the tricks' (field notes, 14 April 2015). We interviewed an MC who confirmed that there were only very few women who were standing for elections independently. If his constituency were to be reserved for women, he would simply nominate his wife: 'If people vote for her, people know they actually vote for me; the men are the main actors here.' He added: 'Women can never do this dirty work' (field notes, 17 February 2013). In their study of women MCs in Indian megacities, Ghosh and Tawa Lama-Rewal (2005: 81) mention that only a minority of women became an MC as per their own decision. All this is not to deny that women do obtain tickets on their own merit and that we met several serious, hard-working and committed women MCs who got elected after having built up a solid local reputation, for instance as doctor or social worker. Women who got into politics may do very well and succeed to be again elected from a general (M/F) ward. The quote system may well, given time, lead to more and more powerful women MCs, as seems to be happening with women councillors as a result of similar quota in rural governments. We met a rather gloomy male ex-corporator who, against his expectations, saw his 'proxy' MC wife being very successful, putting him in the shade. But it will never be simple or easy, if only because of gender norms where it is men and not women who are assumed to enter and operate in the public domain. Other constraints mentioned in our talks over time with women MCs were problems to combine the life of a mother with domestic duties as well as social norms and gender-based values. Women are much more restricted than men in frequenting important (informal) meetings: in a bar, in a car, in the evening, or even go and meet people on her own. Not least, many missed support and/or training to help them understand things like budgets and BMC rules and regulations.

4.2 Informality and corruption in Mumbai governance and the BMC

Before tracing the activities of MCs in relation to non-slum and then slum actors, I need to provide an overview of the very specific, complex and changing context in which MCs operate. *The Economist* does not mince its words by stressing the decay of politics in Mumbai and Maharashtra – while recalling that Mumbai is still the 'New York' of India as its commercial, financial and creative capital. In line with the concern that drives this book, the newspaper argues:

> The state's lead is not a given. Another 20 years of misrule – venal coalition politics, delayed airports and roads, slums and rural poverty – would be ruinous. And the collision that Maharashtra has experienced for two decades, of money, migration and hereditary political power, is one that much of India now faces. It is a test case: can broken governance be fixed? . . . . The problems run deep. First there is graft. It exploded along with Mumbai's property prices in the 1990s. Illegal gains from using bribes to bend planning rules in the city run at perhaps $ 5 billion a year, or 3 per cent of GDP. . . . Politics there is brutal. Grubbier Congress types dislike Mr Chavan and want to build a war chest for state and national elections due by 2014. He must also deal with a shifty coalition partner in the state assembly, the NCP, run by the Pawar family. Since 1999 the two parties have run the state together. Their squabbles over patronage and more have delayed projects and gummed up decisions.[5]

Besides, and this relates to my discussion of informality in the introduction and Chapter 1, much if not most governance of Mumbai is informal, as well depicted by Echanove (2013: 30):

> In Mumbai, the line between the informal economy and the formal economy is certainly an imaginary one. It is not, as often argued, that the two are deeply enmeshed, but rather that the entire economy and the public administration are, so to say, informal. For instance, no building is erected in Mumbai without at least 50 per cent of the land being paid in 'black'. Accountants specialize in hiding projects by reporting fake losses, dummy consultant fees, and offshore banking. The financial sector itself, which is supposed to be at the heart of the 'formal' economy, is fully deregulated. A significant share of skilled employment comes from foreign companies that outsource services to avoid having to pay higher salaries and employment benefits in their home countries. Land deals throughout the city are dependent on building permits delivered by the municipality and require kickbacks to be paid at all levels of the administration.

The Mumbai chapter of the Siddiqui and Bhowmik (2004) book makes depressing reading as corruption, already at that time, is shown to play a role in most city administration and most sectors – especially of course those relating to land and real estate. For instance, 'about half the money earmarked for *development activities* in the BMC is pocketed by corrupt officials and elected functionaries' (italics added to emphasise that this refers only to the specific BMC budgets for development works). The authors refer to Pinto (2000) who agrees on high levels of corruption in the BMC, consisting of blackmail, threats, extortion, as well as collective commissions extracted from contractors. I quote from the comprehensive study of all administrative facets of the BMC by Pinto and Pinto (2005: 513):

> It is well known how in the Standing Committee, contracts are finalised only after deals are struck and cuts fixed with contractors. While officials blame Councillors for making quick money, the officials too have their ways and means of personal gratification by bending rules and regulations, and punishing in devious ways those who do not line their pockets.

This latter line, written by two Mumbai's governance experts, is especially telling: not only is there an all-embracing culture of corruption in BMC, but they talk of 'the extent to which the rot has spread' (Pinto and Pinto 2005: 513). It is depicted to be 'systemic' or the only game in town, as negative incentives are created for those not engaging in corruption – where the label 'perverse' is quite accurate. It may in fact be the innocent or non-corrupt who are framed or accused. The latter may be considered by those corrupt as people portraying an annoying example of moral or ethical superiority or, more seriously, as a potential threat as whistle-blowers or traitors. Ironically it may be precisely such – what is called in the Indian media 'honest' or 'upright' – officers who are framed and suspended on corruption charges:

> This happened to a Ward S Inspector of Shops and Establishments, who incurred the anger of two fellow officers due to his actions against unauthorised shops. He then received threats from them, and they laid a trap for him in July 2012, after which he was suspended. Even while the BMC eventually concluded that he was innocent, 'that he was a victim of dishonest acts of others', he was not re-instated, it proceeded to 'mechanically suspend him without considering the facts', and the High Court ordered his immediate

re-employment and paying arrears due, stressing the shame and drastic impacts of a sudden dis-honourable suspension. It later appeared that the two cheats earlier managed to trap another officer who was found innocent.[6]

So here we have an honest officer, deliberately trapped because of doing his job as per the formal rules, becomes an outcast in the BMC and has to go to court to be re-employed and compensated for serious errors made. Even while not an easy topic, I tried to understand how officers cope in a context where participating in or ignoring/condoning illegal acts, frauds and sharing of informal spoils appears standard – not what is avoided or prevented. I tend to think that most of them found a way to either join the game or quietly avoid or stay clear of things where possible. Pro-active protesting and whistle-blowing seem rare, and as we saw it is actively discouraged. An officer said to be honest told me 'I feel like the only man wearing underpants in a room full of naked people who stare at me as being indecent' (field notes, 14 February 2013). Of course, as we will see later, the transfer industry also works to move upright 'troublemakers' to harmless locations in the bureaucracy, so problems may sort themselves out. But in this informal world of corruption, things may not be what they seem and I would never claim to have fully understood its mechanisms, extent and layers. An official may be wrongly accused for malfeasance for another, personal reason. Another suffers from informal sanctions for overplaying a hand by demanding more than is accepted per informal norms and rules (institutions) of corruption. It illustrates the working of 'informal institutions', the existence of a shadow administration with its own rates, expectations, and well-known systems of rewards or punishments which help enforce such informal rules, norms and values.

That the standing committee, as the most important and supreme decision-making BMC body, is plagued by corruption – both in incidental cases and apparently also when the annual budget is negotiated – is discouraging. It has representatives of all parties but is dominated by the leaders of the bigger parties. Nainan (2006: 13–14) reports that the committee chairman and members are expected to make contributions to their political parties so that 'the standing committee operates as a node in the network collecting money from contractors and feeding it to their parties' (Nainan 2006: 13–14). Informed sources maintain that the annual BMC budget is normally accepted only after much horse-trading – between the various political parties represented in the committee and then between the committee and the commissioner – including reservations for cuts.[7]

It may be good at this point to broaden our perspective and reflect on the nature and degree of corruption in India generally. The book by Debroy and Bhandari (2012: 7) on the *DNA* of Indian corruption argues that 'corruption has taken over India' (which is in line with Gupta 2012). Ways and means have achieved a high level of sophistication, with ongoing and routinised interactions and implicit informal contracts backed up by sanctions including official transfers. They argue that the political system, the bureaucracy and the technocracy are truly integrated, having eliminated the checks and balances designed into India's constitution. Lower-level bureaucracy and the police are seen to thrive on bribes and *baksheesh,* higher levels on grease money and scams. 'It is simply that the lower bureaucracy is neither accountable nor rewarded for delivery and efficiency and the citizen knows it' (Debroy and Bhandari 2012: 17).

> The lower level shares some of the rewards with its superiors to allow them to continue; the superiors share with the politicians, who in in turn share with small time street leaders, media[8] and even the electorate. The State withers away and in many parts of India, what is left of the state, it appears, is only held together due to corruption and a sophisticated system of sharing the spoils. . . . 'Needless to say, there are a few who do not directly indulge in such behaviour. But survival instincts make them look the other way, those who fob not are either eased into non-descript positions or hounded and pursued by a system that depends on their acquiescence.
>
> (Debroy and Bhandari 2012: 7–8)

Their book has a chapter entitled 'Robbing the Poor: Welfare and Graft', which refers to the 2008 India corruption study, according to which households with incomes below the poverty line paid Rs 8.8 billion to avail of 11 public services that were covered. Maximum corruption is experienced with the police, land records and registration and housing – next water supply, the rural employment scheme (MGNREGS), forestry, electricity, health, the PDS, banking, and primary school education (Gupta 2012: 43–44).

The BMC transfer industry: the market for well-earning jobs

In India, public-sector officials (IAS officials, policemen, engineers) can be transferred after some time from one position to another, which might be useful to make sure that employees work where they are most effective or do not build up adverse vested interests. Unfortunately, the transfer system has evolved in a most harmful way, for one thing where good people may be shifted for the sole reason of performing well or as per formal rules. Even worse, or as a token of ultimate collusion, money can be paid to seek a transfer to a position where an official expects to be able to make lots of informal earnings. Das (2001: 131) uses the label 'transfer industry', implying a lively business model. I already quoted Hansen (2001: 151) to the effect that Mumbai policemen actively look for postings in high-crime areas (prostitution, drugs) with ample opportunity to extract money from people who do illegal things, with the basic rule: the more serious the offence, the higher the rate (yet no crime is solved). Similar dynamics apply in certain BMC departments. It could be a WO posted in a poor city ward with low budgets, few if any major housing or infrastructure projects. He might be ready to pay a large sum to be posted in a rich ward, where the sum total of 'cuts' flowing illegally is known to be much higher. Such practices are not limited to Mumbai. Kishwar (2005: 130) refers to the Delhi situation:

> So also with transfers: a Regional Transport Officers posting at a lucrative highway could cost anything from Rs. 500.000 to 2 million. . . . Appointments, postings, and transfers are in fact a big industry – with politicians and bureaucrats routinely making crores of rupees from it. If one were to audit a senior bureaucrat's or a chief minister's working day, one is likely to find that 90 per cent of their workload pertains to handling these job auctions and transfer deals.
>
> (Kishwar 2005: 130)

She mentions that, at that time, the costs to get a peon job was Rs 40,000–50,000; a school teacher job in many states cost Rs 100,000 or more. A low-level policeman job went for a couple of lakhs. All *sarkari naukris* (government jobs) have fixed rates. An anonymous survey among officers of elite Indian services such as the administrative IAS, foreign IFS, police IPS, and revenue IRS services brought out that:

> An overwhelming 80 per cent of them agreed that the 'political corruption takes place because there are always some civil servants willing to collaborate in it'. . . . 'A majority of respondents felt that corrupt officers get away without being punished. It was also felt that corrupt officers are able to get the most sought after postings.

Harassment of honest officials through baseless complaints and investigations turns out to be a major issue in several services.'[9]

I have not studied such sensitive and very well hidden practice in detail, but over time heard many stories on the matter, sometimes with rates. For an anecdotal impression, where there is no guarantee that amounts are correct I present what was picked up over the years also from other sources. Siddiqui and Bhowmik (2004: 137) note: 'In case of transfers and postings to lucrative wards (for example, in the Western suburbs), the transfer bribes rate could be as high as Rs. 500,000' (this was around the year 2000). Way back in 2004 we learnt from an assistant engineer in the R-ward that the transfer to his job cost him Rs 200,000. The transfer to the position of WO (AC) was Rs 500,000 for a poor ward: 'Normally and in a rich ward like K-West (Andheri) this should be Rs. 2.5 million' (field notes, 15 December 2004). On 31 January 2005 we learnt the going rate for a transfer to the position of DMC to be Rs 2.5 million. To pay back that kind of money 'the meter to earn back starts from day one'. However, our informant added that not all applicants had to pay (all) that money; 'if you are well connected you get posted anyway', while referring to 'godfathers'. The current going transfer rate for the position of WO (AC) could apparently be as high as something like Rs 20 million or about $300,000 (field notes, 6 March 2013). It will be explained below that this position is extremely lucrative: a cut of all transactions in the wards office accrues to this official, normally an estimated 2–3 per cent – but then there are numerous transactions. A BMC ward official reported on 6 February 2005 that WOs receive 25 per cent of all the money that is spent in his wards area out of the municipal councillor and MLA funds (which is one reason to explain why corruption is so high here). Nainan (2006: 5) confirms that money is paid for officials seeking jobs in the BMC:

> Officials entering into the municipal system require buying of the post with a set amount of money often going to politicians at the state level. There is a direct relationship between the price of each post and the monies the officials can make in that position or how lucrative the post is. Transfers of officials also require payments to be made either to high level officials or to politicians, these transactions and negotiations are often done by intermediaries . . . , these may be Personal Assistants or political party members and at times this role is also played by members of the media fraternity.

A related dynamic is about postings generally where one would hope these to be merit based, so that gradually Mumbai's administrative capacity would be strengthened. Unfortunately this seems far from the case and this is not something new. Pinto and Pinto (2005: 509) refer to a letter written by a well-respected MC and BMC mayor around 1985 indicating that 'just about 10 per cent of candidates selected by the Maharashtra Public Service Commission were on merit basis and the rest were all ministers' men. It was also alleged that big money changes hands in matters of selection'.[10] Transfers for which most money is paid are with the BMC building department and the SRA.[11]

> The Building Proposals Department is, therefore, a very sensitive department which has high stakes in development activities. It is also singled out for very high levels of corruption. In fact, there is a real scramble for postings in the Building Proposals Department and there are tremendous pressures from ministers, powerful politicians and builders' lobby for placement of staff of their choice at strategic points.
>
> (Pinto and Pinto 2005: 188)

They provide details on the logic and dynamics of how the transfer system works (Pinto and Pinto 2005: 194).

> Civic Activists and commentators claim that a Sub-Engineer (in the Building Proposals Department) who is dutiful, strict and vigilant is transferred and a pliant one is brought in by influencing the administration either through high political pressure or by money power. The cash flow involved is astronomical. The Sub-Engineer who is able to raise this amount, obviously is hell-bent on recovering it. . . . There is competition between one builder and another for the quantum of money payable for speed money (to approve a building proposal). As a result of this, the speed money market has gone up considerably . . . this enables the greedy engineering staff to extract as much money as possible. They openly say, they need the money to pay the higher ups including the top politicians. The Vigilance Cell which is supposed to control this racket has also become part of this corrupt system.

It may happen that a contractor is instrumental in the transfer of a certain official or engineer who has proven to be dedicated to him. Part of or all cash needed is paid by the contractor who so buys a long period of easy working, no questions asked. Hence, some staff of the BMC engineering department almost work like employees or consultants for private developers (Nainan 2006: 10). She provides indications of an 'invisible revolving door' between developers, BMC planners and engineers; a blurring of interests and activities between the public and private sector. In contrast, a builder or contractor could complain to an MC, MLA or MP that a certain officer is making problems in the flow of illegal earnings and that he should be transferred.

MCs and 'the mafia' or underworld

Whereas the corruption mechanisms in BMC are relatively well known and by and large in the public domain, another dimension even harder to grasp is the role of 'the mafia' (Nainan 2012), 'the underworld' or organised crime groups (OCG) (Weinstein 2008). The underworld of Mumbai is mentioned as an important and well-entrenched part of the power and governance structures of Mumbai by Siddiqui and Bhowmik (2004: 182–83), for example as it uses gangs to evict occupants from apartments and plots of land. Its activities appear to have initially been centred on smuggling, to later branch out into the 'Bollywood' film industry (Weinstein 2008: 30), the construction sector, prostitution, and the hotel industry. Weinstein (2008: 25ff.) traces the evolution of the Mumbai mafia from the first slum lords or *dadas* in Dharavi and their engagement with smuggling, brothels, gambling, illegal liquor, and gold. Eventually, they started to claim land which was sub-divided and sold to new migrants. She links the mafia operation to the 'informal governance' literature, including patron–client relations. Mafia-related 'social brokers' came to play critical bridging roles between the poor/ recent migrants and city agencies. This occurred in the fields of justice, housing and local administration and in arrangements bordering the illegal, sometimes embedded in broader criminal structures (Weinstein 2008: 25ff.). Even while the concrete evidence presented on present-day mafia/OCGs activities and relations is limited, Weinstein makes the case that today the OCGs have branched out strongly into real estate, starting after the liberalisation of the Mumbai economy and the increasing role of the private sector in city governance. Weinstein's analysis of the early days of interaction between criminal organisations and Mumbai politicians is consistent with the assessment of Hansen (2001: 98–99), who reflects on the ascendency of the Shiv Sena party:

> The situation was complicated by the deep involvement of sitting councillors and local leadership in contracting, construction and real estate, as well as crime and smuggling. For most municipal

councillors, therefore, the stakes in local politics were considerably higher than before they entered the civic body.

Confirming the role of the underworld in land transactions, Whitehead and More (2007: 2431) indicate that landownership in Mumbai is concentrated in very few hands, so that 'about nine developers and trusts control all available private land in Mumbai Island'. Nainan (2012) makes frequent references to 'the mafia', but details on its nature, composition and how it is engaged today remain a bit hazy. She confirms for the micro-level how criminals entered politics especially through the Shiv Sena but also other parties: 'As a result, several political leaders who emerged from the gangs have strong connections with the organised crime world of the city' (Nainan 2012: 107). The mafia is made up of *dadas,* dons and goondas, who may appear as neighbourhood-level leaders and as heads of Shiv Sena party offices (*shakas*), engaged in protecting illegal slum squatters in exchange for money. It may be assumed that, in varying degrees and from case to case, corporators are engaged with such groups where they are part of definitely powerful networks (cabals in Nainan 2006) of builders, state agency officials and higher-level politicians such as MLAs and MPs (almost half of the former had criminal records).[12] I conclude this section with a striking statement on mafia–politician relations from a political party leader:

> 'Now the politician has become mafia and mafia has become politician, and in the name of development they are robbing the nation. This is their idea of a public-private partnership. It is not a problem of governance. There is a design in this theft', according to a BJP leader from Karnataka State.[13]

4.3   The BMC, corporators and builders/contractors

While the BMC is a massive organisation, itself in charge of many civic services such as road construction and managing and maintaining public schools, it does not have a construction department which builds and repairs things: this is contracted out to contractors. It is not surprising that BMC corruption seems concentrated in the domains of construction and land which is conform global experience. Other departments seem (much) less affected, except those where officials and MCs meet with the public. Corruption is also believed to be considerable here, depending on the service requested, the urgency of the request and the possibility that a request comes with the recommendation of a powerful agent, for instance a corporator. A useful initial distinction can be made between passive and active corruption. Passive corruption is when people willingly pay ('speed') money as requested to get work done quickly. Active corruption is when officials and politicians force people to pay for services that are free of cost (e.g. certificates) or that they forcefully take cash simply because it is possible (e.g. *hafta* for hawkers; police bribes). The scope for the latter is a straight power calculation: if the bribe-taker judges that a bribe payer has no (protective) contacts or networks, risks are low. This is why the poor are such easy victims. And even if things go wrong – and if things are within accepted everyday boundaries and corruption rules – a cover up can normally be arranged. Against this background I will dwell on 'administrative' corruption in the BMC, arising from the interactions (nexus) between politicians, officials/engineers and builders/contractors.

As already explained in Chapter 2 (Section 2.4), the cooperation between MCs and ward officials seems marked by informal dynamics of influence and corruption, where 'workable' patterns have evolved over the years between actors who often know each other quite well. For example, wards offices contract a contractor – who has to meet certain criteria within specified classes – for all works in a year, but the contractor may be the brother of a corporator (field notes, 23 December 2004). The key relationship here is a triangle between an MC who proposes works, a ward official such as a junior or other engineer and the contractor/builder to carry out the work. The work is financed either from the general WO budget allocation up to Rs 500,000 or from the corporator discretionary fund, presently Rs 6 million. All three actors may share the informal proceeds through common strategies to cream off budgets that evolved over time. Some examples of ward-level corruption are listed here from Siddiqui and Bhowmik (2004: 136–39).

- Petty works contractors form a cartel and quote rates 30–40 per cent below the official estimates in collusion with corrupt officials, who approve their non-existent works as being 'satisfactorily completed' and clear the outstanding bills;
- The practise of the 'revised estimate', where contractors seek additional funds just before the end of the financial year, based on token proposals which are hurriedly approved and funds sanctioned, which then disappear in the pockets of contractors and officials;
- A number of ACs (WOs) are known to take heavy bribes for protecting illegal constructions; as a result, they have become owners of flourmills, industries and farmhouses;
- In 2001, 17 BMC engineers were suspended after it was found they paid contractors for work that was not done.

I am led to believe that in all contracts between BMC and contractors bribes are already included, with rates and amounts relatively fixed and well known. The data I collected are again presented more as a rough indication of the 'mechanisms' of malfeasance rather than of precise rates, which change over time, perhaps obeying informal laws of opportunity, demand and supply. Van Dijk (2011a: 40) mentions that corporators receive 2–5 per cent of the costs of all civil works and that another 25 per cent is divided among others who are involved in the contract, from junior engineer to assistant engineer up to the WO/ AC. Siddiqui and Bhowmik (2004: 137–38) mention that 47 per cent of the value of BMC tenders is given as kickbacks, with the following breakdown on the situation around 2000. Over the years I have tried to find out more data and I have added these percentages (in brackets) by way of more recent anecdotal evidence.

- The junior engineer receives 2 per cent for scrutinising the estimate (2–5 per cent);
- The wards account unit clears it for 3 per cent (1–2 per cent);
- The chartered accountant allots the funds for 5 per cent (not applicable);
- The DMC sanctions it for 2 per cent (1–2 per cent);
- The Junior engineer then drafts the bill at 8 per cent (is included in the above first item);
- The sub-engineer and assistant engineer take 10 per cent for signing the bill (4–5 per cent);
- Other official recipients include the head clerk (2 per cent) (2 per cent); the WO (AC) who withholds 3 per cent (2 per cent), the Vigilance Cell takes 2 per cent for the No-Objection Certificate (2 per cent);
- Relevant councillors for 'not crying foul': 10 per cent (3–5 per cent).

According to Nainan (2006: 5)

> A fixed rate of payments gets developed between the officers and the contractors, in exchange for which officers ensure that estimates are developed, projects are sanctioned, work orders issued, and payments are made at the end of the work in a very smooth manner.

She offers a list of cuts: 6–7 per cent to the JE; 2–3 per cent to the sub-engineer and AE with the WO receiving 2 per cent of the project costs (Nainan 2006: 10). Whereas it appears as if normally a 'win–win' situation exists where MCs/politicians, officials and contractors all benefit more than they should under public contracts, the system may be hardest for contractors, the only actors here for whom contracts are the only means of subsistence. They often face problems as the BMC can be very slow, sometimes a contractor already starts work while advancing his initial investment, and there are risks that he may lose out. If all goes wrong he may reduce work quality to break even. Regrettably, indications are things are not getting better.[14] Where kickbacks are concerned, an interesting list by Debroy and Bhandari (2012: 79–80) is quite comprehensive and includes monies channelled on to the Minister and his Personal Assistant in the Indian state of Jharkhand. I reproduce this list, once more to indicate the mechanisms (never mind the precise 'cut' rates) in one Indian state, but which might also operate elsewhere:[15]

> Commissions are typical of all projects involving tender. There are commissions when obtaining the tender paper, getting it approved, and then while taking payment after presenting the bill. Tender-based development works have a commission of 13–15 per cent. The maximum rates of commission are in irrigation and the special division. In both cases, the Minister takes 5–10 per cent. Typically, the contractor obtains payment after the deduction of 40 per cent as commission, the cashier gets a salami amount if Rs. 100–500, while issuing a tender form. The contractor pays Rs. 20.000–10.000 in the name of paper scrutiny. Then the tender paper goes to the estimate officer. From there to the Executive Engineer and the Superintendent Engineer. . . . For tenders above Rs. 25 lakh but less than 2 *crores,* the approval authority is the Chief Engineer (CE). After charging 0.5 per cent, the EE sends it to the CE, where 3–5 per cent commission is charged. This 3–5 per cent is distributed as 0.5 per cent to the minister, 1.25 per cent to the CE and 0.62 per cent to the Technical Advisor. 0.31 per cent goes to the monitoring cell, which includes SE and AE. . . . For tenders above Rs. 2 *crores,* the CE's office charges 1.5 per cent. 0.5 per cent of this goes to the departmental secretary and 0.5 per cent goes to the monitoring cell, the CE retaining the remaining 0.5 per cent. Once the committee has approved, the tender goes to the Minister. The Minister charges 2 per cent and the Minister's PA charges 0.25 per cent.

For my quest to investigate the incidence of machine politics (Scott 1969) in the assumed close ties between corporators and 'business interests', Nainan's (2012) insights are very relevant. She refers to the 'political income' of MCs: all money needed on a weekly and monthly basis to finance the running costs of any MC (contributions to the party, to followers, to maintain an office, transport, presents). She feels that:

> Private developers – not government projects – provide the lion's share of the 'political income'. These exchanges of financial means for political power and related access to decision-making processes are not limited to payments by contractors. The political income that political parties are able to gather also includes income from slum residents and private builders engaged in slum redevelopment. As all private projects also need government approval, councillors play the role of intermediary between officials and builders, and in other cases between the builder and the local brokers. Some councillors also invest with small and medium builders, so that politicians reappear as financiers and partners of builders.
>
> (Nainan 2012: 159)

This concludes my review of administrative malfeasance in Mumbai. The dynamics illustrate and highlight an inevitable decline in Mumbai's administrative and engineering capacity to develop and implement suitable plans, policies and projects. For the rich, global city that it is, this shows in its generally dismal management. As noted in a series of PRAJA (2012, 2014b) reports, a majority of *Mumbaikars* are none too happy about all this. Let is now consider other activities and domains of the city's political representatives.

4.4   Corporators as political entrepreneurs and their citywide networks

Municipal corporators are frequently portrayed as the 'godfather' or 'top patron' of his or her constituency, a bit like someone with the status of a Raja managing a fiefdom. This would be consistent with the degree of respect and status involved, the paraphernalia of power and the fact that a solid MC is deeply embedded in his or her constituency and has a finger in all pies. Following independence and the consolidation of democracy within municipal governance, corporators have become increasingly important in city governance: 'State and city political leaders have recognised that their power is based on their ability to intervene in settlements: by discreetly halting demolitions on the one hand, and through the construction of roads, sewage lines and water lines on the other' (Anand and Rademacher 2011: 1757). They

gradually evolved from essential mediators into very present political entrepreneurs who, like spiders in a web, have extensive networks
including central city actors and agencies, contractors and private-
sector firms, slum leaders, mafia groups and the police. Not least, they
are critical agents for the urban poor in the numerous Mumbai slums,
where they act as patrons and brokers to bridge access gaps between
the poor and critical municipal and state agencies. I established that
MCs need both 'political capital' such as formal and informal trust-
based networks and physical capital such as lots of rupees to finance
their political shops – such as party contributions or repayments to
builders or businesspeople following pre-election promises. But money
is also needed to accommodate their voters, to invest in the future
which may entail a career as MLA, but not in the last place to save
and prepare for the possibility that one is not re-elected. We know an
MC who built up a construction firm in his first election term, another
started a TV cable network, yet another ran a water tank business. The
latter made good money providing slums with drinking water. Before
elections he even provided it free of cost. When we met him in his spa-
cious house after losing the 2012 elections he told us that this did not
worry him financially.

Spiders in citywide webs: the networks of corporators

MCs as intermediaries or brokers can only become effective, elected
and re-elected if they are able to play a useful role in and as the centre
of a web of actors, all somehow linked geographically to a constituency which is their prime arena. The MC networks can be divided into
eight categories (based on Van Dijk, in de Wit and Van Dijk 2010; see
also van Dijk 2006), which include their personal networks as already
discussed before (family, friends, school ties); the political party networks of the MC (city, state and central); the politicians of other parties (ward, city, state) and bureaucratic networks (ward, city, state).
Money networks include the 'clients' of the MC where contractors/
developers are most important as indicated, but also shopkeepers,
slum lords and what we might call mafia or (semi) criminal networks.
Then there are networks of street-level party workers including local
slum leaders. Most powerful here are MC's 'inner-circle' local-level
party brokers, but indispensable too also 'satellites': mostly young men
who are associated with local leaders and the MC for sundry services if
and when needed. Another network is made up of all sorts of organised
citizen groups: RWAs, NGOs, CBOs, ALMs, *mahila mandals,* self-help/

credit/savings groups, trade unions, professional organisations, religious groups and specific ethnic groups. Last but not least any MC is linked to individual citizens for whom he or she is mostly a patron or broker, but some of whom are also important sources of information or money. I agree with van Dijk (2006: 118) that MC networks are mostly localised and that only few of them have ties with political and bureaucratic networks beyond the city level. They would normally have little information on and interaction with central and state-level policies and programmes. Being key agents of local governance already keeps most of them pretty busy for long days – while many male corporators run some business too.

Corporator slum activities contextualised

In a perceptive comment, Sivaramakrishnan (2004: 17) provides a sweeping but accurate depiction of the changing relations between India's urban poor and the state:

> Yet the question remains how relevant are all these efforts for the urban poor. Though it is well recognised that without access to political power, the poor cannot and do not participate in their own governance, the channels of accessing political power continue to be limited. Squatter and slum settlements have long been regarded as an opportunity and a platform both for politicians and the slum residents to acquire and exercise political power. However, this well-trodden path has suffered many diversions caused by fluctuating political loyalties, pressures of the real estate market, land grabbing mafia, rising costs of improvement or redevelopment works and the inability of most governments to be consistent for any length of time. The phenomenon of 'cut off' dates whereby slum residents are included or excluded from relocation benefits is one example. In Delhi and Mumbai such cut off dates have been moved back several times.

McFarlane (2008: 91) believes that slum people are not treated as 'proper citizens' and that there is a fundamental policy – I would say administrative – ambivalence. On the one hand authorities are constrained by a legal compulsion where 'a full recognition of the legitimacy of informal settlement would undermine and threaten the structure of legally held property'. This contradicts with the everyday reality where authorities do have important social, economic and political reasons to provide services to the poor, ranging from ethnic ties, the availability of low cost labour and the readiness of poor people to vote for particular political candidates. As a result, a range of services and facilities are extended on a case-to – case, ad hoc, or exceptional basis, without jeopardizing the overall structure of legality and property'. We see here what I have termed 'the mediated state': not general rules but individual discretion determines state allocations. Poor people not only face access problems to claim entitlements; poor people are also not treated well by BMC and other (e.g. PDS, SRS) officials, confirming what Narayan (2000) already noted. Siddiqui and Bhowmik (2004: 136) found that the BMC office bearers hold strong negative attitudes towards the poor and the women:

> which is reflected in their tendency to manipulate the needs of these groups, ranging from reluctance to take note of their issues and address these, . . . belittling them, and holding them accountable for their substandard conditions or for the larger problems of the city ('You have no right to get water, and yet we provide it to you for free').

As noted in Chapter 3 it seems to be quite rare for individual slum people to independently contact the BMC wards office. While generally rare for slum persons to visit a ward or other agency office, it does happen that a group of aggrieved or angry slum people do join forces and go and demand a solution to an urgent problem, as proof that collective action is possible:

> We interviewed a ward official who said: 'when people come in mobs, immediate attention is given by the MC to solve the problem'. Another: 'poor people who go to the MC often come in mobs. The rich are decent and come for drainage blockings, garbage accumulation, and nuisance of neighbours. Influential people would insist that their problems are attended immediately without even waiting for the minimum period'. Another official said: 'officials *and* corporators are in touch with the people and they know the needs of the people.'
>
> (de Wit field notes, May 2006)

Such differences between the poor and middle classes may well be explained by the differential urgency of needs or in terms of a lower-class manifestation of frustration. There is another side as noted by Kumar and Landy (2009: 124–25):

> Unlike poor slum dwellers, middle class voters usually do not seek personal favours: they look for their representatives' intervention

in order to get better roads or streetlights in their localities . . .
hence, services rendered in their localities are different from those
provided in slum areas (for the votes of a large number of poor
people can be won with meagre monetary incentives).

They argue that in slum areas individual needs very often get precedence over public goods (schools, clinics, roads, drinking water).
In the slums, politicians rather intervene in personal matters such as
arranging a job, financial assistance in case of serious illness, using
influence with law-enforcing agencies in case of trouble, and so on.
For these reasons, the poor remain obliged to their patrons and make
no demands – or at least refrain from openly siding with those wanting
to put direct (collective) pressure on representatives. For these reasons
poor neighbourhoods are left with waterlogged or muddy lanes and
choked drainage (Kumar and Landy 2009: 124–25).

Having elaborated the demand side and access problems for poor
people, I will now consider the mirror image in the supply side of the
local state machinery, where corporators figure large in terms of mediation and bridging gaps. In Chapter 2 (Section 2.4) I already considered
the usefulness of BMC democratic forums: the BMC plenary council and
neighbourhood WCMs. In the latter MCs were shown not to ask many
questions. The main topic discussed was re-naming roads which points
to a general mismatch – of representation – between discussion topics
and problems ward-level people actually experience (PRAJA 2011). As
far as known, problems for slum or poor people were not discussed. Neither do these forums seem to have or aspire much of a policy role. It is
true that BMC (and WCM) mandates do not include key urban poverty
matters of land and slum improvement/redevelopment or 'cut-off dates',
but that should not stop corporators to reflect on, discuss or make suggestions on such critical broader issues of (city) governance. Consistent
with my research frame with mediated state and 'political machine' perspectives, MCs and their party colleagues seem little interested in policy processes or to propose policy other than short-term concrete (and
concrete-based) proposals and projects. It almost appears as if they only
get interested after budgets have been allocated and take it from there,
which fits the model of 'the street-level politician' (Berenschot 2010).
Taking existing conditions, budget lines and schemes for granted, it seems
they see their main vocation as channeling policy benefits to the poor and
other richer claimants, mostly on an individual 'particularistic' basis.

We need to check this further by now targeting corporator-urban
poor relations and interactions. Can evidence be found for the statement that: 'The difference between slums of despair and slums of

progress are the differences in interests and muscle and money power between corporators? (see Anand 2011b: 547; de Wit and van Dijk 2010: 10). Or that corporators run useful, even critical 'one stop shops' for slum people as windows into supra-slum-level opportunities and services?

Corporators' slum-level political and patronage networks

As noted, any corporator needs an effective two-way local network, on the one hand to know and monitor developments, opportunities and problems of his or her ward and its various pockets (notably election booth areas). On the other hand he needs to link to ward people when he wants things from them – mostly votes, but also support during and in between elections. A corporator can be seen as one link in a chain of citywide pyramidal patronage networks, where they themselves are on top of a neighbourhood-level pyramid, with several layers below. MCs have a network of loyal party supporters, whom they select, groom and look after and who represent eyes and ears at street level. Things come together in a local party or MC office, where Shiv Sena has the most developed local party offices or *shakhas*. Often very lively and popular meeting places, this is where information is shared, problems solved and party and friendship ties maintained. According to Eckert (2002: 5–6), such *shakhas* (literally 'branches') 'have become dominant centres of local self-governance . . . they attempt to fulfil what the state promised but did not deliver: infrastructural measures, such as garbage collection, water connection, public toilets, they initiate employment schemes, youth activities, and festivals'. Bedi (2007: 1538) says that the Shiv Sena party relies on local patronage systems operating in each neighbourhood through 'a remarkably vital *shakha* network'. She found that both male and female leaders spent much of their time and energy to make sure that 'they are known (and to some extent feared) in their localities'.[16] The SS is quite successful in organising party cadre and sympathisers in and around its local offices, partly as there is a high premium on 'visibility', seen as sustained support for the party and its leadership. Anand (2011b: 548–49) suggests that the state extended itself into Mumbai's slums over the last two decades via the activities of its elected representatives, where facilities provided – often as part of their Area Development funds – mostly bear their names:

> Because settlers (*slum dwellers*, [italics added]) are critical to the electoral success of political parties, the city's dominant outfits

have worked to bring the services of the state (water, electricity, hospitals, schools) to settlements in a highly visible manner. They often do this by supporting, and seeking the support of dadas and other leaders in the settlements. This is accomplished not only by working to accommodate their ad hoc demands for the state's resources but also by nominating them to run on party tickets in city and state elections.

(Anand 2011b: 547)

Visibility, dedication, loyalty, and respect for party leaders as well as their rank and file help build political capital. It improves chances that the political party hierarchy puts you up for re-election or field you for higher office. While the Shiv Sena boasts a larger women membership, the party also employs poor women to promote its pro-poor image:

It is interesting that most of these 'extras' brought in for *morchas* tend to be very poor women who live in Sena dominated slums and probably perceive that they will get some basic amenities such as water or roads in their areas if they show up as supporters of a *morcha*. It is this high visibility of the urban poor at visible events such as *morchas*, which continues to reinvent the Sena image as the 'common person's party' for the *Sainiks* themselves as much as it does for the press and media opportunities.

(Anand 2011b: 547)

Other political parties also have local party offices, but, with the exception of the MNS party, they are not many, not as vibrant, and not as well organised as the *shakhas*. Corporators of all parties have an office to work from, some of which look quite lively even if it is a room at the ground floor of his or her house, where, as we shall see, people with complaints are welcome. A corporator is rarely alone; there is always a coterie of trusted long-term allies who can be relied upon to execute – even sensitive and delicate – jobs well. They deal with important issues on behalf of the MC and also act as brokers between the MC and inhabitants of the electoral ward, as well as key contacts outside his or her core-constituency.[17] Below this level of power and authority come party or corporator supporters, young men who serve as (emerging) middle-level brokers between the MC (office) and people in their streets and areas. They refer or help solve everyday issues of slum dwellers or are requested to collect various rents/fees for informal services. In exchange for the client's loyalty to the party and sometimes a fee the issue is addressed if possible. At the level of a smaller neighbourhood, slum pocket or a few streets people may be loosely organised in party-linked 'housing cooperative societies', youth groups, sports or women associations which are not normally very active. They wake up when needed for instance for party events or celebration. Some of them become operational and active before elections as conduits for the allocation of freebies or 'machine inducements' (details in Chapter 5). Key agents here are local leaders in close contact with the MC and/or party office. Best characterised as a 'leader-centred network' such loyalists form the lowest-level part of the MCs network.

An overview of general corporator activities and incomes

Nainan (2006: 14) mentions that

> All interviewed councillors admitted that councillors who knew how the system functions and were able to exhibit high nuisance value would reap a good political income. Knowledge of the rules and policies related to housing and slum development, along with muscle power, were considered to be necessary skills for any successful councilor.

On this note I will now mention key areas where MCs are generally active, before narrowing down my focus to their slum work. Basically a corporator needs to balance and navigate between several needs and expectations. For starters and a prime concern is a personal (and family) interest to lead a good life and make more earnings than political costs. There are the demands and expectations of the party ('the Shiv Sena central party management which has five SS corporators in this ward expects Rs 100,000 monthly from each of them'; field notes, 23 February 2012); the demands and expectations from his or her voters; and the demands and expectations of his or her financiers – ranging from builders to bribe/*hafta* collectors. As illustrated by Bawa (2011: 498):

> An elected representative who runs a tanker business or whose election campaign has been supported by the tanker lobbies or whose party cadres are primarily private water suppliers will tread a cautious line between fulfilling informal group's demands for municipal water and balancing his personal and support groups' interests.'

Corporators will be aware of any land or building transaction, of interventions in services (water, electricity) and infrastructure and other events in his ward. Most likely he or she will (need to) be consulted, perhaps approve matters and almost always take a cut: 'Straddling the boundaries of the (in)formal and the (il)legal, councillors are able to re-inscribe their powers in the settlements (slums) by mediating and facilitating access to the procedures of government' (Anand 2011b: 550–1). One important asset of the MC is what was referred to as 'nuisance power'. For example, he may put pressure on a builder to pay more money in return for covering up the addition of an unauthorised floor. In case the builder refuses, the MC can always threaten to come back with a BMC engineer and order him to stop work altogether on some pretext or other. The builder will have little option but to pay up. As elaborated later when considering election campaign funding, builders and developers are an important target group for any corporator. An insightful account of corporator–builder relations is provided by Nainan (2006: 12).

> Councillors admitted giving their '*Ashirwad*' or 'blessing' to builders undertaking any works in the councillor's electoral ward. This is a fee to the councillor for keeping out of conflicts or any question which is likely to emerge in development projects. In most of the slum redevelopment carried out there is a section of the community which is either not eligible or not willing to participate. The developer uses various mechanisms to deal with this population. This may include violence, threat, buying consent or just juggling figures so that certain bogus beneficiaries appear on the beneficiary list. Other rules which are broken are building extra floors, or narrower staircases, or buying out slum residents from their huts. . . . The local councillor could play an important role by representing the grievance of the residents to the officers. However, as the number of affected households are generally very small and 'silence money' large, councillors have admitted to being paid to keep out of this process. In some instances, they represent the developer as co-partner in the municipal corporation or prod the slum dwellers into accepting the builder.

Other areas of corporator engagement include taxes, permits and licences and the general bending of rules. Many semi-illegal actions can be discussed with the MC who may then be able to neutralise any negative impacts – for example by informing BMC engineers that an illegal construction is OK. MCs are normally very close to the local police – here too they may cooperate, for instance, in allowing an illegal bar to stay open or share the collections raised by fining hawkers. MCs and the police almost unavoidably connive if the former is somehow engaged in (condoning) illegal activity relating to things such as smuggling, alcohol, prostitution, or drugs (see Hansen 2001). One must assume that the MC knows about such matters through his or her local networks, eyes and ears. Even while entirely informal, Mumbai does have a formal machinery in which such things are forbidden, can be detected and could suddenly blow up in the media. Especially in case of large-scale operations or when important political, film or mafia personalities are involved, these remain sensitive and delicate matters. Some corporators are reported to cooperate with the police to protect them from the consequences of un-permitted or illegal acts or to put pressure on or punish selected people. Impacts would be that they earn money and that the illegal act is not punished – justice is for sale, another commodity. The most widespread form of petty corruption affecting the poor is the collection of *hafta* (illegal weekly/regular payments) from hawkers to allow them to start, maintain or expand their local business – which indeed is often illegal in a formal, legal sense: 'It is a well-planned operation and involves multiple actors – the police, concerned municipal officials (in particular, the municipal recovery inspector), local politicians (often the councillors) and goons' (Siddiqui and Bhowmik 2004: 142). The formal recorded amounts collected as hawkers' fines are estimated by them at Rs 120 million (by 2000), but illegal and informal *hafta* collections are pegged at about Rs 1,200 million. That makes it a massive, very profitable racket. The sad flip side is a similarly enormous tax on such poor people. Debroy and Bhandari (2012: 84ff.) consider it as 'the organised extortion of the unorganised sector', where 'haftas to both the municipal authorities as well as the police are standard and can account to anywhere between 20–50 per cent of the revenues'. This, apart from unexpected raids and that wares and push carts are impounded resulting in income losses for weeks: 'the inhuman nature of such practices cannot be underscored enough' (Debroy and Bhandari 2012: 86). Weinstein (2008: 35) confirms the practice of *hafta* collection by the police and BMC staff among the numerous Mumbai hawkers, while noting that the mafia (OCG) was engaged too.

4.5 Corporators' slum-level patronage networks and activities

The compulsions of Mumbai corporators, who need to build up and sustain political and rupee capital while meeting a variety of expectations are well captured in this quote by Nainan (2006: 13):

> 'Political costs' are expenditures that the councillor is required to made to maintain his voters after winning the elections. The

expectation of the councillors who represent a slum are many, they include provision of basic amenities, protection against evictions, admissions to schools and colleges, employment and dealing with the police, and family and matrimonial conflicts. For some of these services the councillor may expect payment while others are done to maintain his 'good-will'; quite a few of these tasks are not within his formal role as a municipal councillor and are seen as informal role, and thus it is not a surprising that the councillor is perceived as an elder brother or sister as they are often addressed as a 'Bhai', 'Dada', 'Bhau' 'Daddy'. Councillors' image emerges from merging of a godfather and a modern day Robin hood, who takes from those who can and gives it back to the weaker ones using some for himself and saving a little for the upcoming elections.

The statement usefully brings out well the more positive qualities of Mumbai's corporators. Neatly fitting the 'Janus-faced' character of corporators (which I already noted for Madras slum leaders in de Wit 1985), two perspectives exist. Some see them as basically helpful: the one person who is ready to listen and support slum people in a sea of indifference, as a critical and much needed 'one-stop window' for poor people's multiple problems. In contrast, others emphasise their exploitative and self-interested nature. Always looking for money, engaged in shady and illegal deals, they only support the poor for vote bank reasons. Let us assess MC work against these two divergent views. Where their embedding in slum areas is concerned, I distinguish and will now address four broad activity fields: daily consultation hours, making the slum rounds, incidental support on demand, and the application of the discretionary Corporator Area Development Fund. To set the stage, I take from Boo (2012: 52) a typical and accurate depiction of the image of the constructed and accepted image of a corporator. We need to keep in mind that MCs come in different sizes and shapes and that the slum here is not a typical one in that it is a threatened 'minority slum', at risk to be evicted.

They understood Mr. S. (the corporator) to be corrupt. They assumed he'd faked his caste certificate. 'But he alone comes here, shows his face', Annawadians said. Before each election, he'd used city money or tapped the largesse of a prominent American Christian Charity . . . to give Annawadi an amenity: a public toilet; a flagpole; gutters; a concrete platform by the sewage lake, where he usually stood when he came. And each time he visited, he told residents how hard he'd been fighting to hold of the bulldozers of the airport authority, which had razed huts here in 2001 and 2004. In the scheme of the airport modernization project, and of the governance of Mumbai, the Corporator was a bit-player, a pothole-filler of a politician. But he loomed larger than the prime minister in the political imagination of the Annawadians. He needed their votes; they needed to believe in his power to protect them.

The corporator consultation meetings

Much of the MC patronage and protection-related business takes place invisibly, where problems may be addressed following phone calls and arrangements with leaders or *dadas* in respective slums. At two occasions one can see the MC in full action, which is during daily open meetings and on slum rounds. Apart from solving problems, these are displays of visibility and power, showing people – that is voters – that he or she cares. Just like the Shiv Sena has local party offices, all corporators have a location where people know they can find him or her at specific times. People who come here mostly have personal requests, where people need an urgent referral to a (better) school, a government agency or government scheme. But we also learnt that more or less desperate people come and seek support in seeking a job for a son after the father died or a woman at the end of her wits to seek support against her abusive, beating husband. Many requests are about documents and certificates, not least for slum people to prove their identity.[18] Debroy and Bhandari (2012: 62–63) offer a useful list (plus the bribes to be paid) of all possible certifications, identifications and permissions that all Indians, rich or poor, need to obtain access to the state: birth certificates, death certificates, electricity, water and sewage connection proofs, vehicle registration, driving licence, map clearance of house or multi-storied building, copies of papers relating to land registration and mutations. All such requests can be dealt with formally and will require several visits to relevant offices. Poor people may or may not be entertained there personally. Often unaware where to go and aware of their 'handicaps' they may opt to work through a local leader or to contact the MC, against payment of a small commission and/or a promise to vote for the MC in the next elections. Anand (2011b: 552) illustrates how this works in terms of obtaining water connections:

> If settlers can claim tenancy prior to the cut-off date, councillors write letters of support on settler's behalf, to strengthen their applications. If settlers do not have the necessary documents, councillors organise forged copies, to send along with letters for a

price. Thus, while the legality of settlers matters, as does their ability to pay for connections, it is their relationship with councillors and other charismatic leaders in the settlement that enables their access to the public system.

A final important service a corporator can provide is help organise the paper work for a voter registration proof so that people can vote in elections. This is about the puzzle as to how it would be possible for politicians to support the emergence or growth of an illegal slum (pocket) with a view to vote bank support there. It interestingly implies that slum households who (illegally) encroach city land somehow manage to obtain identity proof as well as a Voter Identification Card which are not easy to obtain, as shown in Chapter 5. It appears that MCs can indeed organise a fast track application procedure to obtain the Election Photo ID Card within two-three months. It is said to involve the election officer, an application form, verification of submitted papers and endorsement at the election commission's office. If correct, this is a win-win arrangement for the MC in terms of a guaranteed vote and for the poor person so suddenly recognised as a voting 'citizen' (field notes, April 2015).[19]

Making the rounds

Following such a morning meeting, many corporators may then make a round of parts of their constituency, to check on possible problems and grievances and to oversee works that are undertaken in the area. Often the MC is accompanied by a ward office junior engineer who brings along specific local and technical knowledge. All corporators we interviewed indicated that they spent time in their constituencies, in varying degrees, while about half of them indicated that they were especially targeting the poor and/or the slums in their constituencies. Some said that they visited slums each day, others twice daily, but all make regular if not daily rounds, except perhaps one outspoken MC (a Brahmin) who has an anti-poor reputation:

> Do not let them fool you, they have more money than you and me, they just do not care about how they live or what effect they have on the city.
>
> (field notes, 5 February 2009)

As noted, MCs and ward office officials/engineers have very different work perspectives, and in most cases, the latter rely on the corporator's localised street-level knowledge either because they do not know the ground realities very well or they are too apathetic to find out for themselves (see de Wit and van Dijk 2010: 4).

Incidental support

Apart from such institutionalised meetings, anything can happen any time that needs the corporator's attention. As confirmed by many MCs they are always busy; they can be disturbed at all times. Whatever else I have said about them, it is definitely not that they are lazy or indifferent. To be a corporator one needs to be willing to work very hard while making long days; be sharp in terms of memorising deals, rates, opportunities; be ready for the manipulations and tricks of both colleagues and undermining opposition party tricks. They manage the risks associated with secretive, 'underground' actions as anything can backfire with many 'sharks' watching. Many are versatile, street wise and powerful persons who have only grown into the job as they can cope with its many pressures.

On average, Van Dijk (2006) mentions, MCs report to be available for citizens at least 17 hours a week and a majority more than 25 per week. Several MCs said that in practice they are available '24 hours a day to their constituency' while late night phone calls from a frantic constituent are not uncommon (de Wit and Van Dijk 2010: 16). Siddiqui and Bhowmik (2004: 175) mention that 92 per cent of the MCs they interviewed said to spend one-two days a week in their constituencies, which seems to be less than we have observed. As indicated, many slum dwellers reported that when their MC is not available, they discuss their issues with local party office workers. Issues that are listed as topics where both male and women MCs may help or intervene as listed by van Dijk (2006: 85) include police harassment, goonda harassment, securing formal and informal housing, slum registration and for women slum dwellers she reports domestic violence, sexual harassment, dowry issues, divorce matters, abandonment by family or husband, rape and police and goonda harassment. Women corporators are seen as more active in women related issues while slum women attach value to being able to discuss certain matters with a woman, not a man. Finally, a corporator will be immediately notified about street or even slum-level disputes, quarrels or fights, for example a clash of local gangs of different caste groups.

> Our corporator did not have a cycle to his name earlier. Today he has two cars but we vote for him because when there is a crisis

and he says he will help, he does. He even comes in the middle of
the night if he is called.

(Mathias 2012: 11)

The MC *discretionary fund – area development funds*

Indian politicians at all levels dispose of their personal 'discretionary'
funds which they can use – given specific rules and conditions – in
their constituencies for what they see as urgent priorities. Amounts
are considerable and many have questioned the wisdom to endow so
much virtually unrestricted discretionary power over public funds to
individuals, by and large outside democratic control and requisite safeguards of transparency and accountability. Notwithstanding, amounts
have generally only risen, which applies to the Mumbai BMC too. Corporators used to receive Rs 10 to 12.5 million over their five-year term.
This compares very nicely against the meagre amount of Rs 500,000
which is the amount up to which an entire WCMs can decide.[20] Yet,
in a very controversial move, all BMC corporators agreed early 2015
to raise their personal entitlement to Rs 1 crore each year – with the
SS standing committee chairman appropriation as much as 17 crore.[21]
The move made it necessary to reduce the BMC budget for other items
and was notable for its brazen portrayal of open power where the Shiv
Sena dominated standing committee appropriated most of the allocations to its party.

Rules for the Area Development funds stipulate that these be used
for specific tangible improvements: making/keeping areas clean,
roads, footpaths and BMC building repairs, improvement of gardens
and markets. From available evidence it can be deduced that MC
Funds are more prone to manipulation and misuse than regular BMC
funded activities and projects, even if the choice of investments by and
large follows the formal rules. One issue is that much of the MC Funds
are not spent on actual improvements or constructions but is creamed
off through informal collusion among MCs, wards officials and contractors, leading to shoddy or incomplete works paid by the remainder.
Work may only exist on paper and cannot be found back on the streets,
or work is done and for no good reason repeated after a short period.
In contrast, solid improvements and constructions can be created which
are appropriated by the MC or his or her party members, for example a gym near a *shakha* which is obviously not used by poor men or
women. Proposals for spending under MC Funds come up for discussion in the wards committees but, as noted, MCs appear to approve

all proposals for these funds without much debate as they do not want to come in each other's way. The result is that there is little collective, 'democratic' scrutiny as to the urgency, need and suitability of the expenditure to solve a local problem, let alone as to whether there might be irregularities.

Van Dijk (2006: 82) mentions that there is a tendency for MCs to spend their fund on visible works, sometimes giving that priority over less visible but more urgent works. Public participation in choosing works was absent in the area she studied. She found that the most popular works sanctioned included pathways, drainage and toilet block repairs/construction (Van Dijk 2006: 84). Anand (2011b: 549) believes that city and state representatives have spent significant amounts of their discretionary local area development funds on linking the city slums to the Mumbai water system (which projects conspicuously bear their names). Most MCs have their own contractor, who may carry out works for him/her and their colleagues over several years, so that intimate relations based on trust can evolve. Nainan (2006: 11) reports that '6 per cent of the (MC Funded) project fund is given to the councillor for looking the other way on quality of repairs and construction'. A respondent in a northern ward office mentioned that WOs receive 25 per cent of all money that is spent from MC and also MLA funds in the ward area (field notes, 6 April 2005). A newspaper[22] reports that the major part of corporators' funds over the past five years – roughly Rs 993 million – were spent on drainage projects, with civic sources saying that drainage spending allows for the maximum fudging of fund figures. MCs also spent much on 'community development', a category including building cement passages, compound walls, fencing, as well as libraries, gyms, welfare centres and *balwadis*. However, some such latter provisions had been converted in a personal or political party office, or a members-only gym. All this fits a gloomy pattern of performance for what are elected representatives and 'city servants', but it seems to confirm a general pattern regarding Indian municipal councillors:

> Many officials suggested that the priorities of Councillors in terms of the construction and maintenance of civic infrastructure are determined not only by their immediate value impact and real necessity, but also by the Councillor's own financial interests. . . . The nexus between officials, contractors and councillors was the object of recurring complaints by women MCs against their male counterparts, especially in Mumbai and Delhi.
> (Ghosh and Tawa Lama-Rewal 2005: 118)

Corporators, slum land and housing

In their chapter on the Mumbai Megacity, Siddiqui and Bhowmik (2004: 139) provide a sobering picture of its governance, which appears to lack in all aspects of good governance, and they are critical of the city's councillors:

> Although corporators are the link between the people (particularly the poor) and the BMC, the services provided by them have to be paid for. Without the corporator's permission, a household cannot extent the house, even if a formal permission has been obtained; the corporator still has to be paid a handsome amount.

An important dimension for all Mumbai slums is that, as per BMC rules 'no external repairs and reconstruction are possible irrespective of landownership without prior permission from the Municipal Corporation', which compels all slum residents to approach it for permissions and repairs. In the case of slums on private land, permissions for repairs are required from the private landlord as well. Implications are that masses of people would need to interact with the BMC in case of any housing change, which is neither quite possible logistically, nor in terms of already noted access problems of the poor. So it is the corporators who have become the local approving agents for a variety of shelter issues. A M-ward informant explained that if he wants to build a house without official licences and permits, he simply contacts the MC he is close to. The MC will then inform the BMC not to block this construction. His corporator then contacted a 'shady contractor' who was ready to construct (semi-) illegal constructions. The MC will charge fees to allow/cover up (semi-) illegal or at least unauthorised constructions (Van Dijk 2006: 51). At that time rates were Rs 2,000 for each new illegal construction of huts or add-ons, Rs 5,000 per chawl room and Rs 20,000 for a flat in an illegal apartment building.[23] She mentions that rates in the slums may differ, depending on the nature and strength of builder-corporator links. Bjorkman (2013: 28) refers to a woman corporator who was denied a new ticket to again stand for elections for alleged wrong doing and the local MLA said:

> Hasina? The public rejected her. She asked for the ticket, but we did a survey in the area – her image was tarnished. . . . During her tenure as corporator Hasina had become famous for extorting exorbitant cash payments from families making renovations or

extensions on their homes – an activity that, since the neighbour-hood is treated a 'slum' is considered to be illegal.

We may safely assume that the collection of fees to condone illegal constructions itself was not the problem, but rather the 'exorbitant' bribes, which must have differed much from regular, institutionalised rates normal for such cases. This is yet another pointer to accepted systems of rules, norms and values governing completely informal and corrupt transactions, with sanctions to go. Desai (2002: 99–100) provides details of the 17 different steps needed to obtain approval to construct a building: a bureaucratic nightmare including many different documents, proofs and statements from many agencies. Transactions are done much more quickly but informally by contacting the MC, who then 'manages' the four 'government functionaries': the building inspector, the clerk, the WO (AC) and the (zonal) DMC: 'The corporators were given 20 per cent partnership in the building proposal or a fixed amount that was then distributed amongst the chain.' The rates were fixed according to size, locality, builder status and quality. There were also rate cards for renovations, additions like balconies, rooms and so on (Desai 2002: 99).

MCs *and slum water supply*

According to Anand (2011b: 546), upper and middle-class Mumbai citizens obtain water through property developers, who hire experts and liaisons to 'convince' city officials to sanction water connections before they occupy their (new) homes. This is in sharp contrast to arrangements for slum people who generally believe they may only get water a decade or so after settling: 'After they are deemed to be critical to the electoral successes of political representatives, and after they have been functionally administered by *dadas* (big men) for several years.' He explains that it is quite problematic for people in un-registered settlements – and for people without proof of living in Mumbai before 1995 (Anand 2011b: 549–50) – to obtain water. The good news is that it is possible – informality also opens doors for those un-registered, undocumented or 'illegal'. By and large all *Mumbaikars* have access to water, even those in new and recent slums and this was endorsed in 2014 by a court.[24]

Bawa (2013) stresses the institutional and political context of water supply, indicating that services and resources are sometimes delivered through legal channels to some groups. In other cases (for instance in non-registered slums) the MCs ally with engineers, officials and plumbers to serve groups without legal access. However, even people with such proof and consequent scope for legal access may not actually obtain it. She presents an overview of all documents required to obtain a water connection legally and formally, but 'every application tacitly requires a letter of support from a politician' (Anand 2011b: 550), so that it becomes difficult to get a connection without the support of an MC or MLA, which again underlines their discretionary powers. So even if slum dwellers are well established, 'after years of delicate clientelism, popular voting, and social mobilisation, their relations with councillor-*dadas* and their political parties continue to play a significant role, particularly around water supply'. I quote from a very instructive interview Anand (2011b: 551) held with a Shiv Sena leader, nicely bringing out the water supply mechanisms and their logic. It reveals local thinking about the role and expectations of the corporator. You better not neglect him, as not only money but respect is involved:

> Here the plumbers know that in the final instance you need a councillor's letter. The procedure has been *made* (italics added) in the BMC. The BMC can sanction water connections without the councillor or the Shakha Pramuk. But if they give it, then they won't get any *maal* (*stuff, colloquial for money*) in the middle. So they have made a 'system'. The system is that you tell the councillor or political party member [you want a water connection]. That way, the local councillor is respected, he will get *maal*. [Otherwise he will object, saying] If you give it direct, what will my position be here [in the settlement]? There is an understanding – that if you do this, like this, things will come in this way. The system. So people say instead of [having to come] eventually to the councillor, let's do it first. So the system – of ration cards, forms etc. – these are all *procedures* (italics added), so [that] people say it's better to go to the councillor. It is the system. Some people say it's about the money. There is the money but that is not the only thing going on.

Anand (2011b: 552) also dwells on the critical factor of ethnicity in service delivery to Mumbai slums based on his study of a Muslim dominated slum with migrants from Uttar Pradesh and Bihar. As per the law and applicable rules, the slum was registered and should be getting normal water supply but it did not. Another nearby slum had mostly Marathi-Hindu inhabitants, was as yet un-registered and would not normally be eligible for a water connection but this one was provided with illegal connections. An engineer said that slum dwellers here were 'our people', who were clean and cooperative. In contrast, he felt that the Muslim slum people 'their people, coming from the outside' lived in dirty conditions. They fought when engineers tried to work there and hence all work was stopped (Anand 2011b: 552). This refers to the important theme of identity in slums, as introduced in the slums Chapter 3. It is a reminder that issues of identity can take precedence over slum rights and assumedly even money.

I first located Mumbai's corporators in their formal institutional city context in Chapter 2 and now completed a detailed review of their formal but overwhelmingly informal everyday activities which confirm the value of the mediated state perspective. What remains is the question: why and how do they get elected? How to explain that such controversial persons and key agents of informality are elected time and again in formal democratic elections? For an answer, the next chapter delves into the unruly proceedings of the 2012 municipal elections. Its presentation is informed by perspectives of machine politics to check the role and origin of campaign funding and of patronage democracy where discretionary service delivery meets with voting systems.

Notes

1 In terms of principal–agent theory, the MC is an agent, serving the principal (voters), but the latter may fail to control the agent due to information asymmetry, a lack of control and enforcement tools.
2 Things are not necessarily better in other cities. For Ahmedabad, see Berenschot (2009). For Chennai see 'Jayalalithaa Warns Corrupt Councillors', *The Hindu,* 20 June 2012. The Tamil Nadu chief minister 'had information that AIADMK councillors were collecting money from every possible source. "When a multi-storeyed building is constructed, you go and collect commission. If a person stores sand or gravel in front of his house for construction purposes, you demand money from him," she said'.
3 Cf. Boo (2012: 51): 'In the previous year's elections, restricted in Ward 76 to low-caste candidates, the Corporator had won handily. . . . He wasn't low caste though. He'd simply manufactured a new caste certificate, a new birth place, and a new set of ancestors to qualify for the ballot. At least ten candidates in other city wards, mostly Shiv Sena, had done the same.' But justice was done: after a court case by the 2nd runner up, an actual Dalit, he was expelled as MC (Boo 2012: 221).
4 Pandurang Mhaske, 'Defaulting Ex-Corporators Ignore BMC Notices, Ex-Mayor in the List', *DNA,* 8 December 2010.
5 'Cleaning up Mumbai and Maharashtra: The Degeneration Game. Can India's Economic Powerhouse Ever Be Cleansed of Its Venomous Politics?', *The Economist,* 6 October 2012, www.economist.com/node/21564268 (accessed on 24 March 2015).

6 'High Court Quashes Suspension of BMC Staffer', *Times of India*, 13 October 2013.
7 Field notes from interviews at BMC on 13 December 2004. See also Chapter 3 where I reported on the controversy that the BMC council decided to rather starkly increase the budget for 'Discretionary MC Funds'. We shall see that it is precisely these funds which are most corruption prone at the level of the ward office.
8 They argue that the Indian media are part and parcel of corrupt practices: 'paid news' where advertisements are disguised as news, 'private treaties' where media houses have commercial relationships with firms, blackmail where a series of negative articles are published until a payment is made, suppressing news, biased reporting etc. are all well-known and have existed in India for some time'.
9 'Babus Admit to Corruption within Ranks', *Times of India*, 24 August 2010.
10 Das (2001: 131) mentions that a newly appointed Maharashtra minister stopped all transfers in his department in 1995 on the ground that over 10–15 crores had changed hands in these transactions.
11 'CM Transfers 159 Officials in a Single Day', *Indian Express*, 4 January 2005. The Maharashtra chief minister Desmukh issued orders to transfer officials in the departments for which he was responsible:

> Of those, revenue and urban development are considered 'cream' departments in the Mantralaya jargon. Certain posts in the revenue department authorized for clearing land transactions and in the urban development department responsible for imposing or lifting reservations on urban land are the most coveted posts among Mantralaya bureaucrats. Sources said the transfers were not affected in a traditional manner. . . . Apparently, Deshmukh handpicked the officers to hold key posts in the four departments.

12 According to data as presented by PRAJA (http://www.praja.org/praja_downloads/Praja per cent 20Newsletter per cent20Aug'2013 _English.pdf, accessed on 8 May 2014) about half the MLAs elected from Mumbai have criminal records: 15 MLAs out of 32 had criminal cases (FIRs) registered against them before elections as per their election affidavits (one case not confirmed) by December 2012.
13 'Lords of the Underworld', *Times of India*, 25 March 2012.
14 'Bribe Demands Hold up Building Projects in City; Some Officers in BMC Seek 30 Lakh to Sign a File', *Times of India*, 9 September 13: 'The degree of "demands" from a section of officials in the BMC's building proposal (BP) department to clear files increased since last year. While the municipal commissioner's office grants clearances swiftly (within a week) major obstructions are faced at the ward level. . . . Construction activity in the city has virtually ground to a halt as venal officials in the BMC's building proposals department sit on project clearances. . . . "It is torturous corruption," complained a well-known architect. . . . "It is becoming increasingly difficult to work with the BMC," he added.'
15 Nainan (2012: 110) dwells on the powerful position of the state CM: 'The Chief minister of any state government is expected to raise funds for his

own political party and Bombay's land was a potential source of such funding.' She considers him the most powerful actor with 'strong patronage networks amongst media, officers and private entrepreneurs'.

16 An informant told us that the SS Party holds annual performance reviews to assess what a member has done in a year, and what future plans are (field notes, 17 December 2004).

17 This includes sensitive assignments as to sorting out the details of illegal deals, ways and means of payment, sometimes making sure that transactions cannot be traced to the MC himself or herself (see Bjorkman 2013 for the election context).

18 See Chapter 3 (Section 3.7) for a range of documents needed to be eligible for the SJSRY scheme, and the problems of people to prove that they were living in a slum before a certain cut-off date. See Berenschot (2009: 110–12) for a vivid account of Ahmedabad corporator meetings with neighbourhood people.

19 I only have one source for these facts, and found no references otherwise, so this is another matter to be studied more.

20 'Corporators Sue BMC for Uneven Fund Allocation', *Mumbai Mirror*, 25 March 2015. In a rare move, BMC opposition party MCs approach the High Court to protest against what they see as an unfair allocation of the discretionary funds available with the (ruling party packed) Standing committee, grossly favouring the ruling SS and BJP party corporators.

21 'BMC May Not Be Able to Buy Reserved Plots, As Corporators Get Funds', *Hindustan Times*, 9 April 2015, reports: 'The Civic Standing Committee has diverted more than Rs 200 crore for corporators to take up local ward work.'

22 'How Corporators Spend, Drain away Your Money', *Times of India*, 15 January 2007.

23 'MNS Corporator, Associate Held for Accepting Bribe', *Mumbai Mirror*, 17 February 2013, quotes an ACB press release: An MC and two party workers were arrested for demanding and accepting a bribe of Rs 12,000 from a slum dweller in relation to the repair of her house to protect it against the rain. When they demanded Rs 20,000 to allow her to continue the work and not complain to the BMC, they were caught by the ACB.

24 'Bombay High Court Asks BMC to Supply Water to Even Illegal Slums', *DNA*, 16 December 2014: 'Stating that authorities cannot differentiate between occupants of illegal shanties and those living in authorized houses and providing water supply is a fundamental right enshrined under Article 21. . . . court directed the BMC to provide water supply to all slum-dwellers, whether legal or illegal.'

5 Politics or poli-tricks? Local democracy and slum voting in the 2012 Mumbai municipal elections

The final data chapter of this book wants to tie up and exemplify its several strands of argument and narrative, keeping in mind my focus on (political) power and the theses of patronage democracy and machine politics. It aims to juxtapose the relations between the urban poor, corporators with their local agents, and private-sector firms, asking the question as to how they deal with local democracy in its most visible and concrete manifestation of local elections. The key question raised is: how are elections conducted formally, and what are the more pronounced informal election dynamics in terms of things like vote banks and vote buying? And how do slum people react to such largely informal dynamics? I will portray the local elections as spectacles of citywide festival-like activities with rallies, mass-meetings, party flags and loudspeakers, when money flows more easily and lots of people already benefiting by simply being engaged one way or another. They have been described as a massive market for votes – but also as the only time that the poor and marginalised can actually expect a benefit from a politician. At the same time, this is a deeply serious – sometimes violent – occasion as the culmination of local power struggles. It is by all means a fiercely fought political fight as to who can garner the most money, best mobilise influential local party workers and agents, to emanate the reputation, capacity and foremost the power to make things happen. I have already explained in Chapter 4 (Section 4.1) that it is costly and not quite easy to obtain a ticket from a party to stand for elections. It helps when one has a good reputation locally, that there are good (ideally family) connections with higher party levels and that one is known to be wealthy: 'It is next to impossible for a candidate to start without any money.'[1] Yet all this is not normally enough to finance the very costly election campaigns which costs may run up from Rs 2 million to sometimes Rs 4–6 million per candidate, large chunks of which are applied in what is called vote buying or for channelling benefits to voters or vote banks before Election Day. So elections are about money, about cash. In an article on the meaning of money in elections, Bjorkman (2013: 48) suggests that Mumbai elections 'inhabit a deeply-political landscape in which the city's most pressing challenges facing city residents – of urban land, access to housing, infrastructural development and urban economy are thought out, performed and acted upon'.

This chapter will trace dimensions of power and money in the Mumbai municipal (or 'local') elections held in February 2012. I will try to uncover the sources of all the money circulating before the elections, starting from the assumption that many corporators are supported by private-sector firms. This, in turn would provide more evidence that we can speak of a 'political machine' in terms of J. C. Scott (1969) where business elites finance politicians in return for (later) support. And if we find such a 'financial corporator–business nexus', a relevant question is what this means for local democracy, accountability and the scope for adequate long-term policy making. But, true to this book's benchmark, this chapter wants to also appraise the reasons for poor slum people to vote for this or that candidate. How to explain their political behaviour? What does it say about the way they see democracy, and whether it actually helps them in their quest for livelihoods and upward mobility? The study is framed in already introduced patronage democracy and mediated state perspectives, but I will review a few perspectives pertaining to micro – in this case booth-level election/voting aspects here, such as the notion of the vote bank and the presumed efficacy of providing cash for votes. I suggest that voters can sometimes be punished for voting a certain, 'wrong' way, conceptualised as 'perverse accountability' (Stokes 2005).

5.1 Perspectives on vote banks, vote buying and booth-level election dynamics

Underlying electioneering in Mumbai are a number of assumptions to check first. One is the existence of vote banks as viable units for targeting benefits; another is the assumption that, if people receive 'election goodies', this very fact will lead them 'quid pro quo' to vote for the dispensing party/candidate. A final assumption which is mostly taken for granted – but which seems to drive, even accelerate the entire vote-buying business – is that all parties and candidates act the same way. Gowda and Sridharan (2012: 232) believe this leads to a 'mad scramble' to raise and spend election money, an 'electoral spending arms race' where parties try to outspend each other with all sorts of inducements. As a reminder of the larger picture as to what is at stake from the perspective of a typical election candidate for the corporator position I present an insightful quote from Nainan (2006: 5):

> Politicians who don't have any other source of income for political work from their post other than payments by contractors require to raise money to buy tickets for elections, campaigns, maintaining their constituency and to move up the political ladder, and as payments to their party bosses for higher positions in the political party. Expenditure on elections and maintenance of the constituency with the use of muscle or money requires regular sources of income, here too political parties do not differ, as all parties require their elected members to generate an 'X' amount of money on a weekly or monthly basis, often creating much pressure for the politician who then continues to find means of raising these funds, sometimes it could be from developers, business houses, shopkeepers, hawkers etc. Corporators and MLAs receive X per cent of the costs of the projects which are undertaken in their wards by any agency (municipal, housing board) and private developers. Often one source is not enough so politicians use multiple sources to fill their kitties. . . . The 'rupee price' of successful politics is indeed very high as each candidate first pays his political party to get a ticket – this itself means payment to senior leaders – and once the ticket is allotted, costs include expenditures for campaigning and payments to agents and voters. Funds for the municipal elections come from money lenders, contractors and developers. Oral and written agreements are made with funders which include repayments in the form of contracts, bending of rules, clearance of development projects and other items of interest to the private sector.

Vote banks

It is clearly impossible for any candidate to link to all voters, even in the more limited context of a municipal ward with around 52,000 inhabitants on average. I will show later how each candidate can only be successful with a small army of close associates, agents and party workers to act as eyes, ears and hands, but even so many potential voters may be missed. It is not so long ago that many rural people in India would simply vote as stipulated by their landlord or 'owner' so that vote blocks would be 'delivered' by powerful persons. This may already be seen as some type of 'captive audience' vote bank. Such convenient arrangements cannot be found in India's big cities today, but efforts to identify and categorise people into demarcated groups with common identities have persisted in the notion of vote bank (defined earlier in Chapter 4, Section 4.1). It links to the importance of identity and patronage in Indian politics, assuming first that local voters can be defined as a group by common characteristics such as religion, caste, ethnicity or income in a limited geographical space. Such a group is assumed to have relatively common needs and expectations, which are neither met uniformly nor through formal channels. So it requires an agent such as a local leader, broker or politician to interact and engage in service delivery. In short voters, parties and 'middlemen' are our election stakeholders (Bjorkman 2013: 9) while I will bring in the more invisible election financiers. She quotes R. Guha in noting recent changes in what is seen to constitute a vote bank:

> We still use the term coined by Srinivas; however, we mostly mean it now to capture a solidarity that is horizontal rather than verti-cal. 'Vote Bank' is not what a single patron demands; rather it denotes a collective political preference exercised by a particular interest group. In India, this interest is defined principally by pri-mordial identity – of caste or religion or language. But one can also think of 'vote banks' being constituted by shared material or moral interests.
>
> (Bjorkman 2013: 12)

Such changes are seen to have led to a loosening of vertical patronage relations and a related articulation of 'horizontal social identities', and a tendency of identity groups 'to market *themselves*' (it. Bjorkman 2013: 13). This, inter alia, is yet another reference to 'market' as if votes are a commodity. Breeding (2011) traces vote bank politics from the 1950s until today and finds that they remain an important plank of party politics – with many differences. Plenty references are made to vote banks in Indian newspapers and journals. They are part of life, or anyway of the dominant political discourse. An implied risk is that too much is made of their actual existence, for example that politicians are busily targeting them but that there is actually no such uniform group and/or that the (positive or negative) incentives provided do not actually have much impact. One example from the media is given here, which might also be seen to reflect middle-class perceptions and concerns.[2]

The BMC demolished around 300 illegal shanties near Bandra Reclamation last month, on the order of the Chief Minister, but they have been rebuilt within two weeks. . . . The people who live there are mainly migrants from Bangladesh and Nepal, and also from within the city. Bandra residents believe the creation of the slum is a major attempt by politicians to build a vote bank, keeping in view the 2014 assembly elections. . . . 'Migrants are pouring into the city almost daily. The truth of this slum is simple. Elections are near and the slum's occupants will serve as a vote bank; 100 per cent of the slum's vote will be for politicians who shut their eyes to the building of illegal shanties', said Anil Joseph, chairperson of the Perry Road Residents' Association. 'Residents said that in the past, politicians have made voting arrangements by issuing fake photo passes and ration cards to slum-dwellers and then approving slum rehabilitation schemes'. The newspaper adds: 'A politician's hunger for votes is almost always the reason behind a new slum coming up. This is abetted by a section of corrupt officials.'

The case raises questions as to the possibility to arrange voter registration for migrants or recent settlers by politicians. I refer back to Section 4.5 where I mentioned that there are indications that MCs can indeed facilitate people to obtain a fast track photo voter ID card. To conclude I quote Bhowmik[3] who feels that the notion of slum dwellers as a powerful vote bank is a myth – from the perspective of the urban poor. 'They are, in fact a much needed vote bank because of their numbers. Politicians threaten them with eviction if they don't vote for them. . . . The political ramifications could be huge if the poor were as powerful as they are made out to be.'

Cash for votes: actual and symbolic implications

In her micro-study of vote banks Breeding (2011: 73) refers to a Karnataka survey, where 49 per cent of respondents reported receiving a private vote bank benefit, poor people more so than rich(er) people: cycles, sewing machines, sarees, stainless steel vessels. Such benefits are provided also at other times than just before elections, such as 'ration cards without qualifying for them, and other private benefits such as money for school fees'- which look like the kind of services the Mumbai corporators are routinely helping organise anytime. However, in an important caveat, Breeding (2011: 73) suggests that 'the expectation for reciprocation upon receiving a (vote bank) benefit is just as symbolic as the gesture of the vote bank benefit itself.' She concludes that today the vote banks in India's political system are inefficient:

benefits are mostly provided as a result of the competitive demands of other parties and historical practice. That vote buying can be layered with cultural meaning is mentioned by Geddis too (2008: 142): 'like a tradition of gift giving or mutual respect, a redistribution between a wealthy ruler and the poor ruled; and even an implied threat that it would be unsafe to resist.'[4] Such a view parallels Bjorkman's (2013), who aptly explores the symbolic *and* actual meaning and role of money in Mumbai's local elections, concretely linking this to slum-level actions and relations.

One meaning or message of having or showing ample cash by a candidate vis-à-vis his or her agents, party workers and people who offer to deliver a block of votes (a vote bank) is to convey his or her 'access to powerful, moneyed networks as well as a show of generosity'. The money so provided is not a one-time purchase; it rather serves to cement a (an enduring) relationship of reciprocity (Bjorkman 2013: 36). For voters and social workers alike, cash symbolises 'networks of access to the worlds of opportunity and promise in the city's mysterious economies' (Bjorkman 2013: 40). It signals access to 'to the most *crucial* kind of urban knowledge: of how to navigate the opacities, dangers, and promises of the city's little-understood but palpably real economies' (Bjorkman 2013: 39, italics added). In terms of power, cash signals 'accomplished power': rumours of cash being distributed are equally important as distribution itself, which rests on reputation (Bjorkman 2013: 43). Another, not necessarily conflicting perspective stresses payment of money/bribes to voters as some sort of one-time compensation for missed governance, which is also based on a type of reciprocity which is assumed to typify the Indian voter:

> An electorate that suffers inefficient delivery of governance and welfare services (which arguably is to a large extent due to corruption) needs to be rewarded, and so a significant part of the returns from RNA corruption are spent in elections and shared with the electorate as rewards to their local leaders and elders, as gifts to the individual voter, as cash payments etc.[5] The intention is very clear, the principle of reciprocity operates. The politician's message is: 'the government is not delivering and I am not sure I can get you the safety, the access to basic needs, the environment for you to earn a decent living, so let me give you this at the very least'. There is no explicit contract, no written document and so on, the rational Indian voter accepts it and using the time honoured principle of reciprocity, gives his vote.
>
> (Debroy and Bhandari 2012: 16)

A familiar view was expressed by an official (field notes, 17 February 2014): if a politician gives you cash for a vote, it works like a buy-off: one forsakes the right that the politician is accountable or representative for you: 'You got your share, now don't come back and bother me with complaints on my performance.' In both cases there is an unwritten understanding that possible claims to representation and accountability on which foundation western 'liberal democracy' rests – I elected you so you represent me and tell me what you do for me – are no longer valid, or redeemed.[6] A final perspective also starting from reciprocity stresses the candidate as a patron. Just like Chandra (2007) in terms of her patronage democracy thesis, Nainan too (2006: 5) considers elections as a time to settle bills; the patron is rewarded for what he or she has done in between elections:

> At the time of the elections the patron's debt are paid back (by the slum people, *JdW*) as votes, as the political leader who now appears as a candidate for elections. Promises are made and money is paid to residents of the slum in exchange for votes.

Voter accountability and perverse accountability: booth-level dynamics

Having established that lots of money is spent prior to elections and that such money can be seen to serve several purposes, often targeting vote banks, we now need to explore what the guarantees are that such massive financial investments will give expected returns in terms of actual votes for one candidate. Kitscheld and Wilkinson (2007: 2) argue that clientelist accountability is a transaction to exchange a citizen's vote for direct payments or continuing access to employment, goods and services. But I agree with Bjorkman (2013) who argues that clientelism/patronage is not the same as outright vote buying which can very well happen outside any relationship. Most writers agree that it is the poor who are the targets of patronage democracies and political machines, fully in line with the Chandra (2004) view that, unlike those most vulnerable and poor, richer and less vulnerable groups have the 'exit option'. Stokes (2005: 315) argues that candidates and parties expect diminishing marginal returns if they target higher-income groups (also Nichter 2008: 30). But in all cases the question remains as to whether and if so how candidates and parties can monitor individual voter choice on which so much depends. Chandra (2007: 89) is suspicious and feels that – in view of the high stakes – we should expect strong efforts to subvert the secrecy of the ballot by exploiting loopholes in the design of the voting procedure. For example, where agents or parties cannot check individual voting, aggregate results from smaller voting booth areas do give some idea to the long-term local expert observer. And even while the ballot is secret, voters may not have the *'perception'* that their vote is secret. Chandra suggests that voters are equally distrustful of election officials and procedures as they are of officials and politicians generally. Kitscheld and Wilkinson (2007: 14ff.) agree that there are many ways to monitor individual and group voting, especially in patterns of successive elections (also listing a whole array of globally prevalent pre-election gifts ranging from liquor to clothes). Concrete strategies are listed by Berenschot (2009: 151), for example that a combination of attentive party workers in a polling booth station and the distribution in India of what is called pre-marked voting slips by party candidates do give some idea of how individuals and groups voted. Stokes (2005: 317–18) is quite convinced that in the secret ballot Argentine elections she analysed, voting is a less than fully anonymous act: 37 per cent of voters believed that party operatives can find out how a person voted. This need not be a problem, unless there is a political culture as well as opportunities to use or misuse such sensitive knowledge: it may lead to what is called 'perverse accountability':

> Democratic accountability is when voters know what parties have done in office and reward or punish them conditional on these actions. When parties know, or can make good inferences about, what individual voters have done in the voting booth and reward or punish them conditionally on these actions, this is perverse accountability.
>
> (Stokes 2005: 316)

There are indications in India today that voters do run the risk of being punished for the way they voted, and I will list two concrete issues here. The first is the size of the Mumbai election booth population which cannot be more than 1,500 persons,[7] which is a relatively small number, and, in addition a limited area (this could mean a slum pocket gets transformed into a political arena). Corporators, their close advisors and their very vigilant party workers make up a powerful team of election experts, who normally have witnessed and 'managed' many elections already. I will show below that they have a pretty good idea as to voter inclinations: the loyalists, the opportunistic waiters who take any benefit, the voters who take advise from social workers or the operation of *dadas* who 'deliver their votes as a block' (see Bjorkman 2013: 32) etc. Such a team has certain expectations, promises may have been made by people earlier to vote this or that way, pressure may have been applied. The latter can be captured under the term 'muscle power', which refers to subtle or not so subtle signals or actual force on people prior to elections to vote a certain way. This can take on the form of threats or violence in a context of 'infra-power' as detailed in Section 3.5 (see Gupte (2012: 201). So in the analysis of elections, the focus should not only be on vote buying, which might be most important for so called 'floating, undecided voters', but also on the use of threats which is more suitable for (poor) people with real needs or issues of security.[8] Hence, if it is established from a careful study of actual voting patterns in a booth area that it looks pretty likely that people there voted against promises, expectations or threats, this may lead to punishment. This could be when a certain powerful candidate wins (again) and he finds (suspects) that one slum pocket voted for another candidate. However, as far as I have been able to assess, this is most likely in hotly contested key voting areas and I have no evidence that such practise is widespread in Mumbai.

A second, but related issue is that the assessment of voting outcomes has been made easier with the introduction of the electronic voting machine (EVM). This is argued for example by Berenschot (2006) who feels that the recent computerisation of the elections helped politicians who now have fairly precise information about the voting in all small areas of their constituencies. Prior to that, people put their choice manually on a ballot paper, bearing the party symbols and it was not possible to trace any vote to a booth any more. This has changed fundamentally now that the voting results for each such small booth area are published on line for all to see. In another and related development, the EVM has come become under scrutiny as some argue that it can be manipulated. Whether true or not, once such a rumour starts, distrust is bound to increase in a context of competition, suspicion and secrecy, where any conceivable trick has been or will be tried (see Quraishi 2014: 191ff.).[9] A magazine quoted experts as saying that EVMs are fundamentally un-secure.[10] At this point of time, the Election Commission 'wants to use a new machine which prevents disclosure of voting pattern during counting to enhance voter secrecy', by using a devise that mixes votes at the time of counting.[11] That practices relating to 'perverse accountability' do occur in India is mentioned even by a state Law Panel:

> The Law Panel, in its report on electoral reforms has recommended amendment to the Conduct of Election Rules to give EC powers

to use Totaliser for mixing of votes where it apprehends intimidation and victimisation of electors in any constituency. The current system reveals voting trends in each polling station, thus leaving the voters in that vicinity open to harassment, and post-election victimisation.[12]

Equipped with general notions on Indian democratic practices in Chapter 1, complemented here with booth-level issues of voting, the role of money in voting and voting secrecy, I will now describe the 2012 municipal elections in Mumbai. They can be seen as a massive formal administrative BMC operation, which provides the context and parameters for an explosion of informal dynamics.

5.2   Corporators and their local agents: party workers and social workers

With so many tiers of governance, there could be elections somewhere in India almost every month, but there are reasons that the elections of Mumbai are seen as a special case. This is one of the richest Indian cities, with a massive annual municipal budget and without debts. It is an attractive place to govern – a fact that was often emphasised in media reports relating to the elections, with a discourse that underlined Mumbai as a very important 'prize' to win, implying great riches for those victorious. This is especially critical for the Shiv Sena party which ruled the BMC for 20-odd years. Mumbai is its key bastion and power basis which it cannot afford to lose, so the party's stakes are always very high – which may show in its strategies. This perception for candidates and parties alike that 'Mumbai is like a hen with golden eggs',[13] helps explain why the battle for votes is so very fierce. While it must certainly be regarded an honour to rule one of the most powerful municipalities of South Asia, the actual attraction seems more worldly in the form of informal/illegal earnings as amply illustrated in earlier chapters. It is likely that most informal incomes and black money originate in the land and building sector, where it is commonplace to read about the 'builder–official–corporator mafia' in the Mumbai newspapers (e.g. Jagannathan 2012). Some say that it is actually the builders/developers who decide about key urban decisions. 'While Mumbai's governance has steadily nosedived, the city has been under the thumb of a politician-real-estate mafia cashing in on land shortage.'[14]

In earlier chapters the Mumbai corporators were shown to be powerful people and I have labelled them 'political entrepreneurs'. They engage with the allocation of municipal budgets over the various budget lines, the spatial distribution of funds over the municipal area and provide building licences. Of great importance too is the SRS 'slum redevelopment policy', which allows for the removal of old, dilapidated buildings or slum huts, to be replaced by new housing blocks or high rise apartments, where builders/developers can earn large sums of money. With much of the process informal, effective mediators who can be trusted to organise and manage this sensitive and complex arena of private and public stakeholders are in high demand – even while there is no such formal position under the rules:

> Despite the absence of an open, direct involvement of a political party or a Corporator, everyone knows that money exchanges hands each time a (redevelopment) project is cleared in the civic corporation and passes through ministerial channels at the state government level. So, a host of residents expect a local Corporator to bring in a favourable 'party' to redevelop and ensure that residents get 'a good deal'.[15]

Even if corporators themselves do or could not actively engage in all such mediation work, they have their agents at the slum, neighbourhood and street level, forming the link between the people/voters and the MC, with their local offices or the *shakhas* for the Shiv Sena (Bedi 2007). Different terms are used for the various people working for and with corporators: slum leaders, party workers, agents, mediators and even *goons*. Partly following Bjorkman (2013: 23) I reserve the word *karyakarta* – party worker – for a person known to be with a specific party and I present the example of the ambitious party worker Mrs Asha (with her alcoholic husband) in Boo's slum study (2012: 19):

> The corporator had helped Asha to a job in a municipal school. 'In return, she spent a good deal of class time on her cell phone conducting Shiv Sena business. She could mobilise a hundred women for a last-minute protest march, and deliver two thousand neighbours to the polls. The Corporator thought she could do more. He asked her to handle a petty Annawadi problem, and then another, somewhat less petty, and yet another, not petty at all, at which point he gave her a bouquet of flowers and his wife giving her the fish eye. Asha took these things to be signs of an imminent triumph . . . she had an influential patron. In time, she imagined, even the men of Annawadi would have to admit that she was becoming the most powerful person in this stinking place'.

In contrast, I suggest using the term 'social worker' for well-connected and locally active men and women, not associated with any party – but willing to cooperate. They may act as 'independent' and trusted local advisors to poor and/or illiterate people often not (completely) aware of all candidates, what they are actually supposed to do, or what democracy actually means or is supposed to engender – apart from one politician winning.[16] Such social workers may be generally helpful, neighbourly persons not at all interested in politics, but some do and play roles in 'delivering votes' as depicted well in Bjorkman's 2013 case study:

> As Abdul's trajectory indicates, establishing oneself as a social worker begins with acts of generosity: running errands for the police and water department earned him the privilege of distributing water around the neighbourhood. Distributing water earned him the trust of community leaders, who began to compensate him for his services. His reputation as a reliable supplier of water made him an indispensable asset at election time, as parties competed to attach the party name to Abdul's reputation, thereby winning the votes of the families who had come to trust in Abdul's abilities as social worker.[17]

5.3 Mumbai's political parties and politics

In a review of the forces shaping Mumbai politics, Vora and Palshikar (2003: 179) identify the key factors as communalisation (i.e. the emphasis on identity factors, notably between Hindus and Muslims, including the 1992–93 riots, and the role of the Shiv Sena party), the decline of the trade union movement (following the closure of most textile mills), the rise of the informal sector, the lumpenisation arising from unplanned capitalist development and a rising criminalisation of society and polity. Mapping key changes over time, they see a shift in political loyalties, with the Congress party increasingly less able to rely on the votes of Muslims and Dalits, who used to form its relatively stable vote bank. They consider the political space in which deprived groups are allowed to participate as very limited, exclusive and narrow and altogether irrelevant to the aspirations of marginal groups. The position for groups such as Muslims, Dalits and slum dwellers is one of 'limited inclusion and substantive exclusion' (Vora and Palshikar 2003: 180). It is beyond the scope of this chapter to provide details of all the parties which participated in the 2012 local elections, and I refer to Chapter 4 on the Mumbai corporators for the evolution of the Shiv Sena party which first won the Mumbai local elections in 1985. I will nevertheless add a bit more recent background on the party and its most recent offshoot the Maharashtra Navnirman Sena (MNS) party. Necessary background information on other parties such as the Congress and the National Congress Party NCP is provided too.

Introducing the contesting political parties

From the early 1970s Mumbai (then Bombay) politics was dominated by the Congress and Shiv Sena political parties. The latter was founded in 1966 by Bal Thackeray (who died in 2012), initially as a platform for dissatisfied (middle-class) Marathis about or against the alleged influx of at that time mostly South Indian migrants. It can be briefly defined by four distinct characteristics: first a successful, occasional use of xenophobic discourses of local/Marathi pride, often with an aggressive, intolerant, no-nonsense style (Hansen 2001: 48ff.). Secondly, the SS soon developed a successful network of local offices and units which assisted citizens – which are today's SS *shakhas*. I may note here in passing that Hansen cautions that their influence is overestimated (Hansen 2001:55). They are more like 'a self-help network with families, male peer groups, business undertakings, and other informal organisations' (Hansen 2001: 48). Violence is third characteristic, at the minimum as rhetorical style but in actual practice too, as can be seen from incidents dating back to the 1960s. Notably, these include Shiv Sena involvement in the 1992–93 Mumbai riots, which put up Hindus against Muslims leading to around 900 casualties. I noted before (Section 4.2) that many Shiv Sena leaders were formerly community leaders engaging in gang-like activities (including protection, settlement of disputes, enforcement of agreements and expulsion from properties) – who still nurture strong connections with the organised crime world of the city (Nainan 2012: 107). As a final trait, Hansen mentions a complex and ambiguous relationship with electoral politics and political institutions, one recent indication of which was the opportunistic alliance with the Dalit party in the 2012 local elections as discussed later. Yet it has allied with the like-minded BJP party since 1988, and this alliance has persisted over time. Appadurai (in Gupte 2012: 205) depicts the evolution of the SS from being 'mainly a group of urban thugs. . . to [becoming] a regional and national political force'. The party was initially associated with extortion and protection rackets, and slums were targeted for the expansion of these activities. Patel (2003: 23–24) traces the early years in relation to the Mumbai slums:

> The Shiv Sena's entrance in the slums occurred in the early 1970ies, where the issue of obtaining land to build slums became critical. Simultaneously, there was a boom in the housing industry, with an expansion of middle class and upper class housing. The Sena was able to organise *dadas* to encroach on the land and organize settlements both for the construction of slums on private and government land and obtaining land to sell it to builders. Violence or the threat of violence was very important for the continuity of this business. With the increasing reach and spread of the extortion and protection business it needed the help of gangs. By the late seventies there is a clear indication that Mafia gangs that earlier formed part of the smuggling trade had entered into the land and housing market and had forged an alliance with sections of the Sena. . . . Within the slum there grew a culture around the *dada*; a culture of brotherhood. For the young male underemployed slum dweller, the Shiv Sena represented the family and its local chief the father or the elder brother, the *dada*.

She goes on to say (Patel 2003: 25) that 'Today, the Shiv Sena is not in control of the formal institutions of power, yet it commands the informal processes of power'. Presently, in 2015 it would seem that the party is in firm control of both the formal and informal institutions governing Mumbai, with Mumbai its recognised key asset and stronghold. The party managed to move into mainstream politics, shedding much of its controversial, sometimes extremist past strategies and to broaden its appeal. Presently it attracts both the Mumbai Marathi middle classes and large voter groups in the slums: 'SS could comfortably combine the support of the urban white collar middle class and the underclass from the slums' (Palshikar 2004: 1502). On a positive note, the party provided a venue of identity and self-confidence among the poor, a sense of energy by being part of power, and many, especially young men, became enthusiastic followers and agents. It ruled Maharashtra State in coalition with the BJP from 1995 to 1999 and was in opposition from 1999 when Congress and NCP came to power. The 2014 State Elections were won by a SS-BJP coalition, which formed an uneasy, quarrelsome government under a BJP CM. The Shiv Sena-BJP combine won the BMC civic elections in 1985, and Shiv Sena was the dominant party in the BMC council since 1997. The party faced serious discontent in 2005, when Raj Thackeray, Bal Thackeray's nephew, left the party. He founded his own MNS party. Occasional conflicts and clashes have dominated relations and interactions between followers of the two Senas with roots in bitter rivalry. The original SS is now led by Udhav Thackeray, Bal Thackeray's son, which is proof for the incidence of 'dynastic parties'. The split was mostly the result of personal issues and in terms of ideology SS and MNS are still relatively similar, notably in stressing the 'sons of the soil' pro Marathi agenda.

Other parties contesting the elections include the Samajwadi Party (SP) which targeted the Muslim voters and the Bahujan Samaj Party (BSP), a party with nominally socialist leanings, with most support among the lowest castes and in Uttar Pradesh. The Dalits of Mumbai[18] might vote for this BSP, but their main party is traditionally the Republican Party of India (RPI). That party won 3 BMC council seats in 2007, and, to the surprise of many, it became part of the SS-BJP combine in the context of the 2012 local elections. After all, the SS is seen by many to have an aversion against Dalits (and against Muslims – 17 per cent of voters – and Northern Indians). The reasons for RPI to join the alliance (which turned out a poor strategy for RPI as it was to lose 2 seats) are not so clear, but it certainly confused many Dalits who saw their RPI leader Athavale be so close to what always were adversaries. Fact is that the Mumbai Dalit population has seen many problems in terms of solid political representation with a view to their many social and economic problems. Teltumbde (2012: 21) suggests that Mumbai Dalit politics have degenerated to such an extent that it does not really touch on problems of urban poverty. Rather, Dalit politicians compete with each other to promote their own interests.

As we will see shortly, Mr Chavan, then Maharashtra CM was the main and most visible Congress party face in the 2012 local elections. Finally, there is the NCP (National Congress Party) which broke away from the Congress party in 1999 under leadership of Sharad Pawar who was introduced in Section 2.6 as the reformer CM to liberalise Mumbai governance. Just like the SS, the NCP party too has traits of a 'dynastic party' family affair.[19] After due deliberations, real or portrayed bickering and complex negotiations, two large coalitions emerged, a coalition between Congress and NCP on the one hand, and, as already explained, a coalition of the Shiv Sena-BJP-RPI parties on the other.[20]

5.4 Candidate selection, tickets and women corporators

The key question for an aspiring candidate in any party is how to obtain a ticket to stand in a constituency, and I provided details before on the most common arrangements, mechanisms and strategies in Section 4.1. Key conditions are long-term party membership with both built-up credit with voters and good (possibly family) relations with other political leaders or 'godfathers'. The latter may in fact invite their 'friends' to stand for election. It helps a lot to be rich so that the candidate can mostly self-finance the campaign and be (seen to be) able to later contribute to the party. But caste and gender play a role as a considerable number of constituencies were reserved for women (50 per cent) and for low-caste/Dalit candidates. As identity is a major consideration, parties prefer candidates with a caste, language or religious background fitting the population mix of a ward. Such factors are the basis of awarding tickets through arrangements differing from party to party. It may take the shape of an auction to the highest bidder which amount is payable to senior party leaders, or that tickets are allocated in a top-down fashion by the party leadership – as was done by the Congress–NCP party combine. Yet another model in the 2012 elections was where trusted party workers were rewarded with a ticket after showing great dedication and popularity within a particular neighbourhood – as was the SS party practice. In all these arrangements, financial considerations may or not play a role and reputations may sometimes be even more important than actual resources. It is certain that well performing and powerful sitting corporators (some are re-elected many times) were often considered safe candidates and got a ticket almost automatically (consider the case of the powerful and hard to contest corporator Fareed[21] in the election studied by Bjorkman 2013: 40–41). Her study also provides proof that the (overly) negative reputation of a candidate may result in a party denying a ticket (Bjorkman 2013: 28).[22] It is important to reiterate that Shiv Sena and MNS are more like 'cadre based parties', in contrast to other parties with a much less developed party basis at grassroots levels such as the Congress and NCP.[23] The SS and MNS parties ultimately relied on numerous party workers (*karyakartas*) throughout the slums and richer city areas working for the party on a voluntary basis. Driven by incentives such as affinity with party ideology, a deep respect or admiration for the party leader or corporator, they no doubt also have self-interested plans for (political) incomes and career. Such admiration up to veneration is quite marked for the SS and MNS leadership. We know most about the (biggest and dominant) Shiv Sena party set-up, with a very well organised and maintained decentralised party hierarchy, starting at the neighbourhood level, up to the level of the constituency. This, inter alia, is consistent with the idea of a 'tentacle-like organisational structure' typical for machine parties as suggested by Stokes (2005: 317ff., see Section 1.5). A committed and talented party worker can rise through these levels and be rewarded with ever higher party positions and possibly an election ticket. The Shiv Sena and MNS, with a clear ideology both to represent Marathi's and to oppose migrants coming to and living in Mumbai, showed a clear preference for Marathi candidates (in the Shiv Sena 131 out of 135 candidates; 213 out of 227 in the MNS). This was much less for Congress, which had 81 Marathi and 85 non-Marathi candidates (e.g. Gujaratis, Muslims and Christians). The BJP fielded 36 Marathi as well as 27 non-Marathi candidates. The SP concentrated on Muslim votes and fielded 38 Muslims, as well as 8 Marathi candidates.[24]

Things were made even more complex in that the ratio of women-reserved constituencies which had been 33 per cent from 2000 was now raised to as much as 50 per cent. The fact that so many constituencies were reserved for women gave rise to complex considerations for instance as to whether women candidates would come forward, or be up to the task to be a corporator. But as noted before in Section 4.1. in practice it was often more important how much pressure an incumbent or former corporator would bring to bear to push his wife, sister or daughter to be given a ticket. This would then enable him to carry on his political (and very rewarding brokerage) activities with the woman corporator his 'proxy' or 'puppet' representative (see de Wit and Holzner 2003, see Section 4.1). In the wake of the 2012 Mumbai polls, the Shiv Sena party, which is known for an active policy to engage women in party and *shakha*-level activities, appears to have had least problems to identify women candidates. This is consistent with its strategies to engage women at the level of its *shakhas* and neighbourhoods. The Congress is reported to have had problems to field women candidates 'as there was tremendous pressure among male candidates vying to contest in the elections'.[25] The women reservation system, according to Mathias (Mathias 2012: 12) led to two problems. First, 'seats which had sitting women corporators who had nursed their constituencies were given to male candidates'. I take this to mean that such incumbent women could very well stand again but with little chance, even if they were popular. One might argue that money power wins over soft, people minded power already here. The second problem was that 'all parties had to fall back on the kith and kin of male leaders/workers'. Mathias mentions two cases. The SS put up a 21-year-old OBC women student who won the seat, while admitting that her brother had been an SS member for 15 years and that he had been instrumental in getting her the ticket: 'no marks for guessing under whose "guidance" she will do her civic work' (Mathias 2012: 12). One Mrs Azmi who won a Kurla ward seat, had never done any political work. It was her corporator husband who had been working hard in the ward area but it was reserved for women this time. Her husband's brother (who won a seat in the next ward) said 'She will be the face of this ward. However, my brother will be handling all the work'. A newspaper reported that education levels of the vast majority of the 1,300 women candidates were quite low, with only around 110 who studied until graduation and beyond. Most others did not complete secondary or higher education, which might be an indication that women had joined politics from backgrounds where education was of less importance.[26] Still, in most cases and with so much at stake, it appears as if parties were very careful to field candidates which were seen to have a real chance to win, so that considerations of past performance/popularity as well as issues of religion, caste and ethnicity did play a role. However, indications are that many male MCs who could not stand themselves, did push forward women family members to stand instead and that voters were quite aware of this. Apparently, they were not too disturbed that they were expected to vote for a woman but to rely on the man as the invisible and informal power. No doubt powerful corporators want to keep their political capital intact by hook or crook (remember the fake caste certificates in the case of Dalit-reserved seats). In terms of a possibly useful positive discrimination strategy for women and of democratic principles, all this is a bit of mockery, another instance where formal arrangements are bended informally in the face of comparatively brute, masculine, and personalised power. Much more detailed research is needed here into the extent and precise dynamics of such cases and how other candidates, 'proxies' and voters perceive all this. For now the proxy arrangement seems to work: people don't seem to mind much and the crucial fact is that such informal arrangements are condoned by the parties. With so much at stake I cannot imagine that they tolerate a system that would undermine their electoral chances.

If given a ticket, the next requirement for a candidate is to find the money for the very costly election campaign. If an incumbent, he, she or they may already have collected sufficient funds over the past five years to self-finance most costs. Some candidates sell land or housing or resort to pawning their jewellery or sell assets. One report[27] mentions that 'Candidates beg, borrow and raise lakhs in funds', noting that first timers depend on their own savings, friends, relatives and neighbours to raise funds and that senior candidates borrow from developers and contractors. The evidence from our 2005 corporator survey brought out that most candidates said to finance the main part of their campaign costs themselves. This, inter alia, favours rich candidates over possibly very sincere, committed, pro-poor and less wealthy candidates. One example is an independent candidate saying that for him the official election spending limit of Rs 500,000 was sufficient. He spent Rs 57,000 in the 2007 campaign when he got elected: 'I would not know what to do with more money.'[28]

> One NCP candidate Mr Vani created excitement when he urged voters to vote for a rich person: if you elect a poor person you will get a *dalal* (a relatively negative word for broker) who will pocket most money he receives and not a corporator.
>
> (Mathias 2012)

When a candidate does not command the requisite funds him/herself, there is a need to look for sponsors. Considering the vast sums needed, this seems to concern a majority of cases. A well informed election watcher estimated that in the 2007 municipal elections funding by political parties of candidates was quite limited and was mostly about party materials such as flags, posters and handouts. Candidates themselves mostly sorted out their money needs. Much money was contributed by builders, some of whom 'own' a candidate (field notes, 10 March 2008). On the one hand all candidates in a constituency expect contributions – sometimes in addition to the regular *hafta* or 'protection monies' – from shops and businesses in their area where the latter are mostly ready to pay up as some kind of insurance. After all it is better now not to antagonise any candidate (given an assessment of chances to win); this could make a big future problem if he or she wins. These, however, are smaller amounts and, as per all sources, the big money really needed mostly comes from builders or developers and other businesses operating in the ward area. They qualify for this in terms of owning sufficient money, much of it as black money which can now be invested conveniently towards a purpose with huge anticipated returns. It follows from their interest to gain the future support of friendly corporators in issues like building licences, construction issues, land-use changes, legalising illegal transactions, tax matters and such where they are the ultimate masters of the constituency. Generally, a 'sponsor' will be careful to invest in a candidate who is likely to win and, consistent with predictions by Gowda and Sridharan (2012) and what was noted before in Chapter 1, Section1.7, sponsors may support the two or three most likely victors, ideally without anyone of them knowing. But a sponsor may also have an eye on a specific opportunity in a ward where they cannot avoid the corporator. Says Mr Tawde, a BJP leader:

> If builder's interests are central, it does not serve the people. Not surprisingly, you find several candidates who are sponsored by

builders. The developers choose their candidates who would later serve their business interests when elected to the BMC.[29]

Nainan (2012: 159) mentions that 'builders are known to fund election campaigns of councillors, easily costing several hundred thousand rupees'. Political functionaries are quoted[30] as saying that developers interested in state-run SRA schemes are keenly interested in these elections, preferring powerful candidates:

> The normal practice of the builders' lobby is to open the purse strings for every party. They are particularly generous with candidates known for their clout and muscle power.

So while candidates may be able to assemble sufficient funds from sources mentioned, much of such funding is essentially local. There appears to be some kind of division of labour here following the hierarchy of governance levels, with power and money increasing upwards. MC election campaigns are financially supported by stakeholders who want to make sure to have cordial local, ward/neighbourhood-level agents in case of some problem or opportunity in the future. This could be a developer with plans for a certain constituency area or an eye on a lucrative slum or other redevelopment project. I already noted that it is not just businesspeople keen to invest in, or engage with MC campaigns where the latter have positioned themselves very expertly for that. Considering the powers and range of corporator pursuits and expectations one can hardly avoid to act, however differently, flexibly or opportunistically from case to case. Aspiring shopkeepers, poor people in neglected slum pockets, ambitious young unemployed men – it is wiser for them all to engage with local power configurations.

But there are levels of political activity, and from the perspective of parties, MLAs and MPs, local elections are small fry. The latter are more likely to have powers or to be party bosses in citywide or national political – and business – arenas. There are indications that it is parties – and not local corporators – who permit or bless political arrangements with private-sector firms at city or state level. It seems that it is parties that entertain relations with specific or favoured firms or business houses which is about the real big money. This is another complex field of considerable opacity, but very critical for study if we want to understand governance and political shifts leading to increased exclusion. Data are hard to come by, and it is again Nainan (2012) who provides evidence, for example that the Mumbai political parties have their own favourite contractor or builder firms, which may operate in tandem to take on works beneficial to both.[31] In the case of a potentially lucrative slum redevelopment project 'builders gained access to the slums through the local councillors and political agents' (Nainan 2012: 159). The Shiv Sena had the best papers in the area, but there was also an active Congress presence. A prime concern for builders in such cases is to get the support of 70 per cent of the slum people, which invariably leads to lots of – sometimes pretty rough – informal wheeling and dealing (see de Wit 2016):

> Each political party supports its own builder; as a result, the residents are divided between a Congress-promoted builder and the one supported by Shiv Sena. The Shiv Sena builder has practically won the election along with the Shiv Sena councillor, but, in order to obtain majority support of the slum occupants, even with strong political backing the builder has to negotiate with almost all of the smaller politically affiliated groups of slum occupants.
>
> (Nainan 2012: 159)

Nainan shows in some detail how and why private builders and developers pay or advance most of the costs for elections, but concrete evidence generally, in terms of hard facts, amounts or cases is obviously scarce. In our election research we came across the case of a wealthy businessman who decided to support the campaign of a talented but poor Shiv Sena candidate in one Mumbai ward. This would help him manage his many shops in the area, many of them in fact illegal encroachments. Another reason for the businessmen's strategy was to undermine the chances of the incumbent corporator who had unhelpfully lodged cases against some such encroachments during his tenure.

Finally there were reports that higher-level politicians such as Members of Parliament may see chances in financially supporting candidates in key constituencies in what may be called higher-level political patronage. Informal patronage relations then span all the way from Delhi to a Mumbai ward, all part of accumulating power through building political capital. This is certainly the case where it was reported that some MPs actually fielded their sons as election candidates, another indication of 'dynastic politics'. If such candidates win, investment returns will be helpful in monetary terms first and later in terms of electoral support where the corporator's son can pull strings for his father and/or his party at local levels. All this goes to show the prime importance of financial considerations and calculated investments of (black) money into local elections with a view to future monetary profit. It is also further evidence for my thesis to consider Mumbai's politicians 'political entrepreneurs'. Rather than acting as per democratic principles of representation and accountability, their major concern is to acquire money personally and to spend it profitably. Naturally one finds such persons in any party and in any country, and the political entrepreneur is by no means a figure limited to India – indeed I worry that they are on the rise globally. Yet where Mumbai goes, it has all the appearances as if the political entrepreneurial corporator is the dominant type. Even more problematic, norms, rules, expectations and (perverse) incentives have gradually evolved into dominant institutions in terms of the 'rules of the political-financial game'.

5.5 Election campaigning: manifestos, strategies and ward-level organisation

All contesting parties had an election manifesto, which however mostly played a role in the media and during the numerous election meetings of parties where leaders addressed crowds. It is my impression that manifestos, just like party ideology, played a very limited role at the level of slums and households – and the everyday electioneering business. One might assume that voters see through such ideals, plans and promises they only know too well. Indeed, poor and slum voters are quite used to hear election promises only to be broken or never anymore heard about – one possible reason why they target more immediate campaign benefits – if any. It was noted that the Shiv Sena party refrained from clearly and openly voicing the 'sons of the soil' and Hindu focused ideas which it had strongly defended in the past. At least for these elections it was believed the party moved away from a more militant pro-Marathi and anti-migrant agenda – according to some as a result of a pragmatic calculation that Marathis no longer form a majority in Mumbai. Possibly the unlikely alliance with the Dalit dominated RPI party also led the party to avoid extremism and controversy. Even so, such issues did crop up at election meetings and roadside rallies. Its manifesto did refer to more fly-overs, enhanced water supply, cleaning rivers, improved roads, 'well women clinics' and the like. Of the manifestos, the MNS one was the most clear – and strict – about slums. It advocated steps towards the removal of encroachments, the enforcement of the actual use of reserved land for its designated purpose and a stop to the growth of new unauthorised slums. Like most manifestos it was critical of the BMC – an easy scapegoat – but marked by a wish to better manage and control city governance. It suggested improved means for citizens to formally complain about illegal practices and wrong doings in the BMC and to enhance awareness of BMC decisions.

As expected for a city where the slum and chawl dwellers are perceived as the main overall vote bank, there was ample attention for slum issues in the manifestos. One issue of contestation was the recurring theme of a 'cut-off date' (see Section 3.3): the legally specified date after which 'unauthorised' slum dwellers have no formal rights in the city. The Congress party promised to extend the 'cut-off date' from the then 1995 limit to 2000 – however subject to Supreme Court ruling. The BSP went so far as to demand that the Government regularise slums up to 2010, and give 500 sq. ft. free homes to slum dwellers.[32] Predictably, this was opposed by middle-class citizens, for example in the northern R/N-ward, with large encroachments of slums within the coastal protection zone, who were reported to protest against the use of slums as vote banks.[33] The Congress–NCP manifesto further proposed reducing the limit along the coast where slums could be regularised. The coalition advocated a single window facility for documents for slum people in slums in existence prior to 1995 and to reserve 5 per cent of BMC revenues for slum development. Forty thousand toilets were proposed to be constructed in Mumbai, adding 10,000 each year. The SS–BJP–RPI manifesto was much less vocal on slums,[34] but rather elaborate on (health) provisions for women, which assumedly impacts slum women mostly. Some observers noted the lack of attention in any of the manifestos for what were arguably the metropolis' key challenges: the larger, deeper, structural and long-term issues of the city. Examples noted were the need for large long-term investments in water supply, sanitation systems and housing; the need for governance reform including a larger voice of people (for example to create neighbourhood-level area councils (*sabhas*) as suggested in the centrally proposed Nagaraj Raj Model bill), or for financial reform, for example the fate of the very important *octroi* tax and expanding personal taxes. Instead, the manifests' issues seemed relatively parochial,[35] localised and tailored more towards the city's poor and slum people. In an article 'Why Mumbai's elections are irrelevant to this City-State', Jagannathan (2012) refers to Mumbai, which 'is unfortunately governed by a mass vote mentality that is entirely rural in character'.

Campaigning

The election campaigning was marked by much mudslinging and nasty personal attacks by party leaders. In the Congress–NCP coalition, Congress Chief Minister Mr Chavan – the chief architect of the alliance – dominated the campaign. This alliance was not so stable as feelings of animosity or uneasiness lingered among the rank and file of both parties, with dissatisfaction about the (top-down) allocation of tickets. The CM took some risk in being quite visible in the campaign. One of his main planks was to accuse the Shiv Sena of large scale corruption in the Shiv Sena dominated BMC – which some found less credible in view of the important role/voice of the state government vis-à-vis BMC. NCP's Mr Pawar (a former CM) joined this line of attack and assured the voters that a probe would be organised if their parties came to control BMC.[36] He accused the SS of being responsible for Rs 40,000 crore or Rs 400 billion (where the annual BMC budget is about Rs. 33,000 crores) worth of irregularities over the past 5 years.[37] A newspaper wondered what had prevented the Congress and NCP leaders to do so earlier, as the Congress–NCP combine had been ruling Maharashtra since 1999, and as the BMC is controlled by State appointed officials: 'In the last ten years, not a single municipal commissioner or his deputy has submitted a default report.'[38] Mr Chavan challenged SS leader Thackeray to make public his assets and was surprisingly outspoken about corruption, for example when he boldly stated in an interview: 'I am told there is a tanker mafia, and a vested interest in ensuring leaks in supply chains (of water).'[39] However, his party did not follow this up with concrete and viable policy initiatives. MNS leader Raj Thackeray also accused the SS of corruption: 'For the Shiv Sena, the Mumbai civic body is nothing but a hen that lays golden eggs.'[40] In turn, Shiv Sena leaders attacked their estranged nephew in his offshoot party MNS, while the BJP Mumbai Unit Chief Mr Purohit claimed that the 'Congress-NCP is an unholy alliance to loot the city'; aiming to rob India's richest municipal corporation.[41]

But real election action was not at all with the possible impact of a manifesto or well-known political accusations; as noted most parties are 'machine' parties more engaged with money and incentives than with ideology or policy issues. Most time and energy was centred around the constituency-level office of each party, where the candidate and a core team of trusted party leaders and workers would spend days and more and more nights to plan the campaign. This is about planning day and evening meetings and street corner rallies, places for the candidate to go for street visits and to chalk out strategies for each booth area. There is a lot of work to do with, on average, 37 polling booths of maximally 1,500 voters in each constituency, with up to 44,000 voters in the 227 city constituencies.[42] They spied on the activities of the other candidates and organise the campaign in terms of distributing party propaganda materials (flags, brochures, ribbons).

A key activity was to study the voters' list, which activity is the basis for the eventual turnout-buying and vote-buying strategies.

The State Election Office published the voter lists (or rolls) as a massive document, an indication for formal local capacity to more or less satisfactorily do the job. After all, it contains the names of on average 44,000 voters in each ward. Often bound in a folder, it contains all registered voter names plus some details and often photographs of each voter in each constituency.[43] This became the key strategic document for the team of each candidate, if only to copy the names onto individual voter slips, which are handed to voters on Election Day, prior to them entering the polling booth. For that reason, all parties have tables around the booths, which double as lively meeting places for party leaders, candidates and supporters. Even while a voter can simply enter the booth without such a slip, he or she needs to know his or her registration number which you can get on line. But most people do not or cannot even do that and they accept a voter slip from their preferred party – or any other party – with their number. It also makes it easier for less literate/illiterate voters to make sure they vote for the party of their choice – their main clue might otherwise be prominently portrayed party symbols, such as the hand for Congress or the BJP lotus. So before entering the booth, most people go to the table of the party of their choice and take the slip – from which the party symbol is removed. Hence, the number of voters coming to your party table already gives a rough idea how things are moving on Election Day. And party people may give or force some advice on each voter.

In addition, the voter's list is used to screen the listed voters and to assess them in terms of whether they are actually likely to vote, where it may happen that voters are still listed from a slum that was evicted, died, are unable to vote, or are known to never vote. Another check is as to whether they are loyalists – known to anyway vote for one specific party or candidate whatever happens, or whether they could reasonably or otherwise be influenced by other considerations. Party strategists and street-level party workers assess who are 'floating voters', who could be influenced with sweet talk, promises, bribes, inducements or threats to vote for the candidate. Such considerations help determine which areas/neighbourhoods/pockets and streets will become the focus of attention during campaigning. But the main decision as to where campaign money is to be spent depends on the nature of the contestation between the various candidates in each constituency. Experienced city-level party analysts monitor election preparations across all 227 constituencies. They draft lists of what are considered 'safe' ones that will be won almost certainly (for example where a well established corporator or his female family member stands); ones that will be lost almost certainly and the critical category where the contest is between two or more candidates who could both/all win. It is these latter constituencies which will see most pre-election action, campaigning and agents actively canvassing, up to the street level and household.[44] It is here that pre-election clashes or violence are most likely, sometimes leading to police presence in 'sensitive booths'. But action is everywhere in the entire city, to be seen and heard all over and in all wards, as well illustrated by Bjorkman (2013) in a ward where a new (woman) entrant took on a well-established powerful incumbent corporator – with the latter winning.

From the day that the elections were announced to the end of campaigning on 14 February 2012, all candidates toured their con-stituencies, focusing key areas and neglecting areas where they (had) calculated that there was little to win – including pockets thought to be safe already, middle-class areas and apartment blocks. Where more wealthy voters go, it was already noted that the Mumbai (and other) middle classes vote far less than the urban lower-income groups (Chap-ters 1 and 4; Mooij and Lama-Rewal 2009).[45] For this reason, but also as they are harder to catch in their multi-storied blocks and behind gates and watchmen, they are not targeted that much by the candi-dates, certainly relative to slum and chawl voters. Both mechanisms seem to be leading to what can be termed a self-defeating cycle down-wards, where we need to study as to whether richer Indian people might be increasingly irrelevant to (local) democracy. Yet, as shown below, they are not completely neglected, which can be a function of a campaign to win over a hotly contested area. All such work and all such campaigning require a lot of active people and ideally there is a whole crowd of motivated party workers and young 'hangers-on' to move into action now. But there are indications that parties could not, as in the past, easily rely on such loyal party workers:

> The story of the karyakartas decline encapsulates the degenera-tion of the city's political culture. . . . Today, everything revolves around money. Young workers cut a deal with the candidates. Ide-ology is nowhere in the picture.[46]

Such trends seem to affect most parties including cadre-based parties such as SS and MNS, but not so much a Dalit party like RPI.[47] As regards the 2014 Medha Patkar campaign as candidate MP for the AAP in Mumbai, Punwani (2014: 13) notes that 'even in cadre-based parties as the Shiv Sena, leaders complain that workers need more than a *vada-pav* to come out in the streets for a two-hour agitation' and that the going rates for employing election workers range from Rs 200 to Rs 500 with meals thrown in. Parties make financial arrangements for their workers, for example paying Rs 5,000 for the whole campaign to young men, with higher ups and experienced veterans receiving Rs 10,000 up to Rs 200,000.[48] Auto rickshaw drivers now transform into election campaigners and were paid Rs 400 (double their average daily wage).[49] Candidates hired men and women to work for them at the street and neighbourhood level, paying Rs 400–500 per day, plus food. People suddenly metamorphosed into political agents, receiving Rs 200 for 3 hours to accompany candidates on slum visits or to be part of a crowd, in a package that includes the expectation to vote for them and to mobilise any other person for the same. Incidentally, this may be a boon to many informal workers (like domestic servants) or unemployed youth. Suddenly engaged in exiting as well as well-paid work, some take leave to cash in on extraordinary windfalls. A Mankhurd 14 member slum household was campaigning for Rs 100 per day:

> 'We start campaigning work right from 8am and continue till 1–2pm. We then take a break for two-three hours and go out again from 4–5pm until the canvassing ends. Normally, we should get Rs1.400 per day', Nanda said. However, it's not always easy money and sometimes, it's no money at all. Lakshmi added that hired campaigners may not get paid every day. 'You know how politicos are. They assure a lot, but do little.' In the same article the MNS and Congress parties deny paying hired campaigners: they have loyal party workers for that.[50]

This apparent commercialisation of election activities – at the expense of or in lieu of volunteers lining up to support 'their party' and 'their leader' – may be related to what has been termed a 'de-politicisation of the electoral process', where ideological positions, policy preferences and public opinion hardly matter for political parties (Prabash 2010: 88). In his view, there has been a centralisation of party decision making by a handful of leaders:

> The implication is that moving with leaders rather than working with people became the sole criterion for electoral positions for party cadres who, therefore, shifted their activities from grassroots to party headquarters. Thus naturally dried up the supply of party

workers from the society, ultimately severing the linkage between parties and the mass of the people.

Still, such campaign activity alone does not win elections, as everything is relative to what other candidates do. It is imperative for all candidates to analyse the power, appeal and specific selling points of the others and to assess whether this can be reduced or neutralised with tailor made strategies. We already saw that this operates at the level of party-coalitions, where SS and BJP joined forces with the RPI party which is seen to have a solid Dalit vote bank. They have made calculations showing this as a secure strategy to attract a large number of Dalit votes, which could tip the balance in multiple-candidate contests. Similarly, candidates would scan their areas for popular local leaders or influential citizens known to have a hold over groups of voters. For instance, in one constituency a popular Muslim leader had been a long time trusted ally of the Congress Party, always requesting his fellow Muslims to vote Congress – with the Congress candidate already counting on his support this time around. In a major blow to him, the surprising news came that the Muslim leader had suggested his supporters to instead vote for the SS candidate. This request was even announced after Friday prayers in the local mosque in the presence of the Imam. No one doubted that he had been rewarded handsomely (field notes, 15 February 2012). Another example is provided by Bjorkman (2013: 32) in her conversation with an independent social worker Mr Khan, which inter alia supports an assumption that (some) poor people are actually at a loss as to what to vote and even what to make of democracy at all:

> Khan (who had worked for another party in the MP elections): I work for myself and my people here. Kamble (the local Congress corporator) supports us. Me: But how do you convince people to vote for him? Khan: I just tell them how to vote and they do. Me: Why don't they just nod and then vote for who they want? They don't know who they want, so they ask me. They trust me to tell them who will protect us – who will do their work.

Another important phenomenon here is the 'rebel' and 'independent' candidate. The rebel candidate has left (or has been removed from) his or her former party and decides to stand as an independent candidate, calculating that he (or, less often she) can stand a chance to win elections based on a certain loyal group of voters/vote bank. One must see this in the context of several candidates contesting in one constituency, where on the average 10–17 candidates contested across the 227 wards. It may not be clear or quite important whether such a candidate has any chance of winning. What counts is the question as to whether and to which degree (s)he will eat into the votes available for all candidates, doing anticipated harm to specific candidates in terms of 'nuisance value'. In such cases, it may happen that a candidate/rebel is contacted by another candidate with the offer to join forces in return for a handsome amount of money, depending on the former's popularity and the anticipated reliability of his claim over voters (the amount of Rs 2 million was reportedly given in one such case as per my field notes, 12 February 2012). Even if a rebel stands alone and does win a seat, he or she is mostly happily welcomed back into the party, which may consider this a 'win-win' situation – and especially if a few seats more help a party or alliance to have a majority in the BMC council. And that is the overriding ultimate goal for all parties.

In the 2012 elections, of all parties, Shiv Sena had most rebels, all saying they were disappointed with the party,[51] but the disenchantment in Congress also led to the emergence of rebels (Mathias 2012: 11). Another dynamic concerns independent candidates who may simply decide to stand or who are stimulated to stand by their supporters and who may then work very hard and often with (very) limited budgets to garner votes. One independent candidate in one chawl area was offered a handsome sum to cross lines but declined to accept. In the end he lost with a wide margin, but he and his dedicated followers were proud to have done well as it was, as a positive sign that people do believe that local democracy can work.[52] Pressure on independents increases with the number of candidates in a constituency.

> Having multiple contestants also means candidates are often subjected to blackmail and extortion while arriving at a compromise formula with stray independents. Many corporators admit to having greased palms of independents to coax them into not contesting.[53]

5.6   Money and muscle power

Finally, a key strategy to win elections at the level of the voters is to manipulate 'money, muscle and machine power'. As per the State Election Commission (SEC) guidelines, the limit of election spending in Mumbai was raised to Rs 500,000, up from Rs 135,000, which many people still find unrealistically low.[54] Estimates of the actual amount spent in each constituency are a manifold of this, with a commonplace estimated average of Rs 20 million[55] but a very high and unlikely estimate of Rs 150 million, 'taking the total expenditure to Rs 3,000 crore.'[56] As noted, some such money is needed for election materials such as banners and flags and for food and drinks for party/election workers. With trends that the willingness to engage in voluntary work is reducing and expectations of compensation in food (*biryani*) and drinks (beer and quality liquor) on the rise, money needs rise too. Money is further needed for cars and jeeps to carry around the candidate and his or her entourage on campaigning. On Election Day numerous auto rickshaws and buses are hired to bring voters to the booths. Candidates make rounds of neighbourhood campaigning, but also organise larger rallies on central spots where MLAs, MPs or other party functionaries are present. These, too, are costly events, including lots of *garlands* and audio and video expenses. 'Corner meetings' where candidates stop and engage with voters are cheaper. Part time sloganeers and auto-drivers need to be hired, and it may be seen as unavoidable – but costly – to buy away or co-opt a candidate seen as a strategic threat. I may note that a strategy often applied by sitting governments (i.e. ruling machine parties) to hastily implement pre-election feel-good schemes or crash-construction drives to influence voters not (only) with individual goods but also 'club goods', did not appear to have been applied in these local elections. This, in contrast to evidence that the ruling Congress–NCP coalition at the Maharashtra state level did engage in such machine-type activity prior to the 2014 MLA elections (which it lost).[57] While I mentioned that promises were made in manifestos and speeches, I have no evidence that the BMC (i.e. the ruling Shiv Sena) ordered the pre-election construction, cleaning or maintenance of public assets or services. The main strategies seem to have been corporator centred, for instance where corporators are believed to condone (or actively support) the emergence of new slums, which are then assumed to favour that corporator. But probably more is or has been going on here than meets the eye. No doubt corporators channelled benefits in terms of facilities and constructions paid from their discretionary Area Development Fund to strategic pockets – before or in between elections as noted, with or without their names prominently visible on a stone pedestal (Chapter 4, Section 4.5).

But the main election expense – and counting – is the apparently unavoidable payment of money and other benefits (goodies, freebies) to the voters, with most estimates of a low amount of Rs 1,500 to a rare estimate of a very high Rs 5,000 per vote.[58] A newspaper mentioned that Rs 1,000 is paid for the vote of a common man, 1,500 for a senior citizen or handicapped person's vote and Rs 2,000 for the person who casts a bogus vote.[59] The amount is a factor of variables such as the budget of the candidate and the perceived need to win a certain number of votes in a particular booth area, which again relates to the degree of competition in a specific constituency. But, as Bjorkman (2013) cautions, it may not only be the sheer amount of money that counts, but also the belief in, assumptions on or reputation of a ward candidate making the actual impact. She mentions the case of a woman candidate who missed out on the votes deliverable by a social worker, as her agent was unable to channel the needed cash to this social worker. This, she suggests, (Bjorkman 2013: 39, 43) called into question her critically important 'accomplished power', translated as having access to networks of power, knowledge and authority crucial to navigate everyday life in the city. Cases like that can be seen to support the thesis of 'a patronage democracy' or 'a mediated state', which start from the recognised discretionary power of a politician over desired resources and requisite channels to mobilise these. Such symbolic connotations however do not mean that amounts are unimportant. Amounts will rise when two well-known or powerful candidates oppose each other, with high stakes for victory in terms of reputation, political incomes and further careers. Voters are clearly getting more demanding, perhaps realising that they should be offered more when helping a selected few into positions where benefits *can* be huge. Foreign branded liquor has replaced country liquor; the regular rate of one saree and Rs 500 for a woman voter is no longer enough.[60] This may explain why some candidates/agents take the trouble to ask voters to swear in the name of a Goddess or in the presence of children to actually vote for him, before handing over the cash.[61]

> After loosening their purse strings to woo voters, politicians are now a worried lot. Two days ahead of civic elections, they are not sure whether all the money, liquor and other goodies splurged on voters will translate into votes. They are invoking divine powers to ensure voters are on their side. Before handing over cash, candidates ask voters to swear in the name of 'Kul Devi' (Goddess of the village or family) or any other God a community believes in so that they would vote for them. . . . 'We took an oath in the name of food grains,' said Dhanuka, a slum dweller of Colaba. Desperate candidates are targeting mainly women as they are soft-hearted and religious. Moreover, they have a say in the family. 'Voters are getting cleverer. They take money and other goodies from more than one party. People are not as loyal as they used to be', said a candidate.

However, it is critical to note that the actual distribution of such good-ies may not be quite visible. This would, first, attract the attention of election watchers (who could report to the Election Commission). Besides, lots of commotion would emerge if all parties go around with crates of whiskey bottles, bags of cash and bulky saree bundles. Many candidates prefer to distribute 'coupons' or vouchers which can be exchanged for goods, for example a coupon exchangeable at a specified liquor shop. In one slum area people could receive coupons marked A, B or C, representing increasing amounts. Candidates organise so called 'meetings' in specific hotels which are really occasions where money changes hands. Items that were distributed in these and other clever ways as per local reports included quarter bottles of liquor,[62] kitchen utensils, stainless steel sets, student notebooks, bangles, and *bindis*. However, low-income voters take a pragmatic look at all this. One Ms Shaikh is quoted as saying:

> When we go to their offices, when they are corporators, they hardly pay attention to us. Now when they need our votes, they come to us with gifts. We have decided to take everything that comes to us, but finally vote for whoever we think right. We are tired of their false promises, election after election.[63]

One constituency witnessed a fierce clash when Congress party work-ers discovered that the SS was bringing money into the area and in the ensuing fight one candidate and some workers were wounded. Follow-ing this another candidate stopped the distribution of *sarees* (women dress) which he had purchased wholesale. They were stacked unused after the elections, a sad symbol of a defunct machine inducement. A similar inter-party clash in another slum resulted in a policeman get-ting wounded but this was not reported in the newspapers. It could be an indication that elections were not conducted quite so peaceful as everybody (fortunately) maintained.[64] The distribution of tangible 'incentives' such as sarees and liquor is mostly done in personal trans-actions, where, naturally, a degree of secrecy is critical and this would also apply to cash. However, paying cash to individuals seems rare and impractical in the dense Mumbai slums and chawls. From a practical, logistical viewpoint, it is already a huge operation to raise (or trans-fer from diverse public, private and business sources) and transport the (black) money, to keep it safe under conditions of secrecy and to bring it to often inaccessible and thickly populated (slum) areas where 'everybody knows everybody'. It would be quite complex and too visible to contact households separately, at a time when each party/

candidate is keeping watch over anything happening by day or night. Three arrangements seem most common. I have already explained that most parties have community organisations such as youth and sports groups, women *mandals* or self-help groups (Chapter 3.5). These may be less active normally, but now often become a conduit to allocate money-for-votes. Amounts ranging from Rs. 10,000 to 25,000 may be given to the leaders, who are trusted to channel that strategically to members and sympathisers (field notes, 10 February 2012). Secondly, candidates hand money – following negotiations – to non-party agents, local leaders and people like the aforementioned social workers who seem trustworthy and say they can deliver votes. Such dynamics are illustrated very well by Bjorkman who depicts the many small and big negotiations and transactions to 'buy' block votes (2013). Trust plays a role for voters who take the agent's word to advise them well on the best choice. Such transactions can be framed as vote bank politics where voters are all known to the agent and are likely to have a similar 'identity' background such as caste, religion or ethnicity.

> One corporator informed us that he would not pay money to slum persons individually: 'we rather pay to groups: youth groups, women associations, neighbourhood *mandals* or CBOs, in amounts ranging from Rs. 10.000 to Rs, 30.000'. He told us that middle income groups did not vote much, perhaps 10 per cent of them; and then they often had a special reason or interest if they did.
>
> (field notes, February 2012)

Another way – which may overlap with the former – is that the cash is given to trusted local party agents/*karyakartas,* who are then expected to channel it on to the voters. At this point it is critical to note that in fact a lot of gambling is going on here. Trust is not in great supply and one might assume that it is almost unavoidable that lots of money is kept behind by agents and social workers in a competitive context of great secrecy, opacity, a complete lack of accountability and what can be seen as an investment gamble. Evidence is naturally hard to come by, but the fact that such money may be provided by outside sponsors like builders or businesspeople in the form of unaccounted for black money might be another factor here. As noted, some see such election largesse as a monetary transfer from the elites to the poor. Bjorkman (2013: 45) puts it like this:

> Whether and how much cash is distributed to voters . . . sits largely [with] the discretion of the social worker; the candidate giving the

money does so as a two-part gamble – first that the social worker has influence to the extent (s)he professes, and second, that (s)he will use that influence to the candidate's benefit. 'Giving money is a gamble because everybody flips, . . . sometimes people take money from one candidate and then distribute it in the name of another. But you have to try – if you spend money then maybe the people will vote for you.'

(Bjorkman 2013: 43)

A similar comment is made by Guha Ray (2009: 7): 'In fact, the cash-for-vote arrangement often works as a hit-and-miss syndrome in India since booth capturing is out and you actually do not know who is doing what.' During our slum-level interactions, some informants said that some agents/social workers actually pay out most money, but there were more reports that such agents keep rather large sums for themselves: 'It depends on the agent's leniency,' said one party worker. One observer made a distinction between three types of agents here. 'The worst fellows are the party workers who may keep half the money.' We then have another group of wheeling and dealing social workers who are well portrayed by Bjorkman (2013). They seem less reliable but may be more trustful as they work outside parties' protection and have a reputation to keep up as being at least somewhat reliable. A final group are the 'sincere' social workers who have built a reputation of trust with local voters and who neither receive nor allocate cash.[65] Almost certainly a lot of money simply disappears. We were told that some parties such as SS are believed not to worry much about it and do not check much as long as voting patterns are favourable.

On the whole, voters seem to play along the game passively, or actively seek out where and how the best inducements can be found. Some recounted that money that was not paid out before the elections might be paid later in terms of area facilities or other support. Agents engaged here are reputed to be strong, if not brave persons. They need to be known to have a claim over 'their' people and be relatively clear headed, especially those seeking the limits of earning by playing double and risky games. The agent/social worker needs to negotiate with the candidate, to sell his assets such as votes at the highest possible price in a pressure cooker atmosphere. It was reported that it may happen that the agent 'sells' 'his votes' to several candidates, walking a fine line between the various candidates, keeping friendly with all. In one constituency we were told that policemen may take cuts from the agent, which is like a *hafta*-like insurance that they won't make a problem. Voters too accept money and other goodies from different parties/agents. This does not appear to be too risky, especially not if it is the agent who distributes. Says one party worker: 'No one will control this, if there is an accusation or threat you just deny it, there is no proof and it is all illegal anyway.' The assumption here is that there is no way to find out who voted what: the electronic voting machine cannot be seen by party agents in the booth – but I will cast some doubts on this below. So while voters may – by and large – feel free to vote in the confines of a booth, one final strategy is of 'impersonation', where party workers scan the voter lists for persons they believe will not vote, or, more conveniently, do not exist or died. They may then fake an identity card with that name and pay party workers extra to come and cast that vote. As such risks increase during Election Day, politicians and citizen groups urged voters to vote early.[66] However, there were only few reports on this.

> We talked to a young Shiv Sena party worker Mr. P. on 17–2–2013. He and some friends had been very active before and during the 2012 local elections, as party agents and also to convince people to vote for the SS party (he did not attend school for two months). He told us that the allocation of money in elections depended from case to case. In case of a hotly contested MC battle between two opposing candidates, money would flow easily, and people would benefit happily. In cases of a general anticipation that one dominant candidate is likely to win, rather less or no money may be allocated. This may have the added advantage that a candidate can 'keep her/his hands clean', which may be an asset in case s/he wants to become an MLA later. He mentioned that amounts of Rs. 5.000 for all votes in a household were not uncommon, with Rs. 500 for an individual vote (and not 1,500 or Rs 5,000). Mr P. said that he and his neighbourhood friends had a pretty good idea as to who was voting on whom.

Most pre-election campaigning and distribution of presents/cash for votes occurs in slum and chawl areas, where candidates expect most returns and where voting can be monitored relatively easier. For example, Bjorkman (2013: 38) mentions that all major parties contesting the polls were reported to have distributed cash to social workers in exchange for delivering (lists of) voters towards the end of campaigning. Intelligence remains critical all along but especially on the last evening/night, which was also when most incidents and clashes took place in the city. All parties sent spies into the slums, especially those seen as key to help a candidate to victory. Seema, a candidate and her team 'had posted an estimated hundred boys (one for every four lanes) throughout the area, where they loitered, listened and sent SMSs back to Seema's office with reports of which areas were safely "ours" and which ones needed some more "attention" ' (Bjorkman 2013: 37).[67]

But it is a mistake to think that only poor voters are targeted. Party agents and social workers with clout in such areas might knock on middle-class house doors and offer cash. Middle-class occupant associations of apartments were promised that the candidate, if elected, would provide facilities or utensils needed for the annual apartment festivals. We learnt from one middle-class informant that a candidate's agent promised to pay an agreed amount of money to an apartment representative if the latter agreed to deliver a certain number of votes. Offers were made to build roads in colonies, dig bore-wells and paint buildings. Senior citizens were taken on fully catered day-long pilgrimages to Mumbai's religious shrines (Mathias 2012: 12). Agents of candidates contacted housing societies and people active in local groups: 'Many close associates of candidates are fixing up appointments with housing societies and office bearers of social groups to bribe voters.'[68]

> Emissaries of the candidates have been meeting key residents of buildings and slum leaders who can ensure at least 100 votes in their favour and offered them money and sponsored trips. Some met members of the managing committees of major housing societies in the western suburbs and promised to pool in funds to repaint the society or erect a security gate if the candidate is elected.[69]

The latter formulation confirms a special strategy that rewards/ inducements will only be provided *if and when* a candidate is actually elected, which brings in a more clear quid pro quo market element in contrast to the gamble when cash or other goodies are simply allocated more randomly.

Finally, apart from promises, presents and cash to influence voters, there may be the strategic application of what in India is called 'muscle' power, which is related to what some call the 'fear factor'.[70] It is about the use of threat to put pressure on voters. Again this is done at the lowest level of neighbourhoods and streets, by party strongmen or goons, in areas where people may already feel vulnerable and less powerful. Voters may be nervous in and around the booths. In such cases where someone took money from one candidate, party workers of other parties may come and threaten him or her. Some MCs have hired goondas working for them; some are seen to be goondas themselves.[71] Fierce competition between powerful candidates and the degree to which some candidates are willing to play a dirty game are played out here. It could result in such party men cruising an area continuously with jeeps, looking directly and intently at individual people and signalling or telling them to vote for their candidate. Party men may be found lining the streets and booth areas whispering the symbol or list number of their candidate on Election Day. In one case a woman candidate threatened an illegal slum community to vote for her, saying that they would face problems if they did not. Again here, the possibility (not certainty) for the party mathematicians to infer voting behaviours from the EVM booth-level results may indeed instil fear in people – and sometimes with reason as we will see shortly.

5.7   Turnout, election results and 'perverse accountability'

Weeks prior to Election Day, the BMC was engaged in a massive organisation to plan and to organise the elections.[72] Among other things, locations were found for the Returning Offices as well as numerous polling booths in each constituency (in total 8,378). BMC employees were ordered to leave their jobs to go on election duty training and to take charge, all EVMs had to be prepared, checked, stored safely in strong rooms and transported under guidance. Large numbers of policemen – 23,000 in all – were on alert to maintain law and order, especially in booths marked as sensitive. While established parties used their time tested symbols, new parties and any rebel or independent candidate were given a unique symbol, which could include a walking stick, scissors, a road roller or an ice cream. But the most ambitious and sensitive task is to create the above mentioned 'voter list' – which was shown to be so critical to party strategists. It is no small job to create and then maintain a list of all 10 million or so eligible voters in a place like Mumbai, with hard-to-map slums, slums that have come up recently or were evicted and a continuous coming and also leaving of migrants, rich or poor.[73] No surprise then that many people established problems with the list – notably missing their name. As noted, the inclusion of dead people in the rolls might be an opportunity for a party to try impersonation.

> Many people turned up at the voting booth only to discover that their name was missing from the rolls. Of course many dead people did not turn up, but their names were on the rolls. These two types of errors of wrongful exclusion and inclusion could be as high as

20 per cent in Mumbai. This would mean that the legitimate and effective voter strength of Mumbai is 8 million, not 10 million. These errors in voter rolls are large in urban areas, especially in metros. In Mumbai, with its large migrant population, whose land records (and hence voter record) is in their 'native place' the problem is more acute. Some missing names were because of ignorance and laziness.[74]

As already mentioned when discussing 'vote banking' earlier, it is by no means easy for a migrant to get registered as a voter in Mumbai, while officials back home 'in the native place' may make extra problems to fix the papers for minorities, as suggested by Boo:

> The Hijras, who were migrants from Tamil Nadu, saw little differences among the political parties, but were eager to vote nonetheless. Their problem was that district election officials sometimes failed to process registration forms submitted by migrants and other reviled minorities. While Asha (the local Annawadi Shiv Sena woman 'slum lord') and her husband had voter cards and ID numbers that allowed them each two votes in two distinct precincts, many non-Maharashtrians in Annawadi had yet to secure their one vote. Zehruniasa and Karam were local record holders in disenfranchisement, having spent up to seven years trying unsuccessfully to register to vote.
>
> (Boo 2012: 230–231)

Yet, as noted before, corporators seem able to help 'undocumented people' to cook up forms and details resulting in a voter ID pass in a few months, so things are not unequivocal and need further investigation.

Part of the operation to manage city elections for nearly 10 million voters is for the SEC to frame the formal Election Code of Conduct specifying which expenses are allowed. Candidates have to submit daily expense statements, which are on public display. The rules include the duty of candidates to provide a comprehensive account of all their all incomes and assets, which are included in affidavits. Newspapers placed large question marks with such statements with often obviously very low or extremely limited listings. Many rumours circulated to the tune that 'the many cars owned by a candidate have been removed temporarily to another location until after the elections'.[75] One newspaper compared 10 affidavits (however incomplete perhaps) of candidates who stood in both 2007 and 2012 and noted that 'becoming a corporator puts you on the fast track to prosperity'. Some corporators saw an increase in assets of 3,300 per cent.[76] There were reports of candidates tainted by corruption (e.g. five cases in the NCP–Congress).[77] On average 13 per cent of all candidates were reported to have criminal cases against them; 57 such cases were serious.[78] Many candidates were shown to be already very rich *Crore-paties* (having assets beyond Rs 10 million). Such wealthy corporator candidates were found in both NCP and BJP (36 per cent); in Congress at 35 per cent, in SS at 22 per cent, with lower ratios at 15 per cent in MNS, 9 per cent in SP and 6 per cent in BSP.[79] One newspaper reported that the average assets of party's candidates are Rs. 10 million plus for Congress, BJP and NCP.[80]

Then came 16 February, Election Day, which, it is important to note, passed mostly peacefully, with no reports of things like booth capturing, ballot box stuffing and the like. This has sometimes occurred in other cities, for example the 2001 and 2006 Chennai civic elections which witnessed a lot of brazen political violence. The Kolkata municipal elections of 18 April 2015 also present quite a contrasting picture. A policeman was shot, there were allegations of booth jamming, intimidation and vote rigging. Crude bombs were allegedly hurled and shots fired, hurting a candidate and party leader.[81] In contrast, 16 February saw no such mayhem or scenes at all during mostly very peaceful and well organised elections. The formal machinery and democratic institutions were in place and mostly respected – no matter that behind this facade and surface informality was massive. There were stray incidences of impersonating and persons who found they were missing on the voters list. Counting occurred expeditiously and without incidents worth reporting, barring some cases where candidates/agents had reason to believe that EVMs had been tampered with. All such issues could be dealt with before all results were announced and no re-voting proved needed. While the election results were a surprise in terms of an unexpected good showing of the SS-BJP-RPI party alliance, voter turnout was consistent with previous elections at a low 46 per cent. The media established a relationship between income and non-voting: the richest wards in areas like Colaba, Andheri-West, Juhu, and Bandra had least voters.[82] However, to interpret differences across areas is not easy in Mumbai, because one finds sprawling slums and chawls even in many posh localities. One Colaba-based citizen group worked to stimulate voting in their (mostly high-income) area: 'In Mumbai, it is largely the slum dwellers that form the political parties' vote bank, this trend needs to be changed.' For now, slum people are the main voters, even while it is not quite clear whether and how they will get benefits from their elected 'representatives'. For example, 60 per cent of voters voted in the Gandhi Nagar slum.[83] Under the heading 'Slumbai provides some saving grace' a newspaper[84] quoted one Kachi, a fish seller from a chawl:

> 'The only weapon we have is our vote. We are powerless and inconsequential for the most part. If we cast our vote for the right candidate, we can hope to improve our situation'. Another voter says: 'We know that one ineffectual politician will be replaced by another. But we still get excited about voting as we can at least kick out the present guy who has not done his work well.'

The Economist offered the assessment that the BMC elections were met with apathy, especially among India's middle class and rich; only 34 per cent of the citizens in the posh Colaba neighbourhood bothered to vote. It suggested a link to the 'staggering corruption' in the BMC: 'Why did people vote for more of the same? The process of voting may itself be terminally corrupt.' The newspaper refers to men with bags of cash driving around a neighbourhood the night before the poll, bribing voters. Another explanation as to the lower voting rates of more wealthy and literate *Mumbaikars* refers to the limited powers of BMC to actually manage the city:[85]

> 'The problem with Mumbai is that it is a city-state, a coastal business entrepot and a potential global dynamo like Singapore or Hong Kong. But it is unfortunately governed by a mass vote mentality that is entirely rural in character'. . . 'Mumbai's elite – who are India's most global citizens and movers and shakers – certainly do not believe in this structure. That is why they do not vote. This elitism has been wrongly interpreted as antidemocratic, or that the powerful want the city to be run undemocratically, almost like a corporation'. The article questions the purpose of electing corporators, where the BMC Commissioner is appointed by the state government. The politicians in Mumbai as the state capital are seen to be of the wrong kind: 'they derive their power from rural and non-metro Maharashtra. So, to them, Mumbai is merely a place where they can make money. They are interested in the city for the resources it can help them raise; they don't want resources going back into the city'. Other factors listed are that BMC shares power with the GoM Urban Development Department and parastatals like MMRDA, so that responsibility for the city is dispersed and that it is both over-centralised and inadequately decentralised at the same time.

Available evidence suggests – conform many other reports and contributing to my patronage democracy frame – that slum people were once more the most reliable and often enthusiastic voters and I will consider the reasons below. But, in line with Boo (2012: 231) I want to already list one important, deeper reason beyond things like dependency, opportunism or goodies, which stands in extreme contrast to the above compulsions of Mumbai's elite:

> To the excluded Annawadians, political participation wasn't cherished because it was a potent instrument of social equality. The crucial thing was the act of casting a ballot. Slum dwellers, who were criminalised by where they lived, and the work they did, living there, were in this one instance equal to every other citizen of India. They were a legitimate part of the state, if they could get on the rolls.

To the surprise of many, the Shiv Sena-BJP-RPI alliance won 106 of all 227 seats and hence were only 8 seats short of an outright majority in the Council. Most observers felt that it would be no problem for the alliance to rope in independent candidates (for example rebel candidates and the sole victorious 'citizen candidate' promoted by middle-class associations) to form a majority on the BMC Council – which is also what happened. The Shiv Sena was reportedly contacting two of the winning Congress rebels:

> On the basis of the candidates, the Sena will offer them either a chairmanship to the local ward committee or membership to a statutory committee. More development funds for their wards (which includes the notorious discretionary MC funds, JdW) are also on the cards.[86]

Many argued that the Shiv Sena's victory could be attributed in large part to its strong grass-roots presence; 'a civic election is about micro, ward-level issues, and it is the "loyal foot soldiers" and the helpful neighbourhood corporator who make the difference'[87] And even while MNS gained much (from 7 seats in 2007 to 28 now), there were reports that the MNS had been less strong than anticipated at the grassroots level. One MNS leader opined that: 'Our cadres did not perform well and took things lightly.' There was large disappointment for the Congress–NCP combine as it performed worse than anticipated. Some said that it made a fatal mistake to harp so much on corruption, at a time that Congress (then part of the UPA government) at the centre and in the state was plagued by many scams and scandals (e.g. 2G Spectrum scam). Besides, there were the accusations regarding the high profile Adarsh Housing Society scam in Mumbai against (the late) former Congress party state Chief Minister Deshmukh (who had to step down).[88] Another factor relates to the vote bank discourse: 'NCP leaders admitted that one of the party's failures was that it failed to carve out a vote bank in the metropolis, hoping Congress' traditional vote bank would support it.'[89]

Perverse accountability

Some voters in slums and chawls got worried following the election outcomes. As already indicated, the introduction of EVMs appears to have enabled vote pattern watchers – well represented in candidate support teams – to assess with some certainty which streets, pockets or neighbourhood voted for whom, or whether their calculations and expectations were confirmed. What would normally be seen as a form of democratic transparency with public and open knowledge as to voting patterns in each relatively small (1,500 votes) booth area,[90] may actually be threatening to local voters who want to remain anonymous. This remains so for an individual voter, even while party workers might circulate stories or rumours that also individual votes can be traced. But on a larger scale voting patterns can be established better than before, certainly if one considers previous elections. It would seem that the more homogeneous such an area is (e.g. an illegal slum, a Muslim-dominated chawl, a Dalit neighbourhood) the more likely that such an area can be expected to vote in one particular way. I need to emphasise that – even in a massive city like Mumbai – the real struggles of the civic elections are very localised, with very experienced strategists studying voters lists, scanning the households in a street or neighbourhood, identifying people who can be moved by money and/or threats. This restricts the options for (vulnerable) voters who may feel insecure before they vote, or after they voted (and gambled) for the losing candidate – which might be traced back to them in what Stokes (2005) correctly calls 'perverse accountability'.

If it then happens that an area voted for another than the winning candidate – especially if this is against expectations, or when a party feels – rightly or wrongly – that it has a claim over an area – it may happen that the latter may 'punish' that area. This can take different forms, for example neglecting it in terms of providing facilities, influencing water supply or by refusing mediation support. In one such case, voters of a small chawl anticipated such trouble, and they lost little time in contacting the new corporator at their own initiative. They did a bit of a kowtow, offering support in the future and generally looked for openings to (re)create harmony (field notes, February 2012). After all, it is the ruling party and corporator channels linking best to tangible and valuable supra-slum-level assets, services and opportunities, so critical for poor and marginalised Mumbai people. As argued correctly by Berenschot (2006: 19): 'The income and the prospects of inhabitants can change dramatically during elections. The local balances of power can shift enormously when a different political party takes over.' If elections result in the change to a new corporator from another party, this locally means something like a regime change, as the former effective channels and networks to get work done may be all but defunct (see Chapter 4, Section 4.4). People have to get used to the new incumbent, sometimes having to learn that the hard way. Hence, voter intimidation or post-poll retribution can occur, even while not reported for the 2012 local elections. But that such mechanisms operate in Mumbai is confirmed by Bjorkman (2013) and Bawa (2011: 492):

> Sometimes, the State appears in the form of the pipeline man to propertied residents and slum dwellers alike, threatening to disconnect them if his demands are not met. At other times, the state is the politician and his party workers who deliberately disconnect poor people from municipal water in order for their private water supply business to thrive or to enforce loyalty and political support.

5.8   Why do people vote for a candidate? Assessing key factors

On election eve, the State Election Commissioner (SEC) Mrs Satyanarayan gave a frank interview in a local newspaper.[91] One question was: what is the SEC doing about parties distributing money and liquor among voters? She answered:

> The SEC cannot do much except demand the accounts of the parties and ask candidates to disclose how much is spent on campaigning. What saddens me most are the demands made by voters from the candidates – free holidays, goodies and other favours. . . . Why don't you take the help of the state administration and police to end the menace? She said: 'Officers across the state administration are involved in corrupt practices. There are complaints about them enjoying patronage from politicians'. Does his mean the administration has degraded? 'Yes.'

This chapter has shown a significant divide between the huge, largely well organised 'formal' operation of SEC and BMC to allow nearly 10 million voters to cast their votes and the dominance of a plethora of 'informal' dynamics of questionable and certainly illegal party and candidate strategies, vote buying, vote bank manipulation and the use of informal relations and even threats. In the end voter turnout was 46 per cent, which is on the low side, but not differing much from earlier MLA and MP elections in Maharashtra state. Participation patterns confirm the earlier noted polarisation between the urban poor and more wealthy 'citizens'. The latter may be driven by an awareness that the BMC and its corporators are not exactly the chief city movers, by a dislike or aversion of dirty local politics, by a reluctance to line up in a row in the hot sun or by problems to park the car near the booth. But possibly the main reason why they can afford to stay away is that they have very little stake in local 'democracy'. They do not need the corporators, they may hardly need politicians who relate to public sector public goods and services any longer. Many of their services are already privately supplied, and they can link directly with (ward) officials if needed without using mediators in Mumbai's mediated local state.

In a clear contrast, 'it is mostly in the slums and chawls where civic services take on importance that local politics and politicians matter' (Mathias 2012: 11). Slum and chawl people live in the shadow of very powerful local operators, not only the often more remote corporator, but always local leaders, *dadas* and social workers. They double as mediators as life lines of poor people into benefits, opportunities and protection in an often unhospitable and risky habitat, frequently coping with more or less serious 'stress events' like illnesses, job/income loss, accidents, alcoholism or evictions. Their roles may not be important for each and every slum person/household. It is my impression that most people in fact very much want to avoid using them, where they may (more guardedly) share middle-class perceptions as to corruption, selfishness and the like. Lacking slum data on perceptions and personal/household strategies it is an important research question as to how many people actually use mediators in their normal, day-to-day lives, or whether they manage quite well mostly without. But I am convinced that if fate strikes, poor households may have no choice but to fall back on political patrons and brokers. So if only as some form of insurance or future protection – which they share with shopkeepers and builders – they will be more inclined to vote. Besides and not least, this could be their moment to feel like an 'equal citizen' for once. The poor do have a clear and present stake in local democracy, even in the relatively distorted local variation I have tried to picture here.

At the close of this chapter I will try and assess or de-bundle the various reasons why poor people would vote for this rather than that candidate. The list of considerations to vote one way or the other that I compiled looks like this: a voter is always loyal to one party; or is always loyal to one candidate, for example a long-term powerful sitting corporator; attracted to an ideology or intended policy plans; driven by identity factors such that poor voters look for candidates with similar caste, religious or ethnic background; give precedence to the perceived effectiveness of the candidate as a good patron/broker; is motivated by the pre-election goodies/inducements provided; is not aware what to vote and hence relying on the advice of a trusted person such as a social worker; and the quality of the election symbol.

But I need to make it clear from the start that I am not in a position to provide hard and solid answers here. There is no solid, convincing evidence which would also be hard to obtain on what is a very personal, private choice, an expression of agency if you like. Impacts of all factors will be mixed and differ for different persons at different times. Nevertheless, based on lots of discussions and interviews over the years and if only as an assumption to test in further research, I want to tentatively delineate different groups of poor/low-income voters. A first group is already convinced about one candidate or party and inducements have no impact here. They nurture a long-term and stable loyalty, which can be based on (perhaps populist) affinity to a party, candidate or leader (e.g. the late Balsaheb Thackeray of SS, now transferred to Udhay). This loyalty may be based on caste (e.g. the 'Dalit vote bank'), ethnicity (the 'sons of the soil' ideology of Shiv Sena) or religion (where Muslims may rather vote for a Muslim candidate or a secular party such as Congress). A second group is formed by more instrumental voters who are less or not concerned about such immaterial factors or 'populist' appeals, but who weigh the proven or potential efficacy of a candidate to be a useful mediator, fitting the perspective of the mediated state (Berenschot 2010). The key concern here is again not so much the incidental (machine) inducement, but that a candidate can be (has proven to be, has the reputation of) a good mediator, in terms of pulling BMC funds into his or her household and/or area. Ideally the candidate has an established willingness to support people by using or tapping the corporator's network or funds – including the contested Area Development fund. A good example for this in the 2012 elections was a powerful incumbent Shiv Sena corporator who stood for election in a new constituency other than his own – as it was a woman reserved one. In spite of not many people knowing much about him or even normally voting for his party, he easily won the seat. This was partly because of his reputation of being very powerful and arguably also having 'spread around a lot of money', which resembles the aforementioned case of a powerful sitting corporator who was next to inconvincible as depicted by Bjorkman (2013: 41). A third group could be distinguished (where we could include (lower) middle income voters with little to lose) who are more fearlessly opportunistic, not (much) concerned about above factors, who do accept benefits and goodies and *may* vote as promised. Almost by definition, they would not worry too much about 'perverse accountability impacts' feeling brave or having less to lose in terms of dependency relations. Finally, a fourth category is seen to be all those (many?) voters who really do not quite know for whom to vote, what to vote for, puzzled or curious as to what this election tamasha is all about. As brought out nicely by Bjorkman (2013) and in my field notes, such people look out for advice from 'trusted' local persons like reliable social workers or NGO staff members. As another assumption, more people in this category could be (semi-) illiterate, recent migrant and a bit at a loss how to cope with what they see as the actual praxis of local 'democracy'. They could well feel more vulnerable in view of threats and rumours, hence happy to be led through labyrinthine election complexities by someone who seems to know. In addition, they may be rewarded for their vote by sharing in funds obtained from the candidate or his or her associates.

In summary, it appears as if most slum people pragmatically check as to how the wind blows in their constituency and booth area while surveying the field of candidates. For convinced party sympathisers it is easy. For others, an initial factor is identity: is there a promising Muslim or Dalit or Marathi candidate? But, as we have seen this can be overruled by other considerations, mostly the assessment as to whether the candidate (in case of women one checks for her former male corporator husband/father) is a well reputed mediator. Is he approachable, has he or she helped people before, have slum improvements been affected? One observer – whose views are only anecdotal – estimated that perhaps 40 per cent of poor voters vote with a view to linking to an effective mediator, which one could conceive as 'positioning for patronage'. As much as possible they will naturally weigh other factors, notably identity. For the remainder this might be a factor, but they are more pragmatically open to inducements and goodies. Of the remaining 60 per cent, 30 per cent was assumed to accept these and act as per the promise made; the others voted as per their choice, with a beating as the main risk (field notes, 14 February 2012). Whatever the value of such guestimates, I am led to believe that the huge monetary investments in elections do not really pay off well.

Sadly, the role of ideology, of policy plans developed by parties after consultations,[92] of discussions or party meetings to reflect on deeper, structural aspects of governance and poverty seem almost completely absent. This supports a view that sees such municipal elections of as global metropolis as parochial. It is consistent with my thesis that the Mumbai parties are basically 'machine parties', with a focus on winning elections rather than ideology or policy driven agendas. But there is more, as formulated by Bjorkman (2013), who seems to agree with a perspective fitting Chandra's (2004: 3, see Chapter 1.4 and 1.5) patronage democracy thesis: 'Vote for me and I get your work done.' She asks: 'That is, if the election was decided by social workers responding to cash-animated networks and signals, does this suggest that party platforms and ideologies as well as policy ideas were irrelevant?' On the positive side, she remarks that policy-related issues were discussed by the candidate Seema with area social workers and voters on local concerns, in incidental, informal consultations. Yet Seema steered the discussion away from urgent problems and grievances towards her mediator capacities (Bjorkman 2013: 46):

> Yet while the topic of conversation was invariably *issues* – shortage of water, high costs of health care, poor quality of local public schooling – Seema responded not by making *promises*, but rather by attempting to convince her audience that she was possessed of the *capacity* to do work – *any* work – by emphasizing her personal qualities. 'Everyone makes promises. . . .' Seema would repeat, 'but if you give me a chance then I will *show* you what I can do.'

Still there were candidates who stood for elections from a clear position or an urgent matter, as mentioned by Mathias (2012: 12–13). Three domestic servants were put up by the Communist Party of India as candidates. Their initial single agenda was to end alcohol abuse in their respective wards; subsequently they wanted to deal with the problems of domestic servants, water and education. They lost.

All in all, the house and street-level touring, the radiation of power, the distribution of cash and other goodies represent massive investments in time, energy and not least money. This applied to nearly all candidates, whether they liked it or not, this was the time tested way to do it. But it was also commonly agreed that the cash-for-vote system was fraught with imponderables, often no more than a gamble as indicated. Conform the thesis of Stokes (2005: 315) and Nichter (2008: 30), the Mumbai (machine) politicians did target the poor more than higher-income groups as they foresaw diminishing returns with the latter. Yet there is good reason to question the efficacy of all that spending, in terms of influencing both voter turnout (which was low, but indeed highest in the slums) and the actual vote, where it was shown that much of the investments yielded highly uncertain impacts. Other reasons may help explain why the power of money in elections keeps increasing, for instance emphasising not the actual concrete performance/monetary returns of all that cash, but rather its symbolic meaning. In this perspective cash articulates the power position of each candidate, his or her access to and control over networks of power into the highest levels (Bjorkman 2013; Breeding 2011; Geddis 2008). That's all agreed and nice and well, but fact is that the (black) money is there and there appears to be no dearth of it (Gowda and Sridharan 2012). It makes one wonder about the origin of that money and whether there is so much of it that actual impacts are a minor consideration. A possible attraction could be that more of it reaches the urban poor than they would normally obtain free of cost by way of public services. But the huge risk is that, as was noted for health care, public sector jobs and ration cards, votes are also commoditised, that we perceive the emergence of a 'market of votes' as suggested by Chandra (2004), thereby fundamentally undermining democracy. That local democracy as translated in local elections is not of much wider or sustainable benefit for the urban poor (for that matter for all Mumbai inhabitants) is also shown in the absence of attention for urgent and broader policy matters. Current wisdom and praxis seems to hold that boasting ones capacity to mediate on personal issues combined with a few freebies are most effective.

Notes

1 Field notes 12 February 2012.
2 'Demolished Bandra Slums back within a Fortnight; Residents Say Shanties Prove Politics of Vote Bank', *Times of India*, 8 January 2013.
3 'For a New Mumbai, at Great Cost', *Frontline*, 28 January 2005: 48, in an article on the impact of the massive 2004–5 Mumbai slum demolitions.
4 Geddis (2008: 142) questions the 'rational actor' model that some students of vote buying apply: the assumption that the payment of money for a vote influences the subsequent voting. He emphasizes that the implicit agreement for a voter to vote as promised after payment needs to be monitored – as a principal–agent problem. 'One can assume that the better monitoring is possible, the more it makes sense to pay for votes. The use of the secret ballot makes all this rather complex, if not impossible', so Geddis wonders what innovative methods exist to 'breach the sanctity of the voting booth'.
5 See Chapter 1 (Section 1.5), note 20, on a union minister allegedly inducing the voters to take bribes. He had said that 'special people will get

foreign made and ordinary people get local brands . . . sarees for older women, pant and shirts for young boys and all "Ghandivadis" are asking for Rs 5,000. Keep whatever you can get. This is the time when illegally earned money can go to poor.'

6 'If politicians get elected on the basis of short-term contracts – money for votes – they have little reason to care about the formulation of policies, the construction of programmatic parties, and practices of accountability. In the best cases, vote buying establishes a continuous obligation to provide clientelist services to constituencies. In the worst cases, it cuts the nexus of representation between voters and politicians. Once votes are paid for, politicians may feel free of any debt to their voters' (Schaffer 2007: 11; quoted in Bjorkman 2013: 16).

7 Bjorkman (2013: 47): 'Electoral data is available at the level of each of the 40 polling booths in ward 228. With approximately 1,000 voters assigned to each booth, candidates (and researchers) are able to assess with some precision the extent of support from various sections of the neighborhood.'

8 Kumar and Landy (2009: 119) also refer to non-democratic means to manipulate voting processes: One on-going concern is to understand 'how force, compulsion and cheating do not prevent people from casting their votes (with a secret ballot) for political parties' candidates, rather it induces them to do so.'

9 Quraishi was chief election commissioner of India from 2006 to 2012. He addresses several EVM controversies (2014: 197ff.)

10 'EVMs, Blinkered Lights, That EVMs Can Be Tampered with Is Proven, Why Not a Paper Trail?', *Outlook,* 23 February 2015.

11 'For Voter Secrecy, EC Wants New EVM', *Deccan Chronicle,* 4 April 2014. The article mentions that the EC has the backing of the Law Commission but that the government is yet to take a final decision.

12 'Election Commission for New Machine to Enhance Voter Secrecy', *Economic Times,* 3 April 2015.

13 Shailesh Gaikwad, 'For Sena, Civic Body a Hen That Lays Golden Eggs: MNS Chief', *Hindustan Times,* 9 February 2012.

14 'Repair the City: A Professional BMC Can Serve Mumbaikars Better', *Times of India*, 16 February 2012.

15 'Redevelopment Bait Dangled to Lure Voters', *Bombay Times,* 19 February 2012. For a vivid account of the process and stakeholder arenas of one redevelopment project in Mumbai, see Adiga (2012).

16 A Mumbai NGO worker told me (15 February 2015) that many slum people – especially recent migrants, the illiterate and many women – really have no clear ideas as to what actually is 'democracy', how that links to elections, and what all that it is supposed to achieve.

17 She suggests that the effectiveness of social worker's networks can sometimes exceed that of a corporator. 'A powerful social worker has no need for a corporator's signature to get work done, while conversely, an unknown corporator can accomplish little without his social workers' (Bjorkman 2013: 23).

18 Dalits make up about 12 per cent of the Mumbai population (Vora and Palshikar 2003: 162) and comprise 18 per cent of all voters. They are overrepresented in the Mumbai slums as noted in chapter 3.

19 Pawar's daughter Supriya is a MP in Delhi. Pawar's nephew, Ajit Pawar, is an MLA and former deputy chief minister of Maharashtra. Pratap Pawar, Sharad Pawar's younger brother, runs the influential Marathi daily Sakal (wikipedia.org/wiki/Sharad_Pawar, accessed on 24 August 2014).

20 Bjorkman (2013: 25) mentions that after much 'high profile horse-trading', Congress and NCP settled on a formula that gave 169 seats to the former and 58 to the latter party. For the other coalition it was 135 for SS, BJP 63 and 29 seats for RPI.

21 Fareed was credited by almost all for the reach and strength of his networks with local businessmen, municipal bureaucracy, the police and rival party leadership, apart from having his own business and ample personal wealth. He had built up a reputation to be liberal with cash: 'Cash for marriages and dowries, cash for school fees, cash for medical bills, cash for home repairs – 'he is always very charitable', one area resident explained, 'that is how he made a name for himself' (Bjorkman 2013: 40–41). Even while he had a three story palazzo in a working class neighbourhood, he did not reside there, but no matter.

22 The corporator Hasina had grown notorious for demanding exorbitant cash payments from families in need of home extensions. As noted already, she had overplayed her hand as per local informal rules.

23 See Mathias (2012: 10).

24 'For Local Parties, It's Divide and Rule; Sena, MNS to Field over 90% Marathi Candidates to Secure Votes', *DNA*, 7 February 2012.

25 'Mumbai Polls: Congress, NCP Wary of Sena "Nari Shakti" ', *Times of India*, 9 February 2012.

26 Ibid.

27 'Candidates Beg, Borrow to Raise Lakhs in Funds', *Times of India*, 11 February 2012.

28 Ibid.

29 Ibid., Mr Vinod Tawde was the leader of the opposition in the State Council.

30 Ibid.

31 For example, 'according to occupiers and local leaders, Sterling Builder's strength lies in its strong financial backing, but also in the perceived support it enjoys from Shiv Sena' (Nainan 2012: 154).

32 'BSP Eyes Votes from City', *Hindustan Times*, 9 February 2012. The BSP party contested 140 of the 227 constituencies.

33 'Fits and Starts to the Final Frenzy: With Two Days Left, Candidates Gear Up to Buy Votes for Rs. 1,000 to Rs. 2,000', *Hindustan Times*, 14 February 2012. Contested slums include cases like the Ganpat Patil Nagar slum introduced at the very beginning of this book.

34 'Uddhav Gets Off the Tiger's Back', Mumbai Mirror, 18 February 2012.

35 Cf. Jagannathan (2012), 'Why Mumbai's Elections Are Irrelevant to This City-State'.

36 'Corrupt Corporation "Worries" Pawar, CM', *Times of India*, 13 February 2012.

37 'Sena-BJP Looted Rs. 40K Crore: Pawar', *DNA*, 10 February 2012.

38 *DNA* (10 February 2012) reported that Mr Pawar of the NCP accused the SS of being responsible for Rs 40,000 crore irregularities over the past

five years. *Times of India* (13 February 2012) reports that Mr Pawar and Mr Chavan raised the issue of corruption in the SS controlled BMC.

39 'Priorities: Water, Housing and Transport', *Times of India*, 15 February 2012. See also a post-election interview with Mr Chavan in the same paper: 'I had to learn a lot and much of the delay was because of that.'

40 'For Sena, Civic Body a Hen That Lays Golden Eggs: MNS Chief', *Hindustan Times*, 9 February 2012.

41 'Cong-NCP Alliance an Unholy Alliance to Loot City', *DNA*, 11 February 2012.

42 Approximately 10 million people were eligible to vote, which gives an average of 44,000 voters for each of the 227 constituencies.

43 I will discuss the many problems with this list below in terms of missing/wrong names etc., but, either way, it remains an indispensable document as the basis for campaigning.

44 Kitscheld and Wilkinson (2007: 12) refer to such strategies: 'Rather than dispensing moderate benefits widely, it makes sense to concentrate a high proportion on a critical mass of voter constituencies whose support they expect to bring victory.' One informant estimated that, out of a total of an average 44,000 voters per constituency only 10,000–15,000 actually may need to be paid; most candidates don't spent more than one crore he believed (field notes 13 February 2012).

45 I already reported low voter turn-out in the then Madras elections 'the response from the middle and upper classes was on the low side', according to *Indian Express* on 23 May 1984 (de Wit 1996: 142).

46 Ambarish Mishra, 'Leaders Lament "Extinction" of Selfless Workers', *Times of India*, 13 February 2012.

47 It is interesting to read about the apparently selfless investments and authentic enthusiasm in the campaign of slum activist Medha Patkar who was a MP candidate for the Aam Aadmi Party AAP in North Mumbai. The account seems to show that people are still willing to organize and invest without inducements once they recognise a candidate they like and trust (Punwani 2014: 13) 'She never asked us for money', 'we feel we have a stake in her campaign', 'it is our loss if we don't elect her'.

48 'Candidates Beg, Borrow to Raise Lakhs in Funds; While Some Bank on Builders or Friends, Other Resort to Selling Their Properties', *Times of India*, 11 February 2012.

49 'Auto Drivers Turn Campaigners', *DNA*, 11 February 2012.

50 'Shouting Slogans Is This Family's Full Time Job, for Now' and 'Water, Chores a Priority for Women Campaigners', *DNA*, 13 February 2012.

51 'They Rebel, They Win . . . They Are back in the Fold', *DNA*, 12 February 2012.

52 'Parties Try to Piggyback on Independents', *Hindustan Times*, 12 February 2012, which article also mentions: 'A new trend is to poach on independents before votes are cast.'

53 'Three Cornered Contests Likely in 18 Wards', *Times of India*, 10 February 2012. The average number of candidates per constituency is reported to be 17 to 18 with an amazing number of 33 candidates in ward 138. Bjorkman (2013: 7) however mentions an average of 10 candidates per ward.

54 'Candidates Can Now Spend More on Poll Campaign', *Times of India*, 22 January 2012.

55 'Candidates Beg, Borrow to Raise Lakhs in Funds; While Some Bank on Builders or Friends, Other Resort to Selling Their Properties', *Times of India*, 11 February 2012.

56 'Civic Polls Campaigning Comes to End in State', *Economic Times*, 15 February 2012.

57 'State to Review All Schemes Introduced by Cong-Led Government', *Hindustan Times*, 12 February 2015. The new BJP-SS coalition Chief Minister indicated that 'the schemes which were announced by the previous government for the sake of garnering votes ahead of the Assembly election are also being reviewed. . . . The pre-poll schemes and those that have not proved beneficial are also being scrapped or re-launched'.

58 According to my field notes (17 December 2004), in 2004, amounts given for a vote were Rs 100 plus a bottle of alcohol for a slum vote, and perhaps 100 up to maximum Rs 1,000 for richer people/apartments. So there appears to have been a considerable increase even if controlled for (high) inflation. In 2008, I noted: payments: Rs 1,000 for the rich; Rs 500 for lower income group and for EWS 100 plus bottle of alcohol (field notes, 11 March 2008).

59 'Fits and Starts to the Final Frenzy; with Two Days Left, Candidates Gear Up to Buy Votes for Rs. 1,000 to Rs. 2,000', *DNA*, 14 February. The text also refers to 'oath taking ceremonies' on respective Gods in the slums to enhance the chances that voters would actually act on their payment.

60 'Desi Daru Won't Woo Voters, Whiskey Will', *Midday Metro*, 13 February 2012. One party worker is quoted to say: 'We are desperate for votes. We are ready to fulfil their demands. If we don't do it someone else will, and that's to whom the vote will go to. If the man of the house is happy after his demands are met, the whole family will come out in support.'

61 'Netas Make Voters Swear on God Not to Ditch Them', *DNA*, 14 February 2012.

62 'From Traditional Home Visits to Valentine's Day, All Means Are Being Used to Seek Votes. In Slums, Alcohol Is Big Bait', *Times of India*, 12 February 2013. 'It's no secret that by evening, election candidates become Santa Claus. But the gifts can be intoxicating too. . . . Political party agents in slum pockets freely distribute alcohol after sunset. . . [in] slum pockets. . . interestingly, they may take alcohol from all parties, but will eventually vote for a party of their choice,. . . "These days, voters demand that they be given something in exchange for votes. Forget about allegiance to a certain party, it is difficult to get people out of their house on voting day if they do not have any incentive," said a Congress worker from Kurla.'

63 'After Sunset, Candidates Turn into Santa Claus', *Times of India*, 10 February 2012.

64 Field notes 9–10 February 2012.

65 Field notes 11 February 2012.

66 'Be an Early Bird to Prevent Bogus Voting', *DNA*, 7 February 2012.

67 'With 65 per cent of the city's population living in slums or on the street, it is clear where the voters are'. . . . 'Gifts to women and distribution of currency to men'. . . 'No one in our colony slept last night. . All the *bhais* were there, bidding till nearly 5am. Our area is very important because of redevelopment and the people know this. Even housing societies were approached, and senior citizens were pampered' (Mathias 2012: 12).

68 'Time for Netas to Deliver Poll Maal: Party Members Fulfil "promise" by Showing up at Housing Societies past 5pm', *DNA*, 15 February 2012.
69 'Rodent Business: Candidates Hold Secret "*Chuha*" Meetings Well Past Deadline; Though the Deadline for Campaigning Ended on Tuesday Evening, Wafer-Thin Margins in the Closely Contested Civic Polls Drove Candidates to Make Clandestine Last-Ditch Efforts to Woo Voters All Through Wednesday', *Hindustan Times*, 15 February 2012.
70 Personal communication by M. Pinto. This links to the overall factor of 'power in slums', which differs from slum to slum and as impacted by other, outside factors including elections (Gupte 2012).
71 Field notes 13 February 2012, cf. Boo (2012) and Hansen (2001). Naturally, voters known to have accepted an inducement are reminded gently or otherwise.
72 The organisation of the 2007 elections cost Rs 190 million; the 2012 costs were estimated at Rs 350 to 400 million (*Midday Metro*, 15 February 2012). The article refers to 368 booths. There were 368 Polling Returning Officers, 368 Assistant Public Relation Officers, 736 Polling officers, 368 peons, 368 police constables. In all, 2,216 staff, 20 buses, 20 minibuses, 181 taxies and one boat were used on 14 and 15 February.
73 'Low Turnout', *Times of India*, 2 July 2007, mentions that the State Election Commission was one factor to help explain the low turnout with large goof-ups in the voter's list at the time of the previous 2007 local elections.
74 'Heed the Absent Voter', *Mumbai Mirror*, 17 February 2012.
75 Personal communication with middle-class Bandra citizen. See also 'These Affidavits Defy All Logic', *Hindustan Times*, 8 February 2012.
76 'Get Elected, Become Wealthy; Becoming a Corporator Puts You on the Fast Track to Prosperity, if the Affidavits Filed by Many of the Sitting Corporators, Who Are Contesting Again This Year, Are Anything to Go By', *Hindustan Times*, 10 February 2012. Even while the report is not based on scientifically obtained finding, it does provide an indication.
77 'Five Ruling Alliance Leaders Tainted by Corruption', *Times of India*, 8 February 2012.
78 There is an intriguing note on 'Gangster Arun Gawli's Party Kept Its Tally Intact with His Wife and Daughter Being Elected Again' (in South Mumbai), *Hindustan Times*, 18 February 2012.
79 'Hundreds of Crorepatis Take Guard for BMC Poll Battle; Scores of Candidates Face Serious Criminal Cases, Shows Analysis of Their Affidavits; Many Have Not Declared Their PAN' (the Permanent Account Number of the Indian Income Tax Department), *Times of India*, 14 February 2012. These are the outcomes of a survey of 40 per cent of the total of 2,233 affidavits by the Mumbai Election Watch, a project involving organizations such as AGNI, PRAJA and the Association for Democratic Reforms.
80 'Hundreds of Crorepatis take guard for BMC Poll Battle', *Times of India*, 14 February 2012.
81 'Kol Civic Polls Rigged by Government: Opposition', *Times of India*, 19 April 2015. 'TMC workers cordoned off most booths of the Sahid Smriti Colony. . . . They did not allow any opposition polling agent inside the booths since morning. All these booth were out of bounds for the media, while cops looked the other way.'

Local democracy and voting in 2012 elections 257

82 'Voting Turnout Poor', *Times of India,* 17 February 2012.

83 'Local Elections in Mumbai: Gluttons for Punishment', *The Economist,* www.economist.com/blogs/banyan/2012/02/local-elections-mumbai (accessed on 7 March 12).

84 'Slumbai Provides Saving Grace', *Times of India,* 17 February 2012.

85 Jagannathan (2012: 2).

86 'Shiv Sena Approaches Sole Citizens' Candidate Winner', *Times of India,* 19 February 2012.

87 Ibid.

88 See, for example the *DNA* editorial on 18 February 2012.

89 'Big Leap, but Not the Kingmaker; Rise of MNS - Party Ups Tally to 28, Sweeps All 7 Seats in Shiv Sena's Dadar', *Hindustan Times,* 18 February 2012.

90 Election results are reported to a central voting centre on counting day and listed on a BMC website, for all to see, study and assess.

91 'Fair Polls Not Possible as Money, Liquor Flow Freely', *DNA,* 14 February 2012.

92 One of the reasons for the success of the AAP party in the 2015 Delhi State elections was that neighbourhood consultations were held on local key issues, as well as that the party disposed of an army of dedicated grass-roots-level volunteers. In a commentary, *Economic and Political Weekly* (14 February 2015: 7) says: 'One, the Delhi triumph emerged from intensive and sustained grassroots work of a sort which has disappeared in India today. Hundreds of young people, professionals, retired employees and informal sector workers came out to give time and money to AAP for its campaign. Such popular upsurges are almost always predicated on a local politics which addresses very grounded demands, like what AAP's "dialogues" and manifesto did for Delhi.'

Conclusions

'The poor pray for miracles, the rich think they have a right to them'[1]

At the highest level of abstraction, this book aimed to assess to what extent Mumbai's urban poor are affected by processes of social, economic and political exclusion, resulting from current modalities of urban governance, local democracy and related local politics. At a global level, Sassen (2014) explores the logic of inclusion/exclusion as arising from the global capitalist system while targeting the fate of those excluded, the marginalisation of the 'losers' who fail to be included and are 'expulsed'. These processes may not be quite visible as inclusion and exclusion can take place simultaneously in a context of economic growth. The world witnesses a demarcation of areas of growth and development where profits are made and less profitable and increasingly neglected areas without much prospect and at risk to disintegrate in processes of global marginalisation. Inequality is on the rise in both rich and poorer countries, leading to increased impoverishment for many, while undermining the cohesion and safety of large areas as well as the scope for robust democracies and democratisation. Politicians are seen by Sassen to be too accommodative to business elites with indications of a blurring of identities. This view fits with a disturbing report on global inequality by Oxfam (2015: 10), which notes a trend towards 'the capture of growth and politics by the economic elite' in the emerging economies. I wanted to engage with and provide concrete evidence relevant to the understanding of such global forces at work in the limited domain of Mumbai, a global metropolis firmly rooted in India's political economy. Targeting the city's slums and urban poor I examined possible exclusionary trends in 'social dimensions' such as discrimination, identity, caste, and gender issues as well as the provision of adequate shelter and basic services. Where 'politics' go, I assessed how effective the 'voice' is of the urban poor – both through party politics and in other organised or individual initiatives – in claiming services and facilities to which they are entitled, as well as to other 'life chances' for upward mobility. I assumed that a focus on the relations and interfaces between the Mumbai Corporation (BMC), its 227 corporators and the poor would best clarify this democratic dimension as, respectively, the key local governance institution and neighbourhood-level democratic agents, hopefully 'agents of inclusion'. In 'economic' terms I surveyed employment issues; conditions in the informal sector which employs the vast majority of urban poor; as well as dynamics of land, informal housing and credit. Poverty is ultimately about incomes and assets, so I checked whether and how people get access to jobs, credit and property and whether the local state could be seen as enabling people to deal better with poverty in terms of safety nets and amenities. It is here that the question as to suitable policies becomes critical: Is there an understanding among Mumbai policymakers of the concrete and increasingly precarious conditions of *and* trends among the city's poor and vulnerable? Are policies and programmes designed to target not only macro-level developments such as planning, sanitation or slum housing but also those below any conceivable poverty or misery line? If these exist, are they effective in terms of implementation, being translated or transformed through intensely political processes? Confronted by a relatively complex puzzle of administrative levels, actors and informal relations, I set about to at least uncover and illustrate the key 'everyday mechanisms' of Mumbai's administration and democracy. I tried to stick as close as possible to local realities and viewpoints/perspectives, among other things by using a range of public resources such as newspapers and journals – in addition to a wealth of secondary academic sources.

By way of conclusions I here briefly present my account of the puzzle put together, first characterising the changing stakeholders in Mumbai's governance arenas since the start of deregulation policy in the 1990s. I then consider the conditions and agency of and prospects for the city's poor, mapping processes of inclusion and exclusion. The nature of and trends in Mumbai's governance, planning and policy making are considered next, with the inevitable assessment of widespread if not systemic informality and corruption and unrestricted politicisation. Governance as a relatively de-politicised paradigm may conceal significant power dynamics, and I show that ultimately Mumbai's politicians share their powerful position with – or even basing it on – their close relations with real estate developers and builders. More broadly, the fervent pursuit of power and money seems to mark most, if not all, stakeholders. This chapter closes with an examination of local democracy through the changing relations between elected corporators, city officials, the private sector, and the slum voters. The lens through which I observe realities is composed of three distinct but overlapping perspectives, all of which centre on the importance and omnipresence of informal patronage relationships. These include patronage democracy (Chandra 2007), the mediated state (Berenschot 2009) and the political machine (Scott 1969). More broadly I contrast what could be termed 'formal governance' with 'informal governance' where the latter is the dominant governance type. Indicators here include broad, popular democratic representation versus particularistic mediation; citywide policy making versus policy particularisation through street-level politicians; and uniform formal rights, laws and general entitlements versus individualised reciprocity and the exchange of favours. Formal broad-based political parties can be contrasted with vast informal pyramidal patronage networks, and, as noted, there seems to be a growing together of the formal public/state domain and the for-profit private-sector domain and a blurring of the positions of politicians and businesspeople.[2]

Changing arenas of governance and democracy stakeholders

Even while I am mindful of continuities rather than breaches where Mumbai's local governance and democracy are concerned, I do recognise as critical the impact of a new governance regime following the liberalisation of the Indian economy, which is generally labelled India's ongoing path towards neoliberalism. Initiated under Chief Minister Pawar from 1990 where Mumbai is concerned, it led to a re-shaping or emergence of hitherto not always very visible or powerful groups of governance actors, partly as a result of reduced or altered rules and regulations. Mumbai's governance has changed dramatically – also as compared to pre-liberalisation conditions I encountered in another megacity Madras (Chennai) way back in 1984–90 (de Wit 1985; de Wit 1996). I have started from the currently most fashionable 'governance framework', which assumes that it is no longer only the government which plans and administers areas and populations, but that it engages other actors or stakeholders such as private-sector firms, NGOs and community organisations in governing. Its usefulness is enhanced to the extent that each stakeholder is checked for its power relative to the other stakeholders and their relative 'stake' or interest as regards not only a specific good or service but also public budgets, laws and policy (Hyden et al. 2004). This allows a ranking and tracing of trends of stakeholder groups in terms of power and politics as actors are assumed to strive for maximum benefits. However, this is only a heuristic tool which obviously cannot do justice to all people placed in any category; we are talking about millions of *Mumbaikars* each with their specific traits and agency. Some appear in several boxes like a middle-class corporator family with a large business, a poor *karyakarta* with good prospects to become a *shakha* leader or a slum woman taking on the 'PDS mafia' who could be seen as part of 'civil society'.

The stakeholders of importance to this book's theme of poverty, policy and politics are first the poor women as well as the poor men of Mumbai, whose interests and powers I have tried to differentiate where possible. But things are complex in view of a somewhat confusing and unhelpful practice to equate 'slums' with 'poverty'. From local vocabulary and discourses – for example in the newspapers and other media – it might seem as if all slum people are poor and very needy, belonging to poor classes and castes. But it may be better to see many established slum colonies as 'low-income settlements', much like favelas in Latin America or South African townships. BMC staff working with slums see patterns or 'waves' as to when and where slums got inhabited over time, with initial settlers mostly well established and relatively integrated in the city fabric today. By now probably the majority of Mumbai's slum areas are well-established colonies (with a variety of names, with 'slum' the least popular) where people can prove tenure rights and are probably there to stay, if past trends say anything about the future. Their facilities and street-level conditions are almost always shoddy or worse – toilets, water supply, cleaning – as depicted in Chapter 3. Yet people who often settled there from the 1970s may have reasonable incomes and prospects and do not qualify as BPL households. Better to say that slums house a majority of low-income groups (named LIG in my Madras days), in which we also find the urban poor, sometimes in poor pockets or in uniformly miserable poor slums – the 'EWSs' or economically weaker sections. So apart from the middle classes and the urban poor, there is a need to much more clearly distinguish a lower-income class – with its own characteristics, outlook and some vested interest in the city and its opportunities. For example, many such households have very low housing costs in their 'informal areas', paying few fees and taxes. It may well be that households here over time succeeded to achieve upward mobility, for example by investing in education for their children, possibly more able than the poor to pay for privately offered services. I have tried to target and map the 'underclass' of urban poor people, who are labelled as the 'undercity people' in contrast to the 'overcity people' by Boo

(2012: 225). Research here would have to confirm such a distinction, requiring detailed and delicate slum research of a kind largely missing today – where solid data, notably about the number of actual poor BPL people, are missing.

The city's corporators comprise my second most prominent actors group – deeply embedded in their political parties – followed by the many officials or public servants (the archetypical street-level bureaucrats as depicted by Lipsky 1980). They include officials in the BMC and SRA, in the PDS fair price shops and in the police. Together they make up Mumbai's local state, responsible for city governance and the allocation of public funds and benefits to its people. I included Maharashtra state-level ministers and MLAs as important, even if less visible actors. It is them – and not corporators – who decide not only about critical Mumbai matters such as land, housing, planning, and poverty reduction but also something like increasing quota systems for women corporators.

The hard-to-define Mumbai 'middle classes' were seen as another emerging group of actors to benefit from the neoliberal regime. They are sufficiently powerful already to claim a voice in governance, but, confirming an assumption of neoliberal 'networked' governance, they seem to opt out of politics, preferring to directly target local government for services. They include wealthy and well-established 'old' Mumbai families and the 'new rich' including those employed in very profitable newer activities in the ICT, building, globalised/multinational, and banking sectors. In addition, lots of households now thrive on the (much less than hoped for) 'trickle-down' impacts of a lot more money going round, including private-sector teachers and doctors, taxi drivers, travel agents – and politicians. Some theories of democratisation vest their hopes on the middle class as an agent of change to claim and gradually enforce better and 'deeper' democracy and 'good' governance. This book does not support such hopes – at least for now. The Mumbai middle classes seem to have gradually turned away from politics: voting less in elections, relatively absent in the everyday hustle and bustle of party politics, avoiding the corporators as representatives by directly contacting officials of public-sector city agencies like the BMC and wards offices (Baud and Nainan 2008; John 2007). This is partly explained by the simple fact that they rely less on public services: their children are typically in private schools; they go to private hospitals and may have private water, electricity and security (backup) arrangements. In addition they take a dim view of local politics – not quite surprisingly – from what they perceive as corrupt and selfish politicians, dirty power games solely aimed to make money and malfunctioning institutions. The middle classes may then exert their powers more defensively by uniting in – sometimes BMC promoted – welfare associations such as ALMs. One could term them 'civil society organisations' in influencing local/neighbourhood governance. Yet their operation can be detrimental to the interests and livelihoods of slum dwellers and the poor, enforcing exclusionary processes (Zerah 2009a).

Last but not least, and coming up fast, is a diverse group of business firms, business(wo)men and industrial houses, ranging from food chain shop owners in a ward to very powerful citywide or India-wide developer and builder firms and business houses. One actor group by and large missing in my book is what is called 'civil society' in the form of Mumbai NGOs. I have the impression that the influence and powers of the more prominent NGOs have decreased over time and that they are less visible than before, also in initiating and acting upon city discourses and debates. There seems to be less citywide activity in terms of advocacy, urban poor mobilisation and resulting pro-poor development today. But this is not to deny that the bigger, but also many smaller, neighbourhood-level NGOs do very useful work to support slum dwellers and poor people generally.

I have tried to trace changes in the relative power of these diverse actor groups and found that the paramount trend is that power has shifted towards the private sector, particularly those persons and firms linked to land and housing sectors. One dimension is noted by Kumar and Landy (2009: 103): 'The addition of new actors in the "big game" of urban governance under the liberation process creates new opportunities for hidden transactions and corrupt practices.' Indian journals and newspapers regularly refer to the 'builder–politician–official' nexus, and there is little doubt that their relations strongly impact city governance (Nainan 2012; Pethe 2010; Pinto and Pinto 2005). Given the centrality and profit-making potential of the Mumbai land and housing sector, it is only natural that the private sector is engaged here. It is a token of progress that the Indian and Mumbai private sector has evolved so quickly following liberalisation. Much needed economic growth followed, which is essential for development and poverty reduction. Yet at a time when India is on a neoliberal path of seeing the 'market' as a key driving force for development, the private/business sector, at least in Mumbai, may be getting too influential – also in terms of ties with politicians. This links to several sources perceiving India as marked by crony capitalism. Mumbai proved quite keen to engage in 'horizontal' governance shifts (Baud and de Wit 2008), allowing and promoting that private firms and entrepreneurs increasingly engaged in the provision of public services. PPP programmes evolved into a favoured implementation model. This shows in policy such as the slum redevelopment approach and in PCPs such as the SAP slum SWM programme (de Wit 2010a; Zerah 2006). Both were shown to be very corruption prone if only through the 'informal privatisation' of implementation (benefits). Another trend is privatisation or allowing private-for-profit organisations to provide hitherto publicly provided critical services as education and health. In all, one could perceive something like a movement from a 'public state with not-for-profit common good services' to a 'private state with individualised for-profit services' and related commodification trends. These trends already multiplied 'actors in governance' in a rather short time span. This, finally, in addition to the many governance agencies, forms the local state in a complex and already hard to manage institutional architecture: BMC, MMRDA, SRA, MHADA, MSRDC, government of Maharashtra, Indian central government, to name the important ones. In different degrees all these are affected by politicisation; some agencies are 'owned' by a political party. Such trends lead Pinto and Pinto (2005: 494) to ask: who governs Mumbai? Let us first start by focusing the conditions and trends in its slums and for its poorest people. I will then proceed to describe BMC realities and subsequently local politics – places to be scanned for openings in terms of access to services and political 'voice'.

Poor women and men and their prospects: livelihoods, agency and exclusion

The focus of this book is on Mumbai's urban poor, but it was not so easy to set them apart from other citizens. Lacking solid data and slum surveys (which is despite several policy initiatives such as BSUP explicitly requiring socio-economic surveys), it is a calculated guess that an estimated two million people survive at the bottom of the city's pyramid of castes and classes. As noted, not all of the city's six million odd slum people are poor. Large segments of city areas covered with slums represent well-established lower-income colonies by and large supplied with most basic services – even if fragmented, rudimentary, incomplete, broken – of water and sanitation, with a variety of self-built housing. Many households living here enjoy protection against eviction and manage to have relatively stable – if precarious and vulnerable – livelihoods. These are really lower middle-class people, and it has been argued that such households enjoy unfair advantages in not paying taxes or fees and that many enjoy free services on account of politicians not allowing or waiving these for vote bank reasons. On the basis of collected evidence, I argue that Mumbai's urban poor can be found in the slums – but mostly in low-quality unauthorised additions to existing slums, in poor rental slum housing and also in chawls, poor-quality 'illegal' new small slums anywhere in the city and on the streets. Poor households are also found in relatively few low-income-housing (SRA) units created under slum redevelopment – especially in eastern Mumbai's M-ward, which is seen by some as a new ghetto (Ayyar 2013). A vast belt along Mumbai's eastern boundaries accommodates large numbers of poor people, often from other states. Yet rather than location or house/hut type, poverty must be located at the household, even better, individual level. Social class, identity and gender better explain poverty where Dalits, Muslims and recent migrants are more likely to be poor. In all these groups, but also in slightly better-off slum households, women and girls are more likely to be poor and/or bear the brunt of the conditions of poverty. This includes deserted women, widows, single women, and women-headed households. If I am correct in assuming that it is men and not women who are the prime 'patronage agents' in that it is their job to cultivate useful contacts, seek out 'friends of friends' who are 'in the know' or link to 'trusted people', this would put women at another disadvantage to escape poverty. Such poor women and men are the focus of my book, and I established the cruel mechanism that precisely those most poor and vulnerable who lack both resources and useful contacts are most at risk to be thwarted in their ambitions. So we need to keep in mind that what is presented here as 'slum data' and 'slum service delivery trends' and 'slum policy' applies to all Mumbai slums – more or much less established – which include the urban poor who must be assumed to have even less positive indicators.

Bottom of the pyramid in an increasingly divided city

Already, there is a clear divide in poverty and well-being indicators if one compares slum and non-slum areas – as very well documented in the Mumbai Human Development Report (MCGM 2009). A key matter is health, where it is commonly known that 'out-of-pocket' payment for health services is a very critical cause of households falling into poverty (starting with indebtedness) or deepening the misery of existent poverty. Slum health conditions compare very unfavourably with non-slum urban areas. Health agencies reach only 30 per cent of the urban poor, and only about 62 per cent of slum mothers receive post-natal care. Nearly one-third of reported ailments remain untreated; inconveniently located health posts further hinder accessibility (Kennedy *et al.* 2009). Public hospitals and nursing homes are stretched to their limits, with hardly any growth in the BMC health budgets. Indeed, the BMC appears to favour the privatisation of health care, partly from a mindset that the private sector can play a large role in health care, partly as it helps reduce pressure on already scarce state budgets. Today, less than 25 per cent of Mumbai's people use public dispensaries and hospitals. All others use private facilities, which now by far outnumber public health facilities – even while these too experience capacity issues. Such private services are often (far) too expensive for poor households who nevertheless use these as public ones are seen to be inadequate. Experts worry about the commodification of health care, where medical care has become a profit industry being targeted by business houses. By and large, health care privatisation may have benefited the wealthier Mumbai classes – and certainly health-sector investors and professionals – but it has had detrimental impacts on Mumbai's poor as a class, whose health and 'reproduction' costs are no longer taken care of by public health services. A similar tale can be told about education, where formerly well-performing public schools are closed (and their valuable premises sold), while there is a mushrooming of all sorts of private schools, tuition and evening classes, sometimes managed by politicians. In the past five years, the number of Mumbai private schools increased by 32 per cent, while the number of municipal schools rose only by 1 per cent. The MCGM (2009: 88) report notes a wide and growing gap between public and private schools, which together accentuate rather than balance class differences. Poor children study in public primary schools with an allegedly increasing poor reputation – but it needs emphasizing that not all corporation schools are bad. In those fewer cases that they (more boys than girls) do complete eighth standard, and if they have ambitions for further study, and if their parents agree – they are forced to switch to more expensive private schools, obviously a major constraint. Formal and informal 'contributions' and 'capitation fees' are high, creating serious dilemmas for poor households, deeply aware that education is one way out of poverty. They are aware that good jobs are hard to come by and there must be plenty of unemployment and underemployment. Slum people overwhelmingly work in the informal sector where incomes are low and fluctuating and working conditions range from inadequate to dangerous – domestic servant women, building labourers, cleaners, and sweatshop workers. The share of formal-sector employment is falling, along with an increase in casual work and a significant feminisation of the workforce. Nearly half of the people working in the informal sector are migrants (MCGM 2009: 52). Labour mobility is limited, partly as cash is demanded for probably all attractive jobs. Most slum households have lower or higher (and high-interest) debts, sometimes burdening them for many years.

Slum or low-income housing policies are lacking apart from the ill-fated and very expensive SRS efforts. The highest number of completed SRA units I could find in available data was 170,000 units over 15 years, probably developed at a huge unit cost if the costs of public land – which was surrendered to builders – at market rates were truthfully added. This is a far cry from the initial SRA target of 500,000 homes in five years – a drop in the ocean of Mumbai's low-income housing shortage.

Dynamics of exclusion

So on the one hand there are trends that the poor and slum people are left to their own devices, implicitly expected to fend for themselves by paying up for services. On the other hand, their hard work and readiness to be employed – even exploited – forms a massive boon for the city and its more wealthy inhabitants. Seen this way, they are economically very well included indeed, but at the same time experience increasing social and political exclusion. Wealthy 'citizens' can easily employ domestic servants, cooks, drivers, and beauticians at low wages with little or no labour protection. The poor subsidise the rich; the funds that the city has for the poor are hard to come by or evaporate before they translate into medicine or a place in a maternity ward. So the poor are solidly included in Mumbai's economy but are undergoing processes of exclusion at the same time. Concrete dynamics of exclusion are listed here. Arguably the most amazing indication is that the recent 2014 Mumbai Development Plan (DP) does not cover the slums, that is 6–10 per cent of the city area with six or so million people. Bhide (2011) indicates that this is nothing new. From a policy perspective it is startling that – as far as I know – there are no recent slum surveys. And while there is no 'slum upgrading' to improve and consolidate existing 'self-help' housing and facilities, massive slum demolitions which related to grand visions at 'city beautification' affected 45,000 households in 2004, displacing nearly 200,000 people. As indicated by Manecksha (2011), the poor are pushed to Mumbai's periphery, where already most recent migrants have settled. New SRA units are mostly constructed here, in what observers see as massive, poorly planned and constructed 'ghettos'.

Less visible, gradually emerging and hence insidious exclusion drivers include the aforementioned privatisation and related commodification of health and education services affecting all Mumbai people. Then, in terms of law and order, poor people simply do not have access to formal justice. Rather, they fear the police, which has been depicted as a venal force mostly serving politicians and the wealthy. Poor people best steer clear from the police as they mean more trouble the poorer you are. Instead of being seen as the protector of poor and vulnerable people they are more of a feared enemy. Ironically one may need protection against police harm in the form of a no-party social worker or the corporator and his agents – and/or simply a bribe. A lack of accountability, coupled with almost full discretion and impunity, allows the police to deal with low status victims as they deem fit, which is not always a pretty sight. The bribes extracted from poor people – such as bribes to the police and *hafta* on the streets or simply to obtain a birth certificate – can be seen as extra taxes limiting their options further. In this respect, Debroy and Bhandari (2012) speak of 'robbing the poor', among indications of reduced central funding for important poverty programmes such as the Integrated Child Welfare Programme, policies to support mothers and women and urban schemes such as SJYSRY and BSUP. To make matters worse, whatever funds are available for the several schemes and other provisions for the urban poor tend to be systematically skimmed off or captured by the non-poor. This is part of widespread, systemic corruption practices documented in this book by many actors having access to such funds or provisions. The PDS system of ration shops is a case in point. The plans to bring governance closer to the people through decentralised Wards Committees (WCMs) never yielded any benefits in terms of 'voice', better representation or more participation. Indeed, in some slums gatekeeping party workers discourage people to contact wards offices themselves. By and large, Mumbai's poor and slum people are facing huge odds to reverse strong trends, which increasingly seem to undermine their position as a group, as a class, in social, economic and political respects. I will examine ways, means and trends as regards their political inclusion in a later section, but first mention a final factor which is an apparent marketisation and commodification of services and opportunities, many of which uniformly public not long ago.

Commodification of public and governance goods

That Mumbai is evolving into a rather more rough, competitive, money-focused place can also been seen in ongoing processes of commodification. More and more hitherto publicly provided services and facilities are pushed away to the private sphere and/or now come with a price tag: user fees or a very place in a hospital, entry into a good primary school, a good job or a water connection. The good news is that in Mumbai anything can be arranged for people with money – from justice to being an election candidate to housing. The bad news is that services need to be paid for and preferably need a trusted contact. I have noted too many references to 'markets' and the power of money to open doors. Hence, state services will normally be allocated after paying; privately supplied services range from low quality and cost to excellent quality at huge cost. There really is no justice system for poor and slum people, but if they are so unfortunate to get caught by the police and end up in a local court, justice is for sale: 'Innocence and guilt could be bought and sold like a kilo of polyurethane bags' (Boo 2012: 107). Chandra (2004) refers to 'elections as auctions'. Experts perceive processes of commercialisation of health care, where health care is seen to become a commodity and less of a public good: 'Medical care has turned into an "industry".' Transfers to key public-sector jobs can be purchased, sometimes at the behest of a powerful contractor or builder. It is not that the poor only sit idle: they join the game by buying residence proof and illegal ration cards; if needed they also bribe the police for a favourable first inspection report. I have referred to examples of 'informal privatisation', where corporators imposed themselves on slum-based SWM schemes, only to engage their local slum leader allies as CBOs so as to be able to get a stake in budgets. Can we say then that the local state is being informally privatised and/or do we witness the emergence of a corporate state as argued by Ravindran (2013: 244) or of a 'hollow state'? How are the poor coping with such substantial and fast changes, and are they able to exert influence – in a context of informality with a dominant patronage logic?

Agency for men and women and the scope for collective action

I established a trend where state benefits appear increasingly as commodities with a price in the context of a mediated state, often with additional costs of bribes and/or entry-level minimal access rules such as party membership or the promise of one's vote. This itself acts as a major impediment to reducing poverty: transaction costs in time, informal payments and cultivating networks are considerable and prohibitive for those most poor (remember the near-impossible requirements to qualify for SJSRY benefits in Section 3.7). How comfortable it would be if all poor people could simply count on basic entitlements in adequate education and health services, police protection actually guaranteed by law and policy and how much misery, worry and energy would be avoided. Yet, surprisingly, there is little evidence of slum-level protest, agitation, collective action, or manifestations. This raises the question of the agency of the poor and whether they apply 'weapons of the weak' to fend for themselves. Such agency is to be contrasted to the many limiting, stigmatising or even undermining 'structures' and power configurations legitimised by extant norms, values and ideologies. These evolve in many shapes and are articulated and enforced by many actors, be it gender roles and expectations in India's patriarchal society, subtle or not-so-subtle discrimination by caste or religion and in what I believe are relatively few constraints or checks on the application of open zero-sum power.

The many daily constraints I listed so far with a view to escape out of poverty are corroborated by a certain disdain for the poor, who may be blamed for their own predicament and misery. Yet all this is by no means to deny that individual poor men, women and their households can and do succeed to come up, capitalising on opportunities or a windfall. Mumbai's poor people are certainly not simply victims; their parents and grandparents have mostly been poor also, while many have origins outside Mumbai and retain relatives and assets there. They may have seen their fortunes increase in Mumbai relative to formerly experienced pre-migration oppressive forms of discrimination or exploitation. In terms of Sassen (2014), many have been pushed or even 'expulsed' from India's not-quite-flourishing rural areas – with droughts, land grabs or brazen upper-caste domination. Whether pushed or pulled, recent migrants may see Mumbai as full of opportunities, often fed by stories of relatives that, in the long run, there is a place in the city for them too. The poor are capable managers of their few resources, and this book has shown that pursuing and managing personal (vertical) relations is a key strategy to get access to critical and good services, to find a suitable job and to avoid or solve police problems. But I would like to suggest that men and women exert agency differently – even if based on the same foundations of power and money.

In the gendered context of slums and poverty, it appears that it is the men who actively, if probably mostly secretively, seek and maintain patronage or brokerage relations (see de Wit 1996; de Wit and Berner 2009; see also Roy 2004: 165 on 'masculinist patronage'). Slum men seem to have been studied even less than slum women, and I forward as an assumption for further research that they, by and large, exert agency by relying on vertical patronage relations, which are the mirror side or response as to how state benefits of governance and democracy are allocated. It reminds one of India's central bank Governor, who seemed to confirm this by arguing that politicians, even if venal, survive as they are access channels for the poor.[3] Mumbai's local state is a mediated state where state benefits are allocated through myriad of personal relations, bribes and deals. In this context it seems men are key agents to 'position themselves for patronage', whether they do this through being active in politics and parties or not. Indian men, rich or poor, are under considerable pressure to be – and to be seen as – the main earning head of household, which earns respect. Poor men are seriously handicapped here in a context where stable incomes are hard to get by and available work is harsh, exacting and lowly paid. There are indications as if such dynamics could result in stress, frustration or sometimes an addiction to alcohol or other substances, which then undermines their effectiveness. Signs are that alcoholism among slum men is considerable, yet evidence is sketchy. But it is certain that addictions undermine a man's efforts to move out of poverty and that he will be more a burden than an asset for his wife and children – whose agency is undermined as well. Yet if husband and wife don't engage too much in wasteful activities, steering clear of conflicts and the police, households could incrementally come up. Slum men do not seem much engaged in grass-roots-level mobilisation or organisation, possible proof that they bet more on personalised contacts. This is not to deny the existence of local slum organisations, but I tend to believe these are often leader-centred networks with a 'big man' in the centre – almost certainly linked to a political party. It appears they become operational only for external reasons such as elections or the need to have a CBO as a condition to be part of an NGO project/network or a slum project. Possibly the most promising way for a man to exert agency in a patronage context is to join party politics, which can bring benefits such as useful contacts, up to a position in a party office or *shakha* – even to be a corporator. But that is not for all. That position needs a strong, shrewd and slightly hard-nosed type of person, ready to venture into and survive in murky and hazardous back lanes with powerful adversaries.

Women's agency

This book has highlighted the enormous challenges that poor women face – for themselves and for their children. Many if not most effects of the failure of the local state to provide adequate services end up on their plates as per the existent gender relations and ideology – in what may be called 'practical gender needs' (Moser 1995). To the extent that slum women deliver babies and take charge of the upbringing of children, fetch drinking water, look after household health needs, clean huts/ houses and slum lanes, and go to the hopelessly dirty public toilets – in all these activities the state lets them down. Slum girls are expected to support their mothers often from an early age, where they are far too often bypassed by their brothers who are sent to school. Escaping (full) literacy, at risk of obtaining insufficient nutritious food and health care and aware that daughters are seen as a burden rather than the great asset they are (even by their mothers), I consider them the most vulnerable slum actors, most in need of attention. Generally, poor slum women and girls are at greater risk of sexual violence, cases of which are reported less than for higher-class women. As usual among poor women, Mumbai slum women too are less able than men to render labour into income (as their wages are always lower than men) and to render that income into choice (as women/mothers tend to first spend any income on their households). Their scope to translate that choice into personal well-being is then finally very limited (at the end of the long day, the hut is clean and having cared for all). A fundamental constraint on women's power is that it is much harder for them to own property or land in their own personal name, a problem they share with many Dalits.

In terms of zero-sum power, households are micro-arenas, with fathers and sons normally (expected to) having the upper hand over women and girls, in terms of decision making, income allocation and who eats first. Where many households may be assumed to operate in varying degrees of harmony and sharing, there are no doubt cases where men, supported by gender norms and patriarchal values, dominate women. Domestic violence is probably a much greater problem than we know – and it can get real bad with alcohol-addicted men. Yet I would venture to suggest that the powers of women play out in this more private domain of houses and slum streets. Here they have the advantage of local knowledge, here they can and do join forces against abusive husbands, sharing worries and possible solutions. Many slum women are the key decision makers in domains of health care, household financial management, planning for employment as well as agents in education. At the slum level, women seem much less focused on playing the power games relating to cultivating useful networks, to position for patronage and to chase opportunities mostly outside the slums and chawls. Rather, it is the women who may organise in local organisations such as saving groups (where men rarely participate) and play a critical role in what has been named 'community management'. Indications are that women are more supportive to each other with ample daily contacts, mutual advice and a readiness to help others out in daily needs. But such inclusive cooperation seems to occur among women of similar caste, religion or status, so that here too we find inclusion at the same time as exclusion.

Kabeer (1999) defines women's empowerment in having a choice, the ability to act on alternatives, which depends on control over resources and on agency. She de-bundles agency in less tangible manifestations such as capacities for negotiating, subversion, deception and manipulation. For example, women may quietly and tactfully manage husbands to take decisions in their favour, subtly maintaining the impression or fiction that he is in the driver's seat (Kabeer 1999: 447–48). Some hide their savings from a saving group from their (alcoholic) husbands, feeling stronger with some personal reserves. Women are locally seen to have 'pillow power', where even the toughest guy shares secrets and takes advice from his wife. Indicators for women's agency include mobility in the public domain; participating in public action and decision-making capacity. This is useful, but I locate agency – be it for women or men – more squarely in terms of any kind of power: making people do things which they would not do otherwise. And if I am correct that power – and money flows – emanate through pyramidal hierarchies and informal relations linking politicians to BMC budgets and political parties to business firms, the question is whether women are and can be part of these. I think that by and large they are not, and if they are they face considerable glass ceilings as for example seen in the case of Asha (with her drunken husband), aspiring to be the first woman slum lord of her 'undercity slum'. But she failed, first as she lost her key political patron, a corporator who stepped down after being caught for lying about his caste certificate in order to stand from a reserved seat (Boo 2012: 221). In spite of shrewdly applying myriad of micro-strategies relating to networking, money, manipulation and information she also failed to overcome the very strong levelling mechanisms already operating within her slum itself in terms of opportunism, jealousies and competition. One might postulate that power centres on men, and that it is through male power that women may obtain power – an example where the wives of newly elected male corporators suddenly rise in status as the wards' first lady. Depending on the latter's inclinations and suitability, they may be groomed to take over as future MC from here.

It is too early to discard the apparent efforts in Mumbai to provide political representation and 'voice' to women through the 50 per cent women's quota for corporator seats. As yet we don't see this evolving into much personal or general women empowerment. Most indications are that male corporators (and arguably the wider public with clear expectations as to mediation capacity) do not find women fit for the job – where all agree it is rough and tough and potentially hazardous. It was little surprise then that many women corporators act as 'puppets' or proxies' of their corporator husbands or fathers. So while solidarity among poor slum men cannot be assumed, this also applies to women where divisions of caste, religion and status seem to be rigid and not easy to overcome. Naturally this is most problematic for women – especially when they are single – of low caste or of minority status. All these factors taken together seem to underline the mostly powerless position of poor women and slum women generally. Yet I like to confirm that Mumbai's poor women and girls are quite versatile and resilient indeed – even if they have disturbingly little choices/alternatives. They manage/juggle different roles, coping daily with countless challenges and concrete problems (but, admittedly, many more women are depressed than men, cf. Parkar et al. 2008). So, in terms of Moser's (1995) more fundamental and power-related 'strategic gender interests', which refer to such matters as domestic violence, equal inheritance, sharing of reproductive tasks and political voice, by and large, things don't look very well for Mumbai's poor women. This, in spite of playing much more important roles in keeping the city liveable than they get credit and money for.

Slum organisation and problematic collective action

Having examined men's and women's individual agency in terms of ways to overcome their many debilitating and constraining structures, I need to finally dwell on the capacity or prospects for slum people to organise for collective action. My research confirmed earlier findings – in 1984 and 1989 Madras and my work with the Bangalore urban poverty programme – that effective, sustainable common action is actually rare. It is more likely as a defensive reaction – witness the slum-level action against evictions and bulldozers and the citywide mass protests at the time of Mumbai's ill-famous 2004–5 massive slum demolitions. But we seem to see much fewer collective offensive or claim-making actions. Rather than a whole slum uniting to claim drinking water (once and) for all, one finds that individual or groups of households put together money for a (common) water pipe line.

   In my view the vertical orientation towards useful personal and hierarchical relations is the key impediment to horizontal collective organisation (cf. Mistra 2014: 'Patronage Politics divides us'). The risk of free riders is only one factor. Slum-level conditions and dynamics with its internal levelling mechanisms and often rigid divisions in very heterogeneous slums are another one. Very pronounced divisions of identity (caste, Hindu–Muslim, gender), incomes ('the slum elite' versus the very poor), housing (tenants versus 'owners' with the right identity proof papers) exist and are being articulated. To this we must add politics in the very politicised slums, where access to critical services and security is mediated by street, slum or neighbourhood/ward-level political party agents. But another factor that people pragmatically opt for vertical, patronage oriented coping strategies is that they neatly fit with and are enforced by the systems and structures of Mumbai's local state as a 'Mediated State' (Berenschot 2010). State benefits are not provided as uniform entitlements for all, but are often conditional on having an affective mediator (ideally linked to whatever is the ruling party) – and/or paying a bribe.

This is not to deny that there are slum organisations, but membership is often limited to select local groups as we saw for women saving groups. As noted, some are more or less sleeping leader/'big man' or *dada*-centred networks fully embedded in the local political setup. Poor leadership is a major factor here, which, sadly, was shown as very problematic for Dalit people. NGO mobilisation and general activities don't seem quite effective at the city level. For example, there is no umbrella 'urban poor federation' uniting slum people, slum organisations and NGOs alike. I quoted incidences where promising local initiatives are co-opted by local agents or parties, and where status-quo threatening actions easily invite comments, intimidation or outright confrontation and termination. These can be seen as slum and citywide levelling and control mechanisms. Slum people will be cautious if the interests of powerful builders, a corporator, a local goon or mafia outfit could be affected, and they will pragmatically anticipate and adjust their reactions. An example is when a slum pocket was found out to have voted for the 'wrong' candidate (the one who lost). But even in political/party organisations, I noted a trend of 'de-politicisation' and reduced grassroots political mobilisation deserving further scrutiny. Prabash (2010) believes that building up and maintaining grassroots support seems to have lesser priority today, with local party cadre and workers more interested to link and move with the locally powerful. In Mumbai such trends affect parties differently, but, here too, one perceives a commodification and monetisation of party and election work, with slum people more and more demanding to work for parties.

There is no doubt that Indian cities are 'fast emerging as critical zones of contestation', with a miniscule but exceedingly powerful global society, and a huge majority of marginalised and dispossessed (Banerjee-Guha 2009: 106). But, as I noted in Chapter 3, I have not found the evidence that she sees of the dispossessed struggling for entitlements and alternatives, in reaction to the neoliberal discourses and practices of the corporate sector and the rich. I have similar doubts about the assessment by Weinstein and Ren (2009: 426) that struggles around the right to the city are only partially grounded in electoral politics. I have not been able to find evidence of what they see as the frequent 'direct agitations, public protests, and legal petitions' where the poor assert their political presence in Mumbai's urban renewal. I have the idea that there is not much significant action beyond or unconnected to electoral party politics, by and large the only game in town. But before talking politics per se, I will now consider the politics of service delivery of key governance organisations, foremost the Mumbai Corporation.

Mumbai's governance agencies, informality and mediated service delivery

Even following the liberalisation of Mumbai's governance regime, the Mumbai local state remains quite strong and powerful in terms of a range of services, budgets and regulation. Mumbai is a rich city, with a large annual budget and lots of money going around, including central government scheme funding and funding by donor agencies such as the World Bank. Its city corporation BMC is in charge of most critical services for the city – especially for slums and the poor in terms of public schools and hospitals, water, electricity, licencing and city cleaning. Yet, despite all the talk of decentralisation to be discussed shortly, it is quite dependent on the Maharashtra state government which appoints the BMC (IAS cadre) leadership, while setting overall parameters of city planning and poverty reduction. The sole remaining low cost housing agency is the malfunctioning SRA, even while parastatals such as MMRDA and MHADA need to be mentioned also. The police, the PDS 'ration shop' delivery system, and institutions implementing central government schemes such as ICDS, SJSRY or RAY are other important agencies for the poor.

Apart from the fact that informality in several agencies seems more dominant than the enforcement of formal rules, a major complication is that inter-agency coordination is very problematic, and, as almost everything, quite politicised (e.g. see the valuable work by Pethe 2010). Different agencies may be 'controlled' by different political parties. It could therefore happen, for instance that the BMC was controlled by the Shiv Sena party and the 'rival' MMRDA by the Congress–NCP coalition.

But with the state now controlled by BJP/Shiv Sena, contestations and rivalry between such agencies persist, as if they are separate kingdoms. While the diverse Mumbai agencies maintain and protect their mandates and budgets which is in the interest of their staff and politicians, overall urban governance is fragmented, missing overall coordination. One factor is insufficient state capacity to manage increasingly complex forms of 'network governance' (Swyngedouw 2005). One provision of the (1992) 74th urban decentralisation reforms might have helped fill this gap through the establishment of a municipal planning committee. But the state government proved unwilling to establish one, until a MPC (on paper) was recently established as a condition to attract JNNURM funding. Observers agree that it is not performing, with Pethe, Gandhi and Tandel (2011) arguing that the state government fears it would dilute its control over the Mumbai Metro Region. Sivaramakrishnan (2011: 54) refers to the significant disconnect between the MPC and the MMRDA, which agency's mandate shows some overlaps with the MPC. Another potentially welcome reform under the decentralisation reforms was the establishment of sub-city wards committees (WCMs).

Disappointing outcomes of urban decentralisation

As enthusiastically as 'neo liberal' public-private cooperation and privatisation arrangements have been and are being embraced and introduced, so lukewarm if not reluctant was the response to and operationalisation of decentralisation reforms. Civil society actors saw more potential and long-term benefits than state actors. Mumbai corporators, their political parties and the state government do not appear to have been very engaged in what was to become a new local/neighbourhood democratic forum in the form of WCMs. Starting from their short political time horizon, they mostly looked at immediate concerns and impacts (Shetye 2006). The 16 established WCMs failed to develop into 'beehives of local activity' (Pinto 2008), and many *Mumbaikars* are not even aware of their existence or potential. One reason is that was unrealistic to expect that they could cater to the needs of on average 600,000 citizens. Besides, the state government chose to keep the mandate and financial endowments very limited, where it is important to note that WMCs are not in charge of most programmes, policies and (budget) plans of relevance to the urban poor. So on the one hand they were left with very little powers which already acted as a key dis-incentive. Another factor to explain their inconsequential treatment and nature is their limited financial mandate, where wards-level corporator meetings can only decide on matters costing less than Rs 500,000 of public BMC funds. If it is power and money that make Mumbai tick, such fatal facts may explain why corporators find it a waste of time to engage much here. Minutes of their meetings show lukewarm participation and a mismatch between WCM discussion topics and wards-level grievances. No surprise then that there has been a steady increase in the discretionary funding of individual corporators in the very corruption prone Area Development Funds, today at one crore or Rs 10 million. This, too, represents to some extent a kind of 'informal privatisation' of public funds. On the one hand there is reduced democratic control over public funds, on the other such funds have been shown to be cash cows for corporators and their parties, officials and contractors.

But if we consider power dynamics, the establishment of neighbourhood-level WCMs did cause a perceptible shift in the relations between the presently more locally visible and demanding corporators in the ward offices on the one hand and ward officials on the other. Formally only accountable to BMC headquarters and zonal commissioners, the latter now had to deal much more closely with wards-based corporators. Initial relations of mistrust and jealousy seem to have generally given way to mutual adjustment – even if it means sharing the spoils of ward-level corruption and informality. This is not to deny that relations between corporators and officials can be antagonistic, while MCs apply their political clout in managing transfers to remove disobliging officers, or to welcome malleable officers. I already discussed the limitations of quota system for women corporators, who currently dominate the council 122 against 105, expressing doubts as to women's agency to be in full control in a rough and male centred political context. One could consider this as a token of discontinuity where women in India are normally associated with 'the private sphere' with men expected to play 'public roles', with related dynamics of 'open power'. Yet dynamics of power and money operate here too. Even while women make up 53 per cent of all corporators, only 6 out of the 36 members (16 per cent) of the powerful BMC standing committee are women. Despite formal reforms, men somehow managed to hang on to the money strings.

Corporators as street-level politicians in a mediated state

Among all actor groups with a stake in Mumbai's slums, this group of corporators straddles all levels from the slum up to the corridors of the Mumbai local state. Like spiders in citywide webs they seem to typify the extent to which informality has creeped into city administration. My focus on these *nagar sevaks* or city servants allowed probing the workings of the local state, and especially local state-society relations and interfaces between the masses of poor people and state institutions important for them. That they have proved to be masters of survival in pretty rough and competitive contexts further explains my interest: they have been able to bend with city evolution and growth, including proliferating slums, neoliberal reforms, private-sector dominance and an emerging middle class.

My assumption that MCs have a finger in all sort of local governance pies proved correct: while MLAs and MPs are much more powerful and influential at the city and state level, at the level of city wards, MCs are the dominant players, if not actors with the status and paraphernalia of a local *Raja* or *Rani*. I have portrayed them as highly capable and versatile street-level politicians, some of whom have risen from street fighters and *dadas* to become powerful ward bosses. They skilfully combine more sympathetic 'public-oriented' activities such as daily 'people consultation meetings', slum rounds and mediation activities with what can be very rough and dirty money-making activities. This may take such forms that they can be key agents of what, in want of a better term, one might call 'the governance of illegality', as one of their domains is to make money out of people trespassing formal rules or the law: those constructing an illegal hut or building; hawking in the wrong place, in need of an illegal water connection, running a brothel or covering up a crime by conniving with the police. Unfortunately, the police is not seen to do much better in reducing crime, illegal activities or corruption – it appears they are often party to all that (Hansen 2001). It is likely that control over Mumbai's slums is located somewhere between corporators, their parties, the police and other power groups such as local informal mafia/goonda outfits some of which may provide more effective protection than the police. Despite good work here by Hansen (2001), Gupte (2012) and Weinstein (2013) more research into concrete mechanisms of slum 'control' and related administration of power is needed.

The question arises as to how such ambivalent, controversial and basically often relatively unpopular, Janus-faced political actors not only survive but also actually do very well (John 2007). So much so that the position of MC is much sought after. Unfortunately, in probably a majority of cases this is not so much from an idealistic desire to be a true representative for all voters in a ward so as to act on common problems and priorities or to design adequate (pro-poor) policy. Rather, even while I must emphasise strongly that one cannot obviously generalise for all MCs in all 227 quite diverse wards, the overall key reason to join politics seems short-term monetary gain and prospects of a higher-level political career. It may happen that male corporators are elected for several successive terms and grow into well-established and almost incontestable local dignitaries/power bosses (e.g. cases in Bjorkman 2013). If such corporators are unable to stand themselves in constituencies reserved under the 50 per cent women quota system, they are somehow often able to get their wife, sister or daughter elected. That way they keep their profitable local networks and localised money making opportunities intact. As is seen in Indian politics at all levels, here too we see a deepening trend of 'dynastic politics'. It seems based on a democratically unhealthy desire to maintain very lucrative 'political capital' in one family, including earning avenues. Earnings are potentially huge from all sort of illegal transactions – fixing water pipes, getting 'cuts' in relation to construction work; *hafta* collected from hawkers, shops and building firms, as well as mediation fees for MCs and their agents linking poor people in (high) need to relevant hospitals, schools and employers. Even though expected contributions from such incomes to MC parties are considerable, indications are that most manage to grow richer in office.

Corporators form a critical component of Mumbai's 'informal local governance' as they oversee the interfaces and informal relations between people and the 'local mediated state' (Berenschot 2010). In an 'ideal type' western liberal democracy, corporators as elected representatives should be engaged in the broad, somewhat detached and impartial business of policy making based on public needs, monitor such policy and be accountable as to budgetary inputs and outcomes in the field. In contrast, and in line with Berenschot (2010), Mumbai corporators are best seen as street-level politicians. In a way he or she replaces or compliments the street-level bureaucrats whose core business is to make street-level decisions as to licences, to allocate benefits as per policy directives, and to directives. Generally, this is about translating policy into concrete individualised decisions. At the slum level, much of this allocation is done by corporators and their local agents who instruct or request officials (and hospitals, schools, employers, the police) to 'get the actual work done'. By and large, they are not guided by policy dictates or a personal ambition to support those most needy – even whole this can surely be a consideration. Examples are that women MCs are helpful to solve domestic quarrels or dowry issues; that MCs generally contribute selflessly to a wedding, cremation or medical treatment or arrange a job for a boy who lost his income earning father. Corporators would not survive if they did not have this social face, portrayed daily on their slum rounds or during morning meetings at the local party/MC office. This face, magnified to stress benevolence and generosity, is expanded once elections are announced, and will appear with the party symbol on posters all over the ward. It is unlikely that corporators are engaged in actual policy making (see Kennedy *et al.* 2009) and that they read monitoring or evaluation reports – if these were available (which they seem not). This apparent absence of a (longer term) policy or development focus is consistent with the trappings of the machine politics model with its short-term emphasis on winning elections at all costs (Scott 1969: 1155; see Prabash 2010) as discussed below.

Informality and corruption in Mumbai's
governance

The concept of informality has figured large in this book, following several writers who endorse my findings in this sensitive and hard to chart domain (Berenschot 2009; Das 2001; Kumar and Landy 2009; Pethe 2010; Roy 2009b). I understand this as the amalgam of undocumented, (semi-) illegal, secretive, 'corrupt' and mostly particularistic actions and relations, starting from, but transforming, manipulating, corrupting, formal institutions and relations. Governance ethics form a plural mix of formal and informal norms and values, where I believe informality is on the increase in both governance and politics. It is certainly not the case that all government and BMC officials are corrupt, but corruption appears to be a dominant operational modality in agencies and departments related to land, construction and housing (such as the SRA and the ward office Building Proposals Department: Pinto and Pinto 2005). This also applies to departments where the state meets the people (where ward offices have a very poor reputation). This is where bribes and negotiations are played out, and where officials and the aforementioned street-level bureaucrats obtain bribes for what are or should be simply entitlements by policy or law. Blundo (2006) who studied such dynamics in Africa terms this 'informal privatisation'. This refers to reports of officials, School Heads or police men who look like small shopkeepers 'selling' public state services or property at relatively fixed, informal rates – or to the highest bidder. But the context of illegality assumes a premium on trust and a reputation of reliability, best guaranteed in longer term personal or patronage relations. So it helps if there support from a powerful agent like a corporator to recommend the person for support. This mostly concerns petty corruption which is a formidable regressive tax on the poor, and a major factor to keep people in poverty and at risk of exclusion. But, mostly unknown to poor people, other city-level dynamics and trends constitute equal threats in terms of their longer term prospects.

For this we need to move into government organisations and institutions, especially those related the land and building sectors. That these are so extremely profitable has started to affect, and according to some, undermine Mumbai's governance. Where the poor go, one case in point is the slum redevelopment 'policy'. Heralded as the final solution to the slum problem in 1995, it envisioned either in-situ slum relocation through a system of slum land sharing, or construction of low-income housing units elsewhere, applying Transfer of Development Rights. Too many reports indicate large scale misuse of arrangements and facilities of SRS and TDR (Doshi 2012; Nainan 2012; Pinto and Pinto 2005; Suresh *et al.* 2013). It appears that very costly public BMC land was handed over free of cost to builders and developers nominally in the name of slum redevelopment – and the urban poor. This could be seen as a massive subsidy to private-sector firms, with attractive side benefits for politicians and their parties who often facilitate transactions. Where it is certain that these stakeholders earned very handsome profits by building high class towers and flats while re-housing slum people in slum tenements, certainly not all original slum dwellers ended up in a 225 sq. ft. unit. Tenants never got any recognition or right; agents were buying up unit rights long before slum people understood the value of a token or registration paper; units were often bought at an early stage, sometimes by wealthy people and movie stars (Boo 2012; de Wit 2016; Suresh *et al.* 2013). That corruption is widespread at the interface – the nexus – between builders, politicians and officials has been noted in successive scams and scandals. Examples are the high profile Adarsh scam (which led to the dismissal of a CM), buildings collapsing during or after construction and roads or pavements showing flaws soon after construction (Pethe 2010; Tinaikar 2003). It is often only after public interest litigations (PIL) that such irregularities are sometimes exposed, with anti-corruption agencies unable to stop such trends. Indeed, there are reports that it is risky for 'whistle-blowers' which may be termed 'honest officers' to report official or political malfeasance. Evidence shows that this is the dominant operational system especially in selected, well budgeted offices, where it is not the corrupt but the honest who have problems.

One example is what has been termed 'the transfer industry'. Politicians have the power to transfer officials which, no doubt, often leads to merit-based postings. However, a transfer can also signify a means to punish an official (if he or she is unwilling to follow which may be taken as illegal or unethical) or to reward an official (pliable and money minded officers can become to be 'owned' by a corporator with a contractor's consent). The transfer system clearly provides rent seeking opportunities where some officials are known to informally pay money to arrange a posting in a department and/or ward known to have good 'informal earning capacity'. Hence, positions such as the head of a ward office or in the licensing/approval departments of SRA and BMC can fetch high payments, which are divided per relatively fixed and informally known formulas among politicians and party functionaries (Debroy and Bhandari 2012; Nainan 2006, 2012). More research is needed here as to the extent of such practices, precise amounts and trends and impacts on citywide government capacity. But if such systems are thriving, it would enhance a hard to arrest trend where it is not proper performance in a public sector job that counts most any longer. The attraction then becomes merely monetary: a calculation whether a private investment is expected to yield good profits out of creaming off/misusing public budgets. Negative impacts may well be larger. Budgetary allocations may favour the 'money making domains', at the expense of often much more important but low cost and less tangible public administration domains such as health and education – precisely those critical for poor people. For the city as a whole, the combination of the above factors of informality make *Mumbaikars* generally dissatisfied with city administration as for example indicated by successive PRAJA (2011, 2012, 2014a,b) reports. They show little trust in the BMC and its corporators to improve things. Evidence includes a poor and shabby overall infrastructure; that work done is sometimes not actually quite needed or done twice; an overall lack of maintenance (painting, cleaning, repairs) of public amenities (e.g. numerous ill-fated public slum toilets or chawls); very meagre allocations for BMC school education materials and mother-child welfare centres. So while prospects for Mumbai's poor are less than promising, the same seems to apply for general city governance in a city seen as India's financial capital, often leading in India's social and cultural trends.

Absence of long-term policy, weak institutions and government capacity

Evidence from this book confirms the existence of machine politics as conceptualised by Scott (1969) in Mumbai, to be elaborated below. One dimension of the model is that such politics brings about a short-term political orientation, at the expense of 'the pursuit of longer term development objectives'. It is assumed to lead to fiscal deficits and business firms seeking monopolistic positions (Scott 1969: 1155). If checked with Mumbai realities, we seem to see little interest among politicians – but certainly many Mumbai corporators – to engage in vital policy processes. This would mean drafting a policy starting from urgent priorities, implementing it, and finally assessing outcomes and impacts. Many corporators are quite focused on budget allocations, where they seem to prefer budget headings allowing for visible, tangible if not concrete investments over 'soft' ones. As noted for pro-poor policy, there is little interest to systematically target common urgent problems such as mother and child care, the provision of toilets, and collective uniform water supply systems. One would hope that the availability of a wealth of data, information and reports – and the presence of donor agencies such as the World Bank and ADB – would lead to informed policy. In contrast, politicians seem not quite interested in such kind of knowledge, undermining the assumption that 'knowledge feeds into development' (take the case of the rich Mumbai Development Report – MCGM 2009, published by BMC itself). If it is correct that policy making takes a backseat, it would also reduce pressure to maintain, or better, enhance government capacity. Indications are that the city experiences a serious lack of overall capacity, which undermines the scope to properly plan for the city as a whole. This shows in several now dormant 'vision' documents (de Wit 2004) and the way in which the current, ill-fated Mumbai Development Plan was designed (outsourced to a firm), drafted and then published and withdrawn. It contained a plethora of mistakes and even after withdrawal it caused lots of confusion and anxiety among slum and non-slum citizens who saw their areas earmarked for unexpected purposes.

For capacity to be effective, an alignment is needed of adequate human resources, organisations with proper leadership and incentives as in salaries and requisite equipment, which join forces for specific wider tasks in an inter-agency 'task network'. But if all this is in place but not embedded and legitimized in societal norms and values – in institutions as 'the rules of the game' (Grindle and Hilderbrand 1995) capacity will be undermined accordingly. But institutions are also organisations empowered by the state to enforce the rules: the municipality, the courts, the police, anti-corruption agencies and the Election Commission. Measuring such an 'ideal type' capacity concept with the above facts and trends in Mumbai, indicators are negative for almost all dimensions. My findings here confirm the work by Pethe (2010) and Pethe *et al.* (2012) who usefully studied 'legal and illegal corruption' in Mumbai noting that enforcing institutions are virtually irrelevant, that their impacts become negative and/or that they harbour 'perverse incentives'. Examples are the role of the police as regards crime, the 'transfer industry' and well entrenched informal systems of 'cuts'. What is noted by Heston and Kumar (2008: 1252) for India might hold true for Mumbai also, in that state capacity has been undermined by Indian politicians: 'Indeed, there is widespread belief that the politicians are not only corrupt by themselves but are also responsible for corrupting the civil service in their quest for money, whether for raising election funds or for their own coffers.' I am aware that some say it is the other way around, that well established officials – with the benefit of ample knowledge of the intricacies of administration – can hinder positive work by (newly elected) politicians. Again, evidence from case to case is needed to confirm either view. But, in such cases where officials can be proven to be in the driver's seat, this too is a negative verdict of democracy.

Local patronage democracy, everyday politics and political entrepreneurs

In Mumbai the *formal* or procedural dimensions of liberal democracy – freedom of speech and organisation, the existence of political parties, regular competitive elections, Election Commissions, limits to election expenditure – are all in place. In contrast to some other countries, defeated parties here accept the voters' verdict, and step down without demurring. New political parties such the AAP party can come up and win elections. So, as Chandra (2004) argues in article on 'Elections as Auctions', there is nothing much wrong with the formal systems and nature of India's democracy, but it does not work properly for the voters, certainly not for the poor. Indeed, in addition to their social exclusion, even if they vote they are at risk of political exclusion, while the value of their vote seems subject to inflation in terms of what it can buy and protect.

I argue for the urgent need to understand 'new' or post-colonial democracies in their own terms, and not to be blinded by some wished for or assumed quality or value only because elections are held in a country. This is not sufficient proof of a working democracy in terms of western or good governance ideals or promises of representation, fairness and accountability. If we abandon the idea of one type of 'democracy', notably the 'one size fits all' ideal-type of western Liberal Democracy – or its shadow category of the 'illiberal democracy' we will be more open to the variations of assumedly democratic systems – as well as their factual merits and demerits. In this book I tried to show that the 'patronage democracy perspective' much better explains everyday politics and governance as experienced by poor and slum people than the assumptions and workings of liberal democracy. Following others (Witsoe 2013: 4ff.; Michelutti 2008; Paley 2002). I suggest that Indian democracy be considered one example of a 'variety of democracies', like we have 'varieties of capitalism'. Part of India's state formation, Westminster style 'liberal democracy' was transplanted on or 'indigenised' in a highly unequal society marked by a caste and power hierarchies and rigid ideologies relating to caste, identity and gender relations. Whether or not voters want a more 'liberal' and representative democracy, politicians seem all set to maintain or even expand Indian democracy into a 'variety of democracy' which fails not in its formal institutions but rather its performance through informal transformations. It evolved and institutionalised into a patronage democracy, fitting the realities and power relations of a mediated state. Such thinking aligns with the concept of 'vertical governance', where Kumar and Landy (2009: 111) confirm that vertical relations are the main connections between differing levels of power in Indian megacities. Politicians and citizens alike share the idea that mediators are required to connect ordinary people with the organs of the state: 'porosities blurring the boundaries between state and civil society or between state and market reinforce a vertical segmentation of society' (Kumar and Landy 2009: 107).

I have combined the above patronage-based perspectives with those underpinning machine politics. Framed by Scott in 1969 it offers a very useful but suprisingly neglected frame to analyse the role of money and other incentives in elections. This book was partly inspired by a puzzling absence of studies into the sources of the money that politicians use to win elections. Election expenditure amounts increase year after year in what has been termed 'an electoral arms race' and always vastly exceed Election Commission norms. It is true that these are unrealistically low, but, today and counting, real expenditure has skyrocketed with hugely costly campaigns. Black money is one of the main sources of the vast funds that politicians believe are needed to run their campaigns and to finance armies of party and non-party workers for the ground work. Not least, many rupees are needed to pay for the freebies or goodies or plain cash which people may receive in return for (the promise of) their vote. Perhaps unsurprising in view of the topic's sensitivity, I cannot offer conclusive evidence to confirm the common local understanding that this money mostly derives from private-sector firms, which invest in (promising) candidates in the expectation of later (agreed upon) beneficial deals. But all evidence I could gather points that way, such as the case of a ward-level business chain successfully promoting a young candidate, to remove a former corporator who had dared to take action against the former's illegal strategies and shops. My slum studies, my corporators' interviews and secondary sources such as newspapers covering the 2012 municipal elections confirm the assumed nexus here between (big) business firms – notably developers/builders and contractors – and elected corporators (with an important role for their political parties). The machine politics model considers politicians brokers, who represent the interests of businesspeople in return for money, which money is partly passed on by politicians to their prospective voters. As noted before, even after economic liberalisation the local state retains sufficient powers of licensing, budgeting, planning, land control and FSI allocation. This compels not only slum people but also more wealthy 'citizens' and all private-sector firms in Mumbai to entertain good relations with politicians and their parties in general. Where corporators – the masters of the wards – are concerned, any business active in a ward – and certainly if it plans something less than legal – needs the MC's consent or cooperation. Politicians at all levels are known to put pressure on business firms to part with contributions that way. Nainan (2006) believes building and contractor firms and other business houses have a large say in the corridors of power. She perceives a meeting point where private-sector monies and opportunities meet with the short-term (5-year) money and power interests of politicians, and that there are cabals of politicians-builders-officials.

Yet the simple three-actor Machine Politics model needs adjustment, as it no longer fits present-day relatively unregulated and power and profit driven neoliberal governance dynamics. First, instead of a single focus on individual politicians as brokers, we need to take into account the role of political parties which may be the initiators and certainly guardians of such relationships. Benefits in terms of contributions and institutionalised systems of 'cuts' allegedly travel from the level of junior engineers and corporators up to higher administrative and political party levels. More importantly and disconcertingly, the positions of 'politician' and 'businessmen' are converging, so that they no longer fit in two separate boxes only. As argued by Oxfam (2015), this is one factor to explain fast growing inequality globally, as benefits, opportunities and spoils circulate among and are shared by a relatively limited elite of the very powerful, be they capitalist, politician or both. In Mumbai, many corporators earn good money in their five year tenure and use that for investment in a business (Pethe *et al.* 2012). Many corporators – and/or their family members – already engage in a side business while in office, iteratively expanding useful networks and investments. Then, if they are re-elected, they are also businessman/woman, a tension ensues between the roles of a publicly accountable representative and a profit minded investor. At the same time we see businesspeople (even mafia dons; Weinstein 2008, 2013) entering politics, being attracted to the many associated (financial) opportunities and status prospects. Indications are that some corporators are elected even if they have criminal records, which may be part of what some see as a larger trend of a criminalisation of politics in India.

The virtue of public representation is undermined by 'money and muscle politics'. What all prospective corporator candidates have in common is that they somehow control large amounts of money. A political career is only for those who can invest liberally – whether self-financed or as the informal agent of powerful/rich businesspersons. This points to another democratic deficit, in that less wealthy individuals are hardly able to win elections, even if they have a good and clean reputation and if more suitable and pro-poor than regular candidates. One dimension here is the emergence and labelling in India of the 'political entrepreneur' type of politician, which has emerged in many democracies, not just India's patronage variety. Such a person combines political office with the self-interested pursuit of money and power, at the expense of democratic (and ethical) attributes such as ideology, accountability, transparency and equality. Evidence shows that, for Mumbai, the most successful corporators are best able to accumulate and apply power, reason why tracing dynamics of power and its use and abuse gradually emerged as a key book theme.[4]

All this gives an uneasy sense of a 'survival of the fittest' system, where the most powerful stakeholders have their way, whereas fitness escapes the poor in terms of assets, incomes, useful relations and hence power. In contrast, the most powerful city governance stakeholders are more or less able to set the rules, mostly in informal processes, but with state and state institutions not hindering – and mostly condoning – these trends. Rather, as argued by Pethe (2010) current institutions – as in norms and values, ethics and informal rules – harbour 'perverse incentives'. In this respect, some believe that the entire shadow world of informality with its own codes, rules, rates of return and sanctions is/has evolved to be actually relatively convenient and efficient, if compared to formal systems not operating above a threshold level of efficiency. This bears grave risks, where informal strategies and incentives align with or adjust to informal money making opportunities, as in easiness to break the rules, the practice of making money out of transfers, the practise that political parties 'own' agencies and a tolerance for petty corruption. The liberalised regime of a relatively unbridled and un-regulated form of capitalism has put such an emphasis and bonus on money and profits in India that it has been labeled crony capitalism. The governor of the Central Bank of India wondered as to 'whether we had substituted the crony socialism of the past with crony capitalism, where the rich and the influential are alleged to have received land, natural resources and spectrum in return for payoffs to venal politicians'.[5] There is obviously a critical issue here, and much more research is needed to provide Mumbai-based as well as micro-level evidence on such opinions and apparent (negative) trends.

Another research agenda is the degree to which Mumbai's local state drifts towards becoming a 'hollow state' (see Nazar n.d.), where one would need to establish how strong Mumbai's local state was in pre-Pawar and liberalisation years. Today we do perceive a state gradually reducing its public service delivery role in favour of private/profit-based modalities. It is a state shown unable and/or unwilling to control or properly manage the complexities of public-private relationships (cf. Romero 2015), replete with moral hazard issues (SRS as the prime case, but also TDR and FSI practices) and the strong presence of very powerful business houses and building/contracting firms in the corridors of power. On the one hand we witness continuing processes of formal privatisation, for example the proliferation of profit-based private slum schools and ward-level clinics, which quality is often open to doubt. On the other hand there is plenty of evidence of 'informal privatisation' of state benefits as part of the mediated state: politicians and officials pushing themselves as agents in informal delivery systems. State institutions such as the courts, police and election and anti-corruption commissions are not able, allowed, or even willing to effectively uphold or implement extent law and policy. Administrative capacity is being undermined where appointments are based less on merit than on considerations of money or expected obedience to the powerful. Surely this is not in the long-term interest of Mumbai as a prime Indian city, a brand in itself with a positive and confident reputation. In a democracy, it is politicians who are expected to first spot and act upon unwelcome trends – politics takes precedence over governance. That does not apply much to the Mumbai corporators. As shown this results from the way they shape their agency, which needs to be understood against the context or 'structures' in which they are groomed and elected for office. One such given is the well-established vote bank system.

Vote banks and vote buying: do the poor buy such election strategies?

This book has assumed that continuity is more likely than change, that the force of 'path dependency' makes real or fundamental change less likely. This might be discerned too in terms of governance, where it has been argued that the Indian bureaucracy retains many traits of the British colonial administration, for example a tendency towards centralisation rather than decentralisation, the authority and powers of high-level administrators or babus, and conceivably a relatively male or patriarchal bureaucratic culture where women face plenty glass ceilings. Policy processes are top-down instead of bottom up. India has retained the 'constituency' or first past the pole election system. In my view is vulnerable to articulating the importance of mediation and to vote buying when power hungry candidates enter such arenas. Or, more sympathetically, one might hypothesise that the system fits with traditional Indian practice that 'leadership' obeys a model where people/likeminded caste/professional/neighbourhood groups support and pay respect to a local leader. In turn they hope for or expect general, individualised or emergency support. If this makes sense, the 'constituency model' where one 'leader' is elected to be in charge of a limited area would better fit customary state-society relations than a proportional election system where the arena is national. This would impair the personalistic element in elections/representation as candidates might live far away.

Chapter 5 of this book focused the hustle and bustle of local elections, the political extravaganza to sort out who will be in charge of a Mumbai ward. This is a deeply serious – occasionally violent – occasion as the culmination of local power struggles, a fiercely fought political fight as to whom can garner the most money, best mobilise influential local party workers and agents and portray the reputation and capacity to make things happen. Elections have evolved into contestations not so much about ideology or policy alternatives but mostly about money, about cash. Yet cash is another manifestation of power, and the elections are foremost a myriad of little power games, tricks and gambles in the relatively limited urban space of a constituency. In such hotly contested arenas several candidates only have single aim: to be the one to get 'first past the post'; when all that matters is to get the votes, and any tactical or murky strategy will be applied or tested. Much money is needed, first to employ an army of workers. In an apparent trend that loyalty to a party or leader is on the decline, more non-party workers such as auto-drivers and domestic servants are contracted these days to engage in canvassing and attending rallies.

Their expectations in terms of payment, food and drinks are increasing in what could be seen as the commodification of political support. But parties score differently here, where Shiv Sena and MNS enjoy more grassroots support and loyalty than the Congress and NCP parties. Yet all of them have to reward their party workers or *karyakartas* for their election work. Other expenses include car rentals, propaganda materials and printing costs for the election registers. Some parties make use of muscle power where more aggressive or goon-like persons are paid to exert pressure or threats on individuals, streets or slum pockets. Probably the main expense includes the goodies that are offered or promised to the voters, which can range from a bottle of liquor, a saree and cash for poor people, to envelopes and facilities for middle-class apartment blocks. Elaborate and secretive arrangements have evolved where voters can receive such benefits, for example through tokens exchangeable for what I consider 'machine incentives'. Gifts have to reach prospective voters in a context of machine parties competing inside slums and away from Election Commission scrutiny. Altogether, the amounts spent are staggering, amounting to crores of rupees.

I question the efficacy of such pre-election largesse in relation to people's voting behaviour, which is another important as well as fascinating area for further research (theoretically, if investment impacts prove limited for a political entrepreneur, the money could be used otherwise, but there is a hurdle in that most money here is black). On the basis of evidence collected on these informal, opaque and secretive dynamics, I conclude that spending such funds amounts to a huge and unpredictable gamble. Impacts cannot be proven. Considerable amounts of money are handed to agents, social workers and others who are not checked or controlled much, among evidence that the number of slum people – or for that matter middle classes – actually receiving cash or concrete benefits may be very limited: quite a lot of it seems to disappear. Besides, there is little guarantee that 'bought' voters will actually vote as expected/promised (even while mechanisms to later 'punish' voters do occur in what is called 'perverse accountability': Bjorkman 2013; Stokes et al. 2013). I suggest that the urban poor play along with the game, hoping to claim at least one sure concrete benefit from local democracy – apart from other potential but much more elusive benefits. Another area for more research, also to piece together the dimensions but especially the demand side of an Indian 'variety of democracy' is the question as to how poor people (semi-illiterate or illiterate, poor or wrongly informed, approached as part of a vote bank or individually with promises or threats) actually understand 'democracy'. How would they know what is a liberal democracy with its potential to organise people as a group or class with a view to (resolving) collective grievances through free and fair elections. Do they have any idea that parties are expected to aim for certain policies framed in some sort of ideology or vision? It is not likely that politicians are going to explain that to them, as it would not fit their present power basis which rests on the channelling of targeted state benefits to needy individuals or slums in the expectation of repayment through votes – otherwise bribes. Indeed, it has been argued that Mumbai's politicians actively protect slums even if 'illegal', or even allow the emergence of new slums (additions) for these same reasons. This however also shows that the poor can benefit from systems of informality which may 'work' for them (cf. Benjamin 2008 on 'occupancy urbanism).

In terms of everyday politics, I argue that the amounts of cash allocated before elections is likely their least important motive to vote for a candidate. And again, certainly not all poor voters actually score anything. In my view they first tend to look for a person they can identify with, as in a 'known' person ideally reflecting their own identity in terms of religion, caste and ethnicity (language, state origin). Another main consideration – consistent with my premise on the operation of the patronage democracy and mediated state – is that the poor may look for a person with a proven record as a stable and reliable broker, with solid networks to pull many strings. This may overrule identity issues where Muslims might pragmatically vote for a Shiv Sena candidate with a proven reputation that 'one's works gets done'. No matter if he or she is known to be more or less corrupt, which is another reference as to the pragmatism of voters – as well as candidates and political parties to condone or use informality and corruption as long as it serves a higher purpose or more effective strategy. As Bjorkman (2013) nicely illustrates, the role of money in elections may be mostly symbolic. It is about 'accomplished power': not the amount of money alone, but also the belief in, assumptions on or reputation of a candidate in the ward that actually makes the impact. Yet candidates, parties and politicians at all levels of India's democracy seem convinced it is money that counts. In Mumbai, this disputable belief does drive them into the hands of the people with money in the fast-growing private sector, the business houses and builders who are happy to accommodate at a price. So politics – and with it local democracy – is at risk to be captured by or merged with for-profit entrepreneurs at the expense of all *Mumbaikars,* with the most negative impacts on those poor and vulnerable.

Contextualising Mumbai's governance and democracy trends

Tracing the interplay of poverty, policy and politics in Mumbai through uncovering the mechanisms of local governance and democracy has neither yielded a tidy picture nor much scope for optimism. At this point I like to underline that I am quite ready to be proven wrong on the whole or part of my argument. As stated in my introduction, my book paints a broad canvass and covers dynamics not or only poorly charted to date. Hence, this book is also a research agenda where many assumptions – listed or not – and observations need be verified with more evidence. But if this is an accurate depiction of actual governance realities and everyday politics, this is where we need to start in terms of framing and designing change or improvement. This is urgent, if only to arrest deepening inequality and processes of exclusion for the city's poor – but also to make sure Mumbai as a great city maintains its current status as a prime Indian but also global megacity. My focus on the very problematic dynamics of murky politics and informal machinations no way represents a negative verdict of the city as a whole. I would not have taken the trouble to engage with Mumbai if I had been indifferent to it, and I am not: this is a dynamic city with a distinct, strong character and a vibrant culture. Mumbai maintains a sense of urban unity in spite of its massive size and increasingly heterogeneous population. With a population of about three million after independence, the city has been somehow able to accommodate nine more million people in the present BMC area with twelve-odd million people today. By and large most have shelter and a degree of services, whether in spite of controversial or tainted politicians and officials or because of them. The city always had and will always have poor people – if only as many came (and now more slowly come) from elsewhere. Some of the negative trends poor people experience here emerge from or link to the current stage of globalisation of Mumbai as a relatively open global metropolis. Politics and governance is much affected by the evolving rough and money minded global political economy and a neoliberal ideology which India has embraced rather eagerly, with impacts that policymakers should take more seriously. Piketty's (2014) observation that returns on capital are higher than on labour implies that slowly, insidiously, all workers are affected, obviously most harming informal-sector workers the world over. Trends where 'political entrepreneurs' emerge occur everywhere, democracy is unfortunately under pressure in too many countries – both rich and poor.

Unfortunately, processes and dynamics of growing inequality and exclusion are not unique then for Mumbai. I have tried to uncover and illustrate the operative mechanisms, zooming in on micro-level relations within slum households, moving up from streets, 'communities' and wards to present a helicopter view of the massive urban conglomeration with its administrative and political organisations. If we zoom out even further, trends towards increased inequality as shown for Mumbai are at work in most if not all countries, witness recent

294 *Conclusions*

disturbing accounts such as those by Oxfam (2015) and Sassen (2014). On the one hand this book wants to endorse and advocate the urgency to arrest such trends, on the other it hopes to have made it clear that changing things will be very complex. It is critical to start from realities on the ground, for both academics and journalists to provide the facts however unwelcome, and for international donor agencies to make sure their developmental budgets and efforts are most effective – so that they are not unwittingly part of the problems. But it is for the politicians of the world's democracies, including those of Mumbai and India, to take the lead in urgent repairs in both democracy and governance.

Notes

1 Dibdin (1988: 4).
2 Thank you to Ward Berenschot for suggesting these contrasting indicators.
3 'The Governor's Speech: Raghuram Rajan Explains Why Corrupt Politicians Win Elections in India', http://qz.com/248685/raghuram-rajan-explains-why-corrupt-politicians-win-elections-in-india/ (accessed 21 September 2014). It is worthwhile to refer again to the governor of India's Central Bank: 'In a speech I made before the Bombay Chamber of Commerce in 2008, I argued that the tolerance for the venal politician is because *he is the crutch that helps the poor and underprivileged navigate a system that gives them so little access*. This may be why he survives' (italics added).
4 If it can be agreed that also/even poor people seek to accumulate (a sense of) power by allying with or seeking a relation with someone more resource and powerful, the following quote by Dibdin seems relevant:

> The opium of these people was not religion but power, or rather power *was* their religion. Everyone believed, everyone was hooked. And everyone was rewarded with at least a tiny scrap of the stuff, enough to make them feel needed. What people hated in the system was being subjected to other's power, but they would all resist any change which threatened to modify or limit their own. The situation was thus both stable and rewarding, especially for those who were rich in power and could bypass it with a few phone calls, a hint dropped here, a threat there.
> (Dibdin 1988: 248).

5 'The Governor's Speech: Raghuram Rajan Explains Why Corrupt Politicians Win Elections in India', http://qz.com/248685/raghuram-rajan-explains-why-corrupt-politicians-win-elections-in-india/ (accessed 21 September 2014). See also: 'The New Age of Crony Capitalism' and 'Planet Plutocrat', *The Economist*, 15 March 2014: pp. 11 and 54–55. In that year India ranked number 9 globally, down from number 6 in 2013 in a table where Hong Kong, Russia and Malaysia come on top.

Glossary

Anganwadi   Neighbourhood health care and pre-education centre, part of the ICDS scheme aimed at women and child welfare

Babu   Term to refer to government officials, including bureaucrats of Indian Administrative Service (IAS) in India – especially used by the Indian media

Balwadi   Pre-school

Bishi   Saving group; a type of Rotating Savings and Credit Association

Chawl   Multi-storied apartment block with one room units built in the early 1900s as working class housing, now often in dilapidated condition

Corporator   Mumbai name for elected councillor (*nagar sevak* or 'city servant') in the 227 municipal wards, another name for constituencies

Crore   10 million

Dada   Local godfather; Big Man, slum lord

Dalal   Pejorative term for broker, mediator, agent

Dalit   Member of a scheduled caste (former untouchables)

Garland   Decorative wreath or cord with flowers, used at festive and political occasions, which can be hung round a person's neck

Goonda   Goon, thug, strongman

Hafta   Literally means weekly; slang for local bribes and other informal financial transactions

Kacha   Built from temporary/flimsy materials such as thatch, plastic (compare *pucca*)

Karyakarta   Party worker in political party

Lakh   100,000

Mahila Mandal   Women Organisation

Mandal   Organisation

Mantralaya   Administrative Headquarters of the Maharashtra state government in South Mumbai

Marathi   Name of the people and the language of India's Maharashtra's state

Morcha   Organised march or rally; public rally

Nagar Sevak   Marathi name for municipal councillor (MC), named corporator in Mumbai

Nullah   Concrete or brick-lined ditches to divert water and (monsoon) rain away from cities

Peon   Office assistant, messenger, attendant

Pucca   Constructed from durable/permanent materials such as stone, brick, cement, also used generally to indicate 'solid'

Rickshaw   Means of transportation, cart seating two passengers being driven by cyclist; today also 'auto rickshaw': a three wheel motor driven vehicle very common in India

Shakha   Name of neighbourhood party office for SS and MNS party office

Tamasha   Grand show or spectacle or celebration; also used to mean controversy or commotion

Ward   Other word for constituency, that is the 227 Mumbai wards

Zopad Patti   Marathi term for slum, 'encroachment'

Bibliography

3iNetwork, IDFC, IIAM and IIT. 2006. *India Infrastructure Report 2006: Urban Infrastructure*. New Delhi: Oxford University Press.

Adiga, A. 2012. *Last Man in Tower*. New Delhi: Harper Collins Publishers India.

Anand, N. 2011a. 'Ignoring Power: Knowing Leakage in Mumbai's Water Supply', in J. S. Anjaria and C. McFarlane (eds.), *Urban Navigations: Politics, Space and the City in South Asia*, pp. 191–212. London and New Delhi: Routledge.

Anand, N. 2011b. 'Pressure: The Polytechnics of Water Supply in Mumbai', *Cultural Anthropology*, 26(4): 542–64.

Anand, N. and A. Rademacher. 2011. 'Housing in the Urban Age: Inequality and Aspiration in Mumbai', *Antipode*, 43(5): 1748–72.

Anjaria, J. 2009. 'Guardians of the Bourgeois City: Citizenship, Public Space and Middle Class Activism in Mumbai', *City and Community*, 8(4): 391–406.

Anjaria, J. S. and C. McFarlane. 2011. *Urban Navigations: Politics, Space and the City in South Asia*. London and New Delhi: Routledge.

Ayyar, V. 2013. 'Caste and Gender in a Mumbai Resettlement Site', *Economic and Political Weekly*, 4 May (18): 44–55.

Ayyar, V. and L. Khandare. (n.d.). 'Social Networks in Slum and Rehabilitation Sites: A Study in Mumbai, India'. http://siteresources.worldbank.org/. . ./336387. . ./ayyar.pdf (accessed on 18 March 2015).

Baker, J., R. Basu, M. Cropper, S. Lall and A. Takeuchi. 2005. *Urban Poverty and Transport: The Case of Mumbai*. Washington, DC: World Bank Policy Research Working Paper No. 3693.

Banerjee, M. 2012. *India: The Next Superpower?* IDEAS reports, London School of Politics and Political Science. http://eprints.lse.ac.uk./43448/ (accessed on 9 August 2014).

Banerjee-Guha, S. 2009. 'Neo-Liberalising the "Urban", New Geographies of Power and Injustice in Indian Cities', *Economic and Political Weekly*, 44(22): 95–107.

Banerjee-Guha, S. (ed.). 2010. *Accumulation by Dispossession: Transformative Cities in the New Global Order*. New Delhi and Thousand Oaks: Sage.

Baud, I. and J. W. de Wit (eds.). 2008. *New Forms of Governance in India: Shifts, Models, Networks and Contestations.* New Delhi: Sage.

Baud, I. and N. Nainan. 2008. ' "Negotiated Spaces" for Representation in Mumbai: Ward Committees, Advanced Locality Management and the Politics of Middle-Class Activism', *Environment & Urbanization*, 20(2): 1–17.

Bawa, Z. 2011. 'Where Is the State? How Is the State? Assessing Water and the State in Mumbai and Johannesburg', *Journal of Asian and Africa Studies*, 46(5): 491–503.

Bawa, Z. 2013. 'From Watertight to Watered Down: The Case of Public Consultations and People's Participation in Mumbai's Water Distribution Improvement Project', in K. Coelho, L. Kamath and M. Vijayabaskar (eds.), *Participolis, Consent and Contention in Neoliberal Urban India*, pp. 89–114. London, New York and New Delhi: Routledge.

Bedi, T. 2007. 'The Dashing Ladies of the Shiv Sena', *Economic and Political Weekly*, 28 April, pp. 1534–41.

Benjamin, S. 2008. 'Occupancy Urbanism: Radicalizing Politics and Economy beyond Policy and Programs', *International Journal of Urban and Regional Research*, 32(3): 719–29.

Berenschot, W. 2006. 'The Machinations of Municipal Elections in Ahmedabad, India'. Paper presented at the 19th European Conference on Modern South Asia Studies, Leiden University, Leiden, 27–30 June.

Berenschot, W. 2009. *Riot Politics: Communal Violence and State-Society Mediation in Gujarat, India.* Amsterdam: Boxpress.

Berenschot, W. 2010. 'Everyday Mediation: The Politics of Public Service Delivery in Gujarat, India', *Development and Change*, 41(5): 883–905.

Berenschot, W. 2011. 'Political Fixers and the Rise of Hindu Nationalism in Gujarat, India: Lubricating a Patronage Democracy', *Journal of South Asian Studies*, 34(3): 382–401.

Bhatiya, N. and A. Chatterjee. 2010. 'Financial Inclusion in the Slums of Mumbai', *Economic and Political Weekly*, 45(42): 23–26.

Bhide, A. 2006. 'From the Margins: The Experiences of Low Income Communities in Mumbai vis-à-vis Changing Patterns of Basic Services Delivery'. Paper presented at an (IDPAD) Seminar on Changing Forms of Governance in Indian Megacities, TISS, Mumbai, 18–19 January.

Bhide, A. 2011. 'Mumbai: Mumbai Reader 10', Urban Design Research Institute (quoted in Echanove, 2013).

Bhowmik, S. 2010. 'Urban Public Space and the Urban Poor', in S. Banerjee-Guha (ed.), *Accumulation by Dispossession: Transformative Cities in the New Global Order*, pp. 182–297. New Delhi and Thousand Oaks: Sage.

Bisiaux, R. 2013. 'Understanding the Mismatch among Three Definitions of Poverty', *Economic and Political Weekly*, 5 January, 48: 51–59.

Bjorkman, L. 2013. 'You Can't Buy a Vote: Cash and Community in a Mumbai election', *MMG Working Paper 13–01*. http://www.mmg.mpg.de/fileadmin/user_upload/documents/wp/WP_13–01_Bjorkman_Cant-buy-a-vote.pdf (accessed on 9 November 2013).

Blundo, G. 2006. 'Dealing with the Local State: The Informal Privatization of Street-Level Bureaucracies in Senegal', *Development and Change*, 37(4): 799–821.

Boex, Jamie. 2010. 'Localizing the MDGs: Unlocking the Potential of the Local Public Sector to Engage in Development and Poverty Reduction', *IDG Working Paper* 2010–15. Washington: The Urban Institute.

Boissevain, J. 1974. *Friends of Friends: Networks, Manipulators and Coalitions*. New York: St. Martin's Press.

Boo, K. 2012. *Behind the Beautiful Forevers: Life, Death and Hope in a Mumbai Undercity*. New Delhi and New York: Hamish Hamilton.

Breeding, M. E. 2011. 'The Micro-Politics of Vote Banks in Karnataka', *Economic and Political Weekly*, 2 April, 46(14): 71–77.

Campana, J. 2013. *Dharavi: The City Within*. Noida and London: HarperCollins.

Chakravarthi, R. 2007. 'India's Middle Class Failure', *Prospect Magazine* (138).

Chamaraj, K. 2015. 'Undermining RAY', *Uday India*, 14 February, pp. 34–39.

Chandra, K. 2004. 'Elections as Auctions', *Seminar*, 539(1–7). http://www.india-seminar.com/2004/539/539%20kanchan%20chandra.htm (accessed on 19 September 2013).

Chandra, K. 2007a. 'Counting Heads: A Theory of Voter and Elite Behaviour in Patronage Democracies', in H. Kitscheld and S. Wilkinson (eds.), *Patrons, Clients and Policies: Patterns of Democratic Accountability and Political Competition*, pp. 84–110. Cambridge: Cambridge University Press.

Chandra, Vikram. 2007b. *Sacred Games*. New Delhi and London: Penguin Books.

Chatterjee, P. 2004. *The Politics of the Governed: Popular Politics in Most of the World*. New York: Colombia University Press.

Chatterjee, N., G. Fernandes and M. Hernandez. 2012. 'Food Insecurity in Urban Poor Households in Mumbai, India', *Food Security*, 4(4): 619–32.

Clark, G. and T. Moonen. 2014. *Mumbai: India's Global City: A Case Study of the Global Cities Initiative: A Joint Project of Brookings and JPMorgan Chase*. Washington, DC: Global Cities Initiative.

Coelho, K., L. Kamath and M. Vijayabaskar. 2013. *Participolis, Consent and Contention in Neoliberal Urban India*. London, New York and New Delhi: Routledge.

Coelho, K. and A. Maringanti. 2012. 'Urban Poverty in India: Tools, Treatment and Politics at the Neo-Liberal Turn', *Economic and Political Weekly*, 47(47 & 48): 39–43.

Crook, R. and A. Sverrisson. 2003. 'Does Decentralization Contribute to Poverty Reduction? Surveying the Evidence', in P. Houtzager and Mick Moore (eds.), *Changing Paths; International Development and the New Politics of Inclusion*, pp. 233–54. Ann Arbor: University of Michigan Press.

Das, P. K. 2003. 'Slums: The Continuing Struggle for Housing', in S. Patel and J. Masselos (eds.), *Bombay and Mumbai: The City in Transition*, pp. 207–44. Oxford and New Delhi: Oxford University Press.

Das, S. K. 2001. *Public Office, Private Interest: Bureaucracy and Corruption in India*. New Delhi and Oxford: Oxford University Press.

Debroy, B. and L. Bhandari. 2012. *Corruption in India, the DNA and RNA*. New Delhi: Konark Publishers LTD.

Demmers, J., E. Fernandez and B. Hogenboom (eds.). 2004. *Good Governance in the Era of Global Neo-Liberalism: Conflict and De-Politicization in Latin America, Eastern Europe, Asia and Africa*. London: Routledge.

Desai, P. 2002. *Institutional Dimensions of Program Planning and Implementation: Three Cases of Slum Upgradation Programs in Mumbai, India*. PhD Thesis, Amsterdam: Free University.

Desai, P. and J. de Wit. 2007. 'The Slum Redevelopment Scheme in Malad, Mumbai: Evidence from the Field'. Mumbai, unpublished research report.

Desai, R. M. and R. Sanyal. 2012. *Urbanizing Citizenship: Contested Spaces in Indian Cities*. London and New Delhi: Sage.

Desai, V. 1995. *Community Participation and Slum Housing: A Study of Bombay* London and New Delhi: Sage Publications.

De Souza, P. 2011. 'Mumbai Water Services and Income Classes', *Urban World* 4(4): 1–10.

de Wit, J. 1985. *Slum Dwellers, Slum Leaders and the Government Apparatus: Relations between Actors in Slum Upgrading in Madras, India*. Urban Research Working Paper No. 8. Amsterdam: Free University.

de Wit, J. 1996. *Poverty, Policy and Politics in Madras Slums, Dynamics of Survival, Gender and Leadership*. London, Thousand Oaks and New Delhi: Sage.

de Wit, J. 2002. 'Urban Poverty Alleviation in Bangalore, Institutional and Community Level Dilemmas', *Economic and Political Weekly*, 21 September, pp. 3935–42.

de Wit, J. 2004. 'A Realistic Alternative Vision for Mumbai', in R. N. Sharma, R. B. Bhagat and A. Rath (eds.), *The Vision Mumbai: A Concept Plan for Mumbai City*, pp. 49–52. Mumbai: Tata Institute of Social Sciences.

de Wit, J. 2009a. 'Changing Arenas for Defining Urban India: Middle Class Associations, Municipal Councillors and the Urban Poor', *Trialog*, 3–4(102 & 103): 21–27.

de Wit, J. 2009b. 'Decentralised Urban Governance and Changing Roles of Municipal Councillors in Chennai, India'. Paper presented at the International Development Planning Review (IDPR) Conference, University of Liverpool, Liverpool, 6–7 April.

de Wit, J. 2010a. 'Decentralized Management of Solid Waste in Mumbai Slums: Informal Privatization through Patronage', *International Journal of Public Administration*, 33(12 & 13): 767–77.

de Wit, J. 2010b. 'Prospects for India's Urban Poor: Livelihoods and Mobility in Conditions of Informality and Middle Class Competition', *The Urban World*, 3(4): 1–7.

de Wit, J. 2016. 'Builders, the Local State and a Mumbai Slum Community: Slum Redevelopment Dynamics in a Public-Private-Community Partnership Project' (forthcoming journal article).

de Wit, J. and E. Berner. 2009. 'Progressive Patronage? Municipalities, NGOs, Community-Based Organizations, and the Limits to Slum Dwellers' Empowerment', *Development and Change*, 40(5): 927–47.

de Wit, J. and B. Holzner. 2003. *Supporting Decentralised Urban Governance: Training Women Municipal Councillors in Mumbai, India*. ISS Working Paper No. 386. The Hague: Institute of Social Studies.

de Wit, J., N. Nainan and S. Palnitkar. 2008. 'Urban Decentralisation in India: Assessing the Performance of Neighbourhood Level Wards Committees', in I. Baud and J. de Wit (eds.), *New Forms of Governance in India: Shifts, Models, Networks and Contestations*, pp. 37–65. New Delhi: Sage.

de Wit, J. and T. van Dijk. 2010. 'Political Entrepreneurs and the Urban Poor: The Role of Municipal Councillors in the Mumbai Region'. Unpublished Paper presented at the CERES Summer School at the International Institute of Social Studies, ISS, The Hague, 23–24 June.

Dhar Chakrabarti, P. G. 2001. 'Urban Crisis in India: New Initiatives for Sustainable Cities', *Development in Practice*, 11(2 & 3): 260–72.

Dibdin, M. 1988. *Ratking, an Aurelio Zen Mystery*. London: Faber and Faber.

Doshi, S. 2012. 'Gendered Slum Citizenship in Neoliberal Mumbai', in R. Desai and R. Sanyal (eds.), *Urbanizing Citizenship: Contested Spaces in Indian Cities*, pp. 83–109. New Delhi: Sage.

Echanove, M. 2013. *Beyond the Informal: Re-Conceptualizing Mumbai's Urban Development*. MMG Working Paper 13–13. Gottingen: Max Planck Institute.

Eckert, J. 2002. *Governing Laws – On the Appropriation and Adaptation of Control in Mumbai*. Working Paper No.33. Halle/Saale: Max Planck Institute for Social Anthropology.

Frederickson, H. G. 2005. 'Whatever Happened to Public Administration? Governance, Governance Everywhere', in E. Ferlie, L. E. Lynn Jr. and C. Pollit (eds.), *The Oxford Handbook of Public Management*, pp. 282–305. Oxford: Oxford University Press.

Geddis, A. 2008. 'Buying Power, Book Review of Schaffer, 2007 "Elections for Sale: The Causes and Consequences of Vote Buying" ', *Election Law Journal*, 7(2): 141–44.

Ghosh, A. and S. Tawa Lama-Rewal. 2005. *Democratization in Progress: Women and Local Politics in Urban India*. New Delhi: Tulika Books.

Gill, K. 2007. 'Interlinked Contracts and Social Power: Patronage and Exploitation in India's Waste Recovery Market', *Journal of Development Studies*, 43(8): 1448–74.

Goankar, R. 2007. 'On Cultures of Democracy', *Public Culture*, 19(1): 1–22.

GOI/Government of India. 1992. *The Constitution Seventy-Fourth Amendment Act 1992 on Municipalities*. New Delhi: Ministry of Urban Development.

GOI/Government of India and Ministry of Urban Development. 2013. *How to Govern India's Megacities: Towards Needed Transformation*. Vol. 1, Draft Thematic Report. New Delhi: Centre for Policy Research.

GOI/Government of India/Planning Commission. 2011. *Report of the Working Group on Urban Poverty, Slums, and Service Delivery System*. New Delhi: Steering Committee on Urbanization Planning Commission.

Gowda, M.V.R. and E. Sridharan. 2012. 'Reforming India's Party Financing and Election Expenditure Laws', *Election Law Journal*, 11(2): 226–40.

Grindle, M. 2012. *Jobs for the Boys: Patronage and the State in Comparative Perspective*. Cambridge, MA: Harvard University Press.

Grindle, M. and M. E. Hilderbrand. 1995. 'Building Sustainable Capacity in the Public Sector: What Can be Done?', *Public Administration and Development*, 15(5): 441–63.

Guha Ray, S. 2009. 'Offer Valid till Votes Last', *Tehelka*, 2 May (17).

Gupta, A. 1995. 'Blurred Boundaries: The Discourse of Corruption, the Culture of Politics, and the Imagined State', *American Ethnologist*, 22(2): 375–402.

Gupta, A. 2012. *Red Tape, Bureaucracy, Structural Violence and Poverty in India*. Durham and London: Duke University Press.

Gupte, J. 2012. 'Linking Urban Vulnerability, Extra-Legal Security, and Civil Violence: The Case of the Urban Dispossessed in Mumbai', in R. Desai and R. Sanyal (eds.), *Urbanizing Citizenship: Contested Spaces in Indian Cities*, pp. 190–212. New Delhi: Sage.

Hadiz, V. R. 2004. 'Decentralisation and Democracy in Indonesia: A Critique of Neo-Institutionalist Perspectives', *Development and Change*, 35(4): 697–718.

Hajare, H. P. 2002. *Economic and Social Background of Women Corporators and Their Working in Mumbai MahaNagarpalika*. Mumbai: Department of Civics and Politics of University of Mumbai.

Hansen, T. B. 2001. *Violence in Urban India: Identity Politics, 'Mumbai', and the Postcolonial City*. New Delhi: Permanent Black/Princeton University Press.

Haritas, K. 2008. 'Poverty and Marginalisation: Challenges to Poor Women's Leadership in Urban India', *Gender and Development*, 16(3): 457–69.

Harris, J. 2005. 'Political Participation, Representation and the Urban Poor: Findings from Research in Delhi', *Economic and Political Weekly*, 40(12): 1041–54.

Harris, J. 2007. 'Antinomies of Empowerment: Observations on Civil Society, Politics, and Urban Governance in India', *Economic and Political Weekly*, 30 June, pp. 2716–24.

Harris, J., K. Stokke and O. Turnquist. 2004. *Politicizing Democracy: The New Local Politics of Democratization*. Basingstoke: Palgrave Macmillan.

Harris-White, B. 2003. *India Working: Essays on Society and Economy*. Port Melbourne: Cambridge University Press.

Helmke, G. and S. Levitsky. 2004. 'Informal Institutions and Comparative Politics: A Research Agenda', *Perspectives on Politics*, 2(4): 725–40.

Heston, A. and V. Kumar. 2008. 'Institutional Flaws and Corruption Incentives in India', *Journal of Development Studies*, 44(9): 1243–61.

Heuze, D. G. 2011. 'Tej City. Protests in Mumbai, 1988–2008', Rethinking Urban Democracy, special issue of the *South Asia Multidisciplinary Academic Journal*, Nr 5/2011. http://samaj.revues.org/index3213.html (accessed on 7 April 2010).

Hicken, A. 2011. 'Clientelism', *Annual Review of Political Science*, 14: 289–310.

Hust, H. and M. Mann (eds.). 2005. *Urbanization and Governance in India*. New Delhi: Manohar, Centre de Sciences Humaines and South Asia Institute.

Hyden, G., J. A. Court and K. Mease. 2004. *Making Sense of Governance: Empirical Evidence from Sixteen Developing Countries*. London: Lynne Rienner Publishers.

Jagannathan, R. 2012. 'Why Mumbai's Elections Are Irrelevant to This City-State', http://mumbaiboss.com/2012/02/17 (accessed on 12 March 2012).

Jha, S., V. Rao and M. Woolcock. 2005. *Governance in the Gullies: Democratic Responsiveness and Leadership in Delhi's Slums*. Policy Research Working Papers. Washington: The Word Bank.

John, M. 2007. 'Women in Power? Gender, Caste, and the Politics of Local Urban Governance', *Economic and Political Weekly*, 29 September, pp. 3986–94.

Jones, N. and E. Presler-Marshall. 2012. 'Governance and Poverty Eradication: Applying a Gender and Social Institutions Perspective', *Public Administration and Development*, 32(4–5): 371–84.

Joseph, M. 2011. *Serious Men*. Noida and London: HarperCollins.

Kabeer, N. 1999. 'Resources, Agency, Achievements: Reflections on the Measurement of Women's Empowerment', *Development and Change*, 30: 435–64.

Kapadia, K. 1996. 'Housing Rights for Urban Poor: Battle for Mumbai's Streets', *Economic and Political Weekly*, 15 June, pp. 1436–40.

Karn, S. K., S. Shikura and H. Harada. 2003. 'Living Environment and Health of Urban Poor: A Study in Mumbai', *Economic and Political Weekly*, 23 August, pp. 3575–86.

Kennedy, L., R. Duggal and S. Tawa Lama-Rawal. 2009. 'Assessing Urban Governance through the Prism of Healthcare Services in Delhi, Hyderabad and Mumbai', in J. Ruet and S. Tawa Lama-Rewal (eds.), *Governing India's Metropolises*, pp. 161–83. New Delhi and Abingdon: Routledge.

Khan, M. Q. 2005. 'Markets, States and Democracy: Patron-Client Networks and the Case for Democracy in Developing Countries', *Democratization* 12(5): 704–24.

Khan, S. 2013. 'Women, Safety, and the City of Mumbai', *Economic and Political Weekly*, 7 September, 48(12): 12–13.

Kishwar, M. P. 2005. *Deepening Democracy: Challenges of Governance and Globalisation in India*. New Delhi: Oxford University Press.

Kitscheld, H. and S. Wilkinson (eds.). 2007. *Patrons, Clients and Policies: Patterns of Democratic Accountability and Political Competition*. Cambridge: Cambridge University Press.

Krishna, A. (ed.). 2008. *Poverty, Participation and Democracy: A Global Perspective*. Cambridge: Cambridge University Press.

Krishna, A. and D. Bajpai. 2015. 'Layers in Globalising Society and the New Middle Class in India: Trends, Distribution and Prospects', *Economic and Political Weekly*, 50(5): 69–76.

Krishna, A. and J. Booth. 2008. 'Conclusion: Implications for Policy and Research', in A. Krishna (ed.), *Poverty, Participation and Democracy: A Global Perspective*, pp. 147–60. Cambridge: Cambridge University Press.

Kumar, A. 2009. 'A Class Analysis of the "Bihari Menace" ', *Economic and Political Weekly*, 44(28): 124–27.

Kumar, G. and F. Landy. 2009. 'Vertical Governance: Brokerage, Patronage and Corruption in Indian Metropolises', in J. Ruet and S. Tawa Lama-Rewal (eds.), *Governing India's Metropolises*, pp. 105–34. London and New Delhi: Routledge.

Kundu, A. 2006. *Final Report: New Forms of Governance in Indian Mega-Cities: Decentralisation, Financial Management and Partnerships in Urban Environmental Services. A Study Sponsored under Indo-Dutch Programme for Alternate Development*. Unpublished report, New Delhi: JNU.

Kundu, D. 2009. 'Elite Capture and Marginalisation of the Poor in Participatory Urban Governance: A Case of Resident Welfare Associations in Metro Cities', in *Government of India, India Urban Poverty Report 2009*, pp. 272–84. New Delhi: Ministry of Housing and Urban Poverty Alleviation.

Landy, F. and D. Ruby. 2005. 'The Public Distribution System as an Entry Point for the Study of Urban Governance: The Case of the Old City of Hyderabad'. Paper presented at a workshop of the research project 'Actors, Policies and Urban Governance', ASCI, Hyderabad, 20 September.

Leftwich, A. 2005. 'Democracy and Development: Is There Institutional Incompatibility?', *Democratization*, 12(5): 686–703.

Lindberg, S. 2003. 'It's Our Time to "Chop": Do Elections in Africa Feed Neo-Patrimonialism rather than Counteract It?', *Democratization*, 10(2): 121–40.

Lipsky, M. 1980. *Street Level Bureaucracy: Dilemmas of the Individual in Public Services*. New York: Russell Sage Foundation.

Lobo, L. and B. Das. 2001. *Poor in Urban India: Life in the Slums of a Western Indian City*. Jaipur and New Delhi: Rawat Publications.

Lund, C. 2006. 'Twilight Institutions: Public Authority and Local Politics in Africa', *Development and Change*, 37(4): 685–705.

Mahadevia, D. 2013. *Urban Poverty in India and Post-MDG Framework*. New Delhi: Oxfam India working papers series OIWPS–XVII.

Manecksha, F. 2011. 'Pushing the Poor to the Periphery in Mumbai', *Economic and Political Weekly*, 46(51): 26–28.

Mathias, L. 2012. 'Mumbai Elections: Congress Self-Destructs, the Sena-BJP Alliance Triumphs', *Economic and Political Weekly*, 47(10): 10–13.

McFarlane, C. 2008. 'Sanitation in Mumbai's Informal Settlements: State, "Slum" and Infrastructure', *Environment & Planning*, 40: 88–107.

MCGM/Municipal Corporation of Greater Mumbai. 2009. *Human Development Report Mumbai 2009*. Prepared by All India Institute of Local Self Government with support by UNDP and Ministry of Housing and Urban Poverty Alleviation. Mumbai: Municipal Corporation of Greater Mumbai.

MCGM/Municipal Corporation of Greater Mumbai. (n.d.). *Slum Adoption Scheme through Community Based Organization for Slum Sanitation, Clean, Green, Decent and Pollution Free Slums*. SAP, Mumbai: MCGM, SWM department, Official leaflet.

Metha, S. 2004. *Maximum City: Bombay Lost and Found*. New Delhi: Penguin.

Michelutti, L. 2008. *The Vernacularisation of Democracy: Politics, Caste and Religion in India*. New Delhi: Routledge.

MISTRA. 2014. *Patronage Politics Divides Us: A Study of Poverty, Patronage and Inequality in South Africa*. Johannesburg: MISTRA/ Mapungubwe Institute for Strategic Reflection.

Mooij, J. and Tawa Lama-Rewal. 2009. 'Class in Metropolitan India: The Rise of the Middle Classes', in J. Ruet and S. Tawa Lama-Rewal (eds.), *Governing India's Metropolises*, pp. 81–104. London and New Delhi: Routledge.

Moore, B. 1966. *Social Origins of Dictatorship and Democracy: Lord and Peasant in the Making of the Modern World*. Boston: Beacon Press.

Moser, C.O.N. 1995. 'Women, Gender and Urban Development Policy', *Third World Planning Review*, 17(2): 223–35.

Nainan, N. 2001. *Negotiating for Participation by NGOs in the City of Mumbai*. MSc Thesis, Rotterdam: Institute of Housing and Urban Development Studies.

Nainan, N. 2006. 'Parallel Universes: Quasi-Legal Networks in Mumbai Governance'. Paper presented at the seminar on Urban Governance in an International Perspective, University of Amsterdam, the Netherlands, 7 January.

Nainan, N.K.B. 2008. 'Building Boomers and Fragmentation of Space in Mumbai', *Economic and Political Weekly*, 24 May, pp. 29–34.

Nainan, N.K.B. 2012. *Lakshmi Raj: Shaping Spaces in Post Industrial Mumbai: Urban Regimes, Planning Instruments and Splintering Communities*. PhD Thesis, Amsterdam: University of Amsterdam.

Nainan, N. and I. Baud. 2008. 'Negotiating for Participation: Decentralisation and NGOs in Mumbai, India', in I. Baud and J. de Wit (eds.), *New Forms of Governance in India: Shifts, Models, Networks and Contestations*, pp. 115–42. New Delhi: Sage.

Narayan, D. 2000. *Voices of the Poor: Can Anyone Hear Us?* New York: World Bank and Oxford University Press.

Narayanan, H. 2003. 'In Search of Shelter', in S. Patel and J. Masselos (eds.), *Bombay and Mumbai: The City in Transition*, pp. 183–206, Oxford and New Delhi: Oxford University Press.

Nazar, B. (n.d.). *The Hollow State: Dilemmas for Management and Performance Measurement*. http://www.google.nl/url?sa=t&rct=j&q=&esrc=s&source=web&cd=2&ved=0CCwQFjAB&url=http%3A%2F%2Fwww.

barrynazar.com%2Fuploads%2F4%2F7%2F1%2F9%2F4719802%2F the_hollow_state.docx&ei= (accessed on 20 March 2015).

NCEUS and A. Sengupta. 2007. *Report on Conditions of Work and Promotion of Livelihoods in the Unorganized Sector.* New Delhi: National Commission for Enterprises in the Unorganized Sector NCEUS, chaired by A. Sengupta.

Nichter, S. 2008. 'Vote Buying or Turnout Buying? Machine Politics and the Secret Ballot', *American Political Science Review*, 102(1): 19–31.

Nijman, J. 2008. 'Against the Odds: Slum Rehabilitation in Neoliberal Mumbai', *Cities*, 25: 73–85.

OXFAM. 2015. *For Richer . . . or Poorer? The Capture of Growth and Politics in Emerging Economies.* London: Oxfam. http://www.csnbricsam.org (accessed on 9 January 2016).

Paley, J. 2002. 'Towards an Anthropology of Democracy', *Annual Review of Anthropology*, 31: 469–96.

Palshikar, S. 2004. 'Shiv Sena, a Tiger with Many Faces?', *Economic and Political Weekly*, 3 April (10): 1497–507.

Pardo, I. and G. Prato. 2012. *Anthropology in the City: Methodology and Theory.* Farnham: Ashgate.

Parkar, S., V. Dawani and M. Weiss. 2008. 'Gender, Suicide, and the Socio-Cultural Context of Deliberate Self-Harm in an Urban General Hospital in Mumbai, India', *Culture, Medicine and Psychiatry*, 32: 492–515.

Patel, S. 2003. 'Bombay and Mumbai: Identities, Politics and Populism', in S. Patel and J. Masselos (eds.), *Bombay and Mumbai: The City in Transition*, pp. 3–31. New Delhi: Oxford University Press.

Patel, S. 2015. 'Affordable Housing with Spatial Social Justice', *Economic and Political Weekly*, 7 February, 50(6): 61–66.

Patel, S. and J. Masselos (eds.). 2003. *Bombay and Mumbai: The City in Transition.* New Delhi: Oxford University Press.

Patel, S. and A. Thorner (eds.). 2003. *Bombay: Metaphor for Modern India.* New Delhi: Oxford University Press.

Patel, V. (undated). *Gender and Human Development in Mumbai.* Mumbai: SNDT Women's University. http://www.academia.edu/653020/Gender_and_Human_Development_in_Mumbai_Prof._Vibhuti_Patel (accessed on 5 March 2013).

Patibandla, M. 2013. 'New Institutional Economics: Its Relevance to Curbing Corruption', *Economic and Political Weekly*, 48(9): 55–62.

Pethe, A. 2010. *Collusion, Conflicts, Informal Systems and Rent Seeking: The Great Prototype Indian Story of Urban Land Management in Mumbai.* A Governance of Urban Land Management in Mumbai Synthesis Paper, Mumbai University, Department of Economics.

Pethe, A., S. Gandhi and V. Tandel. 2011. 'Assessing the Mumbai Metropolitan Region: A Governance Perspective', *Economic and Political Weekly*, 46(26 & 27): 177–94.

Pethe, A., R. Nallathiga, S. Gandhi and V. Tandel. 2014. 'Re-thinking Urban Planning in India: Learning from the Wedge between the De Jure and de Facto Development in Mumbai', *Cities* 39(2014): 120–32.

Pethe, A., V. Tandel and S. Gandhi. 2012. *Unravelling the Anatomy of Legal Corruption in India: Focusing on the 'Honest Graft' by the Politician.* MPRA Paper No. 39306, https://mpra.ub.uni-muenchen.de/39306/ (posted on 7 June 2012, accessed on 12 November 2015).

Phatak, V. K. and S. B. Patel. 2005. 'Would Decentralisation Have Made a Difference?', *Economic and Political Weekly*, 3 September, pp. 3902–4.

Piketty, T. 2014. *Capital in the Twenty-First Century.* Harvard: Harvard University Press.

Pinto, D. A. and M. R. Pinto. 2005. *Municipal Corporation of Greater Mumbai and Ward Administration.* New Delhi: Konark Publishers.

Pinto, M. 2000. *Metropolitan City Governance in India.* New Delhi: Sage.

Pinto, M. 2008. 'Urban Governance in India–Spot Light on Mumbai', in I. Baud and J. W. de Wit (eds.), *New Forms of Governance in India: Shifts, Models, Networks and Contestations*, pp. 37–65. New Delhi: Sage.

Pinto, M. and J. de Wit. 2006. 'Field Notes of Wards Office Interviews'. Unpublished paper, Mumbai and the Hague: ISS.

Prabash, J. 2010. 'India: Mounting Influence of Money Power in Elections and the Crisis of Representation', *Asia-Pacific Journal of Social Sciences*, 86(1): 85–95.

PRAJA. 2011. *Mumbai Report Card, Municipal Councillors.* http://www.praja.org/. . ./concillors-report-card-november (accessed on 14 January 2012).

PRAJA. 2012. *White Paper on Ward-Wise Top Issues: Where Mumbai's New Municipal Councillors Need to Pay Attention February.* http://www.praja.org/white paper.php (accessed on 29 November 2012).

PRAJA. 2014a. *White Paper: Report on the State of Health of Mumbai.* Mumbai: PRAJA.

PRAJA. 2014b. *Report on 'The State of Affordable Housing in Mumbai'.* Mumbai: PRAJA.

Punwani, J. 2014. 'Electing a Representative: An Account of Medha Patkar's Election Campaign', *Economic and Political Weekly*, 49(19): 12–14.

PWC/Price Waterhouse and Coopers. 2012. *Urban Local Bodies Assessment Report, Financing Strategy and Advice: Group 1: Municipal Corporation of Greater Mumbai.* Mumbai: The World Bank and the Government of Maharashtra, PPIAF-SNTA program.

Quraishi, S. Y. 2014. *Un Undocumented Wonder: The Making of the Great Indian Election.* New Delhi: Rupa Publications/Rainlight.

Rajivan, K. 2013. 'Participation and Consultation in the Context of Municipal Infrastructure Financing', in K. Coelho, L. Kamath and M. Vijayabaskar (eds.), *Participolis, Consent and Contention in Neoliberal Urban India*, pp. 133–40. London, New York and New Delhi: Routledge.

Ravindran, K. T. 2013. 'Direct Democracy versus Electoral Democracy: A View from Delhi', in K. Coelho, L. Kamath and M. Vijayabaskar (eds.), *Participolis, Consent and Contention in Neoliberal Urban India*, pp. 244–49. London, New York and New Delhi: Routledge.

Revi, A. 2005. 'Lessons from the Deluge: Priorities for Multi-Hazard Risk Mitigation', *Economic and Political Weekly*, 3 September, pp. 3911–16.

Risbud, N. 2003. *The Case of Mumbai, India*. New Delhi: School of Planning and Architecture.

Robinson, M. 2007. 'Does Decentralisation Improve Equity and Efficiency in Public Service Provision?', *IDS Bulletin*, 38(1): 7–17.

Romero, M. J. 2015. *What Lies Beneath? A Critical Assessment of PPPs and Their Impact on Sustainable Development*. Brussels: Eurodad.

Roniger, L. 2004. 'Political Clientelism, Democracy and Market Economy', *Comparative Politics*, 36(3): 353–75.

Roy, A. 2004. 'The Gentleman's City: Urban Informality in the Calcutta of New Communism', in A. Roy and N. AlSayyad (eds.), *Urban Informality, Transnational Perspectives from the Middle East, Latin America and South Asia*, pp. 147–70. Lanham and Oxford: Lexington Books.

Roy, A. 2009a. 'The 21st-Century Metropolis: New Geographies of Theory', *Regional Studies*, 43(6): 819–30.

Roy, A. 2009b. 'Why India Cannot Plan Its Cities: Informality, Insurgence and the Idiom of Urbanization', *Planning Theory*, 8(1): 76–87.

Roy, A. 2011a. 'Slumdog Cities: Rethinking Subaltern Urbanism', *International Journal of Urban and Regional Research*, 35(2): 223–28.

Roy, A. 2011b. 'The Blockade of the World Class City: Dialectical Images of Indian Urbanism', in A. Roy and A. Ong (eds.), *Worlding Cities: Asian Experiments and the Art of Being Global*, pp 259–78. Chisester and Oxford: Blackwell Publishing.

Ruet, J. and S. Tawa Lama-Rewal (eds.). 2009. *Governing India's Metropolises*. New Delhi and Abingdon: Routledge.

Saigal, A. 2008. 'Community Caretaking and Women Volunteer Teachers in Mumbai Slums', *Economic and Political Weekly*, 18 October, pp. 69–75.

Sassen, S. 2014. *Expulsions, Brutality and Complexity in the Global Economy*. Cambridge, MA and London: Belknap Press of Harvard University Press.

Schaffer, F. C. (ed.). 2007. *Elections for Sale: The Causes and Consequences of Vote Buying*. Boulder, CO: Kumarian Press.

Schedler, A. 2002a. 'Elections without Democracy: The Menu of Manipulation', *Journal of Democracy*, 13(2): 36–50.

Schedler, A. 2002b. 'Clientelism, Patrimonialism and Democratic Governance: An Overview and Framework for Assessment and Planning'. http://www. grc-exchange.org/g_themes/politicalsystems_ informal.html (accessed on 8 July 2007).

Scott, J. C. 1969. 'Corruption, Machine Politics, and Political Change', *The American Political Science Review*, 63(4): 1142–58.

Shah, S. (n.d.- but after 2007). *Aspects of Urban Poverty in Mumbai, Mumbai*. http://www.susiebenshah.in/PDF/PDF2.pdf (accessed on 6 March 2013).

Shatkin, G. (ed.). 2014. *Contesting the Indian City: Global Visions and the Politics of the Local*. Chichester: John Wiley.

Shatkin, G. T. and S. Vidyarthi. 2014. 'Introduction; Contesting the Indian City: Global Visions and the Politics of the Local', in G. Shatkin (ed.),

Contesting the Indian City: Global Visions and the Politics of the Local, pp. 1–38. Chichester: John Wiley.

Shetye, G. 2006. 'Functioning of Wards Committees in Maharashtra: A Case Study', in K. C. Sivaramakrishnan (ed.), *People's Participation in Urban Governance: A Comparative Study of Wards Committees in Karnataka, Kerala, Maharashtra, and West Bengal*, pp. 211–50. New Delhi: Concept Publishing Company.

Shrivastava, P. S. and S. R. Shrivastava. 2013. 'A Study of Spousal Domestic Violence in an Urban Slum of Mumbai', *International Journal of Preventive Medicine*, 4(1): 27–32.

Siddiqui, K. and S. K. Bhowmik. 2004. 'Mumbai', in K. Siddiqui (ed.), *Megacity Governance in South Asia: A Comparative Study*, pp. 105–88. Dhaka: University Press Limited.

Sivaramakrishnan, K. C. 2000. *Power to the People? The Politics and Progress of Decentralisation*. New Delhi: Konark.

Sivaramakrishnan, K. C. 2004. 'Municipal and Metropolitan Governance: Are They Relevant to the Urban Poor?'. Paper presented at the Forum on Urban Infrastructure and Public Service Delivery for the Urban Poor, Regional Asia, New Delhi, 24–25 June.

Sivaramakrishnan, K. C. (ed.). 2006. *People's Participation in Urban Governance: A Comparative Study of Wards Committees in Karnataka, Kerala, Maharashtra, and West Bengal*. New Delhi: Concept Publishers.

Sivaramakrishnan, K. C. 2011. *Re-Visioning Cities: The Urban Renewal Mission*. New Delhi and Thousand Oaks: Sage.

Smitha, K. C. 2010. 'New Forms of Urban Localism: Service Delivery in Bangalore', *Economic and Political Weekly*, 20 February, 45(8): 73–77.

Srivastava, S. 2009. 'Urban Spaces, Disney Divinity and Moral Middle Classes in Delhi', *Economic and Political Weekly*, 14(26 & 27): 338–45.

Stokes, S. 2005. 'Perverse Accountability: A Formal Model of Machine Politics with Evidence from Argentina', *American Political Science Review*, 99(3): 315–25.

Stokes, S., T. Dunning, M. Nazareno and V. Brusco. 2013. *Brokers, Voters and Clientelism: The Puzzle of Distributive Politics*. New York and Cambridge: Cambridge University Press.

Sudhakar, R. K. 2012. 'Profile of Youth Residing in Two Slum Areas of Mumbai', *The Urban World*, 3(2): 34–49.

Suresh, H., S. Suradkar, A. Bhide, C. Deshpande and S. Singh. 2013. *Interim Report of People's Commission on Irregularities and Illegalities in SRA Projects*. Mumbai: National Alliance of People's Movements.

Suryanarayana, M. and D. Mousumi Das. 2014. 'How Inclusive Is India's Reformed Growth?', *Economic and Political Weekly*, 8 February, 49(6): 44–55.

Swyngedouw, E. 2005. 'Governance Innovation and the Citizen: The Janus-Face of Governance beyond the State', *Urban Studies*, 42(11): 1991–2006.

Tawa Lama-Rewal, S. 2005. 'Reservations for Women in Urban Local Bodies: A Tentative Assessment', in S. Tawa Lama-Rewal (ed.), *Electoral Reserva-*

tions, Political Representation and Social Change in India, pp. 189–207. New Delhi: Manohar and CSH.

Tawa Lama-Rewal, S. 2007. 'Neighbourhood Associations and Local Democracy: Delhi Municipal Elections 2007', *Economic and Political Weekly*, 24 November, pp. 51–60.

Tawa Lama-Rewal, S. 2009. 'Engaging with the Concept of Governance in the Study of Indian Metropolises', in J. Ruet and S. Tawa Lama-Rewal (eds.), *Governing India's Metropolises*, pp. 3–14. New Delhi and Abingdon: Routledge.

Teltumbde, A. 2012. 'Bal Thackeray and Maharashtra's Dalits', *Economic and Political Weekly*, 47(51): 20–22.

Thakkar, U. 2003. 'Commissioner and Corporators: Power Politics at Municipal Level', in S. Patel and A. Thorner (eds.), *Bombay: Metaphor for Modern India*, pp. 248–86. New Delhi: Oxford University Press.

Tinaikar, S. S. 2003. *Report of the High Power Committee: Financial Mismanagement of Municipal Corporation of Brihan Mumbai Resulting in Heavy Deficits in Budgets since 1995–9*. Mumbai: MCGM.

Tiwari, P. 2015. *Toilet Torture in Mumbai's Slums: When Will Our Political and Administrative Leaders End the Daily Assaults on Women's Safety and Dignity?* Mumbai: Mahatma Gandhi Centre/Observer Research Foundation Mumbai.

Udupi, S. A., M. A. Varghese and M. Kamath. 2000. *Attacking Urban Poverty and the Role of the SNDT Women University Mumbai*. Paris: UNESCO International Institute for Educational Planning.

UN Women. 2012. *Critical Gender Concerns in Jawaharlal Nehru National Urban Renewal Mission*. New Delhi: UN Women South Asia Sub Regional Office. http://www.unwomensouthasia.org (accessed on 8 November 2013).

Vakulabharanam, V. and S. Motiram. 2012. 'Understanding Poverty and Inequality in Urban India since Reforms: Bringing Quantitative and Qualitative Approaches Together', *Economic and Political Weekly*, 47(47 & 48): 44–52.

Van der Linden, J. J. 1983. 'Actors in Squatter Settlement Upgrading: Their Interests and Roles', in J. Schoorl, J. J. van der Linden and K. S. Yap (eds.), *Between Basti Dwellers and Bureaucrats: Lessons in Squatter Settlement Upgrading in Karachi*, pp. 249–61. Oxford: Pergammon.

Van Dijk, T. 2006. *Post-74th Constitutional Amendment Ward Governance in Mumbai: How and to What Extent Does This Brand of Decentralisation and Affirmative Action Benefit the Intended?* Academic Thesis, Amsterdam: University of Amsterdam/ISHSS.

Van Dijk, T. 2011a. 'Agents of Change and Obstruction: Municipal Councillors and Urban Development in the Mumbai Metropolitan Region', *Human Geography*, 4(2): 31–47.

Van Dijk, T. 2011b. 'Livelihoods, Capitals and Livelihood Trajectories: A More Sociological Conceptualisation', *Progress in Development Studies*, 11(2): 101–17.

Véron, R., G. Williams, S. Corbridge Stuart and S. Manoj. 2006. 'Decentralized Corruption or Corrupt Decentralization? Community Monitoring of Poverty Alleviation Schemes in Eastern India', *World Development*, 34(11): 1922–41.

Vithayathil, T. and G. Singh. 2012. 'Spaces of Discrimination: Residential Segregation in Indian Cities', *Economic and Political Weekly*, 47(37): 60–66.

Vora, R. and S. Palshikar. 2003. 'Politics of Locality, Community and Marginalisation', in S. Patel and J. Masselos (eds.), *Bombay and Mumbai: The City in Transition*, pp. 161–82. New Delhi: Oxford University Press.

Vreeswijk, R. 2006. *Bombay, Hyperstad*. Amsterdam: Meulenhof en de Volkskrant.

Wade, R. 1982. 'The System of Administrative and Political Corruption: Canal Irrigation in South India', *Journal of Development Studies*, 39(5): 287–328.

Weinstein, L. 2008. 'Mumbai's Development Mafias: Globalization, Organized Crime and Land Development', *International Journal of Urban and Regional Research*, 32(1): 22–39.

Weinstein, L. 2013. 'Demolition and Dispossession: Toward an Understanding of State Violence in Millennium Mumbai', *Studies into Comparative International Development*, 48(3): 285–307.

Weinstein, L. 2014. 'One-Man Handled' Fragmented Power and Political Entrepreneurship in Globalising Mumbai', in G. Shatkin (ed.), *Contesting the Indian City: Global Visions and the Politics of the Local*, pp. 91–121. Chichester: John Wiley.

Weinstein, L. and X. Ren. 2009. 'The Changing Right to the City: Urban Renewal and Housing Rights in Globalising Shanghai and Mumbai', *City and Community*, 8(4): 407–32.

Whitehead, J. and N. More. 2007. 'Revanchism in Mumbai? Political Economy of Rent Gaps and Urban Restructuring in a Global City', *Economic and Political Weekly*, 23 June, pp. 2428–34.

Witsoe, J. 2013. *Democracy against Development: Lower Caste Politics and Political Modernity in Post-Colonial India*. Chicago and London: University of Chicago Press.

Wood, G. 2003. 'Staying Secure, Staying Poor: The "Faustian Bargain"', *World Development*, 31(3): 455–71.

Wratten, E. 1995. 'Conceptualizing Urban Poverty', *Environment & Urbanization*, 7(1): 11–33.

Zerah, M. H. 2006. 'Assessing Surfacing Collective Action in Mumbai: A Case Study of Solid Waste Management'. Paper presented at a Workshop on Actors, Policies and Urban Governance at Mumbai University, Mumbai, 23 February.

Zerah, M. H. 2009a. 'Participatory Governance in Urban Governance and the Shifting Geometry of Power in Mumbai', *Development and Change*, 40(5): 853–77.

Zerah, M. H. 2009b. 'Reforming Solid Waste Management in Mumbai and Hyderabad: Policy Convergence, Distinctive Processes', in J. Ruet and S. Tawa Lama-Rewal (eds.), *Governing India's Metropolises*, pp. 241–69. London and New Delhi: Routledge.

Index

For Product Safety Concerns and Information please contact our EU
representative GPSR@taylorandfrancis.com
Taylor & Francis Verlag GmbH, Kaufingerstraße 24, 80331 München, Germany

* 9 7 8 0 3 6 7 1 7 7 4 1 6 *